PROVISIONAL MEASURES IN THE CASE LAW OF THE INTER-AMERICAN COURT OF HUMAN RIGHTS

PROVISIONAL MEASURES IN THE CASE LAW OF THE INTER-AMERICAN COURT OF HUMAN RIGHTS

Clara Burbano Herrera

intersentia
Antwerp – Oxford – Portland

Distribution for the UK:
Hart Publishing Ltd.
16C Worcester Place
Oxford OX1 2JW
UK
Tel.: +44 1865 51 75 30
Fax: +44 1865 51 07 10

Distribution for the USA and Canada:
International Specialized Book Services
920 NE 58th Ave. Suite 300
Portland, OR 97213
USA
Tel.: +1 800 944 6190 (toll free)
Tel.: +1 503 287 3093
Fax: +1 503 280 8832
Email: info@isbs.com

Distribution for Switzerland and Germany:
Schulthess Verlag
Zwingliplatz 2
CH-8022 Zürich
Switzerland
Tel.: +41 1 251 93 36
Fax: +41 1 261 63 94

Distribution for other countries:
Intersentia Publishers
Groenstraat 31
2640 Mortsel
Belgium
Tel.: +32 3 680 15 50
Fax: +32 3 658 71 21

Provisional Measures in the Case Law of the Inter-American Court of Human Rights
Clara Burbano Herrera

ISBN 978-94-000-0037-7
D/2010/7849/33
NUR 828

ACKNOWLEDGMENTS

This book is part of a larger dissertation. While writing this dissertation, many people have made my research life and my social life interesting and pleasant. This seems the perfect opportunity to express my gratitude to these people.

Firstly and foremost, I would like to express my gratitude to my thesis supervisor, Prof. Dr. Johan Vande Lanotte from Ghent University, whose knowledge, expertise, logic, kindness and understanding has lead me through this experience. I would also like to thank the other members of my support committee and exam board, Prof. Dr. Eva Brems from Ghent University, Prof. Dr. Leo Zwaak from Utrecht University, Prof. Dr. Diego Rodríguez-Pinzón from the American University Washington College of Law, Prof. Dr. Koen Raes from Ghent University and Prof. Stephan Parmentier from the University of Leuven, as well as Prof. Dr. Piet Taelman, Dean of the Faculty of Law of Ghent University, for their support and assistance at all levels of my research.

A very special thanks goes out to Prof. Dr. John Vervaele from Utrecht University for taking precious time out from his busy schedule to read and comment my texts and to Dr. Andrew Drzemczewski from the Council of Europe for the fruitful discussions during the Utrecht Conference, his kindness and time.

I would also like to thank Dr. Pablo Saavedra Alessandri, Secretary of the Inter-American Court of Human Rights, the Judges and staff of the Inter-American Court, who allowed me to experience how the provisional measures are being applied and followed-up in practice.

Thank you so much Brian Turnock and Charles Moyer, who helped me with the English language.

Many thanks to my dear colleagues at Ghent University, all of whom have contributed to this period of my life in one way or another: Andy Van Pachtenbeke, Riet Debel, Rozemie Defrancq, Marie Delplace, Geert Goedertier, Martine Dewulf, Valentina Staelens and Pieter Vanden Heede.

I would also like to thank all my friends in Ghent, San José, Utrecht, Washington DC, Madrid and Bogota: Francisco, Nubia, Erika, Leticia, Betsy, Kathy, Philippe, Bruno, Eloisa, Joke, Valentina, Odenis, Renata, Sven, Frederik and Sandy. I spent many enjoyable and late hours with all of you, and without your friendship I would not have felt so fast at home everywhere. Furthermore, I would like to thank my Colombian friends in Ghent: Julian, Carlos and Alexandra, they have been my part of Colombia in Belgium.

I am grateful to both my families Burbano Herrera, my father, Raul, Lenin and Fidel, and Haeck-Nowe, Liliane and Robert, as well as to Willy and Diane Degraeuwe for the support they provided. In particular, I must acknowledge my partner Yves Haeck, without whose love, advise and comments and unbelievable patience, I would not have finished this book.

My thanks also goes to Kris Moeremans, Isabelle Van Dongen, Tom Scheirs and the rest of the Intersentia team, for their professionalism and their trust in me.

Finally, I recognise that this research would not have been possible without the financial support of Ghent University and would like to express my gratitude to my second alma mater.

Ghent, 1 January 2010
Clara Burbano Herrera

TABLE OF CONTENTS

INTRODUCTION

1. The incorporation of human rights into international and domestic legal instruments represents one of the great conquests of humanity. There remains, however, a large gap between the nominal consecration of certain rights and their effective enjoyment, which raises the question as to what can be done so that rights are not simply rhetorical and what can the international human rights protection systems do to avoid their violation.

The purpose of interim measures is precisely to close that gap. These measures are an institution whose objective is to guarantee the practical effectiveness of rights so that they are not just rhetorical. In the end, what is most significant is the recognition that rights are not only included on an international plane and that States are internationally responsible in the event of their violation, but that all individuals believe that those rights will be protected before they are affected.

2. Provisional measures in the inter-American system may be defined as an instrument, the purpose of which is to avoid irreparable damage to the rights of persons who are in a situation of extreme gravity and urgency.[1] This protection is provided by the State as a result of an order by the Inter-American Court of Human Rights, which may act *ex officio* or at the request of a party.[2] The adoption of a provisional measure does not in any way prejudge the merits of the matter.[3]

---

1 Also referred to as 'protective measures', 'measures of protection' or 'interim measures'.

2 Article 63(2) American Convention on Human Rights.

3 IACtHR, *James et al. Case (Trinidad and Tobago)*, Order of the President of May 27, 1998, Preambular Paragraph 7; IACtHR, *The Miguel Agustín Pro Juárez Human Rights Center et al. Case (Mexico)*, Order of November 30, 2001, Preambular Paragraph 10; IACtHR, *The Urso Branco Prisons Case (Brazil)*, Order of June 18, 2002, Preambular Paragraph 10; IACtHR, *Luis Uzcátegui Case (Venezuela)*, Order of November 27, 2002, Preambular Paragraph 6; IACtHR, *Indigenous Kankuamo Community Case (Colombia)*, Order of July 5, 2004, Preambular Paragraph 13; IACtHR, *Communities of the Jiguamiandó and of the Curbaradó Case (Colombia)*, Order of March 6, 2003, Preambular Paragraph 12; IACtHR, *Lysias Fleury Case (Haiti)*, Order of June 7, 2003, Preambular Paragraph 10; IACtHR, *Indigenous Sarayaku People Case (Ecuador)*, Order of July 6, 2004, Preambular Paragraph 12; IACtHR, *Carlos Nieto et al. Case (Venezuela)*, Order of July 9, 2004, Preambular Paragraph 10 and IACtHR, *The Mendoza Prisons Case (Argentina)*, Order of November 22, 2004, Enacting Part 17; IACtHR, *Adrian Meléndez Quijano et al. Case (El Salvador)*, Order of March 23, 2007, Preambular Paragraph 6; IACtHR, *Tyrone Dacosta Cadogan Case (Barbados)*. See also IACtHR, *Cesti Hurtado Case (Peru)*, Order of the President of July 29, 1997, where the President of the Court decided not to adopt the provisional measures requested by the Commission because it would prejudge the merits of the case. See also infra, nos. 45–46.

Unlike under the UN system and the European system, where provisional measures are for example provided for in the Rules of the International Court of Justice, the Human Rights Committee, the Committee Against Torture,[4] and the European Court of Human Rights,[5] respectively, in the inter-American system these measures are expressly found in Article 63(2) of the American Convention on Human Rights, which states:

> "In cases of extreme gravity and urgency, and when necessary to avoid irreparable damage to persons, the Court shall adopt such provisional measures as it deems pertinent in matters it has under consideration. With respect to a case not yet submitted to the Court, it may act at the request of the Commission."

3. The incorporation of this institution into the American Convention and the language of Article 63(2) leave no doubt as to the binding nature of provisional measures,[6] which have been further developed in the Rules

---

4 At the universal or UN level provisional measures are, *inter alia*, contemplated in Article 41 of the Statute of the International Court of Justice, which provides: "The Court shall have the power to indicate, if it considers that circumstances so require, any provisional measures which ought to be taken to preserve the respective rights of either party." Article 86 of the Rules of Procedure of the Human Rights Committee (the supervisory organ created under the UN Covenant on Civil and Political Rights) states: "The Committee may, prior to forwarding its views on the communication to the State party concerned, inform that State of its views as to whether interim measures may be desirable to avoid irreparable damage to the victim of the alleged violation. In doing so, the Committee shall inform the State party concerned that such expression of its views on interim measures does not imply a determination on the merits of the communication." Article 108(9) of the Rules of Procedure of the Committee Against Torture says: "In the course of the consideration of the question of the admissibility of a communication, the Committee or the Working Group or a special rapporteur designated under rule 106, paragraph 3, may request the State party to take steps to avoid a possible irreparable damage to the person or persons who claim to be victim(s) of the alleged violation. Such a request addressed to the State party does not imply that any decision has been reached on the question of the admissibility of the communication."

5 The European Convention for the Protection of Human Rights and Fundamental Freedoms itself does not contain a provision that would allow the European Court to adopt provisional measures. Traditionally, in the European system these measures have been established in the Rules of the Court and in the Rules of the now defunct Commission. The power of the European Court to adopt provisional (interim) measures is contemplated in Rule 39 of the Rules of the Court. That text stipulates that: "Rule 39 (Interim measures) 1. The Chamber or, where appropriate, its President may, at the request of a party or of any other person concerned, or of its own motion, indicate to the parties any interim measure which it considers should be adopted in the interests of the parties or of the proper conduct of the proceedings before it. [...]."

6 H. Faundez Ledesma, *El Sistema Interamericano de Protección de los Derechos Humanos*, San José, IIDH, 3rd ed., 2004, 586–587; R. Nieto Navia, "Las medidas provisionales en la Corte Interamericana de Derechos Humanos", in *La Corte y el Sistema Interamericano de Derechos Humanos*, R. Nieto Navia (ed.), San José, Corte Interamericana de Derechos Humanos, 1994, 392; A. Cançado Trindade, *Medidas Provisionales. Prólogo del Presidente de la Corte Interamericana de Derechos Humanos al Tomo III de la Serie E.*, 2001, paras. 13,

of Procedure and the Statute[7] of the Commission[8] and those of the Court.[9]

4. Under Article 63(2) the Inter-American Court is the only body with competence to adopt provisional measures. The Court may adopt the measures *ex officio* or at the request of a party. While only the Inter-American Commission may request such measures when the matter is not before the Court, the active standing to request them is much broader when the case is being heard by the Court. Indeed, at that stage of the proceedings, the measures may be requested by the Commission, the victim, his next of kin or representatives and may also be adopted *ex officio*. As will be seen in detail, the participation of individuals was not originally envisioned, but has gradually been introduced through various reforms to the Rules of the Commission and the Court.

5. As a general rule, the Court has ordered States to adopt measures to protect specifically named persons and on special occasions has requested that a group of unnamed persons be protected when they are at grave risk. In those cases, belonging to the group of victims is not determined by a precise knowledge of the name of each individual but by objective criteria, such as ties to the group and the type of risk that would permit knowing who the beneficiaries are when the measures are executed.[10]

6. With regard to the abidance by the measures, the States have complied with the provisional measures in a great majority of the cases. This compliance has generally resulted in that some beneficiaries have received protection by State security agents,[11] and in judicial decisions being suspended while the case is under consideration at the international level.[12] As an indirect result, the

21; J.M. Pasqualucci, *The Practice and Procedure of the Inter-American Court of Human Rights*, Cambridge, Cambridge University Press, 2003, 318; J.M. Pasqualucci, "Medidas Provisionales en la Corte Interamericana de Derechos Humanos: Una Comparación con la Corte Internacional de Justicia y la Corte Europea de Derechos Humanos", *Revista del Instituto Interamericano de Derechos Humanos* 1994, 96–97; J.M. Pasqualucci, "Provisional Measures in the Inter-American Human Rights System: An Innovative Development in International Law", *Vand. J. Transnat'l L.* 1993–94, 823, 824, 849. See also *infra*, nos. 335–340.

7 Article 19(c) Statute of the Commission.

8 Article 74 Rules of Procedure of the Commission.

9 Article 26 Rules of Procedure of the Court.

10 See Peace Community of San José de Apartadó Case (Colombia).

11 See Carpio Nicolle Case (Guatemala), Gallardo Rodríguez Case (México) and Blake Case (Guatemala).

12 See for example, La Nación Newspaper Case (Costa Rica) and James *et al.* Case (Trinidad and Tobago).

complaint[13] has also sometimes resulted in that some beneficiaries have regained their freedom,[14] and in that newly organised trials have lead to a reduction of the death penalty sentence to a prison term of the person(s) concerned.

Unfortunately, the measures have sometimes been ignored with the result that beneficiaries of the measures have been killed, threatened, displaced or even executed by the State in application of the death penalty.

7. There are also certain obstacles that make the protection of the rights not as effective as might be wished and in many cases the measures have not been effective at all. Among the reasons for these obstacles is the beneficiaries' lack of confidence in State bodies and the institutions that should protect them.

8. The analysis of the jurisprudence on the provisional measures covers the period 1987–2009, during which there were 374 orders on provisional measures, of which 71 were initial order(s) adopted in a case, while 9 requests for provisional measures were rejected. The others were maintained, broadened, lifted or reinstated.

9. Analysing the jurisprudence of the Inter-American Court on provisional measures is interesting because, in addition to presenting the legal norms and issues related to the topic, it provides an idea of the reality of the Americas. This study deals with the situation of indigenous communities in countries such as Guatemala, Nicaragua and Colombia, the prison crisis that has arisen from the degrading situation of inmates in jails in Brazil, Argentina and Peru, violations against victims of the armed conflict in Colombia, human rights violations during the dictatorships in Argentina, Guatemala and Peru, problems of discrimination in the Dominican Republic, and the danger that human rights defenders and journalists face in Venezuela. In addition, the analysis will show that the system of justice in most American States does not respond to the needs of their inhabitants.

10. The foregoing is a general summary of what will be developed in this study, the main objective of which is to present and analyze the jurisprudence of the Inter-American Court with regard to the provisional measures issued.

---

13 The Court has never ordered States to set free beneficiaries who are in prison, neither has it ordered new trials. The Court has ordered States to adopt all provisional measures indispensable to avoid irreparable damages to the beneficiaries. Sometimes States have complied with the provisional measures by setting free beneficiaries or by organising new trials.

14 See Suárez Rosero Case (Ecuador), Loayza Tamayo Case (Peru), Gallardo Rodríguez Case (México) and Cesti Hurtado Case (Peru).

11. To meet this objective, the book is divided into 9 parts or chapters. The first part or chapter deals with jurisdiction: who may request provisional measures, who may adopt them, and which States are obligated to comply with them. There is also an analysis of the rights that may be protected and the time and place in which the measures are carried out (**Chapter 1**). This part or chapter is followed by the topic of admissibility, with the three elements that must be proved so that a person might become the beneficiary of provisional measures. They are as follows: a) there needs to be a situation of extreme gravity, b) the situation is urgent, and c) measures are required to avoid irreparable damage to persons (**Chapter 2**). The next two parts or chapters deal with the evidentiary means and the processing of the petition or request for provisional measures respectively. Since neither the American Convention nor the Rules of the Court or the Commission refer to the manner in which a situation of extreme gravity and urgency must be proved, the Court has held that proceedings on provisional measures have their own peculiarities that differ from those under domestic law. Consideration of a request is not subject to the same formalities as in domestic proceedings. Certain elements are incorporated into the evidentiary file depending on the facts of the specific case[15] and the limits necessary for legal certainty and procedural equality between the parties must be borne in mind.[16] An analysis of the jurisprudence shows that there are no clear rules with respect to how a petition should be examined. This is important because the length of time that the Court takes to decide a request depends on how the petition is processed. In some cases the decision has been taken the same day that the petition was presented, while in others it has taken more than 16 days. While the effective protection of human rights is more important than how the petition is processed, a delay in adopting the measures may be a violation of the rights that the measures intend to protect. In other words, the lack of timely protection may result in a violation of the right (**Chapters 3 and 4**). The following part or chapter contains an analysis of the decisions of the Court, how the measures are adopted and the obligations imposed on the States (**Chapter 5**). This is followed by a part

15 IACtHR, *Velásquez Rodríguez Case (Honduras)*, Judgment on the Merits of July 29, 1988, para. 128; IACtHR, *Bámaca Velásquez Case (Guatemala)*, Judgment on the Merits of November 25, 2000, para. 97; IACtHR, *Cesti Hurtado Case (Peru)*, Judgment on Reparations of May 31, 2001, para. 21; IACtHR, *Mayagna (Sumo) Awas Tingni Community Case (Nicaragua)*, Judgment on the Merits of August 31, 2001, paras. 89–90; IACtHR, *Ivcher Bronstein Case (Peru)*, Judgment on the Merits of February 6, 2001, para. 65; IACtHR, *Myrna Mack Chang et al. (Guatemala)*, Judgment on the Merits of November 25, 2003, para. 120; IACtHR, *Plan de Sánchez Massacre Case(Guatemala)*, Judgment on Reparations of November 19, 2004, para. 28; IACtHR, *Carpio Nicolle Case (Guatemala)*, Judgment on the Merits of November 22, 2004, para. 55 and IACtHR, *19 Tradesmen Case (Colombia)*, Judgment on the Merits of July 5, 2004, para. 65.

16 IACtHR, *Paniagua Morales et al. and Vásquez et al. Case (Guatemala)*, Judgment on the Merits of March 8, 1998, paras. 70, 75; IACtHR, *Loayza Tamayo Case (Peru)*, Judgment on Reparations of November 27, 1998, para. 38; IACtHR, *Constitutional Court Case (Peru)*, Judgment on the Merits of January 31, 2001, para. 46.

or chapter on the length or duration of provisional measures and the requirements and conditions necessary to maintain them. Here it may be seen that, notwithstanding the temporary nature of provisional measures, the critical situation in certain countries and the need to protect persons have caused some of them to remain in force for more than ten years (**Chapter 6**). In the next part or chapter the abidance by or compliance with the provisional measures issued by the Inter-American Court are thoroughly analyzed (**Chapter 7**). Parts or chapters eight and nine examine the binding nature of provisional measures and the international responsibility for non-compliance respectively. In these parts, the means used by States to comply with the obligations contained in the orders of provisional measures and the situations in which beneficiaries suffer some type of damage to their rights are analyzed. Finally, there is a summary of the factors that, in our opinion, may be considered the main obstacles to some measures being effective. Among them are the lack of confidence of the beneficiaries in the organs or persons who offer the protection and the lack of political will of some governments to comply with the orders of provisional measures (**Chapters 8 and 9**).

12. The study of the jurisprudence of a human rights figure such as interim measures is undoubtedly relevant, not only because it permits viewing the problems that affect contemporary society. To date, the beneficiaries of interim measures have been, *inter alia*, family members of the alleged victims, witnesses, journalists, political candidates, human rights defenders, members of indigenous communities, prisoners who live in deplorable conditions, the seriously ill or those on hunger strikes, officials of the justice system, aliens under orders of deportation or extradition and those sentenced to capital punishment.

The fact that hundreds of people of various nationalities request interim measures as a last, and sometimes only, measure of protection is a disturbing sign of the desperate situations of many persons, those displaced, in poor health, in the midst of an armed conflict, in a foreign country, because the States have not complied with their obligations. Interim measures today have a key role in many of the cases that are brought before the international human rights system. Surely, neither the judges of these tribunals, the academics, nor the international community in general had imagined the dimensions that this institution has acquired in the jurisprudence over thc years.

In a certain sense, this study attempts to exalt the work of the measures and explore responses so that they might better meet their function of protecting rights effectively. But beyond its academic value, this book hopes to have a practical utility, a social visibility. It is an invitation to each individual to learn the power that the jurisprudence of the Inter-American Court has given to this figure. He or she may then use it, as a useful tool that has the virtue of avoiding the irreparable violation of rights in situations of extreme gravity and urgency.

1. JURISDICTION

1.1. JURISDICTION *RATIONE PERSONAE*

1.1.1. ACTIVE STANDING

13. The authorisation to request the adoption of provisional measures in the inter-American system is governed by the American Convention on Human Rights, the Rules of Procedure of the Inter-American Court and of the Inter-American Commission. Articles 63(2) of the Convention, Articles 26(1), 26(2) and 26(3) of the Rules of the Court[17] and Article 74(1) of the Rules of the Commission[18] are the provisions that grant active standing to the Court, the Commission, the President and Vice President of the Commission, the alleged victims, their next of kin or their representatives to request provisional measures.

14. Who may request the measures depends on exactly before what supervisory body in the inter-American system the matter is under consideration. If it is before the Commission, only the Commission is competent to request protective measures. If, however, the case has been submitted to the Court, the standing is broader in that the Commission, the alleged victims, their next of kin or their representatives may request the measures.[19] The Court may also adopt the measures *ex officio*.

15. The jurisprudence of the Court from 1987 to 2009 reveals that 374 orders were issued, of which 80 were the initial order.[20] In the great majority of the cases (65), the Court adopted the provisional measures at the initiative of the

---

17 Rules of Procedure of the Inter-American Court of Human Rights, adopted by the Court at its XLIX Regular Session, held November 16–25, 2000, which was partially amended by the Court at its LXI Regular Session, held from November 20 to December 4, 2003. The latest amendment was implemented during the Regular Session, held January 19–31, 2009. This reform entered into force on March 24, 2009.

18 Rules of Procedure of the Inter-American Commission on Human Rights, adopted by the Commission at its 109th Special Session, held December 4–8, 2000, amended at its 116th Regular Session, held October 6–24, 2003.

19 Article 25(3) Rules of Procedure of the Inter-American Court of Human Rights, adopted by the Court, which was partially amended by the Court at its LXI Regular Session, held from November 20 to December 4, 2003. This reform entered into force on January 1, 2004.

20 In the other cases, the orders amplify, lift or reinstate the security measures.

Commission. The other 14 were requested by representatives of the beneficiaries or directly by the beneficiary and one was adopted directly by the Court. Of the 65 requests, 61 were accepted and four were rejected.[21]

1.1.1.1. Request for Provisional Measures

1.1.1.1.1. Measures requested by the Inter-American Commission

16. The Commission, at any stage of the proceedings and when it deems it necessary, may ask the Court to adopt provisional measures to avoid a human rights violation. The legal basis for the Commission to request provisional measures of the Court is found in the American Convention (Article 63(2)), in the Rules of the Court (Article 26(2)), in the Commission's Rules (Article 74) and in its Statute (Article 19(c)).

17. The Commission may make the request as a result of its own interest or because it has been asked to do so by an interested party,[22] be it the representatives of the victim, the victim himself or his next of kin or a non-governmental organisation. It is important to emphasize that the Commission, in addition to its competence to request protective measures, may suggest in its request the

---

21 IACtHR, *Peruvian Prisons Cases (Peru)*, Order of December 14, 1992. On the same subject, see Order of January 27, 1993, *Chipoco Case (Peru)*. I/A Court of H.R., Order of December 14, 1992 and Order of January 27, 1993; IACtHR, *Castañeda Gutman Case (Mexico)*, Order of November 25, 2005; IACtHR, *García Uribe Case (Mexico)*, Order of February 2, 2006.

22 IACtHR, *Bustíos-Rojas Case (Peru)*, Order of the President of June 5, 1990, Explanatory Statement 1; IACtHR, *Chunimá Case (Peru)*, Order of the President of July 15, 1991, Explanatory Statement 4, in which the complaint also included a special request for provisional measures to protect the life and physical integrity of members of a human rights organization in Guatemala and their families; IACtHR, *Carpio Nicolle Case (Guatemala)*, Order of the President of June 4, 1995, Explanatory Statement 2, where the complaint before the Commission included a request for provisional measures pursuant to Article 63(2) of the Convention and IACtHR, *Giraldo Cardona Case (Colombia)*, Order of the President of October 28, 1996, in which a witness, who had appeared before the Court to testify on facts that implicated specific State agents in human rights violations, asked the Commission to request the Court to protect his life and physical integrity. See also IACtHR, *Bámaca Velásquez Case (Guatemala)*, Order of the President of June 30, 1998, Explanatory Statement 2. In the Liliana Ortega Case, some organizations, among them the Center for Justice and International Law (CEJIL), requested that the Commission asked the Court to adopt provisional measures because of the increasing acts of intimidation. IACtHR, *Liliana Ortega et al. Case (Venezuela)*, Order of November 23, 2002, Explanatory Statement 2 (e). Since the interim measures adopted by the Commission had not produced the expected results and the Community continued to be threatened and harassed by illegal groups, the petitioners requested the Commission to present to the Court a request for provisional measures. IACtHR, *Communities of the Jiguamiandó and of the Curbaradó Case (Colombia)*, Order of March 6, 2003, Explanatory Statement 3 and IACtHR, *Eloisa Barrios et al. Case (Venezuela)*, Order of November 23, 2004, Explanatory Statement 1.

measures that it believes that the State should take to protect the persons who are in danger.

18. The active standing granted to the Commission to request that provisional measures be adopted in situations of urgency, even when the case has not been submitted to the Court, has the potential to be one of the most innovative advances in the jurisprudence of provisional measures in human rights law.[23] As a general rule, the authority of a tribunal to order provisional measures is restricted to the period when the matter is before it, but the inter-American system does not require waiting until the Court is seized with the case in order that protective measures be adopted.[24]

19. There is a debate as to the moment the Commission's competence to request provisional measures commences. There are three different views on the degree of formality required.

One view argues that the Commission may only request provisional measures after it has formally and expressly accepted the petition that has been presented to it, that is, after having declared the case admissible.[25] Gros Espiell, a former judge of the Inter-American Court, favours this position.[26]

Others, such as Pasqualucci, believe that, since the Commission must act in accordance with the provisions of Articles 44 to 51 of the American Convention, and especially Article 48(f) with respect to the requests and communications that are submitted to it, it must be concluded that, while the norms do not require the Commission to make an express declaration on the admissibility of the case, it should at least make a *prima facie* determination that the petition meets the

---

23 When the case is under consideration by the Commission, the Court may adopt provisional measures at the request of the Commission. At this stage of the procedure, the Court cannot adopt measures *ex officio*. See Article 63(2) American Convention.

24 See H. Fix-Zamudio, *Medidas Provisionales. Prólogo del Presidente de la Corte Interamericana de Derechos Humanos al Tomo I de la Serie E.*, 1996; J.M. Pasqualucci, "Provisional Measures in the Inter-American Human Rights System: An Innovative Development in International Law", *Vand. J. Transnat'l L.* 1993–94, 825; T. Buergenthal, "The Inter-American Court of Human Rights", *Am. U. L. Rev.* 1982, 240.

25 H. Gross Espiell, *Estudios sobre Derechos Humanos II*, Madrid, Editorial Civitas, 1988, 170, quoted by H. Faundez Ledesma, *El Sistema Interamericano de Protección de los Derechos Humanos*, San José, IIDH, 3rd ed., 2004, 513.

26 H. Gross Espiell, *Estudios sobre Derechos Humanos II*, Madrid, Editorial Civitas, 1988, 169–171. See also A. Aguilar, "Procedimiento que debe aplicar la Comisión Interamericana de Derechos Humanos en el examen de las peticiones o comunicaciones individuales sobre presuntas violaciones de Derechos Humanos", in *Derechos Humanos de las Américas*, OAS, 1984, 199, 204. The author asserts that the Commission should avoid the formal admissibility requirements in situations of urgency in order to prevent human rights violations and to fulfill the humanitarian nature of its work.

formal requisites of admissibility,[27] including whether it deals with a serious and urgent matter.[28] The competence of the Commission would thus begin when it examines the petition and determines *prima facie* that it meets the requisites of admissibility.[29]

Finally, there is the much less formal view of FAÚNDEZ LEDESMA, who believes that what is important is to act with the promptness that this type of case requires. Thus, if the gravity and urgency of the circumstances of the request for protective measures are taken into account and the purpose of provisional measures is to avoid irreparable damage to the rights of persons, the Commission would not be obligated to make a previous ruling on admissibility. The Commission could request provisional measures from the very moment that it verifies that there is a risk to the rights of persons. Finally, the author argues that requiring the Commission to rule first on admissibility would not be coherent with the object and purpose of the American Convention.[30]

20. From a practical point of view, almost all of the requests (94%) that were presented by the Commission concerned cases that had already been declared admissible. Of the 65 requests for the adoption of measures, only in two cases did the Commission request the Court to adopt protective measures in spite of not having made a formal declaration of admissibility[31], and in two other cases a petition had not even been submitted to the Commission.[32]

---

27 Pursuant to the American Convention, the formal requirements for admissibility are: a) the remedies under domestic law must be pursued and exhausted, b) the petition has to be lodged within a period of six months from the date on which the party alleging violation of his rights was notified of the final judgment, c) the subject of the petition or communication is not pending in another international proceeding for settlement, d) the petition contains the name, nationality, profession, domicile, and signature of the person or persons or of the legal representative of the entity lodging the petition, e) the petition states facts that tend to establish a violation of the rights guaranteed by the Convention and, f) the petition is not manifestly groundless or obviously out of order. See Articles 46 and 47 American Convention.

28 J.M. PASQUALUCCI, "Provisional Measures in the Inter-American Human Rights System: An Innovative Development in International Law", *Vand. J. Transnat'l L.* 1993–94, 829–830.

29 J.M. PASQUALUCCI, "Medidas Provisionales en la Corte Interamericana de Derechos Humanos: Una Comparación con la Corte Internacional de Justicia y la Corte Europea de Derechos Humanos", *Revista del Instituto Interamericano de Derechos Humanos* 1994, 73. See also J.M. PASQUALUCCI, *The Practice and Procedure of the Inter-American Court of Human Rights*, Cambridge, Cambridge University Press, 2003, 296, 308.

30 H. FAÚNDEZ LEDESMA, *The Inter-American System for the Protection of Human Rights*, San José, IIDH, 3rd ed., 2007, 486–487.

31 James et al. Case (Trinidad and Tobago); Castañeda-Gutman Case (Mexico).

32 García Uribe et al Case (Mexico); Capital El Rodeo I & El Rodeo II Judicial Confinement Center Case (Venezuela).

In James, Briggs, Noel, García and Bethel (Trinidad and Tobago) the Commission explained that it had five complaints pending that alleged that five men had been condemned to death for the crime of murder in Trinidad and Tobago. According to the complaints, there were facts in each case that tended to establish a violation of rights set forth in the Convention. It was specifically stated that the prison conditions of the alleged victims violated the obligations of the State under Article 5 of the Convention, that their trials and sentences were unfair in violation of Article 8 of the Convention, and that the inmates were on death row and their executions were imminent.

In each of the five cases the Commission had adopted precautionary measures[33] and the State, instead of responding to the requests, had only expressed the view that the Commission could not prevent the implementation of a domestic sentence. The Commission justified its request to the Court for the provisional measures by arguing in its petition that, although it was not able to finish its examination of the facts and take a decision in the cases, under the circumstances it deemed the adoption of provisional measures necessary because otherwise the condemned men would be executed, causing irreparable harm, and any remedies that might be adopted would not make any sense.[34]

The Court, in considering the request, took into account that the State had accepted its contentious jurisdiction. It also considered that the State had not responded to the Commission's requests for precautionary measures and, as an important fact, it took into account that the petition was submitted on May 27 and that the executions were scheduled for the following month, which demonstrated the need to adopt the measures. Thus, even though the Commission had not formally declared the cases admissible, the Court accepted the request and adopted provisional measures.[35]

In a subsequent decision (2006), the Court indicated that it can only issue provisional measures in respect of cases that may "be brought to the attention of the Court and its contentious jurisdiction" and that before there exists this minimal possibility, it is indispensable that the procedure has been initiated

33 Precautionary measures are adopted by the Commission and they have the same purpose as provisional measures, which is to avoid irreparable damage to the rights of persons in grave and urgent situations. The legal basis of these measures cannot be found in the American Convention, but in the Rules of the Commission (Article 25 Rules). This means that these measures are not based on the Convention because the Commission adopts its own rules and the adoption of measures doesn't prejudge the merits of the matter (Article 25(4) Rules).

34 IACtHR, *James et al. Case (Trinidad and Tobago)*, Order of the President of June 19, 1999, Explanatory Statement 5 (a), (b) and (f).

35 J.M. Pasqualucci, "Medidas Provisionales en la Corte Interamericana de Derechos Humanos: Una Comparación con la Corte Internacional de Justicia y la Corte Europea de Derechos Humanos", *Revista del Instituto Interamericano de Derechos Humanos* 1994, 72–73.

before the Commission in accordance with Articles 44 and 46 to 48 of the Convention. In that sense, it is necessary that the Commission has at least registered and started to take cognizance of the petition, without it being necessary that the Commission has decided on the admissibility or merits of the petition.[36]

However, in 2008 on two occasions the Court adopted provisional measures despite the absence of a petition submitted to the Commission, stating that the conditions of extreme gravity and urgency were satisfied.[37]

21. It can therefore be concluded that under the current case law of the Inter-American Court, the vision defended by Faúndez Ledesma, i.e. as soon as the gravity and urgency of the circumstances dictate so, provisional measures can be adopted, has prevailed, and even that a formal submittal of a petition to the Inter-American Commission is not even required for the Court to adopt provisional measures.

Table 1. Requests submitted by the Commission

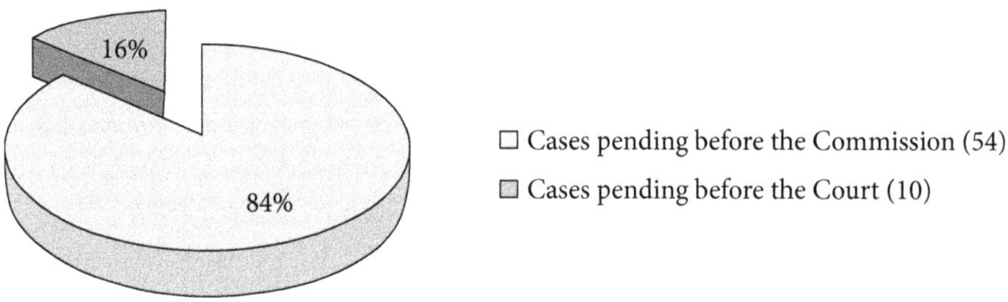

22. Table 1 shows that with respect to the stage of the proceedings at which the Commission requested the measures, in the great majority of occasions (84%), the matters were being examined by it. Of the 64 requests that the Commission submitted to the Court, 54 were matters that were under its consideration and the other ten were pending before the Court.[38]

---

[36] IACtHR, *García Uribe et al Case (Mexico)*, Order of February 2, 2006, Preambular Paragraphs 3, 4 and 5.

[37] IACtHR, Capital El Rodeo I & El Rodeo II Judicial Confinement Center Case (Venezuela), Order of February 8, 2008, Preambular Paragraph 9; IACtHR, 'El Nacional' and 'Así es la Noticia' Newspapers Case (Venezuela), Order of November 25, 2008, Explanatory Statement 6.

[38] IACtHR, *Caballero Delgado and Santana Case (Colombia)*, Order of December 7, 1994; IACtHR, *Blake Case (Guatemala)*, Order of the President of August 6, 1995; IACtHR, *Suárez Rosero Case (Ecuador)*, Order of the President of April 12, 1996; IACtHR, *Loayza Tamayo Case (Peru)*, Order of the President of June 12, 1996; IACtHR, *Bámaca Velásquez Case (Guatemala)*, Order of the President of June 30, 1998; IACtHR, *Ivcher Bronstein Case (Peru)*,

The much higher percentage of cases that were pending before the Commission and that received provisional measures, compared with that before the Court, is mainly because most of the cases were being considered by the Commission and were not pending before the Court. This is due principally to the fact that in the inter-American system the Court can only rule on a case if it has been submitted to it by the Commission or a State Party, and this possibility has been used relatively rarely by the Commission and never by the States.[39] For example, since the Court was installed in 1979 it has heard a total of 109 contentious cases as of 2009, while the Commission in only one year (2003) considered 973 petitions. This large number of petitions being considered by the Commission, most of which in fact are never submitted to the Court, is the reason for this high proportion of provisional measures that are adopted with respect to cases that are under consideration by the Commission and not the Court.[40]

23. With regard to the countries that the Commission has asked the Court to adopt protective measures, as can be seen in Table 2, Venezuela has received the most requests, namely thirteen; Guatemala and Colombia follow with eleven and nine requests each; Mexico with seven; Peru with five; Argentina and Brazil with three each; Ecuador, the Dominican Republic, Barbados and El Salvador with two each, and Honduras, Costa Rica, Nicaragua, Trinidad and Tobago and Haiti with one each.

Order of October 21, 2002; IACtHR, *Helen Mack Chang et al. (Guatemala)*, Order of the President of August 14, 2002; IACtHR, *19 Tradesmen Case (Colombia)*, Order of July 30, 2004; *Tyrone Dacosta Cadogan Case (Barbados)*, Order of the President of April 11, 2008; *Serrano Cruz Sister Case (El Salvador)*, Order of the President of March 27, 2006.

39 The American Convention, which created the Inter-American Court of Human Rights, was adopted in 1969. The General Assembly of the OAS held in La Paz, Bolivia, in 1979, adopted the Statute of the Court (Resolution 448). The Court was officially installed on September 3, 1979 in San José, Costa Rica, where it has its seat.

40 A general vision of the statistics of the Court with respect to the number of contentious cases per year may be found in the 2008 Annual Report of the Inter-American Court of Human Rights.

Table 2. Number of provisional measures requested by the Commission to States

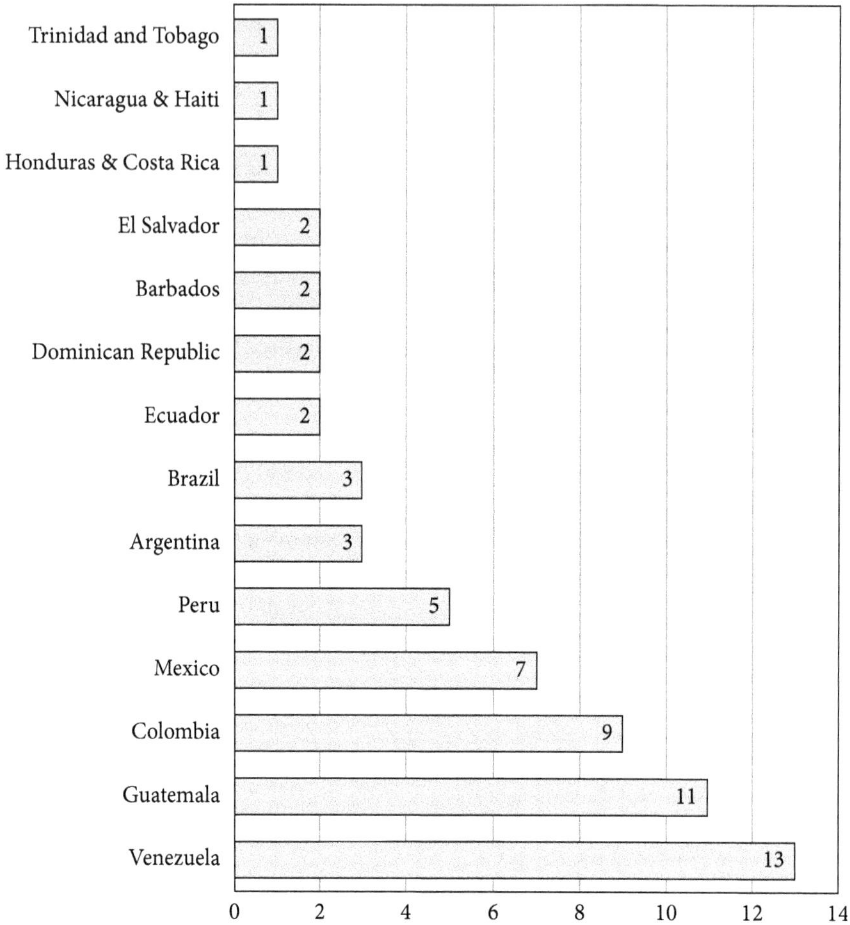

1.1.1.1.1.1. Requests for Provisional Measures when the Matter is pending before the Commission

24. Article 63(2) of the American Convention expressly provides the following:

> "In cases of extreme gravity and urgency, and when necessary to avoid irreparable damage to persons, the Court shall adopt such provisional measures as it deems pertinent in matters it has under consideration. With respect to a case not yet submitted to the Court, it may act at the request of the Commission."

For its part, Article 25(2) of the Rules of Procedure of the Court states:

> "Provisional Measures: With respect to matters not yet submitted to it, the Court may act at the request of the Commission."

25. Although the American Convention and the Rules of the Court refer exclusively to the Commission as the competent organ to request provisional measures when the matter has not yet been submitted to the Court, the Commission's Rules state that when it is not in session,[41] such request may be made by its President or, in his absence, by one of the Vice-Presidents, respecting the order of precedence.[42]

26. The first time that the Commission requested provisional measures with respect to a matter that was not being heard by the Court was in 1990 in the Bustíos-Rojas Case (Peru),[43] in which the Commission asked the Court to order the State to adopt provisional measures to protect the right to life and personal safety of certain persons who were at risk, among whom were witnesses, a journalist who had been injured, and the wife of another journalist who had been murdered.[44]

---

41 Article 74(1) and 74(2) Rules of Procedure of the Commission.

42 Article 74(1) of the Rules of Procedure of the Commission states that the Commission may request that the Court adopt provisional measures in cases of extreme gravity and urgency, and when it becomes necessary to avoid irreparable damage to persons in a matter that has not yet been submitted to the Court for consideration. Article 74(2) states that when the Commission is not in session, that request may be made by the President or, in his or her absence, by one of the Vice-Presidents in order of precedence.

43 IACtHR, *Bustíos-Rojas Case (Peru)*, Order of the President of June 5, 1990.

44 In this case, the President of the Court accepted the request and adopted measures to protect the persons who were in a situation of extreme gravity and urgency, which were then ratified by the Court. See IACtHR, *Bústios Rojas Case (Peru)*, Order of August 8, 1990. See also J.M. Pasqualucci, "Medidas Provisionales en la Corte Interamericana de Derechos Humanos: Una Comparación con la Corte Internacional de Justicia y la Corte Europea de Derechos Humanos", *Revista del Instituto Interamericano de Derechos Humanos* 1994, 82.

27. It is important to point out that the adoption of measures in a matter that is under consideration by the Commission does not obligate the latter to submit the petition to the Court. In fact, the Commission does not always submit to the Court matters in which provisional measures have been issued, either because during proceedings before the Commission a friendly settlement was reached between the parties, as occurred in the Colotenango Case (Guatemala)[45] or because the Commission published an Article 51 Report, as in the Bustíos-Rojas, Chunimá and James *et al.* Cases.[46] Matters have also not been submitted to the Court when the Commission has closed a case because it decided, in accordance with Article 48(1)(b) of the Convention, that the grounds for the petition no longer existed, as occurred in the Reggiardo Tolosa (Argentina)[47] and Clemente Teherán (Colombia) Cases.[48]

28. With respect to the duration of the measures, it is important to emphasize that the Court has exclusive jurisdiction to decide their length. Although the Court may act only at the request of the Commission with respect to matters that have not yet been submitted to it, once the measures have been adopted only the Court can decide on their duration, that is, with respect to maintaining, modifying or lifting them. Therefore, neither the Commission nor any other party have the competence to leave them without effect or to suspend them.[49]

1.1.1.1.1.2. Requests for Provisional Measures when the Case is pending before the Court

29. The competence to request provisional measures when the case is pending before the Court is much broader when compared to that when the matter is being considered by the Commission. When the matter is pending before the Court, the Commission, the alleged victim, his next of kin or representatives may request measures and the Court may also adopt them *ex officio*.[50]

45 In spite of the fact that the Colotenango Case (Guatemala) ended in a friendly settlement, the provisional measures are still in place because the situation of extreme gravity and urgency persists.

46 With respect to a beneficiary of the measures.

47 See <www.cidh.org/comunicados/english/1999/26-99.htm>.

48 IACtHR, *Clemente Teherán et al. Case (Colombia)*, Order of December 1, 2003, Explanatory Statement 10.

49 H. Faundez Ledesma, El Sistema Interamericano de Protección de los Derechos Humanos, San José, IIDH, 3rd ed., 2004, 549.

50 Article 63(2) American Convention; Article 26(1), 26(2) and 26(3) Rules of Procedure of the Court, and Article 74(1) Rules of Procedure of the Commission.

30. The first time that the Commission requested provisional measures was in a case that was being heard by the Court. In 1987 the Commission invoked Article 63(2) of the Convention and requested the adoption of provisional measures to protect certain witnesses who had been receiving threats because of their involvement in the Velásquez Rodríguez, Godínez Cruz and Fairén Garbi and Solís Corrales Cases (Honduras). The situation of the beneficiaries was so dangerous or precarious that the provisional measures were maintained even after the judgments on the merits and on reparations.[51]

31. The Commission's practice has been to request measures when the cases have not yet been decided on the merits and the measures were maintained after that decision.[52] It is also relevant that the Commission does not lose competence to request provisional measures because there has been a judgment on the merits.[53] On this point, the Court has stated on various occasions that provisional measures may be also applied at the supervisory stage of compliance of the judgment. Therefore, regardless of whether there has been a judgment on the merits or on reparations in a case, provisional measures may be requested, adopted, maintained and even broadened.[54] What in the final analysis justifies provisional measures is that they are a response to a situation of extreme gravity and urgency and imminent irreparable damage to persons.[55]

1.1.1.1.2. Measures Requested by the Victims or their Representatives

32. While initially the parties to proceedings before the Court were only the Commission and the State in question, there has been a gradual change beginning with the 1996 Rules of the Court. The evolution with regard to the norms concerning the standing that has been given to the victims, their

---

51 As of 2009, the provisional measures had not been formally lifted. See IACtHR, *Velásquez Rodríguez, Fairen Garbi and Solis Corrales and Godinez Cruz Cases (Honduras)*, Order of the President of November 6, 1988. With respect to this point, it is important to point out that the measures may remain in force even though there has been a judgment on the merits of the matter.

52 Bámaca Velásquez Case (Guatemala), Caballero Delgado and Santana Case (Colombia), Helen Mack Chang *et al.* Case (Guatemala) and Gómez Paquiyauri Brothers Case (Peru), Carpio Nicolle *et al.* Case (Guatemala).

53 19 Tradesmen Case (Colombia) and Mayagna (Sumo) Awas Tingni Community Case (Nicaragua).

54 IACtHR, *Mayagna (Sumo) Awas Tingni Community Case (Nicaragua)*, Order of September 6, 2002, Preambular Paragraph 9; IACtHR, *Loayza Tamayo Case (Peru)*, Order of the President of December 13, 2002, Preambular Paragraph 7 and IACtHR, *Gómez Paquiyauri Brothers Case (Peru)*, Order of May 7, 2004, Preambular Paragraph 10.

55 H. Faundez Ledesma, El Sistema Interamericano de Protección de los Derechos Humanos, San José, IIDH, 3rd ed., 2004, 574–575.

representatives or their next of kin with respect to provisional measures may be divided into three stages.[56]

A first stage would run from 1996 to 2001, during which the representatives of the victims or their next of kin were permitted to present autonomously their arguments and evidence when the case was at the stage of reparations. At a second stage (2001–2004), the Court broadened both the participation of the subjects and the period within which they might act. During this stage, not only were the representatives of the victims allowed to present their own arguments, but the alleged victims themselves and their next of kin were directly authorised to do so autonomously once the case was declared admissible. The final stage began in 2004, when for the first time the norms expressly refer to the participation of individuals in the procedure on provisional measures and enable the alleged victims, their next of kin or their duly accredited representatives to present directly to the Court requests for provisional measures in cases that are being heard by it.[57]

1.1.1.1.2.1. First Stage (1996–2001)

33. This stage is characterised by the fact that, in spite of a lack of norms authorising the victims or their representatives to request provisional measures, they did present some petitions that were accepted by the Court. It is important to clarify that during this period there is a reference to the direct participation, in general, of individuals in the inter-American system, but not to their participation in the proceedings on provisional measures. This general participation was governed by Article 23 of the Rules of the Court of 1996, which authorised the representatives of the victims or their next of kin to participate when the case was at the stage of reparations.[58] On the other hand, the provisional

---

56 The American Convention does not envision an active role for individuals in proceedings before the Court since the States designed the international systems of human rights and participation of individuals was not allowed when the human rights treaties were drafted. It should be emphasized, however, that permitting individuals to present petitions to the Inter-American Commission during the period when the system of protection was created was revolutionary in international law. With the entry into force of the new Rules of Procedure of the Court, once the application is submitted to the Court, the alleged victims, their families or their representatives have standing (*locus standi*) before the Court and, thus, are parties (Article 23(1)). See C. Martin, "La Corte Inter-Americana de Derechos Humanos: Funciones y Competencia", in *Derecho Internacional de los Derechos Humanos*, C. Martin, D. Rodríguez-Pinzon and J. Guevara (eds.), Mexico, Fontamara, 2004, 223–224. See also V. Rodriguez Rescia, "El Sistema Interamericano de Protección de Derechos Humanos", <www.iidh.ed.cr/BibliotecaWeb>, 11–12.

57 Article 25(3) Rules of Procedure of the Court, as amended, effectively on January 1, 2004. This article was not changed during the last reform of the Rules of Procedure of 2009.

58 Article 23. At the reparations stage, the representatives of the victims or of their next of kin were able to submit independently their own arguments and evidence. An interesting article on the role of NGOs and the petitioners in the request for provisional measures during this

measures were contemplated in Article 25 of the same Rules and in general terms, this provision elaborating Article 63(2) of the Convention, did not make any reference to the participation of persons.

34. In this context, the representatives of the victims in the Caballero Delgado and Santana Case (Colombia), invoking Article 23 in relation to Article 25, requested the Court during the reparations stage to review its decision to lift the provisional measures that it had ordered in the case. The representatives requested that the measures be maintained, at least while the case was before the Court. Although the reinstatement of the measures was also requested by the Commission and by the State in question, the Court not only did not object to the petition of the representatives of the victims to reinstate the protective measures, but it expressly considered the terms of their petition.[59]

35. Although during this period the victims could only participate when the case was at the reparations stage, before this stage and even before the judgment on the merits in the Constitutional Court Case (Peru), an alleged victim submitted to the Court a request for provisional measures, under Articles 63(2) of the Convention and Article 25 of the Rules. Despite the fact that the petition obviously came from one of the alleged victims, the Court decided to adopt the provisional measures, but stated that it had acted *ex officio*. The Court ordered Peru to adopt the measures necessary to ensure effectively the physical, psychological and moral integrity of the petitioner.[60]

36. Another interesting point during this stage occurred in the Loayza Tamayo Case (Peru), in which a person not involved in any way in the proceedings suggested to the representative of the victim that protective measures be requested.[61] The President of the Court accepted this petition and ordered that

stage may be found in V. Krsticevic, "El Papel de las ONG en el Sistema Interamericano de Derechos Humanos", in *Liber Amicorum Héctor Fix-Zamudio*, San José, Inter-American Court of Human Rights, 1998, 416–417.

59 IACtHR, *Caballero Delgado and Santana Case (Colombia)*, Order of January 31, 1997, Preambular Paragraph 2, Enacting Part 1. See also, IACtHR, *Caballero Delgado and Santana Case (Colombia)*, Order of April 16, 1997, Explanatory Statement 4, Preambular Paragraphs 1 and 2, Enacting Part 1.

60 IACtHR, *Constitutional Court Case (Peru)*, Order of the President of April 7, 2000, Explanatory Statement 1, Preambular Paragraph 4 and Enacting Part 1. See also, H. Faundez Ledesma, *El Sistema Interamericano de Protección de los Derechos Humanos*, San José, IIDH, 3rd ed., 2004, 550. See also A. Cançado Trindade, "El nuevo Reglamento de la Corte Interamericana de Derechos Humanos (2000) y su proyección hacia el futuro: La emancipación del ser humano como sujeto del Derecho Internacional", in *El Futuro de la Corte Interamericana de Derechos Humanos*, A. Cançado Trindade and M. Ventura Robles (eds.), San José, Corte Interamericana de Derechos Humanos, UNHCR, 2003, 75.

61 IACtHR, *Loayza Tamayo Case (Peru)*, Order of the President of December 13, 2000.

the State ensure the conditions of security necessary for Mrs. Loayza Tamayo to return to Peru without fear of suffering irreparable harm to her physical, psychological and moral integrity.[62]

1.1.1.1.2.2. Second Stage (2001–2004)

37. The Rules of the Court of 2001 introduced important changes on the participation of individuals in the inter-American system.[63] Although the Rules did not refer specifically to participation with respect to provisional measures (Article 25), Article 23 did state that the presumed victims, their next of kin or their duly accredited representatives could present their requests, arguments and evidence autonomously at all stages of the proceedings after the application had been admitted.[64]

There were two important changes during this stage. One had to do with the competence of the victims and their next of kin to participate directly in the inter-American system and the other was related to the possibility of participating during a broader period, by extending it to the admission of the application. Prior to that, only the representatives could participate and that participation was only possible during the stage of reparations.

38. Within this new legal framework, the Commission requested of the Court during the proceedings on provisional measures in the Bámaca Velásquez Case (Guatemala) an extensive interpretation of Article 23 to enable the petitioners to present their own briefs during the proceedings on provisional measures.[65] The Commission argued that Article 23, which permitted the autonomous participation of the victims and their next of kin, could be applied in the proceedings on provisional measures (Article 25). The Court decided that it was possible to receive requests directly from the beneficiaries of the provisional measures provided that they dealt with matters already before it, specifically those cases where the application had been declared admissible. In cases under consideration by the Commission or in matters already submitted to the Court but where the application had not yet been accepted, then neither the victims nor their representatives or next of kin could request the adoption, broadening or

---

62 H. Faundez Ledesma, El Sistema Interamericano de Protección de los Derechos Humanos, San José, IIDH, 3rd ed., 2004, 550.

63 Rules of Procedure of the Inter-American Court of Human Rights, adopted by the Court at its XLIX Regular Session and in force on June 1, 2001.

64 From the moment the application is declared admissible by the Court.

65 Communication of the Inter-American Commission of August 9, 2001. See IACtHR, *Bámaca Velásquez Case (Guatemala)*, Order of September 5, 2001, Explanatory Statement 18. See also IACtHR, *Carpio Nicolle Case (Guatemala)*, Order of September 5, 2001, Explanatory Statement 24, which refers to the Order of the Court of August 29, 2001.

lifting of provisional measures. The Court also stated that, although the beneficiaries themselves had made the request, the Commission by its obligations under the Convention had the duty to present reports on the implementation of the measures.[66]

39. The first request presented at this stage directly by the representatives of the victims[67] was in the Mayagna (Sumo) Awas Tingni Community Case (Nicaragua) in 2002,[68] in which the representatives of the victims argued that the adoption of measures was urgent because the State, in not complying with the obligations that the Court had imposed on it in the judgment on the merits, was endangering the right to the use and enjoyment of the indigenous community of its lands and resources.[69] In view of the specific facts of the case and the fact that the State, in not complying with the judgment on the merits, was endangering the rights of the Community, the Court adopted the protective measures. At the same time, the Court stated that provisional measures could be adopted even at the supervisory stage of compliance of the judgment[70], because there was the probability that irreparable harm to the rights of persons might also occur during that period.[71]

1.1.1.1.2.3. Third Stage (2004–2009)

40. The modification of the Rules of the Court, which entered into force on January 1, 2004, opens the latest stage governing the participation of individuals in the inter-American system.[72] During this period, unlike the others, the norms

---

66 IACtHR, *Bámaca Velásquez Case (Guatemala)*, Order of August 29, 2001, Explanatory Statement 19.

67 In this chapter, the requests for the adoption of provisional measures presented by the representatives of the victims in the Loayza Tamayo Case (Peru) on September 5, 2000 and in the Bámaca Velásquez Case (Guatemala) on September 23, 2003 were not taken into account because, in the strict sense, the petitions did not request the adoption of the provisional measures. In the Loayza Tamayo Case (Peru) the request was for the reestablishment of the measures and in the Bámaca Velásquez Case for their extension. These measures will be examined in the chapter concerning the entry into force and extension of provisional measures in the inter-American system.

68 IACtHR, *Mayagna (Sumo) Awas Tingni Community Case (Nicaragua)*, Judgment on the Merits of August 31, 2001, paras. 89–90.

69 IACtHR, *Mayagna (Sumo) Awas Tingni Community Case (Nicaragua)*, Order of September 6, 2002, Explanatory Statement 4.

70 IACtHR, *Loayza Tamayo Case (Peru)*, Order of the President of December 13, 2000 and IACtHR, *Loayza Tamayo Case (Peru)*, Order of February 3, 2001.

71 IACtHR, *Mayagna (Sumo) Awas Tingni Community Case (Nicaragua)*, Order of September 6, 2002, Preambular Paragraph 9.

72 The first Rules of Procedure of the Court were adopted in July 1980 and were not amended until July 31, 1991. Due to the influence of the International Court of Justice, established for contentious cases between States, the procedure was slow, especially for contentious cases.

refer explicitly to their competence to request provisional measures. Article 25(3) (now Article 26(3)) of the Rules allows the victims, the alleged victims, their next of kin or their duly accredited representatives to present requests for provisional measures directly to the Court with respect to cases that are being heard by it.[73] Three different views may thus be presented to the Court in proceedings on provisional measures: those of the victims or their legal representatives or their next of kin, those of the Commission and those of the State.

41. During this stage, representatives of the victims have presented to the Court 12 requests for provisional measures. This has happened in the Gómez Paquiyauri Brothers Case (Peru),[74] in the Plan of Sánchez Massacre Case (Guatemala),[75] in the Acevedo Jaramillo *et al.* Case (Peru),[76] in the Fermín Ramírez Case (Guatemala)[77], in the Gutiérrez Soler Case (Colombia)[78], in the Mapiripán Massacre Case (Colombia),[79] in the Serrano-Cruz Sisters Case (El Salvador),[80] Miguel Castro-Castro Prison Case (Peru),[81] in the Integrantes del Equipo de Estudios Comunitarios y Acción Psicosocial (ECAP) Masacre Plan De

---

Faced with the vital necessity of accelerating its proceedings, the Court adopted its second Rules of Procedure, which entered into force in August 1991. In January 1993, the Court amended the part on provisional measures to make the procedure more agile and efficient. The third Rules, which entered into force on January 1, 1997, were ground-breaking since they enabled the representatives of the victims or their next of kin to submit independently their own arguments and evidence during the Reparations stage. The Court also adopted new Rules of Procedure in 2000, which entered into force on June 1, 2001. Article 23 of those Rules gives the victims autonomous representation at all the stages of the proceedings before the Court. The reform of the Rules entered into force on January 1, 2004 and allows individuals to present their request for provisional measures directly to the Court in cases already before it. The last reform entered into force in 2009 and it is a confirmation of the reform of 2004. An assessment of the evolution of the Rules may be found in A. Cançado Trindade, "El nuevo Reglamento de la Corte Interamericana de Derechos Humanos (2000) y su proyección hacia el futuro: La emancipación del ser humano como sujeto del Derecho Internacional", in *El Futuro de la Corte Interamericana de Derechos Humanos,* A. Cançado Trindade and M. Ventura Robles (eds.), San José, Corte Interamericana de Derechos Humanos, UNHCR, 2003, 32–37. See also, M. Ventura Robles, "La Corte Interamericana de Derechos Humanos: la necesidad inmediata de convertirse en un tribunal permanente", *Revista CEJIL, Debates sobre Derechos Humanos y el Sistema Interamericano,* 2005, 16.

73 Article 25(3) Rules of Procedure of the Inter-American Court of Human Rights, partially amended by the Court at its LXI Regular Session and in force as of January 1, 2004. The provision was not amended during the reform of 2009.

74 IACtHR, *Gómez Paquiyauri Brothers Case (Peru),* Order of July 7, 2004.

75 IACtHR, *Plan de Sánchez Massacre Case (Guatemala),* Order of July 30, 2004. In this case, the Commission joined the request for provisional measures to protect one of the witnesses in the case who had received death threats.

76 IACtHR, *Acevedo Jaramillo et al. Case (Peru),* Order of November 23, 2004.

77 IACtHR, *Fermín Ramírez Case (Guatemala),* Order of the President of December 21, 2004.

78 IACtHR, *Gutiérrez Soler Case (Colombia),* Order of March 11, 2005.

79 IACtHR, *Mapiripán Massacre Case (Colombia),* Order of June 25, 2005.

80 IACtHR, The Serrano-Cruz Sisters Case (El Salvador), Order of April 6, 2006.

81 IACtHR, *Miguel Castro-Castro Prison Case (Peru),* Order of January 30, 2007.

Sánchez Case (Guatemala),[82] in the Juan Humberto Sánchez Case (Honduras)[83], in the Juárez-Crussat *et al.* Case (Peru),[84] and in the Kawas Fernández Case (Honduras).[85]

Table 3. Requests for Provisional measures

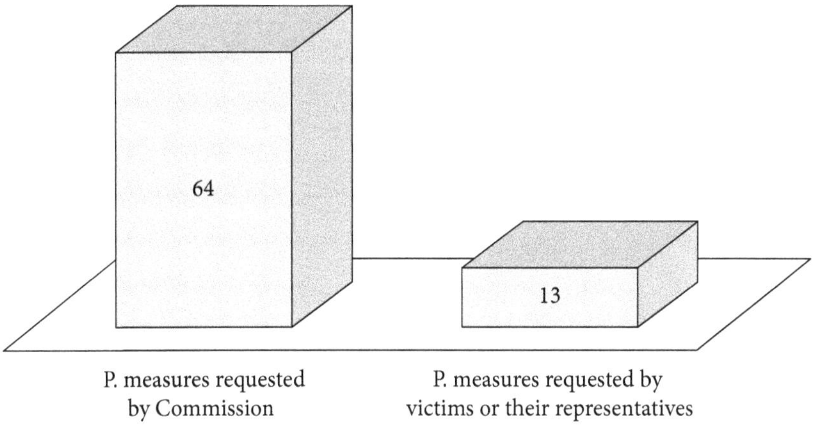

42. In general terms, on the 80 occasions that the Court has ruled on initial requests for the adoption of provisional measures, 13 were petitions presented by representatives of the victims[86] or presented directly by the presumed victim.[87] In this graphic, the earlier-mentioned Case of Caballero Delgado (Colombia) and the Case of Loayza Tamayo (Peru) are not taken into account, because the victims were not asking for the adoption of measures, but their re-establishment. This low percentage is directly related to the circumstance that the alleged victims and their representatives had not until 2004 been explicitly given the competence to ask for provisional measures. It is also due to that that in the above-mentioned year the highest number of requests for provisional measures by the beneficiaries was asked.

82 IACtHR, *Integrantes del Equipo de Estudios Comunitarios y Acción Psicosocial (ECAP) Masacre Plan De Sánchez Case (Guatemala)*, Order of November 20, 2006.

83 IACtHR, *Juan Humberto Sánchez Case (Honduras)*, Order of February 7, 2006.

84 IACtHR, *Juárez-Crussat et al. (Peru)*, Order of May 31, 2006.

85 IACtHR, *Kawas Fernández Case (Honduras)*, Order of November 29, 2008.

86 IACtHR, *Mayagna (Sumo) Awas Tingni Community Case (Nicaragua)*, Order of September 6, 2002; IACtHR, *Gómez Paquiyauri Brothers Case (Peru)*, Order of July 7, 2004; IACtHR, *Plan de Sánchez Massacre Case (Guatemala)*, Order of the President of July 30, 2004; IACtHR, *Acevedo Jaramillo et al. Case (Peru)*, Order of November 23, 2004; IACtHR, *Fermín Ramírez Case (Guatemala)*, Order of the President of December 21, 2004 and IACtHR, *Gutiérrez Soler Case (Colombia)*, Order of March 11, 2005 and IACtHR, *Kawas Fernández Case (Honduras)*, Order of November 29, 2008.

87 IACtHR, *Constitutional Court Case (Peru)*, Order of April 7, 2000.

Table 4. Provisional measures requested by the victims and/or their representatives

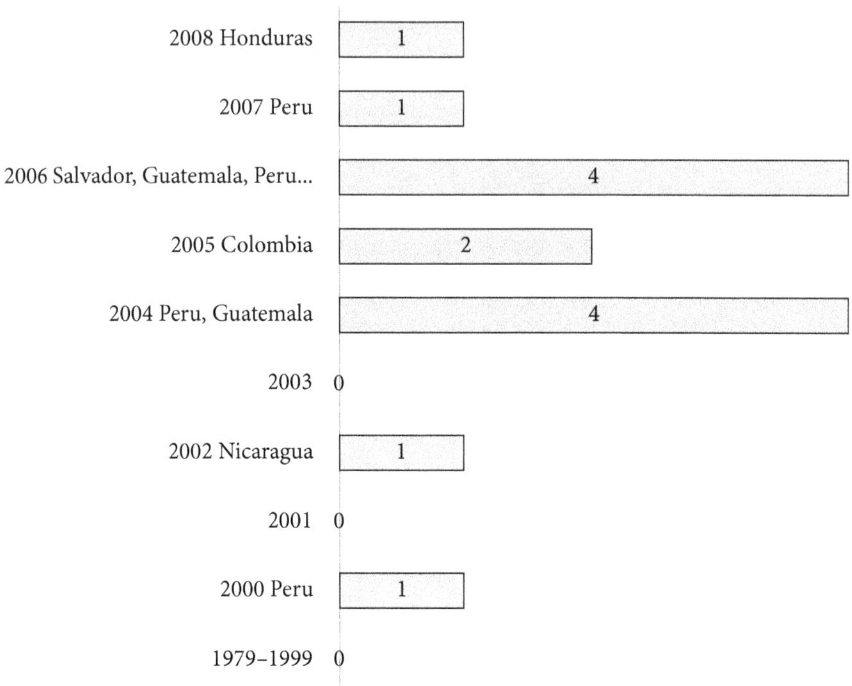

43. The representatives of the victims presented four requests for measures in 2004 and 2006, the most for any one year,[88] which was followed by 2005, 2000, 2002, 2007 and 2008 when the representatives petitioned the Court on two (2005) and one occasion. Five of these petitions concerned Peru, three Guatemala and two regarded Colombia and Honduras, and there was one each on El Salvador and Nicaragua. Four of the 14 requests were rejected by the Court.[89]

The first rejection occurred in the Acevedo Jaramillo *et al.* Case (Peru), in which measures were requested to protect the rights to full freedom and physical integrity of some witnesses and representatives of the victims. The Commission did not support the petition because it did not consider that enough detailed

---

88 In the *Gómez Paquiyauri Brothers Case (Peru)*, the representatives of the alleged victims and their families requested that the Court adopt the measures it deemed appropriate to protect members of the Gómez Paquiyauri family, who had appeared as witnesses, so that they would not suffer reprisals, harassment or persecution. See IACtHR, *Gómez Paquiyauri Brothers Case (Peru)*, Order of May 7, 2004, Explanatory Statement 7.

89 IACtHR, *Acevedo Jaramillo et al. Case (Peru)*, Order of November 23, 2004; IACtHR, *Juan Humberto Sánchez Case (Honduras)*, Order of February 7, 2006, *Juárez Cruzzat et al. (Peru)*, Order of May 31, 2006; IACtHR, *Miguel Castro-Castro Prison Case (Peru)*, Order of January 29, 2008.

information had been furnished to identify an imminent risk of grave and irreparable damage. For its part, the Court held that, since the existence of an extremely grave and urgent situation had not been proved, the situation did not merit the adoption of protective measures.

1.1.1.2. Adoption of Provisional Measures

44. Pursuant to Article 63(2) of the Convention, the Court is the only body with competence to adopt provisional measures that it deems timely in cases of extreme gravity and urgency in order to avoid irreparable damage to persons.[90]

45. The intervention of the Court is restricted to requesting that the State protect those persons who are in a situation of extreme gravity and urgency. The adoption of provisional measures, given their object and legal nature, does not prejudge the merits of the controversy nor does it represent a condemnation of the State.[91] The arguments of the Court in adopting provisional measures do not refer to the merits of the cases, but to the obligations that a State has undertaken as a Party to the Convention.

46. In the Cesti Hurtado Case (Peru), the President of the Court rejected the petition of the Commission that it order Peru to comply with a writ of habeas

---

90 Originally, pursuant to Article 24(4) of the Court's Rules of Procedure, if the Court is not sitting, its President convoked the Court without delay in order for it to rule on the request for provisional measures. This was changed through a reform to the Rules on January 25, 1993 and, with some variations, corresponds to Article 26(5) of the current Rules. The President of the Court, in consultation with the Permanent Commission and, if possible, with the other judges, is now able to call upon the State party concerned to adopt the necessary urgent measures and to act so as to permit that any provisional measures that may be subsequently ordered by the Court in its next session have the required effect. The President's intervention when faced with a request for provisional measures when the Court is not in session is very important because of the urgent nature of the situations that justify resorting to the Court. See Rules of Procedure of the Court, adopted by the Court at its XXXIV Regular Session, held September 9–20, 1996; Article 25(4) of the Rules of Procedure of the Inter-American Court of Human Rights, adopted by the Court at its XLIX Regular Session, held November 16–25, 2000 and Article 25(5) and 26(5) of the Rules of Procedure of the Inter-American Court of Human Rights, partially amended in 2003 and 2009. See also H. Faundez Ledesma, *El Sistema Interamericano de Protección de los Derechos Humanos,* San José, IIDH, 3rd ed., 2004, p. 553; D.J. Padilla, "Provisional Measures Under the American Convention on Human Rights", in *Liber Amicorum Héctor Fix-Zamudio,* San José, Inter-American Court of Human Rights, 1998, 1189; J.M. Pasqualucci, "Provisional Measures in the Inter-American Human Rights System: An Innovative Development in International Law", *Vand. J. Transnat'l L.* 1993–94, 827.

91 IACtHR, *Constitutional Court Case (Peru),* Order of the President of April 7, 2000, Explanatory Statement 1(b)(c) and Preambular Paragraph 12. See also *supra*, footnote 3.

corpus[92] because he deemed that there was a direct relationship between the request of the Commission and the merits of the matter that was before the inter-American system.[93] Similarly, the President of the Court in the Constitutional Court Case (Peru) rejected the petition that requested that Peru be ordered to suspend the trial of one of the alleged victims and to ensure a legal recourse to the adverse decision of an arbitrator.[94] In this case, the President pointed out that the requests referred to trials that were not directly related to the Constitutional Court Case. The Court later stated that if such facts had been submitted to the Court, it could not rule on them, in any event, because that would imply prejudging the merits of the controversy.

Table 5. Applications for provisional measures received, granted and refused by the Inter-American Court

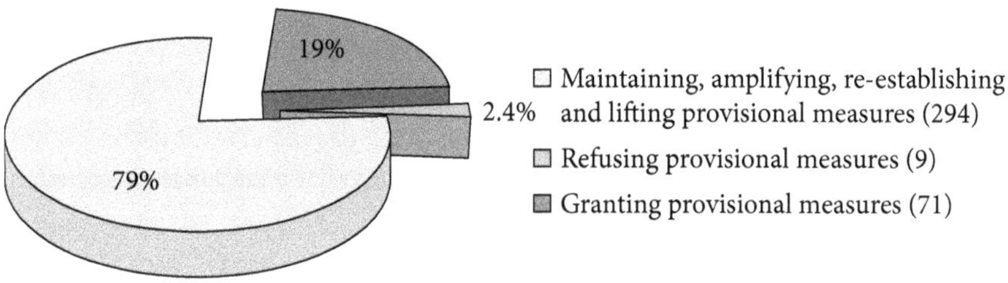

47. As can be seen in Table 5, the general panorama of the activity of the Inter-American Court in the analysed period (1987–2009) shows that the Court has issued 374 resolutions on provisional measures. Of this number, 80 correspond to resolutions is which a request is submitted for the first time. On 71 occasions, the Court accepts the petition and in nine cases rejects the petition. The other 294 resolutions are related to the decision of the Court not to adopt measures but to maintain them, amplify them or reinstate them.

92 The Order was ratified by the Court on September 11, 1997.

93 IACtHR, *Cesti Hurtado Case (Peru)*, Order of the President of July 29, 1997, Preambular Paragraphs 4 and 5.

94 The Order was ratified by the Court on August 14, 2000.

Table 6. Number of provisional measures adopted per year

48. If one takes into account the number of cases in which the Court adopted provisional measures per year, the Statistics show that the major number of measures was adopted in 2004 (13). The significant rise of measures in 2004 is directly related to the reform of the Rules of Court in that year, which gave explicitly competence to the alleged victims, their families and representatives to request provisional measures. In the same way, the rise of requests is related to the situation of the persons that work in a number of media enterprises in Venezuela and the persons that were actively involved as members of the opposition to the Venezuelan president. In this way, 4 of the 13 provisional measures were requested by the representatives of the alleged victims and 4 cases were linked to Venezuela.

1.1.1.2.1. Adoption in cases pending before the Inter-American Commission

49. With respect to cases that are being considered by the Inter-American Commission, the Inter-American Court may only adopt provisional measures at the petition of the Commission, its President or, in his absence, one of the Vice Presidents.[95]

However, it is important in this regard to point out that the adoption of provisional measures in a case does not enable the Court to oblige the Commission to submit that case to its jurisdiction.[96] Given this lack of competence, the Court has recommended on several occasions that the Commission refer cases to it. For example, the Court in the Colotenango Case (Guatemala), at the request of the Commission, had adopted provisional measures to protect certain witnesses, family members and lawyers. Since the measures had been in force for 19 months, the State argued that protective measures were temporary in nature and that, therefore, it was opportune, in view of the time that had lapsed, that they be terminated. Although the Court decided to extend them, it urged the Commission to consider submitting the case to its consideration since the Court lacked sufficient direct knowledge of the facts and of the surrounding circumstances to take the most appropriate decision on the request for provisional measures.[97]

1.1.1.2.2. Adoption in cases pending before the Inter-American Court

50. Requests for the adoption of measures may be presented as soon as the case is submitted to the Court and the Court may adopt provisional measures even when overseeing compliance of its judgments on the merits or on reparations.[98]

---

95 Article 63(2) American Convention; Article 26(2) Rules of Procedure of the Court; Article 74(1) and 74(2) Rules of Procedure of the Commission, adopted by the Commission at its 109th Special Session, held December 4–8, 2000, amended at its 116th Regular Session, held October 7–25, 2002, and at its 118th Regular Session, held October 6–24, 2003; H. Gros Espiell, *Estudios sobre Derechos Humanos II*, Madrid, Civitas, 1988, 170 and T. Buergenthal, "The Inter-American Court of Human Rights", *Am.U.L.Rev.* 1982, 240.

96 IACtHR, *James et al. Case (Trinidad and Tobago)*, Order of the President of May 27, 1999, Preambular Paragraph 7.

97 IACtHR, *Colotenango Case (Guatemala)*, Order of February 1, 1996, Explanatory Statement 4, Preambular Paragraphs 5 and 6.

98 IACtHR, *Mayagna (Sumo) Awas Tingni Community Case (Nicaragua)*, Order of September 6, 2002, Preambular Paragraph 9.

Table 7. **Provisional measures requested when the case was pending before the Commission or before the Court**

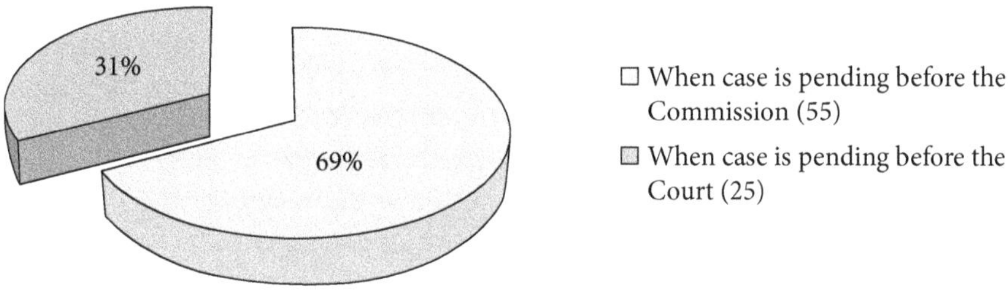

51. To date, provisional measures have been requested on 25 occasions with respect to cases that were being heard by the Court. The measures were requested when the matter was under consideration by the Commission on the other 55 occasions. Eleven of the 25 measures were requested by the Commission,[99] 12 by the representatives of the victims,[100] one directly by the victim,[101] and one directly by the Court.[102] Four of them were rejected.[103] As is mentioned earlier, the high adoption rate of provisional measures with regard to cases before the Commission, is due to the fact that the majority of the cases were pending before the Commission and not before the Court.

52. It is important to point out that, although the Court in its jurisprudence states that it had adopted provisional measures *ex officio*[104] in the Constitutional Court Case (Peru), the Ivcher Bronstein Case (Peru) and the Velásquez Rodríquez Case (Honduras), an examination of each of the orders in those cases leads to the conclusion that the adoption of measures was not the result of the particular interest of the Court but the result of a request made by one of the parties.

---

99 Velásquez Rodríguez, Fairén Garbi and Solis Corrales and Godínez Cruz Cases (Honduras). In these cases the Court adopted just one Order to protect individuals related to three different cases, all of them against Honduras. See also, Caballero and Santana (Colombia), Blake (Guatemala), Suárez Rosero (Ecuador), Loayza Tamayo (Peru), Bámaca Velásquez (Guatemala), Ivcher Bronstein (Peru), Helen Mack Chang *et al.* (Guatemala), 19 Tradesmen (Colombia), Gloria Giralt de García Prieto *et al.* (El Salvador) and Tyrone Dacosta Cadogan (Barbados) Cases.

100 Mayagna Sumo (Awas) Tingni Community (Nicaragua), Gómez Paquiyauri Brothers (Peru), Fermín Ramírez (Peru), Plan de Sánchez Massacre (Guatemala), Gutiérrez Soler (Colombia), Mapiripán Massacre (Colombia), Serrano Cruz Sisters (El Salvador), Miguel Castro-Castro Prison (Peru), Integrantes del Equipo de Estudios Comunitarios y Acción Psicosocial (ECAP). Masacre Plan de Sánchez (Guatemala), Juan Humberto Sánchez (Honduras), Juárez Cruzzat *et al.* (Peru), Kawas Fernández (Honduras) Cases.

101 Constitutional Court Case (Peru).

102 Bueno Alves Case (Argentina).

103 Serrano Cruz Sisters (El Salvador), Miguel Castro-Castro Prison (Peru), Juan Humberto Sánchez (Honduras) and Juárez Cruzzat *et al.* (Peru).

104 IACtHR, *Ivcher Bronstein Case (Peru)*, Order of November 21, 2000.

In the Constitutional Court Case, the presumed victim in a note of April 3, 2000 submitted to the Court, under Articles 63(2) of the Convention and 25 of the Rules of the Court, a request for provisional measures to protect her and her husband. The Court accepted the request and proceeded to adopt the measures. This also occurred during a public hearing at the Court in the Ivcher Bronstein Case, where the witnesses stated that they feared that their rights would be violated and therefore thought it timely to request the Court to adopt provisional measures. The Court ordered the State to adopt forthwith the measures necessary to protect their physical, psychological and moral integrity and the right to judicial guarantees.[105] Finally, in the Velásquez Rodríguez Case (Honduras), the Commission, by a note of 1987, requested the adoption of measures to protect some witnesses who were at grave risk for having testified in the case before the Court.

Table 8. Provisional Measures (P.M.) requested while the case was pending before the Court and their relationship with the judgments

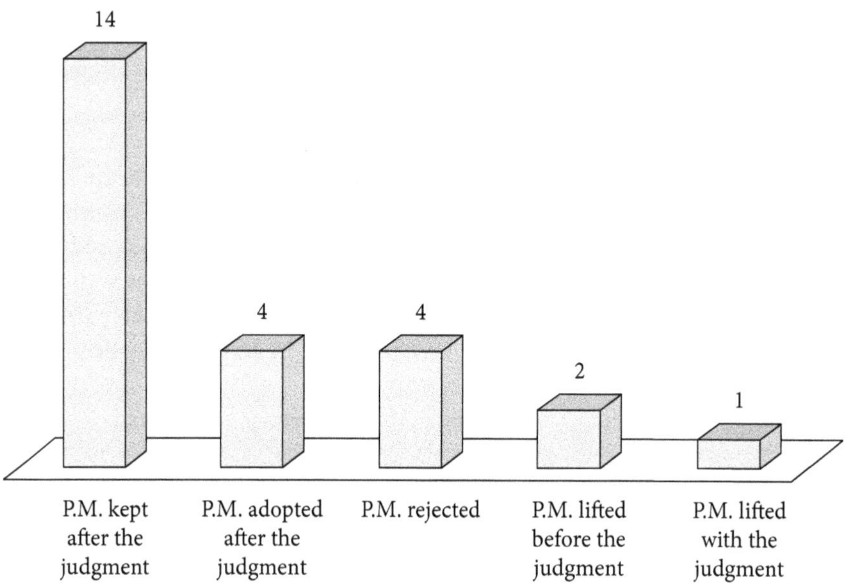

53. As is shown by Table 8, in 14 of 25 cases (56%) in which measures were requested when the case was being heard by the Court, the measures were maintained even after the Court delivered its judgment on the merits.[106] On four

105 IACtHR, *Ivcher Bronstein Case (Peru)*, Order of November 21, 2000, Explanatory Statement 6, Preambular Paragraph 6, Enacting Parts 1 and 2.

106 Blake Case (Guatemala), Loayza Tamayo Case (Peru), Ivcher Bronstein Case (Peru), Velásquez Rodríguez, Fairén Garbi and Solis Corrales Cases (Honduras), Gómez Paquiyauri Brothers

occasions the Court adopted provisional measures after the judgment on the merits (16%), i.e. in the Plan of Sánchez Massacre Case (Guatemala), the 19 Tradesmen Case (Colombia), the Mayagna (Sumo) Awas Tingni Community Case (Nicaragua) and the Integrantes del Equipo de Estudios Comunitarios y Acción Psicosocial (ECAP). Masacre Plan de Sánchez Case (Guatemala). Only once did the Court decide to lift the measures contained in the judgment on the merits.[107] In the Suárez Rosero Case (Ecuador) and the Bueno Alves Case (Argentina) the Court adopted and lifted the measures before deciding on the merits.

1.1.2. PASSIVE STANDING

1.1.2.1. The States

54. All thirty-five States of the Americas have ratified the Charter of the Organisation of American States and are thus member States of the Organisation.[108] The twenty-one States that originally signed the Charter on April 30, 1948 were: Argentina, Bolivia, Brazil, Chile, Colombia, Costa Rica, Cuba, the Dominican Republic, Ecuador, El Salvador, Guatemala, Haiti, Honduras, Mexico, Nicaragua, Panama, Paraguay, Peru, the United States, Uruguay and Venezuela.

The States that have joined the OAS since then are Barbados (1967), Jamaica (1969), Grenada (1975), Suriname (1977), Dominica (1979), St. Lucia (1979) Antigua and Barbuda (1981), St. Vincent and the Grenadines (1981), the Bahamas (1982), St. Kitts and Nevis (1984), Canada (1990), Belize (1991) and Guyana (1991).

Case (Peru), Caballero Delgado and Santana Case (Colombia), Helen Mack Chang *et al.* (Guatemala), Bámaca Velásquez Case (Guatemala), Constitutional Court Case (Peru), Gutiérrez Soler Case (Colombia) and Mapiripán Massacre Case (Colombia). No mention is made of the Cesti Hurtado Case (Peru), Paniagua Morales *et al.* and Vásquez *et al.* Case (Guatemala), James, Briggs, Noel, Garcia and Bethel (Trinidad and Tobago) nor to the Carpio Nicolle Case, because, in spite of the fact that the Court maintained the provisional measures after its judgment, the adoption of the measures took place when the case was under consideration in the Commission and not in the Court.

107 Fermín Ramírez Case (Guatemala). No mention is made to "La Nación" Newspaper Case (Herrera-Ulloa Case) (Costa Rica) nor to the Raxcacó Reyes *et al.* Case (Guatemala) because the provisional measures were adopted when the case was under consideration in the Commission.

108 Antigua and Barbuda, Argentina, Bahamas, Barbados, Belize, Bolivia, Brazil, Canada, Chile, Colombia, Costa Rica, Cuba (by Resolution of the Eighth Meeting of Consultation of Ministers of Foreign Affairs, in 1962 the present Cuban Government is excluded from participating in the OAS), Dominica, Dominican Republic, Ecuador, El Salvador, Grenada, Guatemala, Guyana, Haiti, Honduras, Jamaica, Mexico, Nicaragua, Panama, Paraguay, Peru, St. Kitts and Nevis, St. Lucia, St. Vincent and the Grenadines, Suriname, Trinidad and Tobago, United States, Uruguay and Venezuela.

55. As of 2009, only 24 of the 35 States (68,5%) have ratified the American Convention[109] and of them, 21 (60%) have accepted the contentious jurisdiction of the Court.[110] The States that have not ratified the Convention are: Antigua and Barbuda, Bahamas, Belize, Canada, Guyana, St. Kitts and Nevis, St. Lucia, St. Vincent and the Grenadines and the United States.[111]

56. Trinidad and Tobago on the one hand and Peru on the other hand merit special mention. Trinidad and Tobago has been an OAS member State since 1967 and it ratified the American Convention in 1991, at which time it recognised the contentious jurisdiction of the Court. However, on May 26, 1998, Trinidad and Tobago denounced the American Convention and that denunciation of the Convention made in accordance with Article 78 of the Convention entered into force in 1999. It is also relevant to mention that Peru denounced the Convention in 1999. On that occasion, the Court declared inadmissible the attempt of Peru, by its withdrawal, to exclude from the jurisdiction of the Court all of the cases in which the State had not responded to the applications. The Court held that its jurisdiction "cannot be contingent upon events extraneous to its own actions."[112] In 2001, with the arrival of a new President, Peru again accepted the contentious jurisdiction of the Court.

57. While there is no question that the Inter-American Commission may order precautionary measures with respect to any OAS member State, whether or not it has ratified the Convention, it is not so clear which States are subject to provisional measures ordered by the Court.

One school holds that the Court may adopt provisional measures with respect to those States that have ratified the Convention,[113] while another view holds that the Court may adopt them only with respect to States that, in addition to having ratified the Convention, have accepted its contentious jurisdiction under Article 62 of the Convention.[114] Here it is important to recall that the jurisdiction of the Court does not operate *ipso iure*, and a State is not considered to have accepted

109 Argentina, Barbados, Bolivia, Brazil, Chile, Colombia, Costa Rica, Dominica, Dominican Republic, Ecuador, El Salvador, Grenada, Guatemala, Haiti, Honduras, Jamaica, Mexico, Nicaragua, Panama, Paraguay, Peru, Suriname, Uruguay and Venezuela.

110 Argentina, Barbados, Bolivia, Brazil, Chile, Colombia, Costa Rica, Dominican Republic, Ecuador, El Salvador, Guatemala, Haiti, Honduras, Mexico, Nicaragua, Panama, Paraguay, Peru, Suriname, Uruguay and Venezuela. See <www.oas.org/key_issues/spa/OEAderechoshumanos.htm>.

111 E. Lagos, "La Corte Interamericana de Derechos Humanos a la luz de las decisions de Organos Políticos de la OEA", in *Liber Amicorum Héctor Fix-Zamudio*, San José, Inter-American Court of Human Rights, 1998, 933.

112 IACtHR, *Constitutional Court Case (Peru)*, Competence, Judgment of September 24, 1999, para. 33.

113 H. Faundez Ledesma.

114 T. Buergenthal, R. Nieto Navia, J.M. Pasqualucci and H. Gros Espiell.

its jurisdiction by merely ratifying the Convention.[115] Unlike the Commission, the Court lacks competence over States that have not made a declaration recognising its jurisdiction in the terms of Article 62 of the Convention, that is, by means of a special separate and unconditional declaration, on the condition of reciprocity, for a specified period or for a specific case.[116]

The principal difference between the two positions is that one starts from the idea that the adoption of provisional measures is part of the Court's general function of human rights protection as the supervisory organ of the Convention, while for the other the competence of the Court to adopt provisional measures arises from its contentious jurisdiction. Thus, for the former it is only necessary that the State has ratified the Convention, while the latter insists that it is necessary that the State has also accepted the binding jurisdiction of the Court.

58. The first view, which I fully endorse, is developed and defended by Faúndez Ledesma, who argues that the power of the Court to adopt provisional measures is part of its general competence under the Convention to protect human rights. It is not necessary, therefore, that a State make a declaration accepting the Court's jurisdiction, because mere ratification of the Convention enables the Court to adopt any provisional measure that it deems necessary to protect the rights that are set forth in the Convention.

Faúndez Ledesma does not agree that the measures are part of the Court's jurisdictional function mainly for two reasons. The first is that the measures under Article 63(2) of the American Convention may be adopted in matters that are not being heard by the Court and may even never be heard by it.[117] Thus, if the adoption of provisional measures does not necessarily mean that the case has to be heard by the Court or has to be submitted to its consideration, then it makes no sense to require that the Court has jurisdictional competence over the States. Secondly, the measures are not part of the jurisdictional function because their adoption does not imply a decision on the merits of the controversy between the

---

115 H. Faundez Ledesma, *El Sistema Interamericano de Protección de los Derechos Humanos*, San José, IIDH, 3rd ed., 2004, 605.

116 R. Nieto Navia, "Las medidas provisionales en la Corte Interamericana de Derechos Humanos", in *La Corte y el Sistema Interamericano de Derechos Humanos*, R. Nieto Navia (ed.), San José, Corte Interamericana de Derechos Humanos, 1994, 385. See also D.J. Padilla, "Provisional Measures Under the American Convention on Human Rights", in *Liber Amicorum Héctor Fix-Zamudio*, San José, Inter-American Court of Human Rights, 1998, 1189–1190. We believe that Becerra Ramírez, who considers that the orders for provisional measures adopted by the Court are jurisdictional, also defends this position. See M. Becerra Ramirez, "Las Decisiones Judiciales como Fuente del Derecho Internacional de los Derechos Humanos", in *Liber Amicorum Héctor Fix-Zamudio*, San José, Inter-American Court of Human Rights, 1998, 435.

117 H. Faundez Ledesma, *El Sistema Interamericano de Protección de los Derechos Humanos*, San José, IIDH, 3rd ed., 2004, 519–529.

petitioner and the State.[118] The Court, in adopting provisional measures, simply fulfills its duty to protect the rights of persons by ordering the State to implement certain measures that have as their purpose avoiding damage to the rights of those who are in an extremely grave and urgent situation. This order is issued independently of the international responsibility that is being debated in the course of the matter.

Nonetheless, this position admits that a State, should the case arise, might object to the adoption of provisional measures because it believes that the Court has no jurisdiction to adopt them or because it thinks that there is a lack of jurisdiction with respect to certain specific matters regarding that State. An example would be where a State, upon ratifying or adhering to the Convention, has made a valid reservation, which with respect to that State restricts certain areas from the application of the Convention.[119]

59. The other position is held by Thomas Buergenthal,[120] Rafael Nieto Navia,[121] Asdrubal Aguiar, Jo Pasqualucci[122] and Héctor Gros Espiell.[123] According to them, the Court may only adopt provisional measures with respect to States that

---

118 IACtHR, *James et al. Case (Trinidad and Tobago)*, Order of the President of May 27, 1998, Preambular Paragraph 7; IACtHR, *The Miguel Agustín Pro Juárez Human Rights Center et al. Case (Mexico)*, Order of November 30, 2001, Preambular paragraph 10; IACtHR, *The Urso Branco Prisons Case (Brazil)*, Order of June 18, 2002, Preambular Paragraph 10; IACtHR, *Luis Uzcátegui Case (Venezuela)*, Order of November 27, 2002, Preambular Paragraph 6; IACtHR, *Indigenous Kankuamo Community Case (Colombia)*, Order of July 5, 2004, Preambular Paragraph 13; IACtHR, *Communities of the Jiguamiando and of the Curbaradó Case (Colombia)*, Order of March 6, 2003, Preambular Paragraph 12; IACtHR, *Lysias Fleury Case (Haiti)*, Order of June 7, 2003, Preambular Paragraph 10; IACtHR, *Indigenous Sarayaku People Case (Ecuador)*, Order of July 6, 1004, Preambular Paragraph 12; IACtHR, *Carlos Nieto et al. Case (Venezuela)*, Order of July 9, 2004, Preambular Paragraph 10 and IACtHR, *Mendoza Prisons Case (Argentina)*, Order of November 22, 2004, Enacting Part 17. See also IACtHR, *Cesti Hurtado Case (Peru)*, Order of the President of July 29, 1997, where the President of the Court decided not to adopt the provisional measures requested by the Commission because it would prejudge the merits of the case.

119 H. Faundez Ledesma, *El Sistema Interamericano de Protección de los Derechos Humanos*, San José, IIDH, 3rd ed., 2004, 516.

120 T. Buergenthal, "The Inter-American Court of Human Rights" *Am.U.L.Rev.* 1982, 241 and T. Buergenthal, "The Inter-American System for the Protection of Human Rights", in *Human Rights in International Law, Legal and Policy Issues*, T. Meron (ed.), Oxford, Clarendon Press, 1984, 465–466.

121 R. Nieto Navia, "Las medidas provisionales en la Corte Interamericana de Derechos Humanos", in *La Corte y el Sistema Interamericano de Derechos Humanos*, R. Nieto Navia (ed.), San José, Corte Interamericana de Derechos Humanos, 1994, 385.

122 J.M. Pasqualucci, "Medidas Provisionales en la Corte Interamericana de Derechos Humanos: Una Comparación con la Corte Internacional de Justicia y la Corte Europea de Derechos Humanos", *Revista del Instituto Interamericano de Derechos Humanos* 1994, 70; J.M. Pasqualucci, "Provisional Measures in the Inter-American Human Rights System: An Innovative Development in International Law", *Vand. J. Transnat'l L.* 1993–94, 823–824.

123 H. Gros Espiell, *Estudios sobre Derechos Humanos II*, Madrid, Civitas, 1988, 169–171.

have expressly recognised its contentious jurisdiction pursuant to Article 62(1) of the Convention.[124] Although they are in agreement that mere ratification of the Convention by a State is not sufficient to enable the Court to adopt provisional measures, it is important to mention that their positions differ when there is a doubt as to the Court's jurisdiction.[125]

Nieto Navia believes that it is absolutely necessary that there is no doubt that the State has accepted the contentious jurisdiction of the Court.[126] If such jurisdiction is in question, it must first be clarified in order to examine the topic of provisional measures. He is also of the opinion that it is obvious that proceedings on provisional measures are inextricably linked to the contentious material. He bases his reasoning on Article 62 of the Convention and the Court's practice, in adopting measures of protection, to always refer to the fact that the State is a Party to the Convention and that it has accepted the Court's contentious jurisdiction. An indication that his position is correct is that to date provisional measures have not been adopted with regard to a State that has not met both conditions.[127]

For their part, Buergenthal and Pasqualucci state that the Court may adopt provisional measures after having established, albeit preliminarily, that the State has accepted its jurisdiction.[128] If the jurisdiction is questioned in a case, the gravity and urgency of a situation that would justify the application of provisional measures should encourage the Court to follow the precedent of the International Court of Justice.[129] That tribunal has held that it only has to satisfy itself that

---

124 Article 62(1) ACHR states: "A State Party may, upon depositing its instrument of ratification or adherence to this Convention, or at any subsequent time, declare that it recognizes as binding, *ipso facto*, and not requiring special agreement, the jurisdiction of the Court on all matters relating to the interpretation or application of this Convention". See H. Faundez Ledesma, *El Sistema Interamericano de Protección de los Derechos Humanos*, San José, IIDH, 3rd ed., 2004, 522.

125 T. Buergenthal, "The American and the European Conventions on Human Rights: Similarities and Differences, *Am. U. L. Rev.* 1980–81, 155–156. See also T. Buergenthal, "The Inter-American Court of Human Rights", *Am. J. Int'l L.* 1982, 241.

126 H. Faundez Ledesma, *El Sistema Interamericano de Protección de los Derechos Humanos*, San José, IIDH, 3rd ed., 2004, 521.

127 Although the article referred to is from 1994, it should be noted that as of 2009, all the cases where the Court adopted provisional measures concerned States that had accepted its competence. R. Nieto Navia, *Las medidas provisionales en la Corte Interamericana de Derechos Humanos*, in *La Corte y el Sistema Interamericano de Derechos Humanos*, R. Nieto Navia (ed.), San José, Corte Interamericana de Derechos Humanos, 1994, 386.

128 T. Buergenthal, "The Inter-American Court of Human Rights", *Am. J. Int'l L.* 1982, 241; T. Buergenthal, "The Inter-American System for the Protection of Human Rights", in *Human Rights in International Law, Legal and Policy Issues*, T. Meron (ed.), Oxford, Clarendon Press, 1984, 465–466 and J.M. Pasqualucci, "Provisional Measures in the Inter-American Human Rights System: An Innovative Development in International Law", *Vand. J. Transnat'l L.* 1993–94, 826.

129 J.M. Pasqualucci, "Provisional Measures in the Inter-American Human Rights System: An Innovative Development in International Law", *Vand. J. Transnat'l L.* 1993–94, 826. T.

every indication leads to a *prima facie* basis for its jurisdiction. It is, thus, not obligated to ensure that it has jurisdiction as to the merits of the case.[130] A *prima facie* basis of jurisdiction, when it is questioned, therefore should be sufficient in order for the Inter-American Court to study a request for provisional measures.[131]

Aguiar and Gros Espiell are of the opinion that, when the jurisdiction of the Court is questioned, it is only necessary that the Court believe that it has jurisdiction in order for the measures to be adopted. In that context, the measures may be requested from the moment that the application is submitted to the Court, even when a preliminary objection has been submitted that questions its jurisdiction.[132]

60. The view of Aguiar and Gros Espiell seems to be the position of the Inter-American Court, according to its jurisprudence. In practice, the Court has only adopted provisional measures with respect to States that have accepted its jurisdiction and in each case its orders have mentioned such acceptance at least once. This means that to date the Court has not considered matters related to Dominica, Grenada or Jamaica, which are States that have ratified the Convention but have not accepted the jurisdiction of the Court.

61. Accepting the position that the Court may only adopt measures regarding States that have recognised its contentious jurisdiction would mean that the States regarding which the Court could adopt provisional measures are: Argentina, Barbados, Bolivia, Brazil, Chile, Colombia, Costa Rica, the Dominican Republic, Ecuador, El Salvador, Guatemala, Haiti, Honduras, Mexico, Nicaragua, Panama, Paraguay, Peru, Suriname, Uruguay and Venezuela.

If one would accept the second position, that is the one that holds that it is only necessary to ratify the Convention, this would add Dominica, Grenada and Jamaica to the above list.

Buergenthal, "The Inter-American System for the Protection of Human Rights", in *Human Rights in International Law, Legal and Policy Issues*, T. Meron (ed.), Oxford, Clarendon Press, 1984, 465.

130 Case Concerning Military and Paramilitary Activities in and Against Nicaragua (Nicaragua v. United States of America). 23 *I.L.M.* 468, 473 (I.C.J.) 1984.

131 J.M. Pasqualucci, "Medidas Provisionales en la Corte Interamericana de Derechos Humanos: Una Comparación con la Corte Internacional de Justicia y la Corte Europea de Derechos Humanos", *Revista del Instituto Interamericano de Derechos Humanos* 1994, 71.

132 H. Gros Espiell, *Estudios sobre Derechos Humanos II*, Madrid, Civitas, 1988, p. 170. See also H. Faundez Ledesma, *El Sistema Interamericano de Protección de los Derechos Humanos*, San José, IIDH, 3rd ed., 2004, 511.

62. The States about which there is no doubt that the Court cannot adopt provisional measures are Antigua and Barbuda, the Bahamas, Belize, Canada, Guyana, St. Kitts and Nevis, St. Lucia, St. Vincent and the Grenadines and the United States because, although they are OAS member States, they have not ratified the American Convention. At the present time, Trinidad and Tobago would also be in this group because, as has been explained (*supra*, n° 56), it has denounced the Convention. It must, however, be borne in mind that, in spite of the denunciation, the Court has maintained provisional measures with respect to matters on which it had ordered measures before the denunciation[133] because denouncing the Convention does not relieve a State from its obligations or for acts that occurred during the time that the contentious jurisdiction of the Court was in force.[134]

63. Although 21 States have accepted the contentious jurisdiction of the Court, provisional measures have been adopted regarding only 15 of them during the past 21 years.[135] Although Bolivia,[136] Chile,[137] Panama,[138] Paraguay,[139] Suriname[140] and Uruguay have ratified the Convention and have accepted the contentious jurisdiction of the Court, there have been to date no requests for the adoption of provisional measures with regard to them.

---

133 IACtHR, *James et al. Case (Trinidad and Tobago)*, Order of May 25, 1999, Enacting Part 1.

134 IACtHR, *James et al. Case (Trinidad and Tobago)*, Order of the President of June 19, 1999, Explanatory Statement 3, Preambular Paragraph 3. The Court ratified this decision by Order of September 25, 1999. This is the only case where a State has not complied with provisional measures arguing that the Court did not have competence to adopt them. See IACtHR, *James et al. Case (Trinidad and Tobago)*, Order of August 25, 2000, Explanatory Statement 13. It should be noted that Peru had also denounced the Convention and later, with the new government, again recognized the competence of the Court.

135 Argentina, Barbados, Brazil, Colombia, Costa Rica, Dominican Republic, Ecuador, El Salvador, Guatemala, Haiti, Honduras, Mexico, Nicaragua, Peru, Trinidad and Tobago and Venezuela. It should be underlined that Trinidad and Tobago has denounced the Convention.

136 Provisional measures were not requested, but the Trujillo Oroza Case and Ticona Estrada case were processed.

137 Provisional measures were not requested, but "The Last Temptation of Christ" Case, the Palamara Iribarne Case, the Claude Reyes *et al.* Case and the Almonacid Arellano *et al.* Case were processed.

138 Provisional measures were not requested, but the Baena Ricardo *et al.* Case was processed.

139 Provisional measures were not requested, but the Ricardo Canese, "Juvenile Reeducation Institute", the Indigenous Community Yakye Axa, Sawhoyamaxa Indigenous Community, Goiburú *et al.* and Vargas-Areco Cases were processed.

140 Provisional Measures were not requested, but the Aloeboetoe *et al.* Case, the Gangaram Panday Case, and the Moiwana Village Case were processed.

Table 9. Number of provisional measures adopted per State

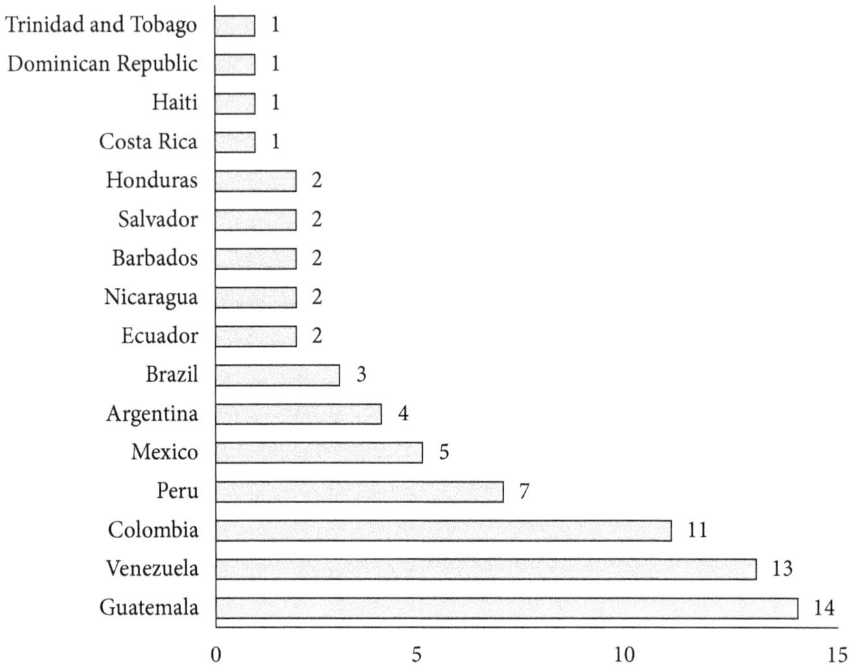

64. An analysis of the number of cases by country shows that Guatemala is the State against which the Court has adopted the most provisional measures, a total of 14.[141] It is followed by Venezuela with thirteen,[142] Colombia with eleven,[143]

---

141 Bámaca Velásquez Case, Blake Case, Carpio Nicolle Case, Colotenando Case, Chunimá Case, Fermín Ramírez Case, Helen Mack Chang *et al.* Case, Plan de Sánchez Massacre Case, Paniagua Morales *et al.* Case, Raxcacó Reyes *et al.* Case, Serech y Saquic Case, Vogt Case, Forensic Anthropology Foundation Case and Integrantes del Equipo de Estudios Comunitarios y Acción Psicosocial (ECAP). Masacre Plan de Sánchez Case.

142 Carlos Nieto *et al.* Case, "El Nacional" and "Asi es la Noticia" Newspapers Case, Eloisa Barrios *et al.* Case, "Globovisión" Television Station Case, Liliana Ortega *et al.* Case, Luis Uzcátegui Case, Luisiana Rios *et al.* Case, Marta Colomina and Liliana Velásquez Case, Penitentiary Center of the Central Occidental Region (Uribana Prison) Case, Yare I and Yare II Capital Region Center Case, Capital El Rodeo I & El Rodeo II Judicial Confinement Center Case, Monagas Judicial Confinement Center ("La Pica") Case and the Guerrero-Gallucci and Martínez-Barrios Case.

143 Alvarez *et al.* Case, Caballero Delgado and Santana Case, Clemente Teherán Case, Peace Community of San José de Apartadó Case, Communities of the Jiguamiando and of the Curbaradó Case, 19 Tradesmen Case, Giraldo Cardona Case, Gutiérrez Soler Case Indigenous Kankuamo Community Case, Mapiripán Massacre Case and Mery Naranjo *et al.* Case.

Peru with seven,[144] Mexico with five,[145] Argentina with four,[146] Brazil with three,[147] Ecuador,[148] Nicaragua,[149] Barbados,[150] Salvador[151] and Honduras,[152] with two each and Costa Rica,[153] Haiti,[154] the Dominican Republic,[155] and Trinidad and Tobago[156] with one each.

With regard to Guatemala, the majority of the measures that were ordered are related to the armed conflict that was taking place in the country. In this sense, the primary objective of the measures was to protect the persons that were threatened and harassed by the de members of the paramilitary Patrullas de Autodefensa Civil (PAC).[157] The first measures were adopted in 1991 and the last ones in 2009. It has to be mentioned that from 1996 on, once the peace agreements in Guatemala were signed, the beneficiaries of the measures were above all the alleged victims, their relatives or witnesses in the cases pending under the inter-American system. The threats in these cases came from the ex-members of the above-mentioned paramilitary groups, which wanted to avoid that Guatemala as a state was held internationally responsible for the acts committed by them.

More or less the same can be said with regard to the provisional measures adopted against Colombia. The majority of those measures are related to the armed conflict that is still ravaging this country. The beneficiaries of the provisional measures are civilians without any link to the armed conflict, who on many occasions have declared that they would keep their neutrality with regard to the conflict. Between the persons protected, one finds indigenous communities, farmers and human rights defenders. According to what can be

---

144 Bustíos-Rojas Case, Cesti Hurtado Case, Ivcher Bronstein Case, Loayza Tamayo Case, Constitutional Court Case, Gómez Paquiyauri Brothers Case and the Ramírez Hinostroza *et al.* Case. The Court on five occasions rejected requests for provisional measures against Peru: Acevedo Jaramillo *et al.* Case, Peruvian Prisons Case, Chipoco Case, Miguel Castro – Castro Prison Case and Juarez Cruzzat *et al.* Case.

145 Miguel Agustín Pro Juárez Human Rights Center *et al.* Case, Digna Ochoa y Plácido *et al.* Case, Gallardo Rodríguez Case, Leonel Rivero *et al.* Case and Pilar Noriega *et al.* Case.

146 Mendoza Prisons Case, Reggiardo Tolosa Case, Bueno Alves Case and Millacura Llaipén *et al.* Case.

147 Urso Branco Prison Case, Persons imprisoned in the "Dr. Sebastião Martins Silveira" Penitentiary in Araraquara, São Paulo Case and Children Deprived of Liberty in the "Complexo do Tatuapé" of FEBEM Case.

148 Indigenous Sarayaku People Case and Suárez Rosero Case.

149 Alemán Lacayo Case and Mayagna (Sumo) Awas Tingni Community Case.

150 Boyce and Joseph Case and Tyrone Dacosta Cadogan Case.

151 Adrián Meléndez Quijano *et al.* Case and Gloria Giralt de García-Prieto *et al.* Case.

152 Velásquez Rodríguez, Fairen Garbi and Solis Corrales Cases and Kawas Fernández Case.

153 Herrera-Ulloa ("La Nación" Newspaper) Case.

154 Lysias Fleury Case.

155 Haitians and Dominicans of Haitian Origin in the Dominican Republic Case.

156 James, Briggs, Noel, Garcia and Bethel *et al.* Case.

157 A kind of paramilitary group.

found in the resolutions, the members of the Colombian army and the members of the paramilitary Autodefensas Unidas de Colombia (AUC) are the people responsible for the alleged acts of violence and threats.

It is interesting to see that the provisional measures indicated against Venezuela were adopted from 2002 until 2009. The beneficiaries in the majority of the cases are persons that were opposed to the Venezuelan government and during this whole period Mr. Hugo Chávez held the presidency. The measures have essentially protected two groups of persons: human rights defenders or activists and persons linked to the communication media.

1.1.2.2. Individuals

65. The Inter-American Court has held on several occasions that in order to ensure effectively the rights enshrined in the American Convention, the States have the obligation *erga omnes* to protect all persons subject to their jurisdiction.[158] This general obligation, in the opinion of the Court, exists not only with respect to abuses of power by the State itself but also with respect to the acts of third persons not associated with the State.[159] An act that violates human rights that is not initially imputable to the State, such as an act of a private person or for not having identified the person responsible, may lead to the international responsibility of the State, not for the act itself but for the lack of due diligence to prevent the violation or to respond to it as required by the Convention.[160]

---

158 With respect to the obligations *erga omnes*, it is interesting to note the concurring opinions of Judge Cançado Trindade regarding the Court's orders of provisional measures in the Peace Community of San José de Apartadó Case (Colombia) of June 18, 2002, the Communities of the Jiguamiando and of the Curbaradó Case (Colombia) of March 6, 2003 and the Indigenous Sarayaku People Case (Ecuador) of July 6, 2004. See also A. Cançado Trindade, "The Evolution of Provisional Measures of Protection under the Case Law of the Inter-American Court of Human Rights (1987–2002)", *Hum. Rts. L. J.* 2003, 166.

159 IACtHR, *Indigenous Sarayaku People Case (Ecuador)*, Order of July 6, 2004, Preambular Paragraph 10; IACtHR, *Plan de Sánchez Massacre Case (Guatemala)*, Order of the President of July 30, 2004, Preambular Paragraph 10; IACtHR, *Luisiana Rios et al. (Venezuela)*, Order of September 8, 2004, Preambular Paragraph 12 and IACtHR, *Mendoza Prisons Case (Argentina)*, Order of June 18, 2005, Preambular Paragraph 11.

160 In this context, the Court in the Caballero Delgado and Santana Case (Colombia) held that the detention and disappearance of Isidro Caballero Delgado and María del Carmen Santana had been carried out by members of the Colombian Army and by civilians acting as military. See IACtHR, *Caballero Delgado and Santana Case (Colombia)*, Judgment of December 8, 1995, paras. 54–63. See also IACtHR, *Velásquez Rodríguez Case (Honduras)*, Judgment of July 29, 1988, paras. 164–169 and IACtHR, *Godínez Cruz Case (Honduras)*, Judgment of January 20, 1989, paras. 173, 178.

Table 10. Who is directly responsible for the situation of danger?

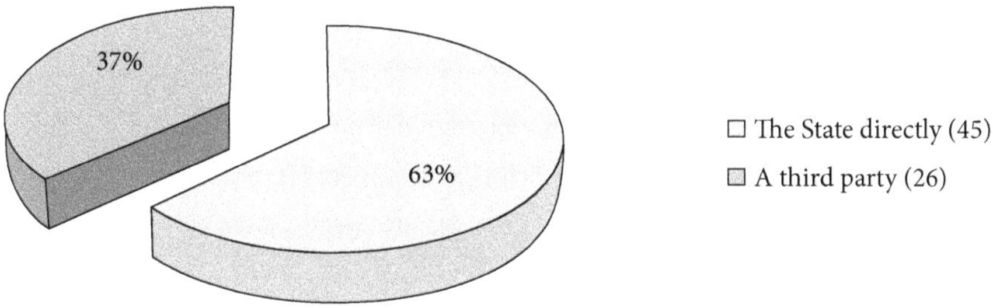

66. As can be observed in Table 10, more than a quarter of the provisional measures were directed towards the protection of persons that had received or were receiving threats by third persons that were no direct state agents. From 1987 to 2009 the Court adopted provisional measures in 26 matters to protect persons whose rights were in danger of being violated by persons not officially associated with the State,[161] such as the so-called civil self-defense patrols in Guatemala,[162] paramilitaries and guerrillas in Colombia,[163] extermination

161 Blake Case (Guatemala), Carpio Nicolle Case (Guatemala), Clemente Teherán Case (Colombia), Colotenango Case (Guatemala), Peace Community of San José de Apartadó Case (Colombia), Communities of the Jiguamiando and of the Curbaradó Case (Colombia), Mendoza Prisons Case (Argentina), Chunimá Case (Guatemala), Indigenous Kankuamo Community Case (Colombia), Indigenous Sarayaku People Case (Ecuador), Giraldo Cardona Case (Colombia), Luis Uzcátegui Case (Venezuela), Serech and Saquic Case (Guatemala), 19 Tradesmen Case (Colombia), Mayagna (Sumo) Awas Tingni Community Case (Nicaragua), The Urso Branco Prison Case (Brazil), Forensic Anthropology Foundation Case (Guatemala), Integrantes del Equipo de Estudios Comunitarios y Acción Psicosocial (ECAP). Masacre Plan de Sánchez Case (Guatemala), Penitentiary Center of the Central Occidental Region (Uribana Prison) Case (Venezuela), Yare I and Yare II Capital Region Center Case (Venezuela), Capital El Rodeo I & El Rodeo II Judicial Confinement Center Case (Venezuela), Monagas Judicial Confinement Center ("La Pica") (Venezuela), Mapiripán Massacre Case (Colombia), Mery Naranjo *et al.* Case (Colombia), Persons imprisoned in the "Dr. Sebastião Martins Silveira" Penitentiary in Araraquara, São Paulo Case (Brazil) and Children Deprived of Liberty in the "Complexo do Tatuapé" of FEBEM Case (Brazil).

162 See IACtHR, *Carpio Nicolle Case (Guatemala)*, Judgment of November 22, 2004, para. 76(1)(2)(3). See also IACtHR, *Blake Case (Guatemala)*, Judgment of January 24, 1998, para. 76 and Amnesty International, *Guatemala: The Civil Defence Patrols Re-Emerge*, 3 September 2002, <http://web.amnesty.org/library/Index/ENGAMR340532002?open&of=ENG-GTM>.

163 The Civil Defense Patrols were created among the civil population. Their purpose was to help law enforcement personnel in anti-subversive operations and defend themselves against the guerrilla groups. The State granted them permission to own and bear arms and gave them logistical support. In the 1980s the goals of many "self-defense groups" changed and they became criminal groups, usually known as "paramilitary groups". See IACtHR, *19 Tradesmen Case (Colombia)*, Judgment of July 5, 2004, para. 84 (a)(b)(c)(g) and (h).

groups in Venezuela,[164] security personnel of an oil company in Ecuador,[165] inmates in Argentina,[166] Brazil[167] and Venezuela[168] and individuals who invaded the territory of an indigenous community in Nicaragua.[169]

---

164 According to the Commission, the so-called death squads or "social cleansing groups" (grupos de exterminio) were made up of Venezuelan State security employees. These groups not only represented an illegal mechanism of social control, but also were part of a criminal organisation inside the police force that extorted money. These groups operated in seven Venezuelan States and threatened the families of the victims and witnesses.

165 According to the Commission, the ancestral territory of the indigenous people of Sarayaku was legally recognized by Ecuador in 1992, through a title of territorial land. In 1996 the State signed a contract with the Argentine corporation, Compañía General de Combustible (CGC) for the exploration and exploitation of oil covering an area of 200,000 hectares of land of which 65% involved the indigenous territory. This contract was signed without prior consultation with the Sarayaku people. Between 1996 and 2002, CGC tried to negotiate its entry to the Sarayaku territory and intended to acquire, through questionable methods, the approval of the indigenous people for its oil exploitation. During this time, members of the village were attacked by the Ecuadorian Army as well as by security personnel of CGC. On one occasion the indigenous leaders were tortured, their hands and feet tied with ropes, were blindfolded and thrown to the ground, forcing them to stay in this position for an hour. See IACtHR, *Indigenous Sarayaku People Case (Ecuador)*, Order of July 6, 2004, Explanatory Statement 2, Preambular Paragraph 10.

166 In this case, the Commission reported that as a consequence of fires, fights between inmates and of unclear circumstances in some of the Argentine prisons, 10 people were killed and 4 were injured during a period of 7 months. Among the victims were inmates and prison guards. The detention centres that are part of the penitentiary systems of Mendoza suffered acute problems of overcrowding, hygiene and bad health conditions. In some cases, as many as six detainees shared a cell, measuring two square meters, with one bed, no natural light or fresh air, with no access to toilets or showers and many suffered from sicknesses related to the lack of hygiene. See IACtHR, *Mendoza Prisons Case (Argentina)*, Order of November 22, 2004, Explanatory Statement 2(e), Preambular Paragraphs 6 and 12.

167 The Court adopted measures to protect the rights to life and to personal integrity of the prisoners of the Urso Branco Prison. According to the Commission, in this prison centre between January 1 and June 5, 2002, 37 people had been brutally assassinated. The prisoners died at the hands of other inmates, some were decapitated and their arms and legs mutilated by use of sharp weapons and others had died from blows of "chunchos" (very sharp weapons made by the prisoners themselves). The Court held that, by virtue of the responsibility of the State to adopt security measures to protect all persons subject to their jurisdiction, this duty was more obvious with respect to persons confined in a State detention centre, in which case the State is the guarantor of the rights of the persons under their custody. See IACtHR, *The Urso Branco Prison Case (Brazil)*, Order of June 18, 2002, Preambular Paragraph 1(a)-(i) and Enacting Part 1.

168 Penitentiary Center of the Central Occidental Region (Uribana Prison) Case (Venezuela), Yare I and Yare II Capital Region Center Case (Venezuela), Capital El Rodeo I & El Rodeo II Judicial Confinement Center Case (Venezuela), Monagas Judicial Confinement Center ("La Pica") (Venezuela).

169 Mayagna (Sumo) Awas Tingni Community Case (Nicaragua).

Table 11. States where the responsible was a third party

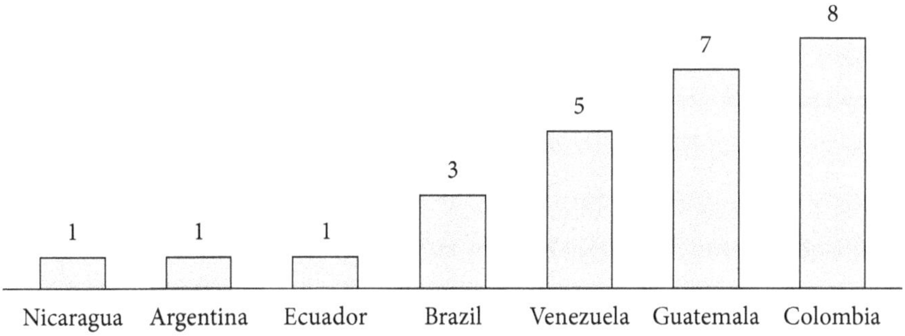

67. The high percentage of measures protecting persons against third persons who have no direct link to the State is linked to the internal armed conflicts that were taking place in certain states. In this sense, one can see that the two states with most provisional measures were Guatemala and Colombia, and the beneficiaries were victims of the conflict. It concerned civilians that were living or working in the combat areas or where the parties in the conflict held territorial control. The objective of the measures was to protect those civilians from the actions undertaken by the members of the so-called 'autodefensas civiles' (paramilitary groups), in the cases against Guatemala and, the guerrilla and the paramilitary, in the cases against Colombia.

68. The Court has adopted on several occasions measures to protect persons from the so-called civil self-defense patrols (PAC), which sprang up during the armed conflict that took place in Guatemala between 1962 and 1996. These patrols were formed at the beginning of the 1980s as groups of civilians forcibly recruited by the Armed Forces and were made up of male peasants coming mainly from rural areas. From 1981 to 1995 the patrols were composed of between 500,000 and one million members. The main purpose of these self-defense groups was to organize the civilian population against the guerrilla movements and control them. They also gave support to the Armed Forces and received resources, arms, training and direct orders from the Guatemalan Army and operated under its supervision. The PAC were legally abolished in July 1996. The conflict is estimated to have caused more than 200,000 victims of summary executions and forced disappearances, a product of the political violence. The Armed Forces and the paramilitary groups, such as the Civil Self-Defense Patrols or Voluntary Defense Committees, committed the great majority of these human rights violations.

The Chunimá Case (Guatemala) was the first case in which the Commission requested that the Court adopt provisional measures to protect the security and physical integrity of witnesses, family members and members of human rights organizations who were being threatened and harassed by members of the PAC and the Guatemalan Army. In its request, the Commission affirmed that from October 1990 to February 1991 members of the civil patrols with the help of the Army had killed four persons belonging to a human rights organization and that the police had refused to execute arrest warrants against some members of the PAC. According to the information gathered by the Commission, the members of the human rights organisation were threatened because they conducted campaigns against the civil patrols. In view of these facts, the President of the Court, in application of Article 63(2) of the American Convention and without referring explicitly to the topic of the international protection of persons for actions not resulting directly from the State, decided to adopt measures of protection.[170]

Notwithstanding the above, the Court had already ordered the protection of persons whose risk of harm did not come directly from State forces. The first case that expressly refers to the obligation of the State to protect persons from the acts of private persons is the Colotenango Case (Guatemala), in which the Commission requested the protection of witnesses in the case and family members of the alleged victims who were being threatened by the PAC because they had been witnesses to an attack by the PAC against unarmed participants in a human rights demonstration. The fathers of two witnesses had been murdered, other witnesses had been seriously injured, others had been detained arbitrarily and others had received death threats. The Court decided to request Guatemala to adopt the measures necessary to ensure that the persons could continue to reside at or return to their homes in Colotenango and provide them with assurances that they would not be persecuted or threatened by State agents or by third persons.[171]

In another case against Guatemala, the Commission requested protection of the rights to life and personal integrity of the witnesses and the special prosecutor who was investigating the murder of Jorge Carpio Nicolle, who had been a journalist and presidential candidate. The Commission stated that he had been

---

170 IACtHR, *Chunimá Case (Guatemala)*, Order of the President of July 15, 1991. The Court by Order of August 1, 1991 ratified this decision. In the Serech and Saquic Case (Guatemala), the Commission also requested measures to protect persons who had an active role in the investigation of the assassination of two pastors. According to the Commission, people were being harassed and attacked by a group of civil patrols and former military commissioners because they considered them to be against the Army. The Court adopted provisional measures, but as it did in the prior case, did not mention the protection of individuals with respect to acts of third parties. See IACtHR, *Serech and Saquic Case (Guatemala)*, Order of June 28, 1996.

171 IACtHR, *Colotenango Case (Guatemala)*, Order of June 22, 1994. Preambular Paragraph 3 and Enacting Part 2.

killed along with three other political leaders while on a visit to several provinces of Guatemala. The deaths occurred after they were intercepted by a group of 15 to 30 men belonging to the PAC. The Court requested that Guatemala inform the military authorities of the Military Zone to which the PAC of San Pedro Jocopilas answered that the PAC should refrain from any activity that puts at risk the lives or personal integrity of the beneficiaries of the measures.[172]

In the Blake Case (Guatemala), measures were adopted to protect the witnesses who had furnished information on the PAC and their responsibility for the disappearance and death of Mr. Blake. The Court requested that Guatemala adopt all necessary measures so that the witnesses who were being threatened could continue to live in their homes. The Court also held that the State must ensure that those persons would not be persecuted or threatened by agents of the State or by persons acting with its acquiescence.[173]

69. The Court has also ordered Colombia to adopt measures to protect persons who were at grave risk as a consequence of the activities of paramilitary and guerrilla groups. It is important to point out that, at the beginning of the 1960s, various guerilla groups emerged in Colombia and, owing to their activities, the State declared "the disturbance of public order and a state of emergency in the national territory." In this context, on December 24, 1965, the State issued Legislative Decree No. 3398. Article 65 of the Decree stipulated that "all Colombians, men and women, not affected by conscription to obligatory military service, may be used by the Government in activities and tasks contributing to re-establish normality." Article 33 of the Decree established that "acting through the authorized commands and when it deems necessary, the Ministry of National Defense may dispose of, as its private property, weapons restricted to the exclusive use of the Armed Forces." The "self-defense groups" were thus established in Colombia among the civilian population and their principal purpose was to aid the security forces in anti-subversive operations and defend themselves against the guerilla groups. The State granted them permission to own and bear arms and gave them logistic support. In the 1980s, many of these self-defense groups changed and became criminal groups, usually known as paramilitaries.

On April 19, 1989, Decree 0815 was issued suspending the application of paragraph 3 of Article 33 of Legislative Decree 3398 of 1965, which empowered the Ministry of National Defense to authorize individuals to carry arms that were for the exclusive use of the Armed Forces. Subsequently, in a judgment of

---

172 IACtHR, *Carpio Nicolle Case (Guatemala)*, Order of June 4, 1995, Enacting Part 3.

173 IACtHR, *Blake Case (Guatemala)*, Order of the President of August 6, 1995, Explanatory Statement 3, Enacting Part 2.

May 15, 1989, the Supreme Court of Justice declared unenforceable that paragraph. On June 8, 1989, the State issued Decree 1194 "extending Legislative Decree 0180 of 1988, to punish new criminal activities, since this was required in order to re-establish public order." One of the preambular paragraphs of this norm stated that "events that have been occurring in the country have demonstrated that there is a new criminal activity consisting in horrendous acts being committed by armed groups, mistakenly called 'paramilitary groups', formed into death squadrons, bands of hired murderers, self-defense or private justice groups, whose existence and activities gravely affect the social stability of the country, and which should be suppressed in order to re-establish public order and peace." It also classified as a crime being connected to or belonging to such groups, as well as instructing, training or equipping "individuals in military tactics, techniques or procedures for carrying out the criminal activities" of these armed groups. In this context, on several occasions the Court required Colombia to adopt whatever measures were necessary to protect the civilian population from the acts of these armed groups.[174]

In the Giraldo Cardona Case (Colombia), the Commission requested the adoption of the necessary measures to protect members of a non-governmental human rights organisation who were constantly being threatened. The Commission stated that since 1992 members of the organisation had been threatened, harassed and persecuted by paramilitary groups and since that time there had been six executions, three disappearances and two persons had been forced to move within Colombia and two other persons had been forced to seek asylum abroad. Under those circumstances, the Court decided to order the government to adopt the protective measures necessary to ensure that the persons could continue "living in their habitual residence and to return to their homes, providing them the assurance that they will not be persecuted or threatened by agents of the government or by civilians."[175] The Court adopted similar provisional measures in the Clemente Teherán Case (Colombia) with the aim of protecting members of the indigenous Zenú community of San Andrés de Sotavento, who, according to the request of the Commission, were being subjected to acts of aggression and threats by paramilitary groups acting under the auspices of large land-owners and cattlemen of the region with the tolerance of the public security forces.

174 See IACtHR, *19 Tradesmen Case (Colombia)*, Judgment of July 5, 2004, para. 84 (a)(b)(c)(g) and (h).

175 IACtHR, *Giraldo Cardona Case (Colombia)*, Order of the President of October 28, 1996, Explanatory Statement 2(3), Enacting Part 2. The Court by Order of February 5, 1997 ratified this Order.

The Court also adopted provisional measures in 2004 to protect the members of the indigenous Kankuamo community made up of approximately 6,000 persons. This community lived in the Southeastern part of the Sierra Nevada Mountains of Santa Marta, located in the Departments of Magdalena, Guajira and Cesar of Colombia. This geographical location exposed its members to continuous acts of violence and threats by armed groups, because it was one of the zones where there was an armed conflict. The dangerous situation had resulted in the indigenous leaders and authorities being the victims of threats, attempts on their lives and assassinations. Armed groups had forcibly recruited indigenous youth and numerous families had had to move in order to protect their lives. According to the information furnished, armed groups had killed 166 Kankuamos between 1993 and 2003.

The Court indicated in this case that the State had the obligation *erga omnes* to protect all persons subject to its jurisdiction. This general obligation extended not only to State bodies but also to the acts of third persons, including irregular armed groups of any nature. The Court held that, given the special characteristics of the case and the general conditions of armed conflict in Colombia, it was necessary to protect all the members of the indigenous Kankuamo community, under the terms of the American Convention, read in conjunction with international humanitarian law.[176]

70. An indigenous community was also protected by provisional measures in Ecuador. The Inter-American Court in that case protected the rights to life, personal integrity and freedom of movement of its approximately 1,200 members, who had been threatened and mistreated by the Ecuadorian army and by security personnel of an Argentine company that the State had contracted to locate and extract petroleum within the territory that belonged legally to the indigenous community.[177]

71. Finally, the Commission in the Luis Uzcátegui Case (Venezuela) requested the adoption of provisional measures on behalf of Mr. Uzcátegui, who had on various occasions received death threats by persons who were part of a criminal organisation within the police forces of Venezuela that extorted money and threatened the families of witnesses and victims. The threats to Mr. Uzcátegui commenced after he denounced the events surrounding the death of his brother through the regional media. Notwithstanding the request of the Commission

---

176 IACtHR, *Indigenous Kankuamo Community Case (Colombia)*, Order of July 5, 2004, Explanatory Statement 2(f) and (g), Preambular Paragraphs 10 and 11. See also IACtHR, *Peace Community of San José de Apartadó Case (Colombia)*, Order of June 18, 2002, Preambular Paragraph 11.

177 See Indigenous Sarayaku People Case (Ecuador).

that the State adopt precautionary measures, the acts of harassment and the threats continued.[178] The Court, in application of Articles 1(1), 62 and 63(2) of the American Convention, adopted the measures to protect the right to life and the right to humane treatment of Mr. Uzcátegui.

1.2. JURISDICTION *RATIONE MATERIAE*

72. Although in principle the jurisdiction *ratione materiae* of the Court to adopt provisional measures is determined by the obligations undertaken by the States Parties to the American Convention and its exercise does not depend on the domestic law of the States nor does it depend on whether the presumed victims have acted in conformity with that law, it is important to underscore that Article 29 of the Convention stipulates that none of its provisions may be interpreted in such a way as to restrict the enjoyment or exercise of any right or freedom that is recognised in the domestic law or in another regional or universal convention to which the State might be a party (the so-called most protective clause).

With respect to the subject matter, the Court may adopt provisional measures that have the purpose of avoiding irreparable damage to the rights provided for in the Convention. It means that a State cannot claim that it need not respect the level of protection offered by the Convention because its legislation establishes a lesser protection, since it is obligated *ratione materiae* to respect the Convention in conformity with the most protective clause.

73. The Court's jurisprudence indicates that it has only adopted provisional measures in cases that have as their objective the protection of the rights embodied in the Convention and that it has not referred to rights found in other international instruments. The only occasion in which the Court referred to the internal law of a State was in the James *et al.* Case (Trinidad and Tobago) to indicate that the execution of the beneficiaries of provisional measures "would create an irreparable situation incompatible with the object and purpose of the Convention." The Court stated that the function of the supervisory organs of the Convention was to ensure that its provisions were observed and adequately applied by the States in their domestic laws and not, as Trinidad and Tobago had argued, to ensure that the States Parties complied with their own domestic laws.[179]

---

178 IACtHR, *Luis Uzcátegui Case (Venezuela)*, Order of November 27, 2002, Explanatory Statement 2 and 3.

179 IACtHR, *James et al. Case (Trinidad and Tobago)*, Order of August 29, 1998, Explanatory Statement 10.

74. On most occasions the provisional measures have been adopted citing Articles 1(1), 62 and 63(2) of the Convention and Article 26 (before 25) of the Rules of the Court. In some cases the Court mentioned Articles 26 and 27 of the Vienna Convention that establish the principle of *pacta sunt servanda*, by which every treaty in force obligates the parties and must be complied with in good faith. The Court has also taken into account the principle that affirms that no State Party may invoke provisions of domestic law to justify non-compliance of a treaty.[180]

75. The adoption of provisional measures is subject to very precise requirements because it requires a situation of extreme gravity and urgency that may cause irreparable damage to persons.[181] There is a question of which rights the Court may protect through provisional measures. Although this topic will be analysed in the section on "Substantive Conditions of Admissibility, Hierarchy of the Right," it is important to mention here that there is a school of thought that considers that not every right set forth in the Convention may be protected through provisional measures, while others argue that nothing in the norms prohibits protecting all of the rights.

The restrictive position is that irreparable damage involves the rights to life, physical integrity, personal freedom and the right to judicial guarantees, given that the violation of those rights have a direct impact on the enjoyment of the other rights and freedoms.[182] On the other hand, the more liberal position holds

180 Digna Ochoa y Plácido *et al.* Case (Mexico), Luisiana Rios *et al.* Case (Venezuela), Liliana Ortega *et al.* Case (Venezuela), Luis Uzcátegui Case (Venezuela), Lysias Fleury Case (Haiti) and Marta Colomina and Liliana Velásquez Case (Venezuela).

181 The Commission, on the other hand, invoking Article 41(b) of the Convention, may take any action that it deems necessary for the exercise of its functions and hence may order precautionary measures in a broader range of situations. See H. Faundez Ledesma, *El Sistema Interamericano de Protección de los Derechos Humanos*, San José, IIDH, 3rd ed., 2004, 517.

182 Faúndez Ledesma believes that a threat to life or to physical integrity is undoubtedly a matter of extreme gravity. A threat to freedoms of association or of movement in State territory, in the context of Article 63(2) of the Convention, does not merit this same consideration. See H. Faundez Ledesma, *El Sistema Interamericano de Protección de los Derechos Humanos*, San José, IIDH, 3rd ed., 2004, 538, 545. Pasqualucci considers that the adoption of provisional measures should be limited to those cases where there is sufficient evidence that a person is at risk of being tortured or assassinated. See J.M. Pasqualucci, *The Practice and Procedure of the Inter-American Court of Human Rights*, Cambridge, Cambridge University Press, 2003, 293; J.M. Pasqualucci, "Provisional Measures in the Inter-American Human Rights System: An Innovative Development in International Law", *Vand. J. Transnat'l L.* 1993–94, 850. Costa Rica contended that provisional measures could only protect the rights to life or to physical integrity. This was one of the reasons that State offered when it requested the Court not to adopt measures to protect a journalist who had been found guilty for four crimes. According to the State, the adoption of measures would be legitimating the use of an extraordinary remedy to annul the execution of a judgment in which neither the life nor the physical

that since all human rights are interrelated and indivisible there is nothing to prevent the adoption of measures to protect any right that is enshrined in the American Convention, provided that the situation meets the requirements of Article 63(2), that is, extreme gravity and urgency and the need to avoid irreparable damage to persons.[183]

In line with this position, the Court theoretically could adopt measures[184] to protect the right to juridical personality (Article 3), the right to life (Article 4), the right to humane treatment (Article 5), freedom from slavery, involuntary servitude and forced labor (Article 6), the right to personal liberty (Article 7), the right to a fair trial (Article 8), freedom from ex post facto laws (Article 9), the right to compensation through a miscarriage of justice (Article 10), the protection of honor and dignity (Article 11), freedom of conscience and religion (Article 12), freedom of thought and expression (Article 13), the right of reply (Article 14), the right of assembly (Article 15), freedom of association (Article 16), rights of the family (Article 17), the right to a name (Article 18), rights of the child (Article 19), the right to a nationality (Article 20), the right to property (Article 21), freedom of movement and residence (Article 22), the right to asylum (Article 22(7)), political rights (Article 23), the right to equal protection (Article 24) and the right to judicial protection (Article 25).

integrity of a person is at stake. See IACtHR, *La Nación Newspaper Case (Costa Rica)*, Order of May 23, 2001, Explanatory Statement 4(c).

183 Cançado Trindade does not believe that there is any judicial or epistemological impediment that would obstruct the protection of any right, provided that the conditions set forth in Article 63.2 of the American Convention are fulfilled. A. Cançado Trindade, "The Evolution of Provisional Measures of Protection under the Case Law of the Inter-American Court of Human Rights (1987–2002)", *Hum. Rts. L. J.* 2003, p. 165. See also A. Cançado Trindade, *Medidas Provisionales. Prólogo del Presidente de la Corte Interamericana de Derechos Humanos al Tomo III de la Serie E.*, 2001, para. 21; A. Borea Odria, "Propuesta de Modificación a la Legislación del Sistema Interamericano de Protección de los Derechos Humanos", in *Liber Amicorum Héctor Fix-Zamudio*, San José, Inter-American Court of Human Rights, 1998, 541–542. See also IACtHR, *Haitians and Dominicans of Haitian Origin in the Dominican Republic Case (Dominican Republic)*, Order of August 18, 2000, Concurring Opinion Judge Cançado Trindade, para. 14.

184 See IACtHR, *Haitians and Dominicans of Haitian Origin in the Dominican Republic Case (Dominican Republic)*, Order of August 18, 2000, Concurring Opinion Judge Cançado Trindade, para. 14.

76. In practice, the Court has adopted measures to protect the rights to life, humane treatment,[185] physical integrity,[186] psychological integrity,[187] moral

[185] In every case in which the Court has protected the right to life, it has also protected the right of humane treatment. See Alemán Lacayo Case (Nicaragua), Alvarez *et al.* Case (Colombia), Bámaca Velásquez Case (Guatemala), Boyce and Joseph Case (Barbados), Bustíos-Rojas Case (Peru), Blake Case (Guatemala), Caballero Delgdo and Santana Case(Colombia), Carlos Nieto *et al.* Case (Venezuela), Carpio Nicolle Case (Guatemala), Clemente Teherán Case (Colombia), Colotenango Case (Guatemala), Chunimá Case (Guatemala), The Urso Branco Prison Case (Brazil), Peace Community of San José de Apartadó Case (Colombia), Communities of the Jiguamiando and of the Curbaradó Case (Colombia), "Globovisión" Television Station Case, Mendoza Prisons Case (Argentina), 19 Tradesmen Case (Colombia), Haitians and Dominicans of Haitian Origin in the Dominican Republic Case (Dominican Republic), The Miguel Agustín Pro Juárez Human Rights Center *et al.* Case (Mexico), Indigenous Kankuamo Community Case (Colombia), Indigenous Sarayaku People Case (Ecuador), "El Nacional" and "Así es la Noticia" Newspapers Case, Digna Ochoa y Plácido *et al.* (Mexico), Eloisa Barrios *et al.* Case (Venezuela), Fermín Ramírez Case (Guatemala), Gallardo Rodríguez Case (Mexico), Giraldo Cardona Case (Colombia), Gómez Paquiyauri Brothers Case (Peru), Gutiérrez Soler Case (Colombia), Helen Chang *et al.* Case (Guatemala), James *et al.* Case (Trinidad and Tobago), Liliana Ortega *et al.* Case (Venezuela), Luis Uzcátegui Case (Venezuela), Luisiana Rios *et al.* Case (Venezuela), Plan de Sánchez Massacre Case (Guatemala), Paniagua Morales *et al.* and Vásquez *et al.* Case (Guatemala), Raxcacó Reyes *et al.* Case (Guatemala), Serech and Saquic Case (Guatemala), Velásquez Rodríguez, Fairén Garbi and Solis Corrales and Godínez Cruz Cases (Honduras), in which the Court mentions the rights to life and personal integrity in the Preambular Paragraphs but not in the Enacting Part, and Vogt Case (Guatemala), Penitentiary Center of the Central Occidental Region (Uribana Prison) Case (Venezuela), Yare I and Yare II Capital Region Center Case (Venezuela), Capital El Rodeo I & El Rodeo II Judicial Confinement Center Case (Venezuela), Monagas Judicial Confinement Center ("La Pica") Case (Venezuela), Guerrero-Gallucci y Martínez-Barrios Case (Venezuela), Mapiripán Massacre Case (Colombia), Mery Naranjo *et al.* Case (Colombia), Ramírez Hinostroza *et al.* Case (Peru), Leonel Rivero *et al.* Case (Mexico), Pilar Noriega *et al.* Case (Mexico), Millacura Llaipén *et al.* Case (Argentina), Persons imprisoned in the "Dr. Sebastião Martins Silveira" Penitentiary in Araraquara, São Paulo Case (Brazil), Children Deprived of Liberty in the "Complexo do Tatuapé" of FEBEM Case (Brazil), Tyrone Dacosta Cadogan Case (Barbados), Adrián Meléndez Quijano Case (El Salvador), Gloria Giralt de García-Prieto *et al.* Case (El Salvador), Kawas Fernández Case (Honduras), Forensic Anthropology Foundation Case (Guatemala), Integrantes del Equipo de Estudios Comunitarios y Acción Psicosocial (ECAP). Masacre Plan de Sánchez Case (Guatemala).

[186] Cesti Hurtado Case (Peru), Constitutional Court Case (Peru), Ivcher Bronstien Case (Peru), Loayza Tamayo Case (Peru), Paniagua Morales *et al.* and Vásquez *et al.* Case (Guatemala), Suárez Rosero Case (Ecuador) and Velásquez Rodríguez, Fairén Garbi and Solis Corrales and Godínez Cruz Cases (Honduras).

[187] Cesti Hurtado Case (Peru), Constitutional Court Case (Peru), Ivcher Bronstein Case (Peru), Loayza Tamayo Case (Peru), Paniagua Morales *et al.* and Vásquez *et al.* Case (Guatemala) and Reggiardo Tolosa Case (Argentina).

integrity,[188] personal freedom,[189] property,[190] freedom of expression,[191] the right to a fair trial,[192] freedom of movement,[193] the right to residence[194] and the special protection of children in the family.[195]

---

188 Cesti Hurtado Case (Peru), Constitutional Court Case (Peru), Ivcher Bronstien Case (Peru), Loayza Tamayo Case (Peru) and Suárez Rosero Case (Ecuador).

189 Carlos Nieto *et al.* Case (Venezuela), Gutiérrez Soler Case (Colombia) and Plan de Sánchez Massacre Case (Guatemala).

190 Mayagna (Sumo) Awas Tingni Community Case (Nicaragua), Indigenous Sarayaku People Case (Ecuador) and Communities of the Jiguamiandó and of the Curbaradó Case (Colombia). In the latter case, although the Court does not explicitly mention the need to protect the territory of the indigenous people in the Preambular Paragraphs, it establishes that the State should adopt measures to stop the cultivation of African palm that was being carried out in the Community's territory. Control of the cultivation was important since it was the primary reason for the displacement of the members of the Community and maintaining the cultivation would make it impossible for the families to return to their Community. Furthermore, the cultivation prevented exploiting the natural resources necessary for their survival. This aspect endangered the life and personal integrity of the beneficiaries of the provisional measures. See IACtHR, *Communities of the Jiguamiandó and of the Curbaradó Case (Colombia)*, Order of March 15, 2005, Preambular Paragraphs 7 and 22.

191 "Globovisión" Television Station Case (Venezuela), Herrera-Ulloa Case ("La Nación" Newspaper) (Costa Rica), "El Nacional" and "Así es la Noticia" Newspapers Case and Lusiana Ríos *et al.* (Venezuela), in which freedom of expression is protected with respect to some of the beneficiaries and the Marta Colomina and Liliana Velásquez Case (Venezuela).

192 Ivcher Bronstein Case (Peru).

193 Indigenous Kankuamo Community Case (Colombia), Indigenous Sarayaku People Case (Ecuador) and Haitians and Dominicans of Haitian Origin in the Dominican Republic Case (Dominican Republic). It is important to point out that in the case against the Dominican Republic the Court mentions the importance of protecting the rights of movement and residence in the Preambular Paragraphs of the Order but not in the Enacting PArt. See IACtHR, *Haitians and Dominicans of Haitian Origin in the Dominican Republic Case (Dominican Republic)*, Order of the Inter-American Court of November 12, 2002.

194 Haitians and Dominicans of Haitian Origin in the Dominican Republic Case (Dominican Republic).

195 *Ibid.*

Table 12. Number of cases in which the above-mentioned rights were protected

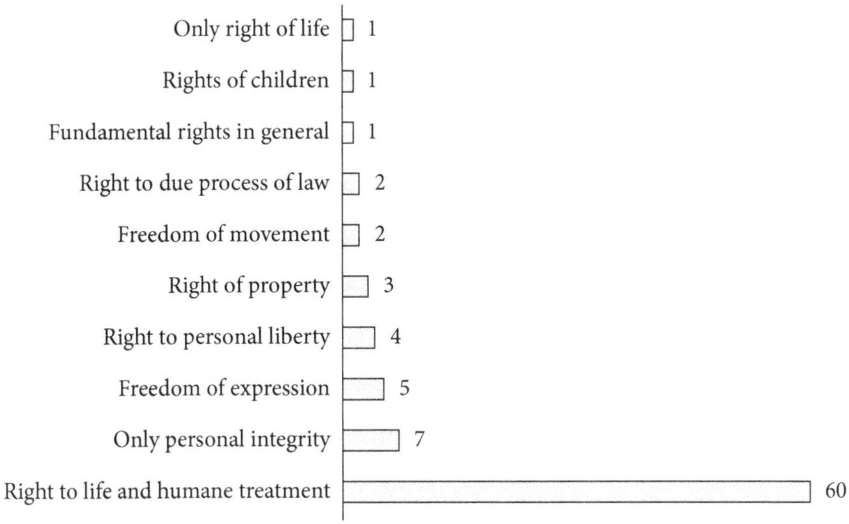

77. The jurisprudence also shows that in the majority of the cases protective measures have been adopted to avoid irreparable damage to the right to life and the right to humane treatment. The Court has protected these two rights in 68 of the 71 cases (84.5%), in seven cases only the humane treatment and in one only the right to life. In five cases, the Court has protected freedom of expression, twice personal freedom, once a fair trial, three times the right to property and one case protected fundamental rights in general, although the preambular paragraphs in that case expressly mentioned the rights to life, to humane treatment and to property. Another case protected the rights of the child in the preambular paragraph, but not in the enacting part.[196] It is relevant to mention that in the majority of the cases more than only one right or freedom is being protected at the same time. Because of that, the sum of the total numbers indicated in this Table does not coincide with the total number of cases (71).

196 IACtHR, Haitians and Dominicans of Haitian Origin in the Dominican Republic Case (Dominican Republic), Order of November 12, 2002.

Table 13. How many times and when were the rights protected[197]

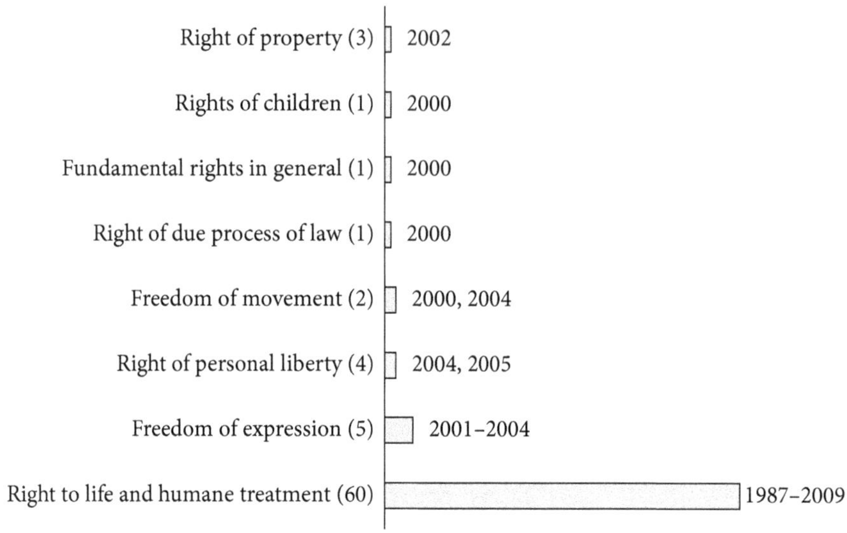

78. Taking into account the period of time, Table 13 shows that during its first twelve years of protective measures (1987–1999), the Court adopted measures to protect exclusively the rights to life and to humane treatment.[198] Only after the year 2000 did it adopt measures to protect other rights. Thus, during 2000 the rights of the child, freedom of residence and movement and the right to a fair trial were protected, in 2001, freedom of expression, in 2002, freedom of expression and the right to property, in 2003, freedom of expression, in 2004, the right to personal freedom, freedom of expression and freedom of movement, and in 2005, the right to personal freedom.

Perhaps during the first years only the right to life and personal integrity were protected, because it was thought that a situation of extreme gravity and urgency could only present itself with regard to a person, once his/her rights to life and personal integrity were in danger. Here it is important to emphasize that the Court did not reject requests for the protection of other kinds of rights, but just that only requests for the adoption of provisional measures regarding these two rights were submitted. Moreover, as has already been said, the three

---

197 The number that appears next to each right indicates the numbers of cases in which this right was protected, while the next number is the year during which the first resolution that was aimed at the protection of the said right was adopted.

198 In this Table, unlike the earlier Table, the total number of times that the right to life and personal integrity was protected is taken into account, independently from the issue whether the resolution made a reference to the 2 or only 1 of them. For this reason, the number is 60 and not 68.

occasions in which the adoption of provisional measures was rejected, was due to the absence of proof or the presence of false information. Therefore, the rejection of some measures was not because of the fact that the Court did not want to protect rights and freedoms that were different to the right to life or personal integrity.

1.3. JURISDICTION *RATIONE LOCI*

79. Articles 1(1) and 63(2) of the Convention authorise the Court, when there is a situation of extreme gravity and urgency that places in danger the rights of persons who are subject to the jurisdiction of a State Party to the Convention, to adopt whatever measures that it deems necessary so that the rights of those persons are not violated.

80. The jurisdiction of the State refers not only to the citizens who are within its territorial limits, but also to aliens who are in its territory, anyone in diplomatic and consular missions abroad or on public ships and planes located outside the territory and its military personnel serving outside the country. Under any of those circumstances, those persons are subject to the jurisdiction of the State and the Court may, therefore, adopt the provisional measures that it deems pertinent to avoid irreparable damage to their rights.[199] Although in theory provisional measures may be adopted in any of the aforementioned situations, in practice they have only been adopted to protect persons who have been within the territory of the State in which there has been a situation of danger.

81. Nonetheless, on some occasions provisional measures have been adopted to protect persons who were not within the territory of a State because they had to leave that State for fear that their rights were at risk.[200] In those cases, the

---

199 Article 2(1) of the International Covenant on Civil and Political Rights of the United Nations (CCPR) grants a more limited jurisdiction than that found in the international human rights instruments of the European and inter-American systems. According to this Article, the State parties must ensure the rights of all individuals within their territory. On the other hand, the American and European Conventions refer to the notion of jurisdiction. Some authors believe that in certain circumstances that interpretation of the CCPR would be unreasonable to the point of being incompatible to the object and purpose of the treaty. D. Rodriguez Pinzón, "Jurisdicción y Competencia en las Peticiones Individuales del Sistema Interamericano de Derechos Humanos", <www.wcl.american.edu/pub/humright/red/articulos/Jurisdccion Competencia.htm>, p. 5, also citing M. Nowak, *U.N. Covenant on Civil and Political Rights. CCPR Commentary*, Engel Verlag, Kehl am Rhein, 1993, 683.

200 In the IACtHR, *Bámaca Velásquez Case (Guatemala)*, Order of November 20, 2003. In this Order, the Court required the State to adopt all measures necessary to protect every individual

measures were restricted to the persons, under the condition that those persons return to the State concerned. The Court indicated to the State of origin, as soon as the persons concerned returned to the territory of that State, that it had to adopt whatever measures were necessary to protect their rights to life and personal integrity.

In the Alvarez *et al.* Case (Colombia), for example, the Commission requested the adoption of measures on behalf of 17 members of the Association of Detained-Disappeared Families (ASFADDES) in a case under considered by the Commission.[201] One of the persons had decided to leave the country because of the continual threats that he had received and his fear of being assassinated, since he had learned of a plan of the military intelligence that had ordered his disappearance.[202] The Court adopted the measures requested by the Commission to protect the 17 members of the organisation, including the person who had left Colombia, provided that the latter person returned to the country.

In the Gutiérrez Soler Case (Colombia) the State was ordered to protect the rights to life, humane treatment and personal freedom of Wilson Gutiérrez Soler and his son in the event that they returned to Colombia.[203] They had been forced to leave their country due to the constant threats that they had received because they had presented a case to the inter-American system. The complaint in the case alleged the torture of Mr. Gutiérrez Soler and his brother while they were detained.[204]

In the Loayza Tamayo Case (Peru), the President of the Court deemed it important that the State ensure to Mrs. Loayza Tamayo the conditions of security necessary for her to be able to return to her country without fearing consequences to her physical, psychological and moral integrity.[205]

---

who was in a dangerous situation and who permanently resided in Guatemala.

201 According to ASFADDES, a non-governmental organisation, which reunites and supports the families of victims of forced disappearances in Colombia and works to achieve progress in Colombia's national policies in this regard. The petition alleged that this organisation in 1992 was pointed out by a Commander as being sympathetic to the guerrillas and from that moment its members have been harassed and threatened. As a result of the threats, the organisation closed some of its offices. In 1997 a bomb with approximately five kilograms of dynamite was placed in one of their offices destroying it completely. See IACtHR, *Alvarez et al. Case (Colombia)*, Order of July 22, 1997, Explanatory Statement 3.

202 IACtHR, *Alvarez et al. Case (Colombia)*, Order of July 22, 1997, Explanatory Statements 4(h) and 5(d).

203 IACtHR, *Gutiérrez Soler Case (Colombia)*, Order of July 22, 1997, Enacting Part 1.

204 The situation described by the Commission pointed out that a bomb had been placed in the house of Mr. Gutiérrez' parents, that they had sent his brother a "book-bomb" and had tried to kidnap his son. For security reasons, his parents had sold their house in Bogotá where they lived and had moved. See IACtHR, *Gutiérrez Soler Case (Colombia)*, Order of March 11, 2005, Explanatory Statement 5(d) and (e).

205 IACtHR, *Loayza Tamayo Case (Peru)*, Order of the President of December 13, 2000, Preambular Paragraph 12, Enacting Part 1. Measures ratified by the Inter-American Court

Finally, in the Carpio Nicolle Case (Guatemala) the children of a witness had to leave Guatemala because of the grave fear of reprisals due to their mother's testimony before the Court. The witness had been threatened and there was an attempt on her life. The Court decided that the State must adopt the provisional measures necessary to ensure effectively the protection of the life and personal integrity of the two children in the event that they returned to Guatemala.[206]

82. In other cases, the protection has been restricted to persons who are in a specific part of the territory of the country in question.

For example, in the Clemente Teherán Case (Colombia) the President of the Court ordered the State, as soon as Nilson Zurita Mendoza (or Nelson Zurita Suárez) returned to the protection of the indigenous Zenú community of San Andrés de Sotavento, to adopt whatever measures were necessary to protect his life and physical, psychological and moral integrity.[207] The same was ordered in the Giraldo Cardona Case (Colombia), in which the Court held that, even though a beneficiary had stated that she did not require protective measures when she was in Bogotá, the State must maintain the measures on her behalf so that they were effective when she was in El Meta.[208]

1.4. JURISDICTION *RATIONE TEMPORIS*

83. There are two views when the Court's jurisdiction to adopt provisional measures commences. One view holds that the jurisdiction begins with ratification of the Convention (*supra*, nos. 57–58), while the other argues that it results from the acceptance of the jurisdiction of the Court, whether by special declaration or by special agreement, and while it remains in force (*supra*, nos. 57 and 59). The majority believes that jurisdiction terminates with the denunciation of the Convention.[209]

As was broadly explained in the section on passive standing, most writers believe that provisional measures may only be adopted with respect to States that have accepted the contentious jurisdiction of the Court (*supra*, nos. 57 and 59). Within this position, some consider it indispensable that there must be no doubt regarding the contentious jurisdiction of the Court in order for it to adopt

---

on February 3, 2001. Bear in mind that at the time of this Order, the Court had already ruled on the merits of the case and the provisional measures had been lifted.

206 IACtHR, *Carpio Nicolle Case (Guatemala)*, Order of July 8, 2004, Explanatory Statement 36, Preambular Paragraphs 16–18, Enacting Part 7.

207 IACtHR, *Clemente Teherán Case (Colombia)*, Order of the President of March 23, 1998, Enacting Part 2.

208 IACtHR, *Giraldo Cardona Case (Colombia)*, Order of June 19, 1998, Preambular Paragraph 3.

209 This matter was thoroughly analyzed in the section on passive standing.

provisional measures.[210] Others argue that when the case is submitted and the jurisdiction questioned, the gravity and urgency of a situation justifies the application of the measures. The Court in that situation would only have to establish to its satisfaction that there exist *prima facie* grounds to examine the request.[211] Finally, a third position is that the Court may adopt the measures when it is persuaded that it has jurisdiction to hear the case and that the Court could even adopt the measures if preliminary objections are made to its jurisdiction.[212]

84. What is certain is that from the very first order of provisional measures adopted in 1987 until the latest orders of 2009, the Court has based its jurisdiction primarily on Articles 1(1), 62 and 63(2) of the Convention. Each order of provisional measures has referred to the contentious jurisdiction of the Court and in no case has the Court adopted provisional measures against a State that has not made a declaration to accept that jurisdiction. The Court sometimes directly cites Article 62 and in other cases, while not citing that Article, it does mention that the State has accepted its jurisdiction.[213]

In one case in which its contentious jurisdiction was questioned, the Court continued adopting provisional measures. This was in the Hilaire, Constantine and Benjamin *et al.* Case (Trinidad and Tobago)[214] where, notwithstanding the preliminary objections presented by the State that contended a lack of jurisdiction, the Court continued to adopt orders of provisional measures to

210 R. Nieto Navia, "Las medidas provisionales en la Corte Interamericana de Derechos Humanos", in *La Corte y el Sistema Interamericano de Derechos Humanos*, R. Nieto Navia (ed.), San José, Corte Interamericana de Derechos Humanos, 1994, 385.

211 T. Buergenthal, "The Inter-American Court of Human Rights", *Am. J. Int'l Rev.* 1982, 241; T. Buergenthal, "The Inter-American System for the Protection of Human Rights", in *Human Rights in International Law. Legal and Policy Issues*, T. Meron (ed.), Oxford, Clarendon Press, 1984, 465–466; J.M. Pasqualucci, "Provisional Measures in the Inter-American Human Rights System: An Innovative Development in International Law", *Vand. J. Transnat'l L.* 1993–94, 826 and J.M. Pasqualucci, "Medidas Provisionales en la Corte Interamericana de Derechos Humanos: Una Comparación con la Corte Internacional de Justicia y la Corte Europea de Derechos Humanos", *Revista del Instituto Interamericano de Derechos Humanos* 1994, 71.

212 H. Gros Espiell, *Estudios sobre Derechos Humanos II,* Madrid, Civitas, 1988, 169–171.

213 Colotenango Case (Guatemala), Alemán Lacayo Case (Nicaragua), Cesti Hurtado Case (Peru), Clemente Teherán Case (Colombia), James, Briggs, Noel, Garcia and Bethel *et al.* Case (Trinidad and Tobago), Gallardo Rodríguez Case (Mexico), Herrera-Ulloa Case ("La Nación" Newspaper) (Costa Rica), Indigenous Kankuamo Community Case (Colombia), Boyle and Joseph Case (Barbados), Caballero Delgado and Santana Case (Colombia), Suárez Rosero Case (Ecuador), Loayza Tamayo Case (Peru), 19 Tradesmen Case (Colombia), Gómez Paquiyauri Brothers Case (Peru), Fermín Ramírez Case (Guatemala), Acevedo Jaramillo *et al.* Case, Gutiérrez Soler Case (Colombia) and Constitutional Court Case (Peru).

214 This application was introduced October 5, 2000 and the preliminary objections on December 9, 2000.

protect various persons whose right to life and right to humane treatment were in danger.[215]

85. No matter the perspective, there are two positions as to when the jurisdiction *ratione temporis* of the Court arises, but the two tendencies agree that such jurisdiction would be lost for the same reason – denunciation of the Convention –, because the only manner in which a State may no longer be a Party to the Convention or may withdraw from the Court's contentious jurisdiction is to denounce the Convention. Thus, in the inter-American system it is possible to ratify the Convention without accepting the contentious jurisdiction of the Court but, once it is accepted, the only way to withdraw it is to denounce the Convention.

It is important to mention that under Article 78 of the Convention, a State may not denounce the Convention until five years have elapsed since the date of its entry into force and the State must give one year's notice. Thus, the denunciation only begins to have an effect one year after it has been presented. The Court, therefore, cannot hear cases that are submitted after the entry into force of the denunciation but does retain its jurisdiction with respect to matters in which it had ordered measures before the entry into force of the denunciation and also with respect to acts that occurred prior to the effective date of the denunciation.[216]

86. It should also be pointed out that the existence of a judgment on the merits or on reparations does not prevent the adoption, broadening or maintenance of provisional measures. The Court has held that protective measures may also be applied at the supervisory stage of compliance of the judgment, provided that

215 H. Faundez Ledesma, El Sistema Interamericano de Protección de los Derechos Humanos, San José, IIDH, 3rd ed., 2004, 528.

216 In the James *et al.* Case (Trinidad and Tobago), in spite of the fact that the denunciation of the Convention by the State had taken effect, the Court extended the provisional measures on three occasions. The Court justified the adoption of the measures by stating that the denunciation did not relieve the State of its obligations regarding acts occurring before its entry into force and, therefore, could be a violation of the Convention. IACtHR, *Case, James, Briggs, Noel, Garcia and Bethel Case (Trinidad and Tobago)*, Order of July 19, 1999, Preambular Paragraph 1. Trinidad and Tobago had been a State party to the American Convention since May 28, 1991 and it recognized the competence of the Court on the same day. The State notified the denunciation of the Convention on May 26, 1998 and according to Article 71(1) of the Convention, the denunciation came into effect on May 26, 1999. See Orders of the Court of May 27, 1999, September 25, 1999 and November 26, 2000. In each of these Orders, the Court extended the measures. See IACtHR, *Hilaire, Constantine and Benjamin Case (Trinidad and Tobago)*, Judgment of June 21, 2002, paras. 12–20. See also H. Faundez Ledesma, *El Sistema Interamericano de Protección de los Derechos Humanos*, San José, IIDH, 3rd ed., 2004, 515.

the facts presented make a *prima facie* showing of a situation of extreme gravity and urgency and the imminent irreparable damage to persons.[217]

Table 14. Provisional measures and judgments

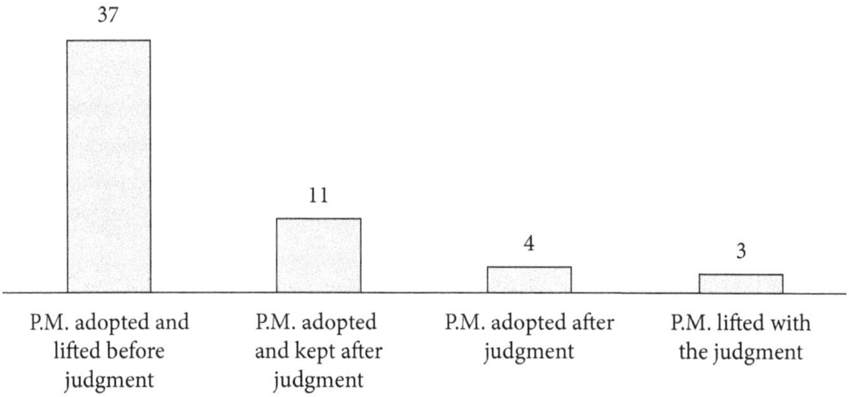

87. With regard to this aspect Table 14 shows that in the majority of the cases (37) the provisional measures (PM) were adopted and lifted before the judgment on the merits (JM) and that, in a quite representative quantity (11), the measures were adopted before the judgment on the merits and extended after that judgment.[218] This happens because the indispensable prerequisite that permits to adopt, extend, or re-establish provisional measures is the configuration of a situation of extreme gravity and urgency that brings persons into danger. If one takes into account that a situation of danger does not necessarily end when the international responsibility of the state is declared, one has to conclude that the Court is not obliged to lift the measures once it renders a judgment on the merits of a case.

88. As of the beginning of 2009, the Court was dealing with eleven cases of provisional measures against six States on which it had already found their international responsibility in a judgment on the merits.[219] The measures were

217 IACtHR, *Bámaca Velásquez Case (Guatemala)*, Order of November 20, 2003, Preambular Paragraph 10; IACtHR, *Mayagna (Sumo) Awas Tingni Community Case (Nicaragua)*, Order of September 6, 2002, Preambular Paragraph 9 and IACtHR, *Loayza Tamayo Case (Peru)*, Order of February 3, 2001, Preambular Paragraph 11.

218 Blake Case (Guatemala), Paniagua Morales *et al.* (Guatemala), Ivcher Bronstein Case (Peru), Hurtado Case (Peru), Loayza Tamayo Case (Peru), Constitutional Court Case (Peru), Caballero Delgado Case (Colombia), Gómez Paquiyauri Case (Peru), James *et al.* Case (Trinidad and Tobago) and Velásquez Rodríguez *et al.* Case (Honduras).

219 In these cases, the Court stated that the cases were under consideration since they were in the supervisory stage of the execution of the judgment. In this regard, the Court had the power to adopt provisional measures provided that the information presented to the Court showed

adopted for the first time in some of those cases when there was already a judgment on the merits.[220]

89. Finally, it is interesting to mention that one State has argued that the Court's jurisdiction to adopt measures ceased when it was certain that the matter would not be submitted to the Court. This was Trinidad and Tobago's position when it did not comply with provisional measures that had as their purpose preserving the life and physical integrity of a group of persons who were on death row.[221] The State justified the execution of one of the beneficiaries by claiming that the Court lacked jurisdiction to maintain the provisional measures with respect to a matter on which the Commission had already published its Article 51 Report.[222] Trinidad and Tobago contended that orders adopted after a case has been the object of an Article 51 Report are null and void because they would have been made when the Court did not have jurisdiction. In other words, it was argued that the acceptance of the Court's contentious jurisdiction is not the only requirement that must be complied with in order to adopt provisional measures,

---

prima facie a configuration of the situation of extreme gravity and urgency and imminent irreparable damage to persons. See IACtHR, *Bámaca Velásquez Case (Guatemala)*, Order of February 21, 2003, Preambular Paragraphs 9 and 10; IACtHR, *Mayagna (Sumo) Awas Tingni Community Case (Nicaragua)*, Order of September 6, 2002, Preambular Paragraph 9; IACtHR, *Bámaca Velásquez Case (Guatemala)*, Judgment on the Merits of November 25, 2000 and Judgment on the Reparations of February 22, 2002; IACtHR, *Caballero Delgado and Santana Case (Colombia)*, Judgment on the Merits of December 8, 1995 and Judgment on Reparations of January 29, 1997; IACtHR, *Carpio Nicolle Case (Guatemala)*, Judgment on the Merits of November 22, 2004; IACtHR, *Mayagna (Sumo) Awas Tingni Community Case (Nicaragua)*, Judgment of August 31, 2001; IACtHR, *Case of 19 Tradesmen (Colombia)*, Judgment of September 12, 2005; IACtHR, *Gutiérrez Soler Case (Colombia)*, Judgment on the Merits of September 12, 2005; IACtHR, *Helen Chang et al. Case (Guatemala)*, Judgment on the Merits of November 25, 2003; IACtHR, *Velásquez Rodríguez, Fairén Garbi and Solis Corrales and Godínez Cruz Cases (Honduras)*, Judgment on the Merits of July 29, 1988, Compensatory Damages, Judgment of July 21, 1989; IACtHR, *Integrantes del Equipo de Estudios Comunitarios y Acción Psicosocial (ECAP) and Masacre Plan De Sánchez Case (Guatemala)*, Judgment on the Merits of April 29, 2004, Judgment on the Merits and Compensatory Damages, of September, 15, 2005.

220 Mayagna (Sumo) Awas Tingni Community Case (Nicaragua), 19 Tradesmen Case (Colombia), Plan de Sánchez Massacre Case (Guatemala) and the Integrantes del Equipo de Estudios Comunitarios y Acción Psicosocial (ECAP) Massacre Plan De Sánchez Case (Guatemala).

221 IACtHR, *James, Briggs, Noel, Garcia and Bethel Case (Trinidad and Tobago)*, Order of August 16, 2000, Preambular Paragraphs 7 and 9. See also IACtHR, *Hilaire, Constantine and Benjamin Case (Trinidad and Tobago)*, Judgment of June 21, 2002, paras. 33, 84(r), 191 and 197–200.

222 Regarding the other beneficiary who had been executed, the State pointed out that it had not received any order to adopt protective measures in favour of Joel Ramiah. The Court considered his execution by Trinidad and Tobago to be an arbitrary deprivation of the right to life that was aggravated because the victim was protected by provisional measures that it had ordered, indicating that his execution should be stayed pending the resolution of the case by the inter-American human rights system. See IACtHR, *Hilaire, Constantine and Benjamin Case (Trinidad and Tobago)*, Judgment of June 21, 2002, paras. 33, 84 and 197–200.

but that it was also indispensable that the case, which was under consideration by the Commission, was capable of being submitted to the Court.[223] The State, on the basis of that reasoning, did not comply with the measures ordered by the Court on May 25, 1999.[224] The Court had held that the situation of extreme gravity and urgency of the case provided the necessary grounds to maintain the measures in order to protect the rights to life and humane treatment of the presumed victims. The Court stated that under the terms of Articles 50,[225] 51[226] and 63(2)[227] of the Convention, read in conjunction with Article 31(1) of the Vienna Convention, every State was obligated to comply in good faith with the international treaties that it has ratified, especially those concerning human rights. The State must, therefore, make every effort to apply the recommendations of an organ of protection of human rights, such as the Commission.[228] The Court held that, in cases that were being considered by the Commission and were

---

223 The Commission informed the Court that it had adopted, in conformity with Article 51 of the Convention, Report No. 44/99 with the respective conclusions and recommendations and had requested that the State respond to an offer of friendly settlement in the case within 30 days. See IACtHR, *James, Briggs, Noel, Garcia and Bethel Case (Trinidad and Tobago)*, Order of May 25, 1999, Explanatory Statement 1(f).

224 Unfortunately, the State did not share the Court's position. Hence, although the Court mantained the provisional measures, the State decided to execute the beneficiary of the measures. IACtHR, *James, Briggs, Noel, Garcia and Bethel Case (Trinidad and Tobago)*, Order of August 16, 2000, Explanatory Statements 11, 12 and 13(a)-(g).

225 Article 50 American Convention on Human Rights states: "1. If a settlement is not reached, the Commission shall, within the time limit established by its Statute, draw up a report setting forth the facts and stating its conclusions. If the report, in whole or in part, does not represent the unanimous agreement of the members of the Commission, any member may attach to it a separate opinion. The written and oral statements made by the parties in accordance with paragraph 1(e) of Article 48 shall also be attached to the report. 2. The report shall be transmitted to the states concerned, which shall not be at liberty to publish it. 3. In transmitting the report, the Commission may make such proposals and recommendations as it sees fit".

226 Article 51 American Convention on Human Rights states: "1. If, within a period of three months from the date of the transmittal of the report of the Commission to the states concerned, the matter has not either been settled or submitted by the Commission or by the state concerned to the Court and its jurisdiction accepted, the Commission may, by the vote of an absolute majority of its members, set forth its opinion and conclusions concerning the question submitted for its consideration. 2. Where appropriate, the Commission shall make pertinent recommendations and shall prescribe a period within which the state is to take the measures that are incumbent upon it to remedy the situation examined. 3. When the prescribed period has expired, the Commission shall decide by the vote of an absolute majority of its members whether the state has taken adequate measures and whether to publish its report".

227 Article 63(2): "In cases of extreme gravity and urgency, and when necessary to avoid irreparable damage to persons, the Court shall adopt such provisional measures as it deems pertinent in matters it has under consideration. With respect to a case not yet submitted to the Court, it may act at the request of the Commission".

228 IACtHR, *James, Briggs, Noel, Garcia and Bethel Case (Trinidad and Tobago)*, Order of May 25, 1999, Enacting Part 1. See also the Concurring Opinion of Judge de Roux Rengifo.

subject to provisional measures, the matter was under the Court's jurisdiction from the moment that it received the request. Thus, regardless of whether the Commission presented the Article 50 and Article 51 Report, the case continued under the inter-American system.[229] According to the Court, Article 63(2) of the Convention only refers to the moment in which the request for provisional measures is made. The Court may, therefore, only act at the request of the Commission with respect to a case that the latter has under consideration, but once the Court's jurisdiction is set in motion, it maintains jurisdiction regardless of any action of the Commission.[230] Once the Commission requests provisional measures, the only restriction in Article 63(2) to the jurisdiction of the Court is that the situation of extreme gravity and urgency continues and that the measures are necessary to avoid damage to the rights of persons.[231]

90. The aforementioned means that with respect to the jurisdiction *ratione temporis*, the Court may adopt whatever provisional measures it deems necessary when it has before it a situation in which the infringement of rights set forth in the Convention is alleged. As provisional measures are employed exceptionally and may only be applied in true situations of gravity and urgency, they may only be extended or maintained while the risk to human rights persists.

---

229 IACtHR, *James, Briggs, Noel, Garcia and Bethel Case (Trinidad and Tobago)*, Order of May 25, 1999, Concurring Opinion of Judge Cançado Trindade, paras. 2 and 3.

230 IACtHR, *James, Briggs, Noel, Garcia and Bethel Case (Trinidad and Tobago)*, Order of May 25, 1999, Concurring Opinion of Judge Cançado Trindade, paras. 5, 6 and 7.

231 *Ibid.*

2. ADMISSIBILITY

2.1. FORMAL REQUIREMENTS OF ADMISSIBILITY

91. The Convention makes no reference to formal requirements that a request for the adoption of provisional measures must comply with. The only reference may be found in Article 26(4) of the Court's Rules, which states that the petition may be presented "by any means of communication."

92. Given the lack of specific rules, the general formalities for the presentation of briefs found in Article 26(1) of the Rules of the Court are applied. Petitions for provisional measures may be presented to the Court[232] "in person, by courier, facsimile,[233] telex,[234] mail[235] or any other method generally used." In the case of presentations by electronic means, the original documents, as well as the accompanying evidence, must be submitted within seven days.[236]

93. A request for provisional measures may be presented to the President of the Court, to any of its judges or to the Court's Secretariat. In any event, whoever receives the request must immediately inform the President. Given the urgency of the matters that are submitted, the request may be presented at any time and the Court should rule on it promptly.[237] Since the Court is not a full-time tribunal, if the request is presented when the Court is not in session, urgent measures may be issued by the President of the Court, after having consulted the

---

232 Pursuant to Article 58 of the Convention, the seat of the Court is determined by the States Parties to the Convention in the General Assembly of the Organisation. The States Parties may change this seat by a two-thirds vote. The seat of the Court is San José, Costa Rica (Central America).

233 The Court's fax is (506) 234-0584.

234 The Court's telephone number is (506) 234-0581.

235 The address of the Court is Avenida 10, Calles 45 and 47, Los Yoses, San Pedro, Costa Rica and the email is: corteidh@org.cr.

236 P.O. Box 6906-1000, San José, Costa Rica (Central America).

237 In the Reggiardo Tolosa Case (Argentina), the Order of the President of the Court was notified to the Government of Argentina, via courier to the Ministry of Foreign Affairs, and through its Embassy in San José, Costa Rica. See IACtHR, *Reggiardo Tolosa Case (Argentina)*, Order of January 19, 1994, Explanatory Statement 3. In the Velásquez Rodríguez, Fairen Garbi and Solis Corrales and Godinez Cruz Cases (Honduras), the Court delivered to the parties the Order to adopt measures from the Bench. See IACtHR, *Velásquez Rodríguez, Fairen Garbi and Solis Corrales and Godinez Cruz Cases (Honduras)*, Judgment on the Merits of July 29, 1988, para. 45.

Permanent Commission and, if possible, the other judges. Under these circumstances, the President requires the State in question to order the urgent measures necessary to ensure that the provisional measures that the Court might adopt at its next session are effective.[238]

94. The Court normally meets in regular sessions, the dates of which are chosen by the Court itself at its immediately previous session. In the event of exceptional circumstances, the President may change these dates after consultation with the judges. Article 12 of the Rules authorises the Court to meet in special sessions convoked by the President on his own initiative or at the request of a majority of the judges.

95. With respect to the languages that are used in the inter-American system, the Rules of the Court distinguish between official languages and working languages. The official languages of the Court, pursuant to Article 20, are those of the OAS (Spanish, English, Portuguese and French) and the working languages are those that the Court decides each year. In a specific case, however, the working language may be that of one of the parties, provided that it is an official language.[239] The petition for provisional measures may thus be presented in any of the working languages of the Court. Those languages are, in accordance with the aforementioned norm, Spanish, English, Portuguese and French.

Table 15. Languages used in the provisional measures

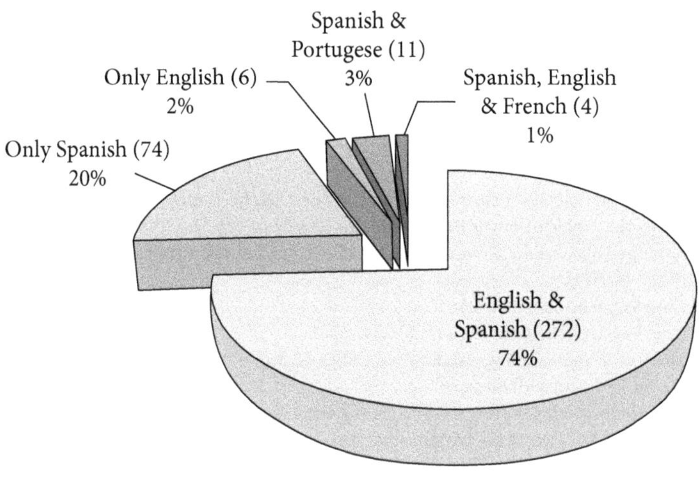

[238] Article 26(3), 26(4) and 26(5) of the Rules of Procedure of the Court.

[239] In spite of the aforementioned, pursuant to Article 21(4) of its Rules of Procedure, the Court may authorize any person appearing before it to use his own language if he does not have sufficient knowledge of the working languages.

96. An analysis of the jurisprudence shows that from 1987 to 2009, the Court adopted 374 orders, of which 81 were drafted only in Spanish, six only in English,[240] 279 in both Spanish and English, eleven in Spanish and Portuguese[241] and four in Spanish, English and French.[242]

The great majority of the orders are drafted in Spanish: the Court has adopted 368 orders in that language (98.3%). It is also interesting to observe that, although the official language of most OAS member States is not English, the Court in a high percentage of instances (76%) uses this language,[243] which is valuable in terms of access to information as it allows persons interested in the inter-American system who read English, but not Spanish, to follow the jurisprudence of the Court.

97. As to content, the request must contain the information necessary to show that there exists a situation of extreme gravity and urgency that justifies the adoption of the measures. The request normally begins by citing the norm that authorises the parties to present the petition, identifying the person or persons who are in a situation of danger, the rights that are to be protected and that the State is obligated to protect, identifying the procedural stage of the case (mostly under consideration by the Commission), followed by an enumeration of the measures that the petitioners deem that the Court should adopt. In the event that there have been precautionary measures, the request contains an indication of the measures and whether they were effective. Finally, there is a description of the facts and arguments leading to the request. The request for provisional measures is sometimes presented separately and at other times the Commission presents it in the application that it submits to the Court.

---

240 IACtHR, *Boyce and Joseph Case (Barbados)*, Order of September 17, 2004, Order of November 25, 2004, Order of February 11, 2005, Order of May 20, 2005 and Order of June 14, 2005; IACtHR, *James et al. Case (Trinidad and Tobago)*, Order of February 28, 2005.

241 IACtHR, *The Urso Branco Prison Case (Brazil)*, Order of June 18, 2002, Order of April 22, 2004, Order of July 7, 2004, Order of September 7, 2004 and Order of September 21, 2005.

242 IACtHR, *Lysias Fleury Case (Haiti)*, Order of the President of March 18, 2003, Order of June 7, 2003 and Order of December 2, 2003.

243 The Court on some occasions has also published in the same case some orders in Spanish and others in English. See Bámaca Velásquez Case (Guatemala), Blake Case (Guatemala), Carpio Nicolle Case (Guatemala), Eloisa Barrios *et al.* Case (Venezuela), Gallardo Rodríguez Case (Venezuela), Liliana Ortega *et al.* Case (Venezuela), Luisiana Ríos *et al.* Case (Venezuela), Marta Colomina and Liliana Velásquez Case (Venezuela), the Miguel Agustín Pro Juárez Human Rights Center *et al.* Case (Mexico) and Peace Community of San José de Apartadó Case (Colombia).

2.1.1. IDENTIFICATION OF THE BENEFICIARY

98. Although at the outset the Court held that it was necessary to individualise the persons who risked suffering irreparable damage to their rights, it subsequently decided that it was necessary to change its position given the real-life situations that were occurring in some of the States Parties. The Court, therefore, increased the range of protection, extending it from beneficiaries who were named to persons who, although not identified by name, could be identified by objective elements. A study of the Court's jurisprudence with respect to the beneficiaries may be classified into three groups: a first group would be the orders that protect persons who are clearly identified by name; a second group would include the orders where the beneficiaries are not named and a third group would be the orders that protect both those persons who are named and those who are not.

Table 16. Kind of beneficiaries protected

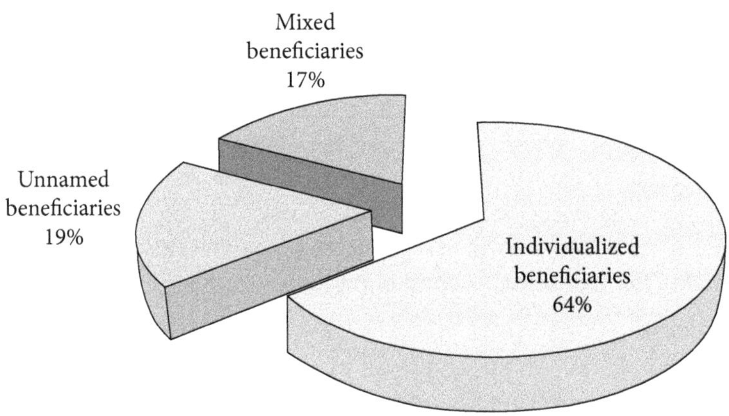

2.1.1.1. Individualised (or Named) Beneficiaries

99. Of the 71 cases to date in which provisional measures have been issued, beneficiaries have been named in more than half (63.3%). From the first orders adopted in 1987 to those adopted in 2009, the Court protected persons who were clearly identified. It is important to clarify that from 1987 to 1997 all the beneficiaries were named, as the Court did not accept the protection of unnamed individuals. Only after 1997 was the range of protection broadened, as will be seen later.

Table 17. Individualised beneficiaries of interim measures

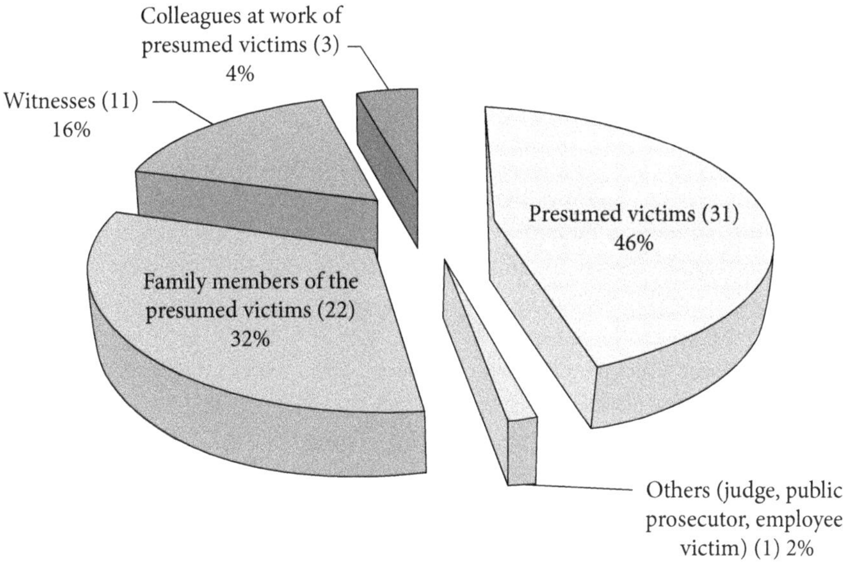

100. In most of the orders, the beneficiaries of protection were identified as the presumed victims in cases that were under consideration in the inter-American system. Of the 45 cases in which measures were adopted that named the beneficiaries, 31 protected the persons who fell in this category. The group of persons that has most benefited from the measures (22 occasions) has been family members of alleged victims, who were shown to have been in a situation of such risk that merited their protection. The Court has also protected on eleven occasions persons who have appeared before it as witnesses, on six occasions, it concerend lawyers; on three occasions it concerned fellow workers of the alleged victims; and on one occasion each, a judge, a prosecutor and an employee of the alleged victim were protected.[244] On 22 occasions, two or more categories of persons were protected at the same time. For example, in the Bustíos-Rojas Case (Peru) the Court protected witnesses, one of the alleged victims and a family member. Another example is the Chunimá Case (Guatemala) where several witnesses, family members, fellow workers and a judge were protected. In the other 23 cases, only one category of persons was protected (i.e. the alleged victim, family members or witnesses).

101. An important case within this group of beneficiaries is that of the Haitians and Dominicans of Haitian Origin in the Dominican Republic (Dominican

244 *Ibid.*

Republic). Here the Commission requested measures on behalf of all Haitians and Dominicans of Haitian origin who were subject to the jurisdiction of the Dominican Republic and who risked being collectively expelled or deported. The Commission indicated that the immigration authorities selected the persons to be deported depending on the color of their skin.

The expulsions were carried out by collective round-ups, without legal proceedings that would have allowed adequate identification of the nationality, immigration status or family ties of those who were expelled and who had to leave their homes without any notice. In general terms, the practice of deportations and expulsions affected two groups: Haitian workers with and without papers and Dominicans of Haitian origin who resided in the Dominican Republic with and without papers.[245]

The petition for the measures, therefore, was presented on behalf of an unnamed group of persons since the manner in which the State carried out the expulsions did not allow distinguishing the members of the group individually and since the persons in question did not present themselves for fear of being identified. The objective of the measures was to suspend the massive expulsions and deportations because of the risk to the life and physical integrity of those deported and their families, especially the minor children who were abandoned after their parents were deported.[246]

The Court rejected the request of protection for unnamed persons. The holding of the Court in this decision is somewhat confusing, not to say contradictory. In effect, the Court based its decision mainly on two aspects. On the one hand, it held that the measures were not appropriate because the beneficiaries had to be named, but at the same time it held that the measures were not appropriate because it had not been shown that the Dominican Republic had a State policy of massive deportations and expulsions in violation of the terms of the Convention. Thus, if it had been demonstrated that it had been State policy, the Court would have adopted the provisional measures, but if that were true, why was the Court emphatic in declaring that the beneficiaries of the measures had to be individualised? If the arguments of the Court were consistent, regardless of whether there was a proven State policy of massive expulsions and deportations, the measures would not have been appropriate. It would, therefore,

245 IACtHR, *Haitians and Dominicans of Haitian Origin in the Dominican Republic Case. (Dominican Republic)*, Order of August 18, 2000, Explanatory Statements 1, 2(d)(g) and 11(c).

246 An analysis of the case may be found in M.E. Ventura Robles, "La Corte Interamericana de Derechos Humanos: Camino hacia un Tribunal Permanente", in *El Futuro de la Corte Interamericana de Derechos Humanos*, A. Cançado Trindade and M.E. Ventura Robles (eds.), San José, Corte Interamericana de Derechos Humanos, UNHCR, 2003, 145–147.

not have been necessary to show such a policy if at the time the jurisprudence of the Court only protected named beneficiaries.

The Court, thus, rejected the general petition in this case to adopt measures of protection for unnamed persons, but adopted them for five persons who had been named because, according to the Court, it could be presumed *prima facie* that those persons were subject to abuses.

2.1.1.2. Unnamed Beneficiaries

102. In view of the particularities of the cases that it began to receive, the Court reversed its view and changed the criterion of protection by extending the range of beneficiaries of provisional measures. Protection was given to members of communities not only as individuals, as had occurred until 1999, but also as members of that community. The Court, thus, accepted the protection of groups of unnamed persons when they were potentially at risk.[247] Proof of belonging to the group of alleged victims is done by using objective criteria, such as the ties of belonging and the type of risks that allow individualising the beneficiaries at the time of execution of the measures.

103. Although the protection extends to a non-individualised group, the Court normally knows the approximate amount of persons forming part of the group (i.e. the beneficiary). For example, in the Peace Community of San José de Apartadó Case (Colombia), the approximate number of beneficiaries was about 1200 and in the Case of the Indigenous Kankuamo People (Ecuador), it concerned about 6000 persons. Exceptionally, this information is not available to the Court. However, other mechanisms permit to know this information. For example, in the Penitentiaries of Mendoza Case (Argentina), although the approximate amount of beneficiaries was not indicated, from the list of detainees that each detention facility has to have, the number of persons could be deduced.

[247] See also, in favour of a change in the jurisprudence, D. Shelton, "Discussion", in *Mesures conservatoires et droits fondamentaux*, G. Cohen-Jonathan and J.F. Flauss (eds.), Brussels, Bruylant, 2005, 170–171.

Table 18. Unnamed beneficiaries

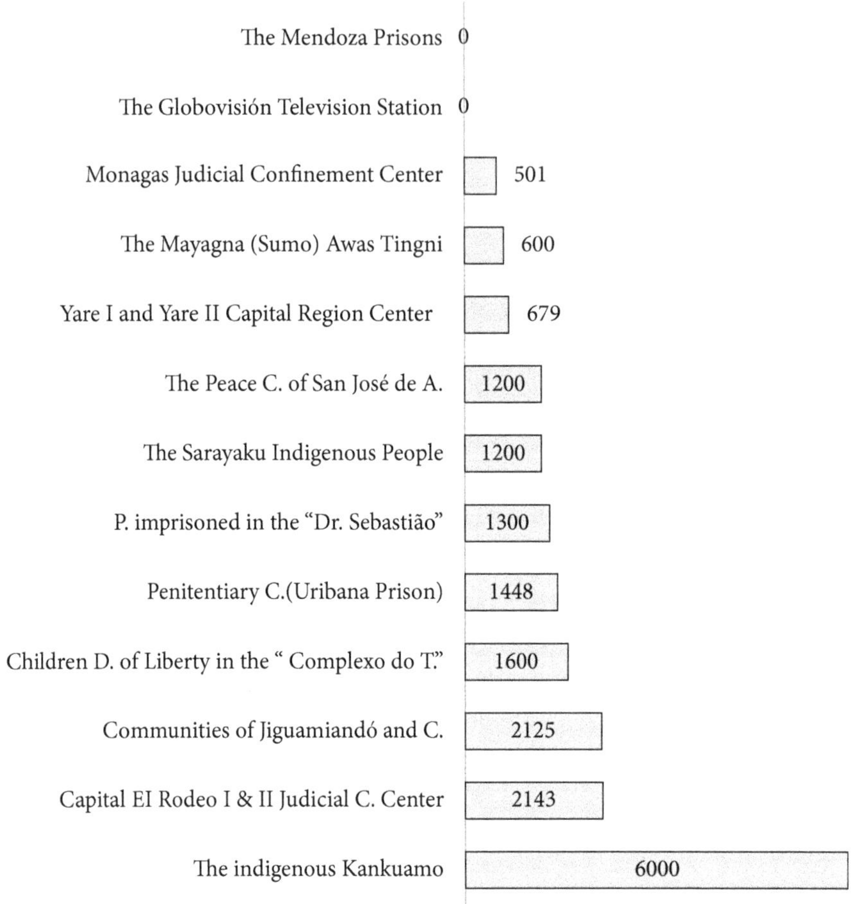

104. As can be seen in Table 18, the Court has adopted this type of measures in 13 cases. For a better understanding and in view of the characteristics of each case, they have been divided in four groups. A first group would be made up of the protection granted to members of communities of civilians who have declared themselves neutral with regard to the armed conflict in Colombia. Another group would be made up of the measures granted to members of some indigenous communities. A third group would be those measures protecting persons involved in the mass media of Venezuela and a fourth group would cover the protection of inmates in some prisons in Argentina, Brazil and Venezuela.

2.1.1.2.1. Members of Organised Communities

105. Within the group of provisional measures that protected members of civilian communities that had declared themselves neutral in the internal armed conflict in Colombia are the Case of the Peace Community of San José de Apartadó (Colombia) and the Case of the Communities of the Jiguamiandó and of the Curbaradó (Colombia). The former case marked the beginning of protection for unnamed persons by the Inter-American Court.

106. When the Commission requested the adoption of the measures in the Peace Community of San José de Apartadó Case, the case was under its consideration. According to the Commission, the purpose of the provisional measures was to protect the members of the Peace Community of San José de Apartadó, which was located in the region of Urabá, Antioquia, one of the epicentres of the internal armed conflict that was/is taking place in Colombia. That Community was composed of approximately 1,200 members who, since the Community had been founded in 1997, had been stigmatised and constantly menaced by the paramilitary violence, in spite of their attempts to isolate themselves from the armed conflict. In the same year that the Community was established, the Commission requested the State to grant precautionary measures in favour of the Community's members since there had been more than 40 summary executions and forced disappearances, for which nobody had been found guilty. In addition, almost three years after having been granted the measures, the Community was still living under dangerous conditions due to the continual threats of armed individuals and because of its utter defenseless. One of the grave problems was that members of the Community were claimed to be guerrillas or persons who aided the guerrillas.

The Commission also stated that, although it attempted to identify every member of the Community, it had only been able to make a list of 189 persons, which was not an accurate count of the persons who were in a dangerous situation. The Commission could not furnish a complete list because the members of the Community had not authorised their names to be divulged because they feared that it would stigmatise them more, which would lead to more violence. Nevertheless, the Commission argued that there was a series of elements that allowed the identification of the members of the Community collectively. Geographically, the Community was located in a specific place – the Municipality of Apartadó – and was formed of 32 "surrounding trails." Another element was belonging to a community and here it showed that the Community was governed by a series of norms, had a system of representation comprised of an internal council of eight peasants who were elected democratically for a three-year term. In addition, the Community was governed by several principles, such as neutrality with respect to all armed actors, no direct or indirect participation in the war, refusal to bear arms, and no offering or manipulating information in favour of any of the armed actors.

The Commission also pointed out that the precautionary measures that it had ordered were of an indeterminate nature, that they had not been opposed by the State nor had the State questioned or alleged having problems identifying the persons that it had to protect. The Commission stated that it was convinced that the State understood the collective dimension of the problem, knew which persons it had to protect, understood the geographical limits, the element of belonging to the Community that its members had and the Community's mechanisms for functioning. For the aforementioned reasons, the Commission requested that the Court adopt measures for all the members of the Peace Community.[248]

The Inter-American Court stated that the case had special characteristics that made it different from others that had been submitted to it and that such peculiarities warranted the adoption of measures to protect all the members of the Peace Community. The Court held that it was an organised community made up of approximately 1,200 persons whose members could be identified and individualised and that all of its members, for belonging to that Community, were at a similar risk of suffering acts of aggression against their lives and personal integrity. These facts and the general obligation of the State under Article 1(1) of the Convention warranted provisional measures of protection on behalf of all the members of the Peace Community of San José de Apartadó.[249]

The Court, thus, extended the protection of the provisional measures in a reasonable manner to a greater range of beneficiaries. It admitted that the measures could be used to protect a group of unnamed persons when they were potential victims of acts of authority or acts of persons linked in one way or another to the authority. Belonging to the group of possible beneficiaries of the measures comes not from precise knowledge about each individual but rather from objective criteria, such as the ties in belonging and the shared risks that would permit individualising the beneficiaries when the measures are executed. It is, therefore, a matter of protecting the members of a community not only as individuals, as is the general rule, but as members of that community.[250]

---

[248] IACtHR, *Peace Community of San José de Apartadó Case (Colombia)*, Order of November 24, 2000, Explanatory Statement 9 (a)-(f) and (i)-(k).

[249] IACtHR, *Peace Community of San José de Apartadó Case (Colombia)*, Order of November 24, 2000, Preambular Paragraphs 7–9. See M.E. Ventura Robles, "La Corte Interamericana de Derechos Humanos: Camino hacia un Tribunal Permanente", in *El Futuro de la Corte Interamericana de Derechos Humanos*, A. Cançado Trindade and M.E. Ventura Robles (eds.), San José, Corte Interamericana de Derechos Humanos, UNHCR, 2003, 148–149.

[250] IACtHR, *Peace Community of San José de Apartadó Case (Colombia)*, Order of November 24, 2000, Concurring Opinion of Judges Alirio Abreu and Sergio García Ramírez, para. 8.

The Court also held that the obligation of the State to protect all beneficiaries of the measures not only existed regarding acts of State agents but also with respect to acts of third persons, in this case members of the so-called United Self-Defense Forces of Colombia (AUC) who were, according to the petitioners, creating a dangerous situation in the Community. The Court later decided to broaden the measures to protect everyone who served the Community. This group of persons was not named either but could be identified by their ties of service to the Community.

107. The Case of the Communities of the Juguamiandó and of the Curbaradó (Colombia) was the second case in which the Court ordered protection for a group of persons who had not been named but who were identifiable because they belonged to the Communities. The Communities were made up of the Community Council of the Jiguamiandó and the families of the Curbaradó, approximately 2,125 persons from 515 families. It was an organised community located in a specific geographical area, the Municipality of Carmen de Darién, Department of Chocó. The members of the Communities could be individualised and identified and in belonging to the Communities they all were at the same risk of suffering acts of aggression against their personal integrity and their lives as well as being displaced from their territory. The State had recognised in this case the collective ownership of their land and their mechanisms of self-government and their identity as a civilian population and as non-participants in the internal armed conflict, with respect to which they had assumed a pacifist position.[251]

Two factors were primarily responsible for the danger. The first was related to battles between the Colombian Army and the members of the paramilitary AUC against the left-wing FARC guerilla group and the second was the cultivation of African palm oil trees within part of the territory that belonged to the Communities. The Commission stated in its request that the members of the Communities were accused by the Armed Forces and by the paramilitaries of belonging to or collaborating with the FARC. For that reason, they were, *inter alia*, threatened with death, illegally detained, harassed, killed, disappeared, displaced and had their goods looted and destroyed.[252] In addition, the private

251 IACtHR, *Communities of the Jiguamiando and of the Curbaradó Case (Colombia)*, Order of March 6, 2003 Explanatory Statements 2 and 5. See also Order of March 15, 2005, Preambular Paragraph 7.

252 Among the events alleged were that in September of 2001 members of the Army and paramilitary forces had stoned and stabbed two persons, cut another's throat and had murdered a handicapped peasant and a pregnant women and in November 2002 the body of a member of the Community was found cut to pieces and his head was found 10 yards away. The persons responsible for these abuses generally wore insignias of the Colombian Army and AUC armbands, which made it easy to identify them. See IACtHR, *Communities of the*

company cultivating the African palms on approximately 1,500 hectares of the collective zone of those Communities, with the aid of the Army and the AUC, were intimidating the members of the Community so that they would collaborate in the production of palm oil or otherwise would abandon the territory. This had resulted in the displacement of many members of the Communities and had paralysed the planting of the Communities' crops, which had exacerbated their food situation.

The Court, following its precedent in the Peace Community of San José de Apartadó Case, adopted provisional measures to protect all the members of the Communities of the Jiguamiandó and of the Curbaradó. The Court held that the beneficiaries could be identified and individualised and as a part of those Communities they all suffered acts of aggression against their personal integrity and their lives as well as being forcibly displaced from their territory.[253] The Court stated that, given the particular circumstances of the case and the general condition of the armed conflict in Colombia, the protection of the provisional measures was necessary for every member of the Communities in light of the provisions of the Convention and international humanitarian law.

2.1.1.2.2. Members of Indigenous Communities

108. In the second group that has received interim protection from the Inter-American Court one can find the Mayagna (Sumo) Awas Tingni Community Case (Nicaragua),[254] the Indigenous Kankuamo People Case (Colombia)[255] and the Indigenous Sarayaku People Case (Ecuador).[256] In each instance the Court

---

Jiguamiando and of the Curbaradó Case (Colombia), Order of March 6, 2003, Explanatory Statement 2.

253 *Ibid.*, Preambular Paragraph 9.

254 In this case members of the Mayagna (Sumo) Awas Tingni Community requested provisional measures to avoid immediate and irreparable damage resulting from third party activities carried out in their territory and the exploitation of their natural resources, which according to the petitioners would endanger the effectiveness of the measures already provided by the Court in its judgment on the merits and thus constituted a threat of irreparable damage to the Community. In addition, it made the "delimitation, demarcation and titling of lands belonging to the Community" difficult.

255 In this case, the Commission stated that the indigenous community had been the victim of continual violent acts, threats and murders by illegal armed groups that operated in its territory. The community had its source of food blocked and its young members were recruited by force by the armed groups, hence many families were forced to move.

256 The Commission pointed out that the territory of the Sarayaku people had been legally recognized by Ecuador in 1992, but that in 1996 the State had signed a contract with the Argentine corporation, Compañía General de Combustible, for the exploration and exploitation of oil covering an area of 200,000 hectares of land, of which 65% involved the indigenous territory. Members of the Ecuadorian Army, together with the company's security personnel, would attack the members of the indigenous community in order to enter their territory and exploit their oil. The use of explosives in the territory had destroyed forest, water

considered that the adoption of provisional measures to protect the unnamed indigenous persons who belonged to those communities was justified.[257] The Court held that the indigenous peoples who were in danger were identifiable according to the information that had been furnished, such as the approximate number of members who made up each community, the geographical location where they were living and the fact that it had been proved that each indigenous person was in danger of acts of aggression as a result of belonging to the community.

109. The Mayagna (Sumo) Awas Tingni Community was composed of more than 600 indigenous persons located in the Northern Atlantic Autonomous Region of the Atlantic Coast of Nicaragua. The members of the Community were at risk because persons outside the Community, with the tolerance of the State, had invaded their territory and were illegally exploiting their natural resources. These facts constituted a situation of extreme gravity and urgency with regard to respect for the property of the Mayagna Community, including resources that were the basis of its subsistence, culture and traditions.[258]

110. For their part, the Kankuamo Indigenous People were comprised of approximately 6,000 persons located in the Southeastern part of the Sierra Madre Mountains of Santa Marta, located in the Departments of Magdalena, Guajira and Cesar. Their reservation of 40,000 hectares was composed of twelve communities and had been recognised by the State in 2003.[259] The geographical location of the Kankuamos had exposed its members to continual acts of violence and threats by illegal armed groups that operated in the zone, which had caused the governors and leaders of the indigenous groups to be victims of threats, attempts on their lives and killings. The Commission alleged that between 1993 and 2003 the armed groups active in the zone had assassinated approximately 166 Kankuamos.[260]

---

sources and sacred places, also provoking the migration of animals and a general decrease in the capacity to survival of the members of the village. Consequently, the right to the usage and enjoyment of the territory had been affected.

257 IACtHR, *Indigenous Kankuamo Community Case (Colombia)*, Order of July 5, 2004, Preambular Paragraph 9 and IACtHR, *Indigenous Sarayaku People Case (Ecuador)*, Order of July 6, 2004, Preambular Paragraph 9.

258 In the *Mayagna (Sumo) Awas Tingni Community Case (Nicaragua)*, the location of the Community and the identification of its members were not in the order of provisional measures but in the judgment on the merits. See IACtHR, *Mayagna (Sumo) Awas Tingni Comunidad Case (Nicaragua)*, Judgment on the Merits of August 31, 2001, para. 103 and Order of September 6, 2002, Preambular Paragraphs 6 and 7.

259 IACtHR, *Indigenous Community Kankuamo Case (Colombia)*, Order of July 5, 2004, Explanatory Statement 2(a), (b) and (d), Preambular Paragraph 9.

260 *Ibid.*, Explanatory Statement 2(g).

111. On the other hand, the Indigenous Sarayaku People (Ecuador) was made up of approximately 1,200 members, who were located in the towns of Shiguacoca, Chontayaku, Sarayakillo, Cali, Teresa Mama, Llanchama and Sarayaku Center, in the Province of Pastaza. The territory of the community had been legally recognised by Ecuador in 1992. According to the information furnished, the Sarayakus were the object of aggression, harassment and threats by the Ecuadorian Army and by security personnel of an oil company that was interested in exploring and exploiting petroleum within the territory of the community.

112. In each of these cases, the Court adopted measures to protect the communities' members without naming them. The Court took into account that it knew the approximate number of indigenous people in the community, that they were located in a specific place within the territory of the State and that every indigenous person was at the same risk of acts of aggression for belonging to his community. In view of these circumstances, the Court deemed it appropriate to order provisional measures of protection on behalf of the indigenous community so as to include all of its members.

2.1.1.2.3. Beneficiaries Working in the Mass Media

113. With respect to the third group, the Court adopted provisional measures to protect the life, personal integrity and freedom of expression of journalists, officials and other employees of the Globovisión television station.

114. In the Globovisión television station case the Commission pointed out that from 2002 to 2004, in spite of precautionary measures being in force, the employees and installations of the company had been the object of various attacks. For example, two explosive devices and a tear gas bomb had been set off within the installations of the station, resulting in a fire and the destruction of three vehicles. On another occasion, attacks interrupted a live television program. The Commission also stated that reporters were continually exposed to aggression while they were covering news stories on location and that under these circumstances two journalists had been injured. The petition stated that the aggressors were government sympathisers and that nobody had been arrested in spite of the fact that the National Guard had been present in the area of the incidents.[261]

Unlike the other cases, the Court in its arguments did not analyse the topic of the protection of unnamed persons but rather emphasized the important role

[261] IACtHR, *Globovisión Television Station Case (Venezuela)*, Order of September 4, 2002, Explanatory Statements 1 and 2, Preambular Paragraphs 7 and 13.

of the mass media in democratic societies. The Court stated that the mass media play a relevant role within democratic societies because freedom of expression is materialised through them and, therefore, it is important that journalists enjoy special protection because how a society is kept informed depends on their independence. The Court, therefore, deemed that adoption of the measures was justified since the rights of journalists, cameramen, officials and photographers as well as the installations of Globovisión were threatened.[262]

2.1.1.2.4. Beneficiaries who are Prisoners

115. The Mendoza Prisons Case (Argentina), the Penitentiary Center of the Central Occidental Region (Uribana Prison) Case (Venezuela), the Yare I and Yare II Capital Region Center Case (Venezuela), the Capital El Rodeo I & El Rodeo II Judicial Confinement Center Case (Venezuela), the Monagas Judicial Confinement Center ("La Pica") Case (Venezuela), the Persons imprisoned in the "Dr. Sebatião Martins Silveira" Penitenciary in Araraquara, São Paulo Case (Brazil), the Children Deprived of Liberty in the "Complexo do Tatuapé of FEDEM Case (Brazil) are the latest cases in which the Court granted protective measures to a group of persons who were not named.

116. In the Mendoza Prison Case, the Commission requested the adoption of provisional measures to protect the life and personal integrity of the inmates, employees and officials inside the Provincial Penitentiary of Mendoza and the Gustavo André Unit of Lavalle. It concerned, *inter alia*, detainees, personnel and public servants that worked in those places.

The Commission stated that in the past seven months there were a series of incidents that led to the belief that persons inside the prisons were in danger. The incidents had provoked the death and injuries of some of the inmates and prison employees as a result of fights between inmates and other circumstances that still had not been clarified by the authorities. In addition, the Commission argued that the detention centers had very serious problems of security, infrastructure, overcrowding and unhealthy conditions. Additionally, a lack of guards placed at risk not only the lives of the inmates but also those of the security personnel.

The Court considered particularly grave the fact that the affected persons were in State detention centers because the State is the guarantor of the rights of persons who are under its custody.[263] The Court held that the beneficiaries were

---

262 *Ibid.*, Preambular Paragraphs 7, 8, 9 and 13.

263 The function of the State as guarantor is an expression generally used in penal matters to refer to a violation by omission: who should respond for certain outcomes, by virtue of the obligations of custody that the State assumes or are attributed to it in a binding manner. This is the case with prisons: the inmate is in the hands of the custodian and is dependant on the will of the functionary who may be benevolent or tyrannical (oppressive); or at the mercy of

identifiable since they were in jail or had entered the prisons under normal conditions, as employees or visitors, and that in places where persons are detained there is a daily registry for each inmate that indicates his identity, the reasons for his detention, the competent authority that ordered the detention and the day and hour of his entry and his departure.[264] The Court, therefore, decided to adopt provisional measures for the unnamed persons because there was a situation of extreme gravity and urgency in the prisons that placed in danger the life and physical integrity of the detainees and the persons who were inside the prisons and because, although the beneficiaries were not named, it was possible to identify each of them.

2.1.1.3. Named and Unnamed Beneficiaries

117. In this group one can find the orders of the Inter-American Court that simultaneously protect both named and unnamed beneficiaries. There are twelve cases in this group.[265] In five cases, the beneficiaries were persons working for human rights organiations;[266] in four cases, family members of persons who were identifiable without being named; in two cases, persons working in the mass media;[267] and in one case, the beneficiaries were inmates, security personnel and other persons who had entered the detention centres.[268]

118. The first case in which the Court adopted provisional measures on behalf of persons both named and unnamed was presented in 1997. In the Alvarez *et al.*

circumstances which often occurs when the custodian abdicates his responsibility as the authority of the detention center and leaves things in the hands of destiny or chance. See IACtHR, *Mendoza Prisons Case (Argentina)*, Order of July 18, 2005, Concurring Opinion of Judge Sergio García Ramírez, para. 2. The Court's jurisprudence has established that the State is the guarantor of the rights of the inmates under its custody. See IACtHR, *Bulacio Case (Argentina)*, Judgment of September 19, 2003, paras. 126–127, 138; IACtHR, *Hilaire, Constantine and Benjamin et al. Case (Trinidad and Tobago)*, Judgment of June 21, 2002, para. 165; IACtHR, *Bámaca Velásquez Case (Guatemala)*, Judgment of November 25, 2000, para. 171 and IACtHR, *Neira Alegría et al. Case (Peru)*, Judgment of January 19, 1995, para. 60.

264 IACtHR, *Mendoza Prisons Case (Argentina)*, Order of November 22, 2004, Preambular Paragraphs 7, 13 and 14.

265 Alvarez *et al.* Case (Colombia), Bámaca Velásquez Case (Guatemala), Carlos Nieto *et al.* Case (Venezuela), Carpio Nicolle Case (Guatemala), The Urso Branco Prison Case (Brazil), The Miguel Agustín Pro Juárez Human Rights Center *et al.* Case (Mexico), "El Nacional" and "Así es la Noticia" Newspapers Case (Venezuela), Digna Ochoa y Plácido *et al.* Case (Mexico), Gómez Paquiyauri Brothers Case (Peru), Helen Mack Chang *et al.* Case (Guatemala), Luisiana Rios *et al.* Case (Venezuela) and Paniagua Morales *et al.* and Vásquez *et al.* Case (Guatemala).

266 Álvarez *et al.* Case (Colombia), Carlos Nieto *et al.* Case (Venezuela), Miguel Agustín Pro Juárez Human Rights Center *et al.* Case (Mexico), Digna Ochoa and Plácido *et al.* Case (Mexico) and Helen Mack Chang *et al.* Case (Guatemala).

267 El Nacional and Asi es la Noticia Newspapers Case (Venezuela) y Luisiana Rios *et al.* Case (Venezuela).

268 Urso Branco Prison Case (Brazil).

Case (Colombia), which was under consideration by the Commission, the Court protected by name 41 members of the Association of Families of the Detained and Disappeared of Colombia (ASFADDES)[269] and, without naming them, the next of kin of a person who had disappeared and all those who, as a result of their work in ASFADDES, were in danger.[270] During the implementation of the measures, two persons who had not been named but who worked with ASFADDES had disappeared. The Court held that, while it was true that the orders of provisional measures had not named the persons who had disappeared, they were generically protected because the Court had established the obligation to adopt whatever measures were necessary to ensure that all persons who worked in the offices of the Association could carry out their functions without danger to their lives or physical integrity. In that respect, it was clear that the State had not complied with its duty of protection.[271]

119. In the Digna Ochoa y Plácido *et al.* (Mexico),[272] the Miguel Agustín Pro Juárez Human Rights Center *et al.* (Mexico),[273] the Helen Mack Chang *et al.*

---

269 A non-governmental organisation, which reunites and supports the families of the victims of forced disappearances in Colombia and works to achieve progress in Colombia's national policies in this regard. See IACtHR, *Alvarez et al. Case (Colombia)*, Order of the President of July 22, 1997, Explanatory Statement 3.

270 *Ibid.*, Enacting Part 1 and 4. Also see, Order of August 14, 1997, Preambular Paragraph 2; Order of December 11, 1997, Enacting Part 5; Order of the President of December 22, 1997, Preambular Paragraph 3; Order of January 1, 1998, Enacting Part 5; Order of the President of August 6, 1998, Preambular Paragraph 3; Order of the President of October 11, 2000, Preambular Paragraph 9, Enacting Part 3; Order of November 12, 2000, Preambular Paragraph 6, Enacting Part 4 and Order of May 30, 2001, Enacting Parts 1 and 2.

271 *Ibid.*, Order of the President of October 11, 2000, Preambular Paragraphs 8 and 9, Enacting Part 3 and Order of November 12, 2000, Preambular Paragraph 6, Enacting Part 4.

272 In the Digna Ochoa y Plácido *et al.* Case (Mexico), the Commission reported that the offices of the Miguel Agustín Pro Juárez Human Rights Center had, on various occasions, received letters containing threats against its workers because of their work defending human rights. The last threat said that a bomb would explode. In this matter, the Court ordered Mexico to adopt without delay, whatever measures were necessary to protect four persons who were named, among them a lawyer and a priest, and also all the persons who worked or visited the offices of the Center to ensure that they were able carry out their work or transactions without danger to their lives or physical integrity. See IACtHR, *Digna Ochoa y Plácido et al. Case (Mexico)*, Order of November 17, 1999, Preambular Paragraph 2, Enacting Parts 1 and 2.

273 In the case of the Miguel Agustín Pro Juárez Human Rights Center *et al.* (Mexico), the Commission requested protection for the parents and 12 brothers and sisters of Digna Ochoa, who had been assassinated after the provisional measures in her favour were lifted. Her family had seen persons and strange vehicles around their homes and had received anonymous telephone calls, which had made them fear for their lives. In addition, the Commission requested that measures be adopted to protect all of the members of the human rights organisation because a message containing an express threat to all of them was found on the body of the assassinated lawyer. According to the Commission, the series of threats, the messages and different forms of intimidation were due to the work of the lawyers in the Center as defenders of human rights, who had denounced military, police and judicial staff for violating fundamental rights. Since the State in its report did not object to the complaint

(Guatemala),[274] and the Carlos Nieto *et al.* (Venezuela) Cases,[275] the Court also adopted measures to protect both named and unnamed persons who were in danger as a result of their association with human rights organisations.

120. In *El Nacional* and *Así es la Noticia* Newspapers, the *Globovisión* Television Station and the Luisiana Ríos *et al.* Cases,[276] measures were adopted

---

and the evidence presented in the Commission's petition showed the existence of a situation of grave danger to the lives and physical integrity of the members of the organisation, lawyers and the family of the murdered woman, the Court thought it was necessary to adopt provisional measures in favour of all the persons in question. A total of 17 individualized persons were protected and, in general, all of the members of the human rights center. See IACtHR, *Miguel Agustín Pro Juárez Human Rights Center et al. Case (Mexico)*, Order of November 30, 2001, Explanatory Statement 7, Enacting Parts 2 and 3. Two years later, the Court, requested by the Commission, lifted the measures that benefited all the members of the human rights center and maintained them regarding the other 17 people. See IACtHR, Order of the Court of April 20, 2004, Explanatory Statement 5, Enacting Part 1.

274 In the Helen Mack Chang Case (Guatemala), the Court protected 12 persons in an individualised manner, among them the families, co-workers and a witness in the Myrna Mack Chang Case being heard by the Court. The Court also adopted measures, without giving precise names, to protect the next of kin of a relative of Mrs. Chang, the families of a witness and the rest of the members of the organisation. The beneficiaries were related to Myrna Mack Chang who had allegedly been murdered by the high command of the Presidential General Staff. Mrs. Mack had founded and worked in the *Asociación para el Avance de las Ciencias Sociales* in Guatemala conducting research on the causes and consequences of the displacement of rural indigenous communities, the living conditions of the victims of this phenomenon, and government policies toward the displaced population. See IACtHR, *Myrna Mack Chang et al. (Guatemala)*, Judgment on the Merits of November 25, 2003, VIII Proven Facts, 134.2 and 134.6. See also IACtHR, *Helen Mack Chang Case (Guatemala)*, Order of the President of August 14, 2002, Enacting Part 2 and Order of the President of April 25, 2003, Enacting Part 1.

275 In this case, the Court adopted measures to protect Carlos Nieto Palma, an attorney and general coordinator of the non-governmental organisation of human rights "*Una Ventana a la Libertad*" and his family. This organisation was dedicated to defending and promoting human rights in Venezuelan prisons and jails. According to the Commission, Mr. Nieto had received death threats and had been harassed by police agents. The Court said that States must provide effective and adequate guarantees to human rights defenders to enable them to carry out their activities freely and hence it was necessary to pay particular attention to acts that limited or obstructed their work. The Court adopted measures to protect Mr. Nieto and his nephew individually and general measures to protect his family. Unlike other cases, the Court gave the Commission seven days to submit a list of the family members on whose behalf the State must adopt the aforementioned protective measures. See IACtHR, *Case of Carlos Nieto et al. (Venezuela)*, Order of July 9, 2004, Explanatory Statement 2 (b) and (c), Preambular Paragraph 7, Enacting Parts 1 and 2.

276 In this case the Court initially adopted nine provisional measures to protect certain individuals who were in a situation of danger because of their relationship to the media. The incidents reported included the murder of a journalist, bullet wounds, threats, explosives placed in media offices and the discrediting of the profession. Two years later, the Commission requested the extension of the provisional measures to protect all the employees who were in the facilities of the communications media or who were associated with journalism. The Commission reported that in Venezuela a Presidential recall referendum had been approved and that this had led to a number of violent disturbances resulting in the death of one person,

to protect persons who had some type of relation with some mass media in Venezuela, either because they were journalists or simply because they were inside the installations or officies of those companies.

In those cases, the Commission affirmed that in Venezuela there had been a significant and progressive increase in threats and attacks by followers of President Hugo Chávez against reporters, particularly those who covered political events and rallies of the opposition and that some journalists had been injured and harassed and the offices of the companies damaged by members of the Movimiento Bolivariano 200 and the so-called Círculos Bolivarianos.[277] Among the incidents were the breaking of windows of the *El Nacional* building and the burning of a newspaper delivery truck. Damage at *Así es la Nación* included the destruction of computers, microwave ovens, telephones, furniture and windows as well as the destruction of twelve cars of journalists and the burning of the warehouse of the returned papers. The headquarters of the television station *Radio Caracas Televisión* had been attacked with rocks and firearms and shots were also fired at persons who looked out the windows of the building.[278]

The Court said that the information revealed a *prima facie* grave peril for all the journalists, officials, workers and other persons who were at the facilities of those companies or who were involved in the operations of those media, that justified the adoption of provisional measures. The Court, therefore, ordered the State to adopt without delay all necessary measures to protect the life, personal integrity and freedom of expression of those persons.[279]

121. Another group of provisional measures was directed at protecting unnamed family members of previously named persons.[280] In those cases, the

---

at least two persons wounded and attacks with rocks and firearms against the offices of the private media. The Court found that the events that took place made it reasonable to presume that both the beneficiaries of the provisional measures ordered by the Court and all the journalists, managers, workers and other persons who were in the facilities of the media or who were associated with journalism were at grave risk, which made the extension of the measures necessary for their protection. See IACtHR, *Luisiana Rios et al. Case (Venezuela)*, Order of November 27, 2002, Explanatory Statements 1 and 2 and Order of September 8, 2004, Explanatory Statements 6 and 7, Preambular Paragraphs 7 and 12, Enacting Part 1.

277 IACtHR, *El Nacional and Asi es la Noticia Newspapers Case*, Order of July 6, 2004. Explanatory Statements 1, 2(a), (b) and (m).

278 *Ibid.*

279 See IACtHR, *El Nacional and Asi es la Noticia Newspapers Case (Venezuela)*, Order of July 6, 2004, Enacting Part 1; IACtHR, *Globovisión Television Station Case (Venezuela)*, Order of September 4, 2004, Preambular Paragraph 13, Enacting Part 1 and IACtHR, *Luisiana Rios et al. Case (Venezuela)*, Order of September 4, 2004, Preambular Paragraphs 7 and 12, Enacting Part 1.

280 The Helen Mack Chang Case (Guatemala) and the Carlos Nieto *et al.* Case (Venezuela) also belong to this group inasmuch as the families of the individualised persons were also

Court initially names the persons whom it considers to be in danger and then refers to the family members of the protected persons to whom the measures are extended. On these occasions, the Court uses only the expression "and their next of kin," but does not say which family members or how many of them. Within this group one can find the Bámaca Velásquez (Guatemala), the Gómez Paquiyauri Brothers (Peru) and the Paniagua Morales *et al.* and Vásquez *et al.* (Guatemala) Cases.[281]

The representatives of the alleged victims in the Gómez Paquiyauri Brothers Case (Peru) requested the Court to adopt protective measures in favour of members of the family of Gómez Paquiyuari[282] and of a witness and his family. The request stated that the persons named were in a situation of extreme gravity and urgency since they had received repeated threats and were being harassed by State agents who were interested that the case under consideration in the inter-American system be closed. The Court decided to adopt measures to protect by name eight family members of the alleged victim and the witness. The Court also decided to protect members of the witness' family without naming them, but at no time did it state to whom it was referring or how many of the family members were covered by the measures.[283]

Similarly, the Court protected family members of the alleged victims who brought cases before the inter-American system and a witness in the Paniagua Morales *et al.* and Vásquez *et al.* Case (Guatemala).[284] The Court named five family members and also stated that the other members of the family should be protected by the provisional measures.[285] In the Bámaca Velásquez Case (Guatemala), the Court decided to protect by name 27 persons, among them a witness and some next of kin of Mr. Bámaca Velásquez. The Court also adopted measures in favour of their family members without naming them. Those persons were in danger because of statements that they had made that implied the responsibility of State agents in human rights violations. After their appearance at the Court, the witness and his family had been the victims of continual threats

protected. They are not analysed in this part, however, since they were considered within the group that was protected for having links with human rights organisations.

281 In this matter, the Commission requested in the same petition provisional measures to protect persons in two different cases that were being considered in the inter-American system. See IACtHR, *Paniagua Morales et al. and Vásquez et al. Case (Guatemala)*, Order of the President of February 10, 1998, Preambular Paragraph 4.

282 The relatives had testified before the Court.

283 IACtHR, *Gómez Paquiyauri Brothers Case (Peru)*, Order of May 7, 2004, Explanatory Statements 6 and 7, Enacting Parts 1 and 2.

284 The witness had been shot and did not know who was responsible for the attack. See IACtHR, *Paniagua Morales et al. and Vásquez et al. Case (Guatemala)*, Order of the President of January 29, 2001, Explanatory Statement 2, Preambular Paragraphs 4, 8 and 12, Enacting Part 1.

285 IACtHR, *Paniagua Morales et al. and Vásquez et al. Case (Guatemala)*, Order of the President of February 10, 1998, Enacting Parts 1 and 2.

and persecutions. Three cousins of the witness were kidnapped and subsequently murdered.[286] The Court believed it indispensable that the State protect the alleged victim's family members residing in Guatemala and that it ensure the conditions of security necessary so that they could continue living in their homes without fear of suffering damage to their lives or their physical integrity.[287]

2.2. SUBSTANTIVE CONDITIONS OF ADMISSIBILITY

122. The Inter-American Court does not have complete discretion to adopt and maintain provisional measures but, prior to adopting the measures, it must, under the terms of Article 63(2) of the Convention, ascertain that each of the following conditions has been met: a) there needs to be a situation of extreme gravity; b) the measure requested is required with urgency, and c) there is a risk that there will be irreparable damage to persons. Thus, not every situation or every potential violation of rights leads to the adoption of provisional measures. Only when it is shown that there is a situation that, due to its extreme gravity, could lead to the irreparable damage of the rights of persons and that it is possible to avoid such damage by the adoption of certain measures does there then exist the basic objective elements that would allow the Court to adopt them.[288]

123. Although these three elements are intimately related, to the extent that the urgency to adopt the measures, given the imminence of a possible prejudice to human rights, is the direct result of the gravity of the situation presented, for methodological reasons an attempt will be made to examine each element separately.

---

286 IACtHR, *Bámaca Velásquez Case (Guatemala)*, Order of the President of June 30, 1998, Explanatory Statement 2, Enacting Parts 1 and 2; Order of August 29, 1998, Enacting Part 2; Order of February 21, 2003, Explanatory Statement 5, Preambular Paragraph 13, Enacting Parts 2 and 3 and Order of November 20, 2003, Explanatory Statement 17 (f) and (g), Preambular Paragraph 5. Enacting Parts 2 and 3.

287 Although the first order that protected the family of the witness was dated 1998, because of the death of some unnamed beneficiaries and the State's difficulty to protect these people, the President of the Court requested the representatives of the beneficiaries to individualize or name the beneficiaries so the State could find them and offer them provisional measures. See IACtHR, *Bámaca Velásquez Case (Guatemala)*, Order of March 11, 2005, Explanatory Statements 17 and 20, Enactings Part 1 and 2.

288 R. Nieto Navia, "Las medidas provisionales en la Corte Interamericana de Derechos Humanos", in *La Corte y el Sistema Interamericano de Derechos Humanos*, San José, Corte Interamericana de Derechos Humanos, R. Nieto Navia (ed.), 1994, 389. See also M.E. Ventura Robles, "La Corte Interamericana de Derechos Humanos: Camino hacia un Tribunal Permanente", in *El Futuro de la Corte Interamericana de Derechos Humanos*, A. Cançado Trindade and M.E. Ventura Robles (eds.), San José, Corte Interamericana de Derechos Humanos, UNHCR, 2003, 145.

2.2.1. SITUATION OF EXTREME GRAVITY

124. The idea of gravity, as employed in Article 63(2) of the Convention, is related in three aspects: with the hierarchy of the right, the violation of which is sought to be avoided; with the relevance of the actions or the omissions that may be attributed to the State presumably responsible and with the presence of a real and not merely hypothetical danger.

2.2.1.1. Hierarchy of the Right

125. The first aspect – the hierarchy of the human right, the violation of which is sought to be avoided – means that the described facts or situations must, in principle, threaten or place in danger rights that are enshrined in the American Convention.[289]

126. There are, however, two positions as to which rights may be protected by provisional measures. One school considers that not every right embodied in the Convention may be protected through provisional measures and the other holds that nothing in the norms prohibits the protection of all the rights.

The restrictive position argues that irreparable damage is that which concerns the rights to life, physical integrity, personal freedom and to judicial guarantees, given that the violation of those rights have a direct impact on the enjoyment of the others.[290] On the other hand, the more liberal position holds that since all human rights are interrelated and indivisible there is nothing to prevent the

289 A. Aguiar, "Apuntes sobre las Medidas Cautelares en la Convención Americana sobre Derechos Humanos", in *La Corte y el Sistema Interamericano de Derechos Humanos*, San José, Inter-American Court of Human Rights, 1994, 101.

290 Faúndez Ledesma believes that a threat to life or to physical integrity is, undoubtedly, a matter of extreme gravity. A threat to freedoms of association or of movement in State territory, in the context of Article 63(2) of the Convention, does not merit this same consideration. See H. Faundez Ledesma, *El Sistema Interamericano de Protección de los Derechos Humanos*, San José, IIDH, 3rd ed., 2004, 538, 545. Pasqualucci considers that the adoption of provisional measures should be limited to those cases where there is sufficient evidence that a person is under risk of being tortured or assassinated. See J.M. Pasqualucci, *The Practice and Procedure of the Inter-American Court of Human Rights*, Cambridge, Cambridge University Press, 2003, 293; J.M. Pasqualucci, "Provisional Measures in the Inter-American Human Rights System: An Innovative Development in International Law", *Vand. J. Transnat'l L.* 1993–94, 850. Costa Rica sustained that provisional measures could only protect the right to life and to physical integrity. This was one of the reasons why it requested the Court to adopt measures to protect a journalist who had been found guilty for four crimes. According to the State, this measure could legitimate the use of an extraordinary remedy to annul the execution of a judgment in which neither the life nor the physical integrity of a person is at stake. See IACtHR, *The La Nación Newspaper Case (Costa Rica)*, Order of May 23, 2001, Explanatory Statement 4(c).

adoption of measures to protect any right that is found in the Convention,[291] provided that the situation meets the requirements of Article 63(2): extreme gravity and urgency and the need to avoid irreparable damage to persons.[292]

127. The jurisprudence of the Inter-American Court demonstrates that there is a clear tendency to protect the rights to life and personal integrity. These two rights have been protected in 68 of the 71 (95.8%) cases. The Court generally orders the adoption of provisional measures when it is shown that the life or physical integrity of persons is in danger.[293] For example, in the Miguel Agustín Pro Juárez Human Rights Center *et al.* Case (Mexico), the Court held that, since it had been confirmed that there had been threats to the life and personal integrity of members and lawyers of a human rights organisation, the situation allowed it to establish a situation of extreme gravity that made it necessary to adopt the protective measures.[294]

Although on most occasions, the Court has protected the rights to life and personal integrity, this does not mean that the Court favours only these rights, but rather it appears to be because the protection of those rights and not others has been requested. On the few occasions in which the adoption of provisional measures has been requested to protect rights other than the aforementioned two, the Court in ascertaining that the situation is extremely grave and urgent

---

291 The following rights are contemplated by the Convention: the Right to Juridical Personality (Article 3), the Right to Life (Article 4), the Right to Humane Treatment (Article 5), Freedom from Slavery (Article 6), the Right to Personal Liberty (Article 7), the Right to a Fair Trial (Article 8), Freedom from Ex Post Facto Laws (Article 9), the Right to Compensation (Article 10), the Right to Privacy (Article 11), Freedom of Conscience and Religion (Article 12), Freedom of Thought and Expression (Article 13), the Right of Reply (Article 14), the Right of Assembly (Article 15), Freedom of Association (Article 16), Rights of the Family (Article 17), the Right to a Name (Article 18), Rights of the Child (Article 19), the Right to Nationality (Article 20), the Right to Property (Article 21), Freedom of Movement and Residence (Article 22), the Right to Participate in Government (Article 23), the Right to Equal Protection (Article 24) and the Right to Judicial Protection (Article 25).

292 Cançado Trindade does not believe that there is any judicial or epistemological impediment that would obstruct the protection of any right, provided that the conditions set forth in Article 63(2) of the American Convention are fulfilled. See A. Cançado Trindade, "The Evolution of Provisional Measures of Protection under the Case Law of the Inter-American Court of Human Rights (1987–2002)", *Hum. Rts. L. J.* 2003, 165; A. Cançado Trindade, *Medidas Provisionales. Prólogo del Presidente de la Corte Interamericana de Derechos Humanos al Tomo III de la Serie E.*, 2001, para. 21; A. Borea Odria, "Propuesta de Modificación a la Legislación del Sistema Interamericano de Protección de los Derechos Humanos," in *Liber Amicorum Héctor Fix-Zamudio*, San José, Inter-American Court of Human Rights, 1998, 541–542. See also IACtHR, *Haitians and Dominicans of Haitian Origin in the Dominican Republic Case (Dominican Republic)*, Order of August 18, 2000, Concurring Opinion Judge Cançado Trindade. Para. 14.

293 H. Faundez Ledesma, *El Sistema Interamericano de Protección de los Derechos Humanos*, San José, IIDH, 3rd ed., 2004, 538.

294 IACtHR, The Miguel Agustín Pro Juárez Human Rights Center et al. Case (Mexico), Order of November 30, 2001, Preambular Paragraph 7.

has adopted the measures. The Court has, therefore, protected freedom of expression, personal freedom, freedom of movement, the use and enjoyment of property and the right to judicial guarantees.[295]

Two cases merit special attention because the Court in the preambular paragraphs of the orders mentions that certain rights should be protected but in the enacting part does not refer to them. One of them is the Haitians and Haitians of Dominican Origin in the Dominican Republic Case (Dominican Republic), in which the preambular paragraph mentions the importance of offering special protection to children and freedom of movement and residence, but the enacting part only mentions the rights to life and to personal integrity. Something similar occurred in the Velásquez Rodríguez Case (Honduras), in which the Court mentioned in the preambular paragraphs that the State must protect the assets of the beneficiaries, but in the enacting part only referred to the measures that were adopted to protect the fundamental rights of those who had testified before the Court as well as those who were summoned to do so.

It should also be noted that to date the Inter-American Court has not ordered the protection of other rights such as the recognition to juridical personality, freedom of conscience and religion, the right to a name and the right to a nationality, not because the Court has rejected such protection but because these types of cases have not been submitted to it.[296]

Finally, it is important to mention the Castañeda Case (Mexico), in which the Court rejected the adoption of provisional measures to protect political rights because it would suppose deciding the merits of the matter.[297]

2.2.1.2. Importance of Acts or Omissions

128. The gravity of the situation is – also – related to the importance of the acts or omissions that endanger the rights of persons[298] and is derived not only from

---

295 Of the 71 cases in which the Court adopted measures, 68 sought to avoid irreparable damages to the rights to life and/or personal integrity; five protected the rights to life, to personal integrity and to freedom of expression; three cases the right to life, to personal integrity and to personal freedom; two the right to life, to integrity and to freedom of movement; three to avoid irreparable damages and to protect the right to the use and enjoyment of land and its resources; in another case, integrity and judicial guarantees were protected and in another case fundamental rights without specifying which ones. On nine occasions, the Court decided not to adopt provisional measures.

296 No reference is made to the rights of children or to the right to a family because, as it will be seen further on, in the case of the Haitians and Dominicans of Haitian Origin in the Dominican Republic, the Court mentioned these rights in the Preambular Paragraphs but not in the Enacting Part of the Order.

297 IACtHR, *Jorge Castañeda Gutman (Mexico)*, Order of November 25, 2005, Preambular Paragraph 6.

298 A. Aguiar, "Apuntes sobre las Medidas Cuatelares en la Convención Americana sobre Derechos Humanos", in *La Corte y el Sistema Interamericano de Derechos Humanos*, San José, Inter-American Court of Human Rights, 1995, 101.

the nature of the right that is in danger but also from the degree of risk to the person.[299] Acts that demonstrate the existence of a grave danger to the rights of persons are, for example, those when the persons are under the control of the State; when they are in a State in which there is an internal armed conflict; where it is proved that there exists a constant persecution of a certain sector of the population, and situations in which it is alleged that the leaders of a community or an organisation are being assassinated.

The Court considers especially grave the damage that may be suffered by persons over whom the State is a guarantor, such as those who are in prisons and other establishments such as detention centres for minors, asylum seekers or illegal immigrants, establishments for the mentally ill in which there is some restriction of freedom and the handing over of the person to the public authorities.[300] Under those circumstances, the threat of damage to the rights of persons who are under the control of the State is especially grave, given that the preservation of their rights depends absolutely on the will of the State. It is a case of "aggravated responsibility," as Judge García Ramírez has named it, which results from the special gravity of the infringements, the circumstances surrounding the facts, the manner in which the violations are committed and who the victims are.

129. The Boyce and Joseph (Barbados), the Raxcacó Reyes *et al.* (Guatemala), the Cesti Hurtado (Peru), the Urso Branco Prison (Brazil), the Mendoza Prisons (Argentina), the Fermín Ramírez (Guatemala), the Gallardo Rodríguez (Mexico), the James, Briggs, Noel, Garcia and Bethel (Trinidad and Tobago), the Loayza Tamayo (Peru), the Suárez Rosero (Ecuador), the Penitentiary Center of the Central Occidental Region (Uribana Prison) (Venezuela), the Yare I and Yare II Capital Region Center (Venezuela), the Capital El Rodeo I & El Rodeo II Judicial Confinement Center (Venezuela), the Monagas Judicial Confinement Center ("La Pica") (Venezuela), the Persons imprisoned in the "Dr. Sebatião Martins Silveira" Penitenciary in Araraquara, São Paulo (Brazil) and the Children Deprived of Liberty in the "Complexo do Tatuapé of FEDEM (Brazil) Cases belong in this category. They all involved persons who were deprived of their freedom. In each case the Court adopted measures and in each of them the preservation of the rights of persons in jail depended on the will and the conduct of the State authorities, thus being the absolute responsibility of the State.

---

299 S. García Ramírez, "Medidas Precautorias", in *Los Derechos Humanos y la Jurisdicción Interamericana*, X (ed.), México, Universidad Autónoma de México, 2002, 129–132.

300 IACtHR, *The Urso Branco Prisons Case (Brazil)*, Order of July 7, 2004, Concurring Opinion of Judge García Ramírez.

An example would be the Urso Branco Prison Case (Brazil), in which it was claimed that, during a period of five months, 37 inmates had been brutally murdered, some of the bodies had been torn apart and body parts had been thrown at prison authorities. During four days 308 inmates had been kept by the prison authorities in the prison yard as punishment, where they received food and water only on a sporadic basis, were beaten and had their hair cut off. The Court took into account the frequency with which homicides occurred in that jail and how they occurred. The deaths were the result of great violence and a notorious loss of control of the prison by the authorities. The Court believed it appropriate to adopt provisional measures above all to preserve the life and physical integrity of the inmates of that jail.[301]

A similar situation occurred in the Loayza Tamayo Case (Peru) where the Court held that the situation in the prison in which Ms. Loayza Tamayo was serving a sentence of 20 years, placed her physical, psychological and moral health in grave danger. The Commission stated that Ms. Loayza Tamayo spent twenty-three and a half hours in an extremely small, damp and cold cell. She was not allowed to have a radio or magazines nor could she receive visitors.[302] In the Cesti Hurtado Case (Peru), it was concluded that the health of a detainee was in grave danger since he was not allowed to receive medicine for a heart problem that he had had for various years.[303] In these cases the Court adopted measures to avoid irreparable damage to the physical, psychological and moral integrity of the detainees.

130. The gravity of the matter is also related to the general situation in the country that is the subject of the petition. The Court has at times referred to the general context of the country regarding a case submitted to its consideration.

---

301 *Ibid.* See also IACtHR, *Mendoza Prisons Case (Argentina)*, Order of November 22, 2004, Preambular Paragraphs 10–12. In this Order the Court establishes that one of the obligations, indispensable to the State as guarantor, is to ensure that the individuals deprived of their freedom enjoy the minimal conditions compatible with their dignity while in the detention centres. See also IACtHR, *Case of the "Juvenile Reeducation Institute" (Paraguay)*, Judgment of September 2, 2004, para. 159. This judgment cites the European Court when it indicated, regarding Article 3 of the European Convention, that the States must "ensure that a person is detained in conditions which are compatible with respect for his human dignity, that the manner and method of the execution of the measure do not subject him to distress or hardship of an intensity exceeding the unavoidable level of suffering inherent in detention and that, given the practical demands of imprisonment, his health and well-being are adequately secured by, among other things, providing him with the requisite medical assistance" (See, *mutatis mutandis*, ECtHR, Aerts v. Belgium, Judgment of 30 July 1998, *Reports* 1998-V, p. 1966, paras. 64 *et seq.*).

302 IACtHR, *Loayza Tamayo Case (Peru)*, Order of July 2, 1996, Explanatory Statements 4 and 7 and Order of September 13, 1996, Explanatory Statement 3.

303 IACtHR, *Cesti Hurtado Case (Peru)*, Order of the President of July 29, 1997, Preambular Paragraph 7.

In the Indigenous Kankuamo People, the Peace Community of San José de Apartadó and the Communities of the Jiguamiandó and of the Curbaradó Cases, the Court held that the special nature of the cases and the general conditions of the armed conflict in Colombia made protection necessary for all the members of those communities.[304] In each of these cases, the members of the communities were victims of threats and harassment by illegal armed groups and the Colombian Army, actions that were carried out within the framework of the armed conflict that continues in that country.

In a similar situation involving human rights defenders in Venezuela, the Commission stated that its petitions for measures were within the context of violence directed at any person who worked in the area of human rights and who, therefore, needed international protection. In view of these circumstances, the Court held that States must grant effective and adequate guarantees to human rights defenders so that they might freely carry out their activities and it was therefore appropriate that it pay special attention to actions that were directed to restricting or impeding their work.[305]

Some petitions claimed that persons who had leadership roles in a community or an organisation had been murdered. The Court deemed these cases especially grave since the killing of leaders menaces all the members and fragments their community. The Court deemed as grave in the Peace Community Case (Colombia) the fact that while the measures were in effect, eight persons had been killed, among them a leader of the Community and his family. The Court stated that the death of those persons, especially the death of the Community leader, could be interpreted as part of a process to menace and paralyse the members of the Peace Community with the aim of breaking it up and placed at risk the survival of the Community and especially that of its members. These circumstances showed a situation of extreme gravity that required effective and urgent measures of protection.[306]

---

304 IACtHR, *Indigenous Kankuamo Community Case (Colombia)*, Order of July 5, 2004, Preambular Paragraph 11; IACtHR, *Peace Community of San José de Apartadó Case (Colombia)*, Order of March 15, 2005, Preambular Paragraph 10 and IACtHR, *Communities of the Jiguamiandó and of the Curbaradó Case (Colombia)*, Order of February 7, 2006, Preambular Paragraph 6.

305 IACtHR, *Case of Carlos Nieto et al. (Venezuela)*, Order of July 9, 2004, Explanatory Statements 2(a) and 3, Preambular Paragraph 8.

306 IACtHR, *Peace Community of San José de Apartadó Case (Colombia)*, Order of March 15, 2005, Preambular Paragraph 24. See also the Giraldo Cardona Case (Colombia), where a president of a human rights organisation, back from exile, was assassinated in front of his home while playing with his daughters. Likewise, in the Clemente Teherán Case (Colombia), among the violent actions were the assassination of a tribal chief from the reservation and that of three indigenous leaders, as well as death threats made against an indigenous person who was candidate for council. See also the Alvarez *et al.* Case (Colombia) and the Helen Mack Chang *et al.* Case (Guatemala).

2.2.1.3. *Real Danger*

131. Finally, extreme gravity must be the result of a real and not merely hypothetical danger.[307] The Court has stated that there is a real danger when one or more persons are in a situation similar to that of another person whose rights have already been violated.

132. An example would be when a witness had received death threats and another witness in the same proceedings was threatened and then killed. The witness who is still alive is in a situation of real danger because in the same case another person who had been in the same position – witness – and who was in the same situation – had received threats – was killed.[308] These cases involve witnesses who have given testimony before the Court or have been summoned to do so or their family members,[309] persons who work for human rights organisations,[310] or in the mass media, detainees,[311] members of indigenous communities,[312] of civil organisations[313] and of Afro-descendant organisations.[314]

---

307 IACtHR, *Peace Community of San José de Apartadó Case (Colombia)*, Order of November 24, 2000, Concurring Opinion of Judges Alirio Abreu and Sergio Ramírez, para. 2.

308 In the first cases where provisional measures were issued, the Court initially verified that a witness summoned to testify had been threatened and later assassinated and that another who had already testified had also been assassinated. The Court held that under those circumstances, other witnesses who had already testified before the Court or who had been summoned to do so were in danger and merited the adoption of the measures. See Velásquez Rodríguez Case (Honduras).

309 Colotenango Case (Guatemala), Eloisa Barrios *et al.* Case (Venezuela), Giraldo Cardona Case (Colombia), Adrián Meléndez Quijano *et al.* Case (El Salvador), Mapiripán Massacre Case (Colombia), Guerrero-Gallucci and Martínez-Barrios Case (Venezuela), Kawas Fernández Case (Honduras), Millacura Llaipén *et al.* Case (Argentina), Ramírez Hinostroza *et al.* Case (Peru), Gloria Giralt de García-Prieto *et al.* Case (El Salvador), Mery Naranjo *et al.* Case (Colombia), Forensic Anthropology Foundation Case (Guatemala) and Leonel Rivero *et al.* Case (Mexico).

310 Alvarez *et al.* Case (Colombia), Bustíos-Rojas Case (Peru), Chunimá Case (Guatemala), Miguel Agustín Pro Juárez Human Rights Center *et al.* Case (Mexico), Guerrero-Gallucci and Martínez-Barrios Case (Venezuela), Mery Naranjo *et al.* Case (Colombia), Forensic Anthropology Foundation Case (Guatemala) and Pilar Noriega *et al.* Case (Mexico).

311 The Urso Branco Prison Case (Brazil), Mendoza Prisons Case (Argentina), Penitentiary Center of the Central Occidental Region (Uribana Prison) Case (Venezuela), Yare I and Yare II Capital Region Center Case (Venezuela), Capital El Rodeo I & El Rodeo II Judicial Confinement Center Case (Venezuela), Monagas Judicial Confinement Center ("La Pica") Case (Venezuela), Persons imprisoned in the "Dr. Sebastião Martins Silveira" Penitentiary in Araraquara, São Paulo Case (Brazil), Children Deprived of Liberty in the "Complexo do Tatuapé" of FEBEM Case (Brazil), Tyrone Dacosta Cadogan Case (Barbados).

312 Clemente Teherán Case (Colombia) and the Indigenous Kankuamo Community Case (Colombia).

313 Peace Community of San José de Apartadó Case (Colombia).

314 Communities of the Jiguamiandó and of the Curbaradó Case (Colombia).

This circumstance has justified the adoption of protective measures on 21 occasions.[315]

133. Another example would be the Communities of the Jiguamiandó and of the Curbaradó Case (Colombia) in which measures were adopted to protect the members of those Communities because some had been killed for belonging to the Communities. Two members had been stoned, another's throat had been cut, a disabled peasant had been killed, as had a pregnant woman.[316] In the case of persons deprived of their freedom in Argentina, the Court considered it timely to adopt measures to protect all the inmates of a penitentiary because 18 inmates had been killed during the period 2004–2005. Similarly, measures were adopted to protect the inmates of the Urso Branco Prison in Brazil because 37 inmates had been killed during a period of five months.[317]

134. The Court has also deemed it a real danger when persons have been victims of attempts against their lives. In 13 of the 71 cases in which it adopted measures, the Court found that the persons had suffered this type of attack. Among the situations were attacks on a presidential candidate,[318] on

---

315 In the Alvarez *et al.* Case (Colombia) it was reported that two members of a human rights organization had been killed. In the Bustíos-Rojas Case (Peru) it was claimed that a journalist who worked for a non-governmental organization had died as a result of an attack allegedly carried out by the military that had threatened him. In the Colotenango Case (Guatemala), the parents of two witnesses in the case under consideration by the Court had been murdered. In the Chunimá Case (Guatemala), five members of a human rights organization had been assassinated supposedly by civil patrols. In the Clemente Teherán Case (Colombia), as a result of a territorial confrontation members of an indigenous community had been assassinated, among them a tribal chief of the reservation and three indigenous leaders. In the Peace Community of San José de Apartadó Case (Colombia), within a 9-month period 47 members of the Community had been killed. In the Miguel Agustín Pro Juárez Human Rights Center *et al.* Case (Mexico), one of the members of the organization had been murdered and a message containing an express threat to all of the members of the organization was found on her body. In the Indigenous Kankuamo Community Case (Colombia), various indigenous persons had been assassinated. In the Eloisa Barrios *et al.* Case (Venezuela), it was reported that two people had been killed. In the Giraldo Cardona Case (Colombia), it was mentioned that between 1992 and 1995 six people had been assassinated, among them was the president of a non-governmental organization.

316 Communities of the Jiguamiandó and of the Curbaradó Case (Colombia).

317 In the Fermín Ramírez Case (Guatemala) the protection of a person sentenced to the death penalty was requested; the State had already executed other convicts in spite of having been beneficiaries of the precautionary measures adopted by the Commission. See IACtHR, *Fermín Ramírez Case (Guatemala)*, Order of the President of the IACtHR, Order of March 12, 2005, Explanatory Statements 1 and 6(b).

318 As a result of an attempt on the life of a presidential candidate, a bodyguard had been killed and other people had been gravely injured. The Court stated that these acts had "invested the events with a high degree of notoriety and credibility". See IACtHR, *Alemán Lacayo Case (Nicaragua)*, Order of February 2, 1996, Preambular Paragraph 3.

journalists,[319] on a Catholic priest,[320] on members of indigenous communities,[321] on witnesses,[322] attacks on offices of human rights organisations[323] and the mass media,[324] as well as on homes of the alleged victims.[325]

Measures were adopted in the Alemán Lacayo Case (Nicaragua) to protect a presidential candidate, who had been the victim of an attempt on his life during the electoral campaign. One of his bodyguards had been killed in the attack and other persons were gravely wounded. In this type of cases, the Court considered that the facts were notorious, credible and grave and showed the existence of a true danger that made necessary the adoption of provisional measures.[326]

135. The above-mentioned cases could be classified as "easy cases" because concluding that there was a true danger or a dangerous situation in principle was not difficult. In cases where the petitioners were not able to show the existence of a true and not merely hypothetical danger, the Court has refused to adopt the measures.

The petitioners in the Acevedo Jaramillo *et al.* Case (Peru) explained to the Court that they were requesting the measures since they had been informed that they were to be tried and that there was an arrest warrant against them. According to the petitioners, this situation was not only directed at intimidating them for having initiated judicial proceedings but also to prevent them from leaving the country to attend, if necessary, hearings that the Inter-American Court might schedule in the future.

The Court held that provisional measures had to be based on the existence of a true situation of extreme gravity and urgency. With respect to the judicial proceedings, the Court stated that it was not possible to speak of the existence of the true danger since the petitioners had only heard that they would be tried. Regarding the attendance of the petitioners at the hearings, the Court stated that when the hearings were convoked, the President or the Court would decide at that time how to proceed in the event that the representatives and witnesses were prevented from leaving the country. The Court did not adopt the measures

---

319 Bustíos-Rojas Case (Peru), "El Nacional" and "Así es la Noticia" Newspapers Case (Venezuela) and Marta Colomina and Liliana Velásquez Case (Venezuela).

320 Vogt Case (Guatemala).

321 Indigenous Kankuamo Community Case (Colombia).

322 Gloria Giralt de García Prieto *et al.* Case (El Salvador) and Ramírez Hinostroza Case (Peru).

323 Alvarez *et al.* Case (Colombia) and the Guerrero Gallucci and Martínez Barrios (Venezuela).

324 "Globovisión" Television Station Case (Venezuela) and Luisiana Rios *et al.* Case (Venezuela).

325 Gutiérrez Soler Case (Colombia).

326 On the other hand, the Court also considers that if the persons have been victims of a series of harassments, detentions, threats or attempts, or if they are in a similar situation as a person whose rights have already been violated, there is a situation of extreme gravity meriting the adoption of the measures. See IACtHR, *Gutiérrez Soler Case (Colombia)*, Order of March 11, 2005, Preambular Paragraph 8.

because the petitioners based their petition of a series of suppositions; that is, on events that, although they may occur in the future, in reality were not yet occurring.[327]

2.2.2. SITUATION OF URGENCY

136. Given the special nature of the cases that are submitted to the Court, an urgent situation implies the impossibility of waiting for a judgment on the merits in order to adopt protective measures because of the risk that during the lapse of this period the damage sought to be avoided occurs. This means that every measure to protect the rights of those who are in danger must be adopted as soon as possible. The urgency of adopting the measures is therefore related to the factor of time.[328]

137. When there is a request for the urgent adoption of provisional measures, there is an affirmation of a great fear that a right is going to be violated and that this situation requires the immediate adoption of measures. This is clear in the cases of persons on death row. For example, in the Boyce and Joseph Case (Barbados) protection was requested on September 17 for four persons who had been sentenced to death. The orders had already been read out and the executions were scheduled for September 21, four days after the request. The Court, in view

---

327 IACtHR, *Acevedo Jaramillo et al. Case (Peru)*, Order of the President of November 23, 2004, Explanatory Statement 7, Preambular Paragraphs 6, 13 and 17, Enacting Part 1. In the Chipoco Case (Peru), the Commission reported that it had received information from a human rights defender, who had collaborated and participated with the Commission in a number of cases, that he would be criminally accused of allegedly having carried out activities supporting subversion in the United States. The Commission explained that once the defender was identified, the arrest could be ordered and if convicted, he could lose his Peruvian nationality and could be sentenced to more than 20 years in prison. The government argued that the complainant had not been criminally accused and that it had only requested his individualisation before the Ministry of Foreign Affairs. The Court stated that since the case was under consideration by the Commission the measures were exceptional. In these cases, it is essential that the Commission, after ascertaining, even preliminarily, the veracity of the acts denounced, present to the Court clear evidence that there exists a situation of extreme gravity and urgency. After considering the information presented to it, the President and later the Court decided not to adopt the requested measures. See *Chipoco Case (Peru)*.

328 In this regard, it is important to recall that one of the reasons why the Court changed its jurisprudence to include the possibility of adopting provisional measures to protect persons who had not been previously individualised, but who are perfectly identifiable by other objective data, is precisely because if one waits to identify each person who is in a situation of grave danger there is a risk that the damage that is attempted to be avoided may take place.

of the urgency of the matter, adopted the measures the same day that they were requested.[329]

138. Another method of analysing the urgency with which provisional measures in the inter-American system should be adopted is by considering how long the Court takes in adopting them. The period between the presentation of the petition and when the Court or, in its absence, the President of the Court issues the first order demonstrates with what promptness the Court has acted in practice when faced with situations of urgency.[330]

Table 19. Time needed by the Court to adopt interim measures

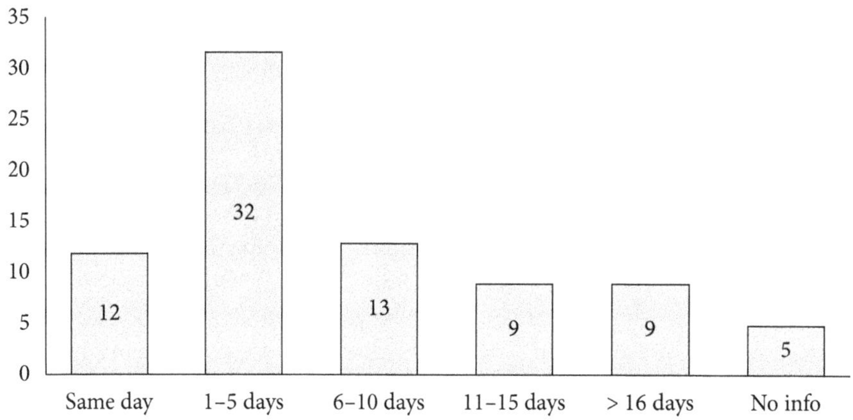

139. As can be seen in Table 19, the Court has adopted provisional measures in twelve cases on the day that the petition was presented. In 32 cases the Court took between one to five days; in 13 cases the Court delayed between six and ten days; in nine cases between 11 and 15 days and in nine cases the Court took more than 16 days to adopt the provisional measures. This means that the protective measures were adopted in more than half of the cases between the day that the

329 The Court's time frame depends on the circumstances of the case. Thus, in other cases regarding the death penalty, the Court took a longer time when compared to that of the case against Barbados. In the James, Briggs, Noel, Garcia and Bethel Case (Trinidad and Tobago), concerning five persons sentenced to death with programmed and imminent executions, the President of the Court took five days to adopt the measures. The Court held that the facts described a situation of extreme gravity and urgency that required the immediate adoption of measures necessary to preserve the life and physical integrity of the alleged victims. In the Raxcacó Reyes *et al.* Case (Guatemala), also concerning a matter of convicts sentenced to death, the Court took 14 days. The time taken by the Court in this case was perhaps longer due to the fact the date of the sentence of the execution had not been not set.

330 The procedure that the petitions for provisional measures follow may be seen in depth in the section on "Procedure".

request was received and five days later. This promptness reflects the urgent nature of the matters that are submitted to the consideration of the Court.

Here the President of the Court plays a very important role since in a significant number of cases he has the responsibility to adopt the initial order.[331] If it were not for the competence that he has been given in these matters, the requests would have to wait until the next session of the Court, which would run the risk that the rights of the person would be violated during that period.

The efficacy in adopting protective measures in the inter-American system is quite high, especially if compared with the time that the Court takes to decide the merits of a case submitted to its consideration or to how long a judge in any country takes in deciding an appeal or in trying a case.

140. The two cases in which the Court has delayed the longest in deciding on protective measures have been the Mayagna (Sumo) Awas Tingni Community Case (Nicaragua) and the Haitians and Dominicans of Haitian Origin in the Dominican Republic Case (Dominican Republic). In one the order was not adopted for 49 days and in the other for 47 days. In the first case, the Court adopted provisional measures with respect to a matter that had already been resolved by a judgment on the merits. This has been the only time that measures were adopted to protect the use and enjoyment of lands and natural resources belonging to an indigenous community. In the latter case, although measures had been requested to protect all the Haitians and Dominicans of Haitian origin who were subject to the jurisdiction of the Dominican Republic because they risked being expelled or deported collectively, the measures only covered those who were individually named.

In deciphering the reasons that could have led the Court to delay so long in adopting the decision, if compared with that in deciding other matters, the following may be pointed out. In the first case, the delay could be related to the decision to protect a right that traditionally was not protected – the right to property. In the second case, the request was directed to protecting a group of persons who were not specifically identified and so the delay could be related to the fact that for the first time there was a request for the protection of a group of persons not specifically named, that is, Haitians and Dominicans of Haitian origin who were in the Dominican Republic.[332]

These two aspects enable those cases to be described as "difficult cases" because they present innovations in the practice of the Court. Under these conditions, to accept the petition implied not only protecting the rights of

---

331 The President of the Court was the first to respond to the adoption of provisional measures in 52 of the cases. See section 4. "Processing of the Request".

332 This was the first time that protection was requested for a non-individualised group of people.

persons but also creating a legal precedent that would broaden the protection of the provisional measures. The Court, thus, needed more time.[333]

2.2.3. THE NEED TO AVOID IRREPARABLE DAMAGE TO RIGHTS

141. In order to adopt provisional measures it is indispensable that the damage to the rights has not yet occurred and that adoption of the measures seeks to avoid an irreparable damage. The fundamental purpose of provisional measures in the international system for human rights protection is to prevent or reduce violations of the rights of persons; it specifically seeks to avoid that they suffer irreparable damage.[334] Irreparable damage means the impossibility of rescuing, preserving or compensating the right threatened by means of some measure after the damage. It should be understood that if the damage has already occurred, provisional measures do not make any sense and it would be necessary to await reparations from the State once its international responsibility has been declared.[335]

142. Under some circumstances, it is easy to comprehend the irreparable damage that is sought to be avoided, as for example when the damage refers to the loss of life or a violation of the right to physical integrity.[336] Thus, with respect to the cases of persons who are on death row, the Court has ordered the State in question to adopt all measures necessary to protect the life of the condemned men while the case is being considered in the inter-American system. The objective of the provisional measures in these cases is to prevent the persons from being executed until it is ascertained whether their trials were held in

---

333 It is interesting to observe, for example, that in these cases the Court requested the observations of both the State and the Commission before adopting a decision. Thus, in the first instance two public hearings were held and the Commission and the State presented their observations to the Court. In the second case, even though no public hearing was held, the Court requested observations on the petition from the State and the Commission. This participation by the States parties and Commission in the procedure also influenced the time required by the Court to adopt the order. Although there is no specific procedure to process the petition, that followed in most cases is to adopt the measures after the petition was presented. The observations of the parties were requested once the provisional measures were adopted.

334 A. Cançado Trindade, "The Evolution of Provisional Measures of Protection under the Case Law of the Inter-American Court of Human Rights (1987–2002)," *Hum. Rts. L. J.* 2003, 163.

335 A. Aguiar, "Apuntes sobre las Medidas Cautelares en la Convención Americana sobre Derechos Humanos", in *La Corte y el Sistema Interamericano de Derechos Humanos*, San José, Inter-American Court of Human Rights, 1994, 102.

336 S. Garcia Ramirez, "Medidas Precautorias", in *Los Derechos Humanos y la Jurisdicción Interamericana*, X (ed.), México, Universidad Autónoma de México, 2002, 129–132.

accordance with the provisions of the Convention. In other words, by means of provisional measures the State is requested to suspend the execution of the men on death row so that, in the case of an eventual determination of the Inter-American Court that the State has violated Article 4 of the Convention, irreparable damage has not already occurred.[337]

143. It is more complicated in other situations to determine whether the damage is irreparable, as for example in matters related to the right to property or the right to honour. In these types of cases, the specific characteristics of the situation must be taken into account to determine whether the damage that provisional measures seek to avoid is irreparable or not.

For example, in the Mayagna (Sumo) Awas Tingni Community Case (Nicaragua) the Court resolved to protect the right to property of the indigenous community because, as it had already stated in its judgment on the merits of the case, it recognised the importance of taking into account aspects of their customs in applying the Convention. The Court deemed it relevant to understand that indigenous communities believe that land is the fundamental basis of their culture, their spiritual life, their integrity and their economic survival. The relationship of indigenous communities to their land is not merely a question of possession and production, but a material and spiritual element that must be enjoyed fully to preserve their cultural heritage and to hand it down to future generations. This means that if the right to the communities' property is infringed, it would cause much more than economic damage because, according to their view of the cosmos, the land is a fundamental part of their life and damage to it under those conditions would affect the very survival of the collectivity.[338]

In the *La Nación* Case (Costa Rica) protection was requested for a journalist who had been found guilty of four crimes and whose name had been ordered entered into the Registry of Delinquents. The fact that the case concerned a journalist whose exercise of his profession depended to a large extent on his credibility and that the crime that he was accused of was related to his profession were aspects that the Court considered important in ascertaining whether the situation could cause irreparable damage. The Court called upon the State not to enforce the part of the sentence that ordered the entry into the Registry while the

337 IACtHR, *Raxcacó Reyes et al. Case (Guatemala)*, Order of September 30, 2002, Preambular Paragraphs 8 and 9.

338 IACtHR, *Mayagna (Sumo) Awas Tingni Community Case (Nicaragua)*, Order of September 6, 2002, Preambular Paragraphs 5, 6 and 7. The Court refers to the following jurisprudence: IACtHR, *Bámaca Velásquez Case (Honduras)*, Reparations, Judgment of February 22, 2002, para. 81; IACtHR, *Mayagna (Sumo) Awas Tingni Community Case (Nicaragua)*, Judgment of 31 August 2001, para. 149 and IACtHR, *Aloeboetoe et al. Case (Suriname)*, Reparations, Judgment of September 10, 1993, para. 62.

case was being resolved in the inter-American system.[339] The Court believed that such entry could cause irreparable damage to the exercise of the profession of the claimant and to his reputation.

144. Circumstances such as the above-mentioned are what have led the Court on some occasions to order the protection of rights where it is not easy to judge whether the damage is irreparable. Provisional measures, therefore, are not only "precautionary", in the sense that they preserve a legal situation, but "fundamental", because they protect human rights. The measures are thus a true jurisdictional guarantee of a "preventive" nature.[340]

The purpose of international protection is not only to decide on State responsibility for violations of the rights of persons but it also seeks to act to avoid the occurrence of such damage.[341] When measures are requested that are not directed at avoiding the infringement of rights but would prejudge the merits of a case[342] or would refer to matters that depend entirely on the will of the State, they are not appropriate.

In the Constitutional Court Case (Peru) the petitioner requested that the Court rule on certain domestic legal proceedings in which she and her husband were implicated. The Court stated that those proceedings were not directly linked to the case that was under consideration in the inter-American system and, even if they were related, it would not rule on the provisional measures as that would imply a prejudgment of the merits.

Similarly, the Commission in the Cesti Hurtado (Peru) and the Suárez Rosero (Ecuador) Cases requested that the respective States be ordered to release various persons who had been detained. The Commission stated that in one case there was a writ of habeas corpus that ordered the cancellation of the arrest warrant of the detained person and that in the other case the preventive detention served

---

339 IACtHR, *"La Nación" Newspaper Case (Costa Rica)*, Order of September 7, 2001, Preambular Paragraph 11.

340 IACtHR, *Peace Community of San José de Apartadó Case (Colombia)*, Order of November 24, 2002, Preambular Paragraph 11; IACtHR, *Alvarez et al. Case (Colombia)*, Order of May 30, 2001, Preambular Paragraph 6; IACtHR, *The Urso Branco Prison Case (Brazil)*, Order of June 18, 2002, Preambular Paragraph 9; IACtHR, *Mendoza Prisons Case (Argentina)*, Order of June 18, 2005, Preambular Paragraph 4; IACtHR, *Luisiana Ríos et al. Case (Venezuela)*, Order of September 12, 2005, Preambular Paragraph 4 and IACtHR, *Peace Community of San José de Apartadó Case (Colombia)*, Order of February 2, 2006, Preambular Paragraph 5.

341 S. Garcia Ramirez, "El Acceso de la Víctima a la Jurisdicción Internacional sobre Derechos Humanos," in *Derecho Internacional de los Derechos Humanos. Memoria del VII Congreso Iberoamericano de Derecho Constitucional. Serie Doctrina Jurídica* 98, R. Mendez Silva (ed.), México, Universidad Autónoma de México, 2002, 118.

342 M.E. Ventura Robles, "La Corte Interamericana de Derechos Humanos: Camino hacia un Tribunal Permanente", in *El Futuro de la Corte Interamericana de Derechos Humanos*, A. Cançado Trindade and M.E. Ventura Robles (eds.), San José, Corte Interamericana de Derechos Humanos, UNHCR, 2003, 150.

was longer than the sentence if he had been tried and found guilty. In neither of the two cases did the Court adopt the requested measures because, by ruling on the Commission's petition in those terms, it would be prejudging the merits of the cases.[343]

Neither did the Court accept a petition to require the Government of Peru to allow the Commission to make on-site visits to three jails that housed persons accused or found guilty of the crime of terrorism. The President of the Court stated that this measure could not be properly considered precautionary or provisional in the terms of Article 63(2) of the Convention because it referred to an authorisation that only the Government could grant and that the will of the State could not be supplied by means of orders issued by the President of the Court.[344]

343 IACtHR, *Constitutional Court Case (Peru)*, Order of April 7, 2000, Preambular Paragraph 12; IACtHR, *Cesti Hurtado Case (Peru)*, Order of September 11, 1997, Preambular Paragraph 5 and IACtHR, *Suárez Rosero Case (Ecuador)*, Order of June 28, 1996.

344 IACtHR, *Peruvian Jail Cases (Peru)*, Order of December 14, 1992, Preambular Paragraphs 5 and 6.

3. THE EVIDENCE

145. Because the circumstances that give rise to a request for provisional measures are of such gravity that they require a prompt reaction and at the same time because the measures are an exceptional mechanism that may only be used in certain situations,[345] the petitioners do not have to furnish all proof of the facts,[346] although they must offer the information necessary to ascertain that the situation is *prima facie*[347] one of extreme gravity and urgency.[348]

The petitioner may not, therefore, simply provide a description of the facts, he must also prove, even preliminarily, that the facts to which he refers are true and must join the pertinent information to the petition.[349] In any event, since the adoption of provisional measures does not involve a ruling on the merits, the evidence that is furnished must be directed solely to show the gravity and urgency of the situation and the probability that it will result in irreparable damage to persons.[350] The amount of evidence, of course, will depend on the type of matter.[351]

---

345 See the requisites described in Article 63(2) of the American Convention.

346 Furthermore, the Court held that when the Commission requests interim measures it does not have to completely demonstrate the veracity of the facts but must have reasonable basis to presume them to be true. IACtHR, *Chunimá Case (Guatemala)*, Order of August 1, 1991, Preambular Paragraph 6.

347 IACtHR, *Alvarez et al. Case (Colombia)*, Order of November 12, 2000, Preambular Paragraph 4; IACtHR, *Carlos Nieto et al. Case (Venezuela)*, Order of July 9, 2004, Preambular Paragraph 7; IACtHR, *"Globovisión" Television Station Case (Venezuela)*, Order of September 4, 2004, Preambular Paragraph 13 and IACtHR, *Eloisa Barrios et al. Case (Venezuela)*, Order of November 23, 2004, Preambular Paragraph 11. See also A. Cançado Trindade, *Medidas Provisionales. Prólogo del Presidente de la Corte Interamericana de Derechos Humanos al Tomo III de la Serie E.*, 2001, para. 18.

348 IACtHR, *Constitutional Court Case (Peru)*, Order of the President of April 7, 2000, Preambular Paragraph 7. See H. Faundez Ledesma, *El Sistema Interamericano de Protección de los Derechos Humanos*, San José, IIDH, 3rd ed., 2004, 564–566. See also A. Cançado Trindade, "The Evolution of Provisional Measures of Protection under the Case Law of the Inter-American Court of Human Rights (1987–2002)", *Hum. Rts. L. J.*, 2003, 165.

349 IACtHR, *Chunimá Case (Guatemala)*, Order of August 1, 1991, Preambular Paragraph 6. See also J.M. Pasqualucci, "Medidas Provisionales en la Corte Interamericana de Derechos Humanos: Una Comparación con la Corte Internacional de Justicia y la Corte Europea de Derechos Humanos", *Revista del Instituto Interamericano de Derechos Humanos* 1994, 103.

350 H. Faundez Ledesma, El Sistema Interamericano de Protección de los Derechos Humanos, San José, IIDH, 3rd ed., 2004, 562.

351 R. Nieto Navia, "Las medidas provisionales en la Corte Interamericana de Derechos Humanos", in *La Corte y el Sistema Interamericano de Derechos Humanos*, R. Nieto Navia (ed.), San José, Inter-American Court of Human Rights, 1994, p. 397.

The information and evidence furnished are of great importance because they form the raw material necessary for the Court to be able to rule on the petition. While the Court does not necessarily have to share the position of the petitioners, its decision depends to a large extent on the information that they submit to it.[352]

146. One of the reasons that has led the Court not to require complete proof on whether the situation under consideration is extremely grave and urgent is that it recognises that it is often very difficult to obtain it. For example, the Convention grants the Commission competence to conduct investigations, which indicates that it could issue studies with the purpose of collecting evidence. However, such a function cannot be exercised within the jurisdiction of a State unless the Commission has the State's consent.[353] This fact demonstrates that some evidence may be obtained only if it has the cooperation of the State.[354]

An interesting example is the Peruvian Prisons Case (Peru) in which the State refused to authorise the Commission to visit several prisons on which it had information that the rights of the inmates were being violated. This led the Commission to request that the Court use provisional measures to obligate the State to allow it to conduct such visits. The Court held that the possibility of the Commission carrying out investigations within a State depended absolutely on the will of the respective State and that such will could not be supplied by the inter-American organs through the adoption of provisional measures.[355] The refusal meant that it would be impossible for the Commission to obtain the evidence that it needed to prove that the situation met the requirements of Article 63(2) of the Convention and also showed the difficulty in obtaining evidence when the State does not cooperate.

147. Another circumstance that makes it difficult for the petitioners to present all the evidence on a situation is related to the very gravity of the cases that are

---

352 J.M. Pasqualucci, "Medidas Provisionales en la Corte Interamericana de Derechos Humanos: Una Comparación con la Corte Internacional de Justicia y la Corte Europea de Derechos Humanos", *Revista del Instituto Interamericano de Derechos Humanos* 1994, 103–104. See IACtHR, *19 Tradesmen Case (Colombia)*, Judgment on the Merits of July 5, 2004, para. 77.

353 Article 48(2) American Convention on Human Rights. See also IACtHR, *Velásquez Rodríguez Case (Honduras)*, Judgment on the Merits of July 29, 1988, para. 136.

354 *Ibid.*

355 IACtHR, *Peruvian Prisons Cases (Peru)*, Order of December 14, 1992, Preambular Paragraphs 5 and 6. See also J.M. Pasqualucci, "Medidas Provisionales en la Corte Interamericana de Derechos Humanos: Una Comparación con la Corte Internacional de Justicia y la Corte Europea de Derechos Humanos", *Revista del Instituto Interamericano de Derechos Humanos* 1994, 107.

submitted to the inter-American system. The alleged victims in some cases prefer not to provide information for fear that their situation will become worse.

For example, in the Clemente Teherán Case (Colombia) the Commission informed the Court that it did not have all of the information at its disposal since at that moment the leaders of the indigenous Zenú community were afraid to give testimony due to the strong presence of paramilitary groups in the zone. Under those circumstances, it was clear that individuals who furnished the information ran a great risk.[356]

148. The Court has generally not been very clear on what type of petitions should be accompanied by stricter evidence. In principle, it appears that the Court has imposed an additional burden of proof with respect to matters that are under consideration by the Commission, since it does not have information on the facts in those matters that are certainly in the possession of the Commission.[357] This circumstance has sometimes gone unnoticed. Nonetheless, the Court has held that in those cases, since the description of facts comes from the Commission, its affirmations deserve the credibility necessary to state that the situation *prima facie* is one of extreme gravity and urgency that justifies the adoption of provisional measures.[358]

In any event, in matters that have not yet been submitted to the Court, the petitioners must indicate that the complaints refer to acts that, if proved, would tend to establish violations of rights set forth in the Convention. The Court must be persuaded that if the State does the opposite of what was sought through the provisional measures, it would be creating a situation that is incompatible with the purposes of the Convention.[359]

149. In general terms, in the great majority of cases in which provisional measures have been requested, the Court has been provided with the information necessary to prove the gravity of the situation and the urgency of the measures. This is confirmed by the observance that of the 80 petitions presented from 1987 to 2009, only four were denied because the situation of risk was not proved.[360]

---

356 IACtHR, *Clemente Teherán Case (Colombia)*, Order of June 19, 1998, Explanatory Statement 6.

357 IACtHR, *Chunimá Case (Guatemala)*, Order of August 1, 1991, Explanatory Statement 7. See also IACtHR, *Chipoco Case (Peru)*, Order of the President of December 14, 1992, Preambular Paragraph 4.

358 IACtHR, *Carpio Nicolle Case (Guatemala)*, Order of July 26, 1995, Preambular Paragraph 4.

359 H. Faundez Ledesma, *El Sistema Interamericano de Protección de los Derechos Humanos*, San José, IIDH, 3rd ed., 2004, 564.

360 Acevedo Jaramillo (Peru), Chipoco (Peru), Miguel Castro-Castro Prison (Peru) and Juarez Cruzzat *et al.* (Peru).

Table 20. Number of provisional measures granted and refused

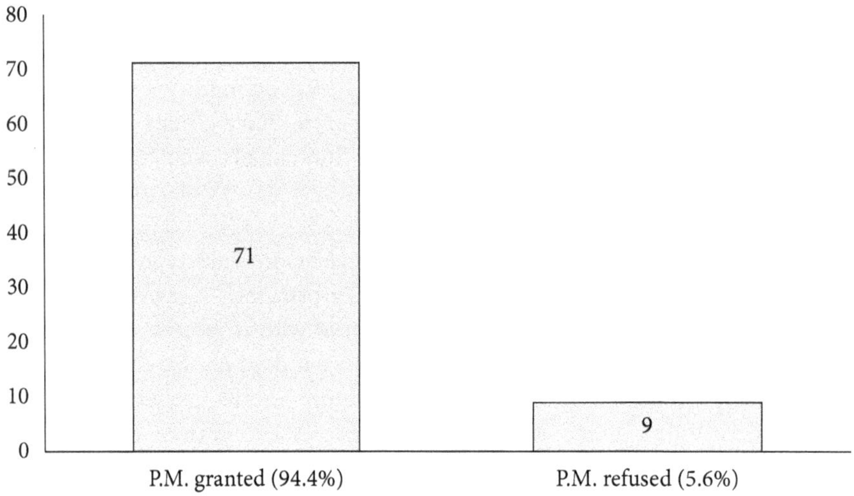

150. With regard to the petitions in which the provisional measures were rejected, only in the Peruvian Prisons Case was the petition not accepted because it did not furnish the minimum amount of information necessary to allow the Court to presume that the situation described by the Commission was true.[361] The Commission had stated that there were serious signs of a grave situation in three detention centres because it had received information that there was a very high incidence of illness, loss of weight, overcrowding, psychiatric and emotional problems of those accused of and those found guilty of terrorism. In addition, the Commission stated that no independent body was able to investigate the situation and that the State had not authorised a visit to the prisons. Since the Commission had not presented proof of the truth of the acts denounced and that its affirmations depended on what it might have observed inside the installations

361 In the other eight cases, the measures were rejected for other reasons. For example, in the Acevedo Jaramillo *et al.* Case because the facts mentioned and the information provided did not demonstrate to the Court that there existed a situation of extreme gravity and urgency. In the Chipoco Case (Peru), the measures were not adopted because the information presented by the State proved that the facts described by the Commission were not correct and in the Carlos Castañeda Case the measures were rejected because according to the Court their adoption would suppose to decide the merits of the matter. Cançado Trindade has also emphasized that the Inter-American Court has rejected provisional measures on very few occasions. See A. Cançado Trindade, "The Evolution of Provisional Measures of Protection under the Case Law of the Inter-American Court of Human Rights (1987–2002)", *Hum. Rts. L. J.* 2003, 164.

or by other proof that to that moment had not been presented, the Court decided not to adopt the requested measures.[362]

151. In some cases where the Court has judged that the information that has been submitted to it is insufficient, it has asked the petitioners to complete it. The Court sometimes states exactly what information it needs. In the *La Nación* Case (Costa Rica), the President of the Court requested the Commission and the State to submit in writing information on the following: a) the urgency of the situation, b) the gravity of the situation, c) the probability of irreparable damage that could be caused to the alleged victims, and d) the implications that a decision of the Court on the adoption of the provisional measures requested by the Commission could have on the judgment on the merits of the case.[363]

152. When the arguments presented by the petitioners have been confusing, the Court has asked that the petition be clarified before taking a decision. For example, in the Fermín Ramírez Case (Guatemala) the Court requested that the representatives of the victims explain what had led them to claim that a judgment of the Constitutional Court of Guatemala, delivered four years prior to the presentation of the petition, was a threat to the rights of persons.[364]

153. When the information presented by the parties is contradictory, the Court in some cases has convoked them to a public hearing[365] and in others it has requested clarification in writing. For example, in the *La Nación* Case the Commission and the State had each furnished the same certification, which in spite of having been issued by the same body differed as to its content. As a result, the Court requested the State to clarify whether the information that it had sent was correct, i.e. whether the alleged victim was entered in the Registry of Delinquents, and, if so, the date of the entry as well as the implications and effects of having been listed.[366] The Court asked only the State to clarify the information, given that it had been a public body that had issued the certifications.

---

362 IACtHR, *Peruvian Prisons Cases (Peru)*, Order of the President of December 14, 1992, Preambular Paragraph 6. The Inter-American Court ratified this Order by means of Order of January 27, 1993.

363 IACtHR, *"La Nación" Newspaper Case (Costa Rica)*, Order of April 6, 2001, Preambular Paragraph 4.

364 IACtHR, *Fermín Ramírez Case (Guatemala)*, Order of March 12, 2005, Explanatory Statements 4 and 5.

365 IACtHR, *Giraldo Cardona Case (Colombia)*, Order of February 5, 1997, Preambular Paragraph 7.

366 IACtHR, *"La Nación" Newspaper Case (Costa Rica)*, Order of September 7, 2001, Preambular Paragraph 12.

154. Finally, the Chipoco Case (Peru) has been the only one in which the Commission has made affirmations that proved to be incorrect. The Commission had stated that a human rights activist had been criminally charged, but the State was able to show that it had merely requested his identification in the Electoral Registry. The President of the Court, after having studied the request and the accompanying documents as well as the information provided by the State, held that the necessary elements to adopt provisional measures did not exist because the alleged victim had not yet been subjected to any judicial proceedings, as affirmed by the Commission.[367]

155. The Court has stated that, although neither the American Convention nor its Statute or Rules specifically governs the evaluation of the evidence, international jurisprudence refers to the competence that the tribunals have to evaluate the evidence within the limits of the rule of sound criticism (*sana crítica*).[368] The evidence, therefore, must be evaluated by the judges taking into account the object and purpose of the Convention – the international protection of human rights – and applying, if applicable, the *pro homine* principle of interpretation, in accordance with the rule of sound criticism.

3.1. EVIDENTIARY MEANS

156. Since the American Convention and the Rules of the Court and the Commission do not explain how a situation of extreme gravity and urgency must be proved,[369] the Court has pointed out that proceedings for provisional measures have their own peculiarities that differ from State proceedings because the objective of provisional measures is to prevent irreparable damage to the rights of persons. The procedure that is followed in the inter-American system is, therefore, not subject to the same formalities as domestic proceedings and, in

---

367 IACtHR, *Chipoco Case (Peru)*, Order of the President of December 14, 1992, Preambular Paragraph 6.

368 Case Concernng Military and Paramilitary Activities in and against Nicaragua (Nicaragua v. United States of America). International Court of Justice. Merits. Judgment I.C.J. Reports 1986 paras. 29–30 and 59–60; IACtHR, *Velásquez Rodríguez Case (Honduras)*, Judgment on the Merits of July 29, 1988, para. 127; IACtHR, *Paniagua Morales et al. and Vásquez et al. Case (Guatemala)*, Judgment on the Merits of March 8, 1998, para. 76; IACtHR, *Blake Case (Guatemala)*, Judgment on the Merits of January 24, 1998, para. 50; IACtHR, *Cesti Hurtado Case (Peru)*, Judgment on Reparations of May 31, 2001, paras. 22 and 23; IACtHR, *Mayagna (Sumo) Awas Tingni Community Case (Nicaragua)*, Judgment on the Merits of August 31, 2001, paras. 87–88; IACtHR, *Constitutional Court Case (Peru)*, Judgment on the Merits of January 31, 2001, para. 52 and IACtHR, *Hilaire, Constantine and Benjamin et al. Case (Trinidad and Tobago)*, Judgment on the Merits of June 21, 2002, paras. 65 and 69.

369 E. Rey Cantor and A. Rey Cantor, *Medidas Provisionales y Medidas Cautelares en el Sistema Interamericano de Derechos Humanos*, Bogotá, Editorial Temis, 2005, 222–223.

incorporating certain elements into the evidentiary file, special attention must be paid to the specific circumstances of the case[370] and to the limits imposed by respect for legal certainty and the procedural equality of the parties.[371] The Court, therefore, usually applies flexible criteria in receiving evidence.[372]

157. As will be seen, the parties have used different means to show that the situation falls under Article 63(2) of the Convention and to demonstrate that the alleged facts are true. The evidence has been organised into two groups. One is direct proof and the other is indirect proof. The first group would include judicial decisions, press clippings, reports of national and international bodies and testimony. The second group would include precautionary measures, internal armed conflict and evidence of a generalised practice. This type of proof is used when these situations permit solid conclusions to be drawn on the extreme gravity and urgency of the situation.[373]

3.1.1. DIRECT EVIDENCE

3.1.1.1. Judicial Decisions

158. The parties presented a judicial decision as evidence in 40 of the 80 requests (50%). The decision was a domestic sentence, a judgment on the merits of the Inter-American Court, a complaint that the alleged victims had presented before the domestic courts or one that had been presented against them. An

---

370 IACtHR, *Velásquez Rodríguez Case (Honduras)*, Judgment on the Merits of July 29, 1988, para. 128; IACtHR, *Bámaca Velásquez Case (Guatemala).* Judgment on the Merits of November 25, 2000, para. 97; IACtHR, *Cesti Hurtado Case (Peru)*, Judgment on Reparations of May 31, 2001, para. 21; IACtHR, *Mayagna (Sumo) Awas Tingni Community Case (Nicaragua)*, Judgment on the Merits of August 31, 2001, paras. 89–90; IACtHR, *Ivcher Bronstein Case (Peru)*, Judgment on the Merits of February 6, 2001, para. 65; IACtHR, *Myrna Mack Chang et al. (Guatemala)*, Judgment on the Merits of November 25, 2003, para. 120; IACtHR, *Plan de Sánchez Massacre Case (Guatemala)*, Judgment on Reparations of November 19, 2004, para. 28; IACtHR, *Carpio Nicolle Case (Guatemala)*, Judgment on the Merits of November 22, 2004, para. 55 and IACtHR, *19 Tradesmen Case (Colombia)*, Judgment on the Merits of July 5, 2004, para. 65.

371 IACtHR, *Paniagua Morales et al. and Vásquez et al. Case (Guatemala)*, Judgment on the Merits of March 8, 1998, paras. 70 and 75; IACtHR, *Loayza Tamayo Case (Peru)*, Judgment on Reparations of November 27, 1998, para. 38 and IACtHR, *Constitutional Court Case (Peru)*, Judgment on the Merits of January 31, 2001, para. 46.

372 IACtHR, *Velásquez Rodríguez Case (Honduras)*, Judgment on the Merits of July 29, 1988, para. 132.

373 IACtHR, *Velásquez Rodríguez Case (Honduras)*, Judgment on the Merits of July 29, 1988, para. 130; IACtHR, *Paniagua Morales et al. and Vásquez et al. Case (Guatemala)*, Judgment on the Merits of March 8, 1998, para. 72 and IACtHR, *Blake Case (Guatemala)*, Judgment on the Merits of January 24, 1998, paras. 47–49.

affirmation that the domestic remedies had been exhausted was also presented as evidence.

3.1.1.1.1. Judgments

159. An attempt was made to show the gravity of the situation by means of sentences in 16 cases (20%). This evidence was presented in almost all cases in which the alleged victim was a prisoner[374] and in all matters in which there was an attempt to protect persons who had been condemned to death.[375]

The Commission pointed out in the Raxcacó Reyes *et al.* Case (Guatemala) that the imminence of the damage was apparent from the finality of the sentences that had condemned the persons to the death penalty. It also noted that, according to the relevant laws in Guatemala, if there were no pending actions to decide a writ of *amparo*, the judge would set the day and hour to carry out the death sentence. Therefore, if the fact that a decision was final and that all the internal domestic remedies had been exhausted were taken into account, it could be concluded that the adoption of provisional measures was the only appropriate means to avoid the execution of the alleged victims.[376] In this case, the four condemned men had availed themselves of the inter-American system alleging that the State had violated Article 4(2) of the Convention because it had imposed the death penalty for a crime for which it had not been provided at the moment Guatemala had ratified the Convention. In this case, the measures had as their purpose not to frustrate the possibility of complying with an eventual determination by the organs of the inter-American system of a violation of Article 4 of the Convention.[377]

Similarly, representatives of the alleged victim pointed out in the Fermín Ramírez Case (Guatemala) that the urgency of the situation was shown by the fact that there was a sentence that imposed the death penalty, that the internal legal remedies had been exhausted and all that remained was to set the day and hour for the execution of Mr. Ramírez. In this case, the adoption of measures was justified not by the fact that the death penalty had been imposed but because it was alleged that the State had imposed the death penalty without the accused having had an opportunity to exercise his right to a defense.[378] The measures

374 Cesti Hurtado Case (Peru), Mendoza Prisons Case (Argentina), Peruvian Prisons Cases (Peru) and Suárez Rosero Case (Ecuador).

375 Boyce and Joseph Case (Barbados), Raxcacó Reyes *et al.* Case (Guatemala), Fermín Ramírez Case (Guatemala) and James, Briggs, Noel, Garcia and Bethel Case (Trinidad and Tobago) and Tyrone Dacosta Cadogan (Barbados).

376 IACtHR, *Raxcacó Reyes et al. Case (Guatemala)*, Order of August 30, 2004, Explanatory Statement 5.

377 *Ibid.*, Preambular Paragraph 8–9.

378 IACtHR, *Fermín Ramírez Case (Guatemala)*, Order of March 12, 2005, Explanatory Statements 1 and 6.

therefore had the objective of avoiding the frustration of an eventual reparation that the Court might determine in favour of the presumed victim for the violation of the Convention.

A violation of Article 13 of the Convention was alleged in *La Nación* Case where a journalist had been found guilty of four crimes due to articles that he had published in a Costa Rican newspaper.[379] The Commission stated that the urgency of the measures was self-explanatory since there was a criminal sentence and a resolution of a national tribunal that warned the alleged victim that he might commit the crime of disobedience if he did not comply with the sentence.[380] The Commission requested that the Court order the suspension of some effects of the sentence, among them the listing of the victim's name in the Registry of Delinquents and the publication in the newspaper of parts of the sentence. The Court considered that the fact that the matter involved a journalist whose work depended on his credibility and that the crime was related to the exercise of his profession should be taken into account. These aspects led it to consider that such inscription should not be made until the organs of the inter-American system could resolve the case.[381]

160. The parties also have used the judgments of the Inter-American Court to show the gravity of the situation. In the Mayagna (Sumo) Awas Tingni Community (Nicaragua), the 19 Tradesmen (Colombia), the Plan of Sánchez Massacre (Guatemala) and the Integrantes del Equipo de Estudios Comunitarios y Acción Psicosocial (ECAP), Massacre Plan de Sánchez (Guatemala) Cases, the judgments of the Court on the merits were taken into account in adopting the provisional measures.

In the Mayagna (Sumo) Awas Tingni Community Case (Nicaragua), the representatives of the alleged victims stated that the petition of provisional measures had as its purpose to protect the Community's right to the use and enjoyment of its lands and resources, as had been recognised by the Inter-American Court in its judgments on the merits and on reparations in that case. The petitioners stated that contrary to what had been expressly ordered in the judgment, Nicaragua had "not avoided detriment to the property located within the geographical area where the members of the Community live and conduct their activities," endangering the effectiveness of the rights recognised by the Court.[382]

---

379 Article 13 American Convention: Freedom of Thought and Expression.

380 IACtHR, *"La Nación" Newspaper Case (Costa Rica)*, Order of May 23, 2001, Explanatory Statement 3 (c) and (d).

381 IACtHR, *"La Nación" Newspaper Case (Costa Rica)*, Order of September 7, 2001, Preambular Paragraphs 7 and 11.

382 IACtHR, *Mayagna (Sumo) Awas Tingni Community Case (Nicaragua)*, Order of September 6, 2002, Explanatory Statements 2 and 4(a).

Similarly, in the order adopting provisional measures in the Plan of Sánchez Massacre (Guatemala), the Court referred to the judgment on the merits on the case that it had delivered some months earlier. That judgment mentioned that persons associated with the case had received a series of threats that made them fear for their safety. This circumstance, together with the brief presented by the Commission and by the representatives of the beneficiaries of the measures, in which they informed that the threats were continuing, led the Court to adopt protective measures.[383]

3.1.1.1.2. Complaints – Investigations

161. With respect to this topic, the petitioners have presented as evidence complaints that the alleged victims had submitted to the authorities of their respective countries, complaints that had been presented against them, and the investigations that the States had carried out with the object of clarifying the facts.

161. Petitioners submitted to the Court complaints that the presumed victims had presented to the national authorities with respect to their situation of danger in 18 cases (22.5%).[384] The great majority of the complaints was submitted to the Public Prosecutor,[385] which means that the situations before the Court were also being considered by the criminal courts of the respective States Parties. On other occasions, the complaints had been presented to the State Ombudsman.[386]

162. The petitioners also presented as evidence the complaints that had been made against the presumed victims in six cases (7.5%).[387] For example, in the Colotenango Case (Guatemala) it was shown that the State had begun judicial

383 IACtHR, *Plan de Sánchez Massacre Case (Guatemala)*, Order of July 30, 2004, Explanatory Statements 2–4.

384 Alvarez *et al.* Case (Colombia), Carlos Nieto *et al.* Case (Venezuela), Cesti Hurtado Case (Peru), Peruvian Prisons Case (Peru), Eloisa Barrios *et al.* Case (Venezuela), Giraldo Cardona Case (Colombia), Liliana Ortega *et al.* Case (Venezuela), Luis Uzcátegui Case (Venezuela), Lysias Fleury Case (Haiti) and the Plan de Sánchez Massacre Case (Guatemala).

385 Alvarez *et al.* Case (Colombia), Cesti Hurtado Case (Peru), Peruvian Prisons Case (Peru), Eloisa Barrios *et al.* Case (Venezuela), Giraldo Cardona Case (Colombia), Liliana Ortega *et al* Case (Venezuela), Luis Uzcátegui Case (Venezuela), Lysias Fleury Case (Haiti), Plan de Sánchez Massacre Case (Guatemala), Miguel Castro Castro Prison Case (Peru), Guerrero Gallucci and Martínez Barrios Case (Venezuela), Ramírez Hinostroza *et al.* (Peru) and Glori Giralt de García Prieto *et al.* Case (El Salvador).

386 Carlos Nieto *et al.* Case (Venezuela), Eloisa Barrios *et al.* Case (Venezuela) and Juarez Cruzzat *et al.* (Peru).

387 Carlos Nieto *et al.* Case (Venezuela), Colotenango Case (Guatemala), "Globovisión" Television Station Case (Venezuela), Indigenous Sarayaku People Case (Ecuador), Constitutional Court Case (Peru) and "La Nación" Newspaper Case (Costa Rica).

proceedings against witnesses in the case and also against organisations of civil society that were supporting them. In the *Globovision* Television Station Case (Venezuela) it was demonstrated that administrative proceedings had been initiated against the station. In addition, in the Indigenous Sarayaku People Case (Ecuador) there was a showing that the oil company had denounced some indigenous peoples in that community.

163. Finally, on some occasions States attempted to prove to the Court their interest in clarifying the facts by showing that judicial investigations had been opened to prosecute and punish the persons responsible.[388] In the Peace Community of San José de Apartadó Case (Colombia), the State argued that the prosecutor had begun several investigations that had as their purpose clarifying the facts and identifying and punishing those responsible. The same was true in the Mendoza Prisons (Argentina) and the Miguel Agustín Pro Juárez Human Rights Center *et al.* (Mexico) Cases. In the Suárez Rosero Case (Ecuador), the State furnished very important evidence that resulted in the provisional measures not being adopted. In this case, the President of the Court had adopted urgent measures and when the Court had to decide whether to ratify them, the State sent a copy of the judicial resolution that had released the presumed victim. This evidence was fundamental for the Court not to adopt provisional measures, as the situation of extreme gravity and urgency had disappeared following that act of the State.

3.1.1.1.3. Exhaustion of Domestic Legal Remedies

164. On seven occasions (8.75%) the parties included as evidence the remedies that the alleged victims had exhausted before domestic judicial bodies.[389]

In the Raxcacó Reyes *et al.* Case (Guatemala) measures had been requested to preserve the life and physical integrity, including the suspension of the executions of several persons who had been condemned to death, so that the consideration of their cases in the inter-American system would not be frustrated. The Commission affirmed that the persons who required protection were waiting that the date be set for their execution. The four condemned men had exhausted the domestic remedies in their respective cases. One of them had presented writs of special appeal, cassation and *amparo* without success; another had exhausted

[388] Acevedo Jaramillo *et al.* Case (Peru), Peace Community of San José de Apartadó Case (Colombia), "Globovisión" Television Station Case (Venezuela), Mendoza Prisons Case (Argentina), Miguel Agustín Pro Juárez Human Rights Center *et al.* Case (Mexico) and Suárez Rosero Case (Ecuador).

[389] Alvarez *et al.* Case (Colombia), Raxcacó Reyes *et al.* Case (Guatemala), Cesti Hurtado Case (Peru), Mendoza Prisons Case (Argentina), "La Nación" Newspaper Case (Costa Rica), Castañeda Gutman Case (Mexico) and Tyrone Dacosta Cadogan (Barbados).

the remedies of appeal, cassation, *amparo* and review, and the other two had filed remedies of appeal, cassation, *amparo* and a request for a pardon to the President of the Republic, which had not been resolved.[390]

Similarly, the Commission stated in its request in the Mendoza Prisons Case (Argentina) that during a period of seven months various inmates and guards had been killed or injured in fires and fights among inmates and generally in circumstances that were not clear. The Commission presented as evidence judicial resolutions of habeas corpus writs that showed the grave conditions of security, infrastructure, overcrowding, detention and health that prevailed in the jails.[391]

3.1.1.2. Information contained in the Mass Media

165. In 15 of the 80 petitions (18.75%) the petitioners presented information from the mass media as evidence.[392] On some occasions the information was from newspapers and in others from a television program.

Unlike what occurs normally in cases being considered in the inter-American system where the Court does not consider press clippings as documentary evidence, while recognising their importance in verifying that the acts referred to are public and notorious and in corroborating the information in the evidentiary file,[393] it appears that the Court gives full consideration to press clippings when it is a question of evaluating them as evidence in the proceedings of provisional measures. The different treatment is perhaps due to the fact that the Court believes that any evidence of a situation of extreme gravity is relevant to determine whether a person deserves the protection requested.

---

390 The Commission deemed that the acts constituted a situation of extreme gravity and urgency that could cause irreparable damages because the execution of the four prisoners would make eventual reparation *in integrum* of their rights impossible. See IACtHR, *Raxcacó Reyes et al. Case (Guatemala)*, Order of August 30, 2004, Explanatory Statements 2 (a), (e) and 3.

391 IACtHR, *Mendoza Prisons Case (Argentina)*, Order November 22, 2004, Preambular Paragraph 7.

392 Alemán Lacayo Case (Nicaragua), Bustíos-Rojas Case (Peru), Chunimá Case (Guatemala), Mendoza Prisons Case (Argentina), "La Nación" Newspaper Case (Costa Rica), Marta Colomina and Liliana Velásquez Case, Plan de Sánchez Massacre Case (Guatemala), Raxcacó Reyes *et al.* Case (Guatemala), "Globovisión" Television Station Case (Venezuela), Miguel Castro-Castro Prison (Peru), Mapiripán Massacre Case (Colombia), Persons imprisoned in the "Dr. Sebastião Martins Silveira" Penitentiary in Araraquara, São Paulo Case (Brazil) and Ramírez Hinostroza *et al.* (Peru).

393 IACtHR, *Velásquez Rodríguez Case (Honduras)*, Judgment on the Merits of July 29, 1988, para. 146; IACtHR, *Paniagua Morales et al. and Vásquez et al. Case (Guatemala)*, Judgment on the Merits of March 8, 1998, para. 75; IACtHR, *Bámaca Velásquez Case (Guatemala)*, Judgment on the Merits of November 25, 2000, para. 107; IACtHR, *Constitutional Court Case (Peru)*, Judgment on the Merits of January 31, 2001, para. 53 and IACtHR, *Ivcher Bronstein Case (Peru)*, Judgment on the Merits of February 6, 2001, para. 70.

In the Alemán Lacayo Case (Nicaragua) the Court adopted provisional measures the same day that it received the petition. The Court took into account that the petition described an attack on the lives of a presidential candidate and his followers and that it had been published in the national and international press.[394] The Court considered the facts on which the petition was based to be notorious, credible and serious, which made necessary the adoption of the measures.[395] The Court did not need any more evidence in this case than the information that appeared in the press and in the request.

In the Raxcacó Reyes *et al.* Case (Guatemala) the Commission contended that the judges in charge of executing sentences had announced in the mass media that the execution of the persons condemned to death would proceed. While it was true that the date of the executions had not been established, it could be concluded from the statements that the dates would soon be set.[396] The Court also considered in the Bustíos-Rojas Case (Peru) that the information furnished, which included press clippings, showed that the situation was extremely grave.[397]

166. The States, for their part, have also resorted to the press as a means of demonstrating that they have taken action to remedy a grave situation.

In the Chunimá Case the Government of Guatemala furnished the Court copies of newspapers that published information on the detention of two persons responsible, according to the petitioners, for the acts of violence that occurred in Chunimá and who had been denounced in the case that was under consideration in the inter-American system.[398]

3.1.1.3. Reports and Studies of National and International Bodies

167. The Inter-American Commission joined to its petition in twelve cases (15%) documents of national authorities or international bodies, such as reports of the Ombudsman, studies of the Inter-American Commission itself or UN

394 IACtHR, *Alemán Lacayo Case (Nicaragua)*, Order of February 2, 1996. Preambular Paragraph 3.

395 *Ibid.*

396 IACtHR, *Raxcacó Reyes et al. Case (Guatemala)*, Order of August 30, 2004, Explanatory Statement 2(b). In this case, the four prisoners sentenced to death had turned to the inter-American system, alleging that the State had violated Article 4(2) of the American Convention, since it had imposed the death penalty for a crime not contemplated for that penalty when it had ratified the American Convention.

397 J.M. Pasqualucci, "Medidas Provisionales en la Corte Interamericana de Derechos Humanos: Una Comparación con la Corte Internacional de Justicia y la Corte Europea de Derechos Humanos", *Revista del Instituto Interamericano de Derechos Humanos* 1994, 106.

398 IACtHR, *Chunimá Case (Guatemala)*, Order of August 1, 1991, Explanatory Statement 8.

Working Groups and reports of local authorities who were directly involved in the situation that was being heard by the Court.[399]

In the Mendoza Prisons Case (Argentina) the Commission stated that other international bodies had also verified the precarious conditions of detention and the insufficient security in the Mendoza prisons. The Commission cited the report of the UN Working Group on Arbitrary Detentions that had recommended urgent measures with respect to overcrowding, studying the possibility of increasing the capacity of the prison system and reducing overpopulation by alternative measures such as early release, conditional release, parole, house arrest, imprisonment during the evening and permission for short home leaves. The Commission also referred to a communication that Amnesty International had sent to the Governor of the Mendoza Province, where the prisons were located, to express its concern on what was taking place and had requested to be informed of the measures that the State was adopting to resolve them.[400]

In the Carlos Nieto *et al.* Case (Venezuela) the Commission contended that, as mentioned in its Report on the Situation of Human Rights in Venezuela, the human rights situation in that country was rather critical. The Commission underscored the considerable number of complaints of attacks, acts of intimidation and threats against human rights defenders. The available information indicated that the defenders and their organisations were frequently harassed, either by direct attacks to their physical integrity or by various means of intimidation, such as veiled threats. The situations in which the activists were selective targets of attacks generally coincided with the absence of serious judicial inquiries to investigate the threats and attacks against them. That situation was often aggravated by the State's refusal to recognise the obstacles that the defenders faced in their work and they, therefore, required special protection.[401]

---

399 Carlos Nieto *et al.* Case (Venezuela), Clemente Teherán Case (Colombia), Urso Branco Prison Case (Brazil), Peace Community of San José de Apartadó Case (Colombia), Mendoza Prisons Case (Argentina), Indigenous Kankuamo Community Case (Colombia), Indigenous Sarayaku People Case (Ecuador), Gallardo Rodríguez Case (Mexico), Lysias Fleury Case (Haiti), Suárez Rosero Case (Ecuador), Penitentiary Center of the Central Occidental Region (Uribana Prison) Case and Monagas Judicial Confinement Center ("La Pica") Case. For example, in the Lysias Fleury Case (Haiti), the Commission referred to a Resolution of the OAS General Assembly on the rights and responsibilities of individuals, groups and organisations of society to promote and protect the universally recognized human rights and fundamental freedoms. See IACtHR, *Lysias Fleury Case (Haiti)*, Order of June 7, 2003, Preambular Paragraph 5. In the Urso Branco Prison Case (Brazil), the Commission referred to a report of the person responsible for the operations within the prison that pointed out that he had found 45 bodies of prisoners, some decapitated and with arms and legs mutilated by sharp weapons and others who had died from blows made with "chunchos" (very sharp weapons made by the prisoners themselves). See IACtHR, *The Urso Branco Prison Case (Brazil)*, Order of June 18, 2002, Explanatory Statement 1(d).

400 IACtHR, *Mendoza Prisons Case (Argentina)*, Order of November 22, 2004, Explanatory Statement 2(j) and (k).

401 IACtHR, *Carlos Nieto et al. Case (Venezuela)*, Order of July 9, 2004, Explanatory Statement 2.

On four occasions reference was made to reports of the Ombudsman, which were relevant because they showed the grave situation facing the persons for whom the protective measures were requested. One case was related to the situation of the prisoner in the Penitentiary Center of the Central Occidental Region (Uribana Prison) in Venezuela and the other cases were related to indigenous peoples, two of which involved Colombia[402] and one concerned Ecuador.[403]

In the Clemente Teherán Case (Colombia) the Commission referred to the Ombudsman's report that stated that the conflict involving the indigenous Zenú community, generated by a controversy regarding the land, had brought about killings, massacres, forced disappearances and the jailing of indigenous leaders.[404]

Similarly, the Commission presented as evidence a resolution of the Ombudsman concerning the indigenous Kankuamo people, which referred to systematic violations of human rights, the arbitrary control of the territories and the forced displacement to which the indigenous communities were being subjected in the Sierra Nevada Mountains de Santa Marta by armed individuals. The Ombudsman had also referred to summary executions and cruel treatment of members of those communities.[405]

In the Indigenous Sarayaku Community Case (Ecuador) the Commission contended that, in spite of a resolution issued by the Ombudsman protecting the rights of the Sarayakus, State agents and employees of the private enterprise that had been extracting petroleum from their territory had taken actions against them.[406]

3.1.1.4. Declarations of Presumed Victims, Witnesses and Experts

168. The fact that a person has a direct interest in the outcome of proceedings or has participated as a complainant in the proceedings before the Commission is not an obstacle to testify. The Court even admits testimony of the victim himself and of his family members. Even though these persons have a direct interest in the case, the Court has held that their testimony must be evaluated and taken into account within the totality of the evidence presented.[407]

---

402 Clemente Teherán Case (Colombia) and Indigenous Kankuamo Community Case (Colombia).

403 Indigenous Sarayaku People Case (Ecuador).

404 IACtHR, *Clemente Teherán Case (Colombia)*, Order of June 19, 1998, Explanatory Statement 2 (b).

405 IACtHR, *Indigenous Kankuamo Community Case (Colombia)*, Order of July 5, 2004, Explanatory Statement 2 (h).

406 IACtHR, *Indigenous Sarayaku People Case (Ecuador)*, Order of July 6, 2004, Explanatory Statement 2 (c).

407 IACtHR, *Haitians and Dominicans of Haitian Origin in the Dominican Republic Case (Dominican Republic)*, Order of August 7, 2002; IACtHR, *"La Nación" Newspaper Case (Costa*

Article 44(1) of the Court's Rules provides that the Court may obtain *ex officio* any evidence that it considers helpful and may especially hear as a witness, expert witness or in any other capacity, any person whose evidence, statement or opinion it deems pertinent. It is even possible for the Court to accept the testimony of persons with criminal records or who are awaiting trial because this is not sufficient *per se* for the Court to deny the competence of the witnesses to testify.[408]

The Rules of Court also provide that the States may not institute proceedings against witnesses or experts or take reprisals against them or their families on account of their testimony or opinions delivered before the Court.[409]

169. The Court, before ruling on the petitions, took into account the testimony of the presumed victims, the witnesses or the experts on eight occasions (10%).[410] In four cases, the testimony was given in public hearings on the merits[411] and in four in public hearings on provisional measures – hearings convoked specifically to hear the parties with respect to the petition for measures.[412]

Most of the victims' family members in the 19 Tradesmen Case (Colombia) stated at the hearing on the merits that they feared reprisals as a result of their testimony to the Court.[413] That testimony led the Court to order in the judgment

Rica), Order of May 21, 2001, Preambular Paragraph 4; IACtHR, *Suárez Rosero Case (Ecuador)*, Judgment on the Merits of November 12, 1997, paras. 32, 33 and 36; IACtHR, *Paniagua Morales et al. and Vásquez et al. Case (Guatemala)*, Judgment on the Merits of March 8, 1998, para. 70; IACtHR, *Ivcher Bronstein Case (Peru)*, Judgment on the Merits of February 6, 2001, para. 75; IACtHR, *Plan de Sánchez Massacre Case (Guatemala)*, Judgment on Reparations of November 19, 2004, para. 40 and IACtHR, *Carpio Nicolle Case (Guatemala)*, Judgment on the Merits of November 22, 2004, para. 71.

408 IACtHR, *Velásquez Rodríguez Case (Honduras)*, Judgment on the Merits of July 29, 1988, para. 145 and IACtHR, *Bámaca Velásquez Case (Guatemala)*, Judgment on the Merits November 25, 2000, para. 117.

409 Article 51 Rules of Procedure of the Inter-American Court.

410 The 19 Tradesmen Case (Colombia), Gómez Paquiyauri Brothers Case (Peru), Gutiérrez Soler Case (Colombia), Haitians and Dominicans of Haitian Origin in the Dominican Republic Case (Dominican Republic), Ivcher Bronstein Case (Peru), Serech y Saquic Case (Guatemala) and "La Nación" Newspaper Case (Costa Rica).

411 That is, in the public hearing of the case where the final arguments of the parties are heard. The Court then delivers its judgment on the merits. The 19 Tradesmen Case (Colombia), Gómez Paquiyauri Brothers Case (Peru), Ivcher Bronstein Case (Peru) and Mapiripán Massacre Case (Colombia).

412 It is important to bear in mind that the alleged victims and experts do not testify in every hearing. Here, we are only taking into account the hearings where this testimony was received: Gutiérrez Soler Case (Colombia), Haitians and Dominicans of Haitian Origin in the Dominican Republic Case (Dominican Republic), Serech y Saquic Case (Guatemala) and "La Nación" Newspaper Case (Costa Rica).

413 The Court held that since it was a question of the next of kin of the alleged victims who have a direct interest in the case, their testimony must be weighed together with all the evidence in the proceedings and not in isolation. See IACtHR, *19 Tradesmen (Colombia)*, Judgment on the Merits of July 5, 2004, para. 79.

on the merits that the State ensure the life, physical integrity and security of those who had appeared before it and their families and provide them with the necessary protection against any person, taking into account the circumstances of the case. Almost two months later, the Court adopted provisional measures to protect the persons mentioned in the judgment on the merits.[414] What basically happens in these cases is that the Court establishes the obligation of protection in the judgment on the merits and formalises that duty by means of an order adopting provisional measures.

The Court also took into account the testimony of witnesses and an expert during the hearing on the merits in the Ivcher Bronstein Case (Peru). The Court stated that such testimony allowed it to establish *prima facie* the existence of threats to the rights of personal integrity and judicial guarantees of Mr. Ivcher Bronstein, as well as of those of members of his family, employees of his companies and other persons related to the facts that gave rise to the case, which necessitated the adoption of protective measures.[415]

170. When the Commission has requested the Court to convene a public hearing in order to hear testimony on the extreme gravity and urgency of a case, it usually indicates the names of the persons who will testify, their capacity (witness/expert) and the purpose of their intervention. The Court forwards the request to the State, which pursuant to Article 49 of the Rules, may object to the proposal. The Court may, however, hear for purposes of information any person who cannot testify as a witness. The Court decides when the parties, the witnesses and experts are to testify. In summoning the witnesses or experts, the Court indicates the object of the testimony or expertise.[416] The relevance of the proposals and objections of the parties is weighed by the Court in ruling on the petition.

In the Haitians and Dominicans of Haitian Origin Case (Dominican Republic) the Commission proposed two experts to provide information on the policy of expulsions to which the alleged victims were subjected and on the frequency and method of the expulsions and their consequences. The State objected to the appearance of the experts because it considered that they were not disinterested persons and were not independent experts or professionals who could offer totally objective and impartial information or opinions, in accordance with Articles 49 of the Rules of the Court and Article 19 of its Statute. After receiving the views of the parties, the Court decided to hear the testimony of the two persons, not as experts as the Commission had proposed, but as witnesses.

414 IACtHR, *19 Tradesmen Case (Colombia)*, Judgment on the Merits, Reparations and Costs of July 5, 2004, para. 280.
415 Ivcher Bronstein Case (Peru).
416 Article 45 Rules of Procedure of the Court.

The Court took into account that, according to statements of the State and the Commission, while the two persons had direct knowledge of the circumstances and the conditions in which the petitioners lived, they had also worked on behalf of the presumed victims.[417]

The State has not always objected to the appearance of a person before the Court. In the *La Nación* Case (Costa Rica) the State agreed with the Commission's proposal that one of the presumed victims appear at the public hearing. The Commission stated that this person would testify on his personal situation and specifically on the facts that would result in a grave situation if the sentence handed down by the Criminal Court of Costa Rica were implemented.[418] The Court decided, since the Commission had proposed the appearance of the presumed victim and the State had not objected, to accept his testimony provided that it was restricted exclusively to the object of the hearing, which was the gravity and urgency of the situation and the probability of irreparable damage if the sentence handed down against him were implemented.[419]

171. The Court once accepted the testimony of a person who could not attend the public hearing since he could not obtain the necessary documents to leave his country. The Commission had, therefore, requested that a sworn statement be accepted as his testimony. When it issued a summons, the Court reminded the State that it was responsible for collaborating so that the person summoned who was in its territory could appear. Under Article 24 of the Rules, the States Parties in a case have the duty to cooperate so that all notices, communications or summons addressed to persons under their jurisdiction are duly executed, as well as facilitating compliance of the summonses of persons who reside or are present in their territory.

Article 44(3) of the Rules of the Court provides that the Court may exceptionally admit evidence at a different time than that indicated if one of the parties alleges *force majeure*, serious impediment or supervening events, provided that the opposing party is guaranteed the right of defense. Since Venezuela had not objected to the reception of a sworn statement in the place of oral testimony and due to the circumstances of the witness and the aforementioned norms, the Court decided to accept the sworn statement as evidence.[420]

---

417 IACtHR, *Haitians and Dominicans of Haitian Origin in the Dominican Republic Case (Dominican Republic)*, Order of August 7, 2002, Enacting Part 4.

418 IACtHR, *"La Nación" Newspaper Case (Costa Rica)*, Order of May 21, 2001, Preambular Paragraphs 1–4.

419 IACtHR, *"La Nación" Newspaper Case (Costa Rica)*, Order of May 21, 2001, Enacting Part 2.

420 IACtHR, *Luis Uzcátegui Case (Venezuela)*, Order of February 20, 2003, Explanatory Statement 14, Preambular Paragraph 9.

172. Finally, before giving his testimony, a witness must swear or make a solemn oath in which he affirms that he will tell the truth, the whole truth and nothing but the truth. Expert witnesses must swear or make a solemn oath affirming that they will discharge their duties honorably and conscientiously.[421] Articles 46 and 47 of the Rules place on the parties that present witnesses, expert witnesses or items of evidence the responsibility of covering the costs involved.[422]

3.1.2. INDIRECT PROOF

3.1.2.1. Precautionary Measures

173. An affirmation that, prior to the request of provisional measures, precautionary measures[423] were adopted that did not give the expected results, is an element of evidence that is usually utilised by the parties to show that the matter is extremely grave. In 43 of the 80 petitions (53.7%) presented to the Court, it was stated that precautionary measures had been adopted that did not provide the desired results and that, therefore, the situation of extreme gravity and urgency continued. The Commission argued that precautionary measures did not meet the objectives desired when, while they were in force, a beneficiary was assassinated, a State implicitly or explicitly refused to comply with them or the situation had not improved although some measures had been adopted.

174. The Commission argued that in eleven cases (13.75%) beneficiaries had been killed while the precautionary measures were in force.[424] The majority of

---

421 Article 48 Rules of Procedure of the Court.

422 Article 46 Rules of Procedure of the Court. See also IACtHR, *Haitians and Dominicans of Haitian Origin in the Dominican Republic Case (Dominican Republic)*, Order of August 7, 2002, Enacting Part 4 and IACtHR, *Fermín Ramírez Case (Guatemala)*, Order of the President of January 23, 2002, Enacting Part 3.

423 Precautionary measures are adopted by the Commission and they have the same purpose as provisional measures, which is to avoid irreparable damage to the rights of persons in grave and urgent situations. The legal basis of these measures cannot be found in the American Convention, but they are established in the Rules of the Commission (Article 25).

424 Giraldo Cardona Case (Colombia), Alvarez *et al.* Case (Colombia), Clemente Teherán Case (Colombia), Peace Community of San José de Apartadó Case (Colombia), Urso Branco Prison Case (Brazil), Communities of the Jiguamiandó and of the Curbaradó Case (Colombia), Indigenous Kankuamo Community Case (Colombia), Eloisa Barrios *et al.* Case (Venezuela), Mendoza Prisons Case (Argentina), Mery Naranjo *et al.* Case (Colombia) and Children Deprived of Liberty in the "Complexo do Tatuapé" of FEBEM Case (Brazil). In the Giraldo Cardona Case, a beneficiary was assassinated while the interim measures were still in effect. See IACtHR, *Giraldo Cardona Case (Colombia)*, Order of the President of October 28, 1996, Explanatory Statement 3(f). In the Alvarez *et al.* Case (Colombia), while the interim measures were still in effect, two people were murdered, two were disappeared and there was an attack

these cases (seven) concerned Colombia. Among the most serious situations were the Urso Branco Prison Case (Brazil) where five prisoners were killed during time of the measures,[425] the Peace Community of San José de Apartadó Case (Colombia) where 15 persons lost their lives and the Indigenous Kankuamo Community Case (Colombia) where it was alleged that eight indigenous persons had died as a result of violence.[426]

175. The measures were also insufficient because States implicitly or explicitly refused to obey them. In twelve cases (15%),[427] States explicitly stated that they would not comply with the precautionary measures because their purpose was to prevent them from implementing a sentence authorised by their domestic legal order.

In the James, Briggs, Noel, Garcia and Bethel Case (Trinidad and Tobago) the State contended that the Commission did not have jurisdiction either through acts or through omissions to prevent in any way the execution of a sentence authorised by the Constitution and laws of Trinidad and Tobago, which had been handed down by a competent tribunal. The State, therefore, argued that it was at liberty to implement a sentence that imposed the death penalty.[428]

Similarly, in referring to the precautionary measures requested by the Commission to protect witnesses in the Carpio Nicolle Case, Guatemala stated that they were not appropriate because under its Constitution the State had the responsibility to guarantee to all its inhabitants their lives and freedom and that it had an internal legal system that governed the means to accomplish that duty.[429] The precautionary measures, therefore, were not necessary to protect the witnesses.

In the Indigenous Sarayaku Community Case (Ecuador) the State informed that it would not comply with the measures because the petitioners were not telling the truth and because they were involved in acts of banditry.

---

on the office of the human rights organization. See IACtHR, *Alvarez et al. Case (Colombia)*, Order of the President of July 22, 1997, Explanatory Statement 3.

425 IACtHR, *Urso Branco Prison Case (Brazil)*, Order of June 18, 2002, Explanatory Statement 1.

426 IACtHR, *Indigenous Kankuamo Community Case (Colombia)*, Order of July 5, 2004, Explanatory Statement 2.

427 Peruvian Prisons Case (Peru), Colotenango Case (Guatemala), Carpio Nicolle Case (Guatemala), Serech and Saquic Case (Guatemala), Cesti Hurtado Case (Peru), "La Nación" Newspaper Case (Costa Rica), Luis Uzcátegui Case (Venezuela), Lysias Fleury Case (Haiti), Indigenous Sarayaku People Case (Ecuador), Eloisa Barrios *et al.* Case (Venezuela), Blake Case (Guatemala) and James, Briggs, Noel, Garcia and Bethel Case (Trinidad and Tobago).

428 IACtHR, *James, Briggs, Noel, Garcia and Bethel Case (Trinidad and Tobago)*, Order of the President of May 27, 1998, Explanatory Statement 3(c).

429 IACtHR, *Carpio Nicolle Case (Guatemala)*, Order of June 4, 1995, Preambular Paragraph 6.

Peru, for its part, explicitly stated that it would not comply with the measures requested in the Peruvian Prisons Case and thus did not authorise the Commission to visit some prisons on its territory.[430]

176. Lack of compliance by a State is also demonstrated by a failure to respond to the petitions of the Commission, whereby the State does not provide its views, does not answer the request or does not adopt any measures: it literally does nothing. Examples have been the Luis Uzcátegui (Venezuela), the Lysias Fleury (Haiti),[431] the Eloisa Barrios *et al.* (Venezuela) and the Blake (Guatemala) Cases.

177. The Commission has also contended that, if experience shows that the precautionary measures do not produce the desired results with respect to a certain type of matter concerning certain States, it may be presumed that they would not be complied with if they were adopted again. The Commission in these cases tries to show that it is not worth adopting precautionary measures because the State would not comply with them and, in view of the urgency of the matter, it is necessary that the Court adopt protective measures.

In the Raxcacó Reyes *et al.* (Guatemala) and in the Fermín Ramírez (Guatemala) Cases the Commission described, as a situation of particular gravity, the fact that the State had executed several persons condemned to death notwithstanding the precautionary measures that had been adopted to protect them. The Commission stated that this circumstance allowed it to conclude that it would be fruitless to adopt precautionary measures because experience showed that Guatemala would not comply with them, since it had been shown that precautionary measures were not effective in this type of matters.[432] The Commission, therefore, attempted to show that there was a situation of extreme gravity and urgency that justified the adoption of provisional measures to avoid irreparable damage to the right to life of the persons who were on death row in Guatemala.[433]

---

430 The Court later held that although the Commission had requested the Government, pursuant to Article 29 of its Rules, to take measures to avoid harm to the persons protected under Article 63(2) of the Convention, some of those measures could not be considered to be "precautionary" and provisional since they referred to the authorisation of the Government to allow the Commission to conduct on-site visits to various Peruvian prisons, a matter governed by Articles 48(2) of the Convention and 44(2) of the Rules of the Commission that required the prior consent of the Government. This consent had not been given and could not be granted by means of a ruling of the President the Court. See IACtHR, *Peruvian Prisons Cases (Peru)*, Order of the President of July 30, 2004, Preambular Paragraph 5.

431 The State limited itself to declaring that it had received the resolution of the Commission.

432 IACtHR, *Raxcacó Reyes et al. Case (Guatemala)*, Order of August 30, 2004, Explanatory Statement 3, Preambular Paragraphs 8 and 9.

433 IACtHR, *Fermín Ramírez Case (Guatemala)*, Order of March 12, 2005, Explanatory Statement 12.

178. The Commission also argued the necessity of adopting provisional measures when the precautionary measures were not able to produce positive changes in the situation. This argument was made on 16 occasions (20%).[434]

In the cases of Carpio Nicolle (Guatemala), Ramírez Hinostroza *et al.* (Peru) and Gloria Giralt de García Prieto *et al.* (El Salvador) the Commission in its request contended that the precautionary measures had been shown to be ineffective due to the continued attacks and threats against the beneficiaries of the measures and the failure of the authorities to investigate and punish the authors of those threats.[435] The Commission also pointed out in the Communities of the Jiguamiandó and of the Curbaradó Case (Colombia) that the actions of the State in response to the precautionary measures had not effectively protected the beneficiaries, who continued being subjected to acts of harassment and violence by paramilitary groups that operated freely in a zone with the strong presence of the Army.[436]

177. The President of the Court considered as an exceptional circumstance that necessitated the adoption of measures in the Serech and Saquic Case (Guatemala) the fact that the Commission had adopted precautionary measures on two occasions without them resulting in the protection warranted since a proper investigation had not been conducted by the competent authorities, nor had a pending arrest warrant been served, nor had certain persons been investigated and prosecuted in spite of having been accused of the death of two members of the Conference of Evangelical Churches, whose case was under consideration in the inter-American system.[437]

3.1.2.2. Internal Armed Conflict

178. The *prima facie* standard of appreciation and the application of presumptions, given the need to protect persons, have led the Court to order

434 Vogt Case (Guatemala), Carpio Nicolle Case (Guatemala), Alvarez *et al.* Case (Colombia), Digna Ochoa y Plácido *et al.* Case (Mexico), Haitians and Dominicans of Haitian Origin in the Dominican Republic Case (Dominican Republic), Luisiana Ríos *et al.* Case (Venezuela), Liliana Ortega *et al.* Case (Venezuela), Marta Colomina and Liliana Velásquez Case (Venezuela), "El Nacional" and "Así es la Noticia" Newspapers Case (Venezuela), Mendoza Prisons Case (Argentina), Communities of the Jiguamiandó and of the Curbaradó Case (Colombia), Children Deprived of Liberty in the "Complexo do Tatuapé" of FEBEM Case (Brazil), Ramírez Hinostroza *et al.* Case (Peru), Gloria Giralt de García Prieto *et al.* Case (El Salvador), Mery Naranjo *et al.* Case (Colombia) and Forensic Anthropology Foundation Case (Guatemala).

435 IACtHR, *Carpio Nicolle Case (Guatemala)*, Order of the President of June 4, 1995, Preambular Paragraph 6.

436 IACtHR, Communities of the Jiguamiandó and of the Curbaradó Case (Colombia), Order of March 6, 2003, Explanatory Statement 4.

437 IACtHR, *Serech y Saquic Case (Guatemala)*, Order of the President of April 24, 1996, Preambular Paragraph 6 and Order of June 28, 1996, Explanatory Statement 3.

provisional measures on different occasions.[438] When the petition is related to an armed conflict that is taking place in a State, the Court has held that that circumstance allows the presumption of the existence of a situation that may produce irreparable damage to the rights of persons. This situation has occurred in five cases (6.25%).

In the Chunimá Case (Guatemala) the State recognised that there was an armed conflict in its territory for more than thirty years and that, as described in the petition, there were acts of violence in Chunimá. The Court held that this general recognition, although it did not imply accepting as true the acts denounced, permitted the presumption of the existence of a situation in which irreparable damage could occur to persons.[439]

Similarly, in the Communities of the Jiguamiandó and of the Curbaradó (Colombia), the Indigenous Kankuamo People (Colombia) and the Peace Community of San José de Apartadó (Colombia) Cases, the Court held that the special nature of the cases and the general conditions of the armed conflict that was taking place in Colombia necessitated the protection of all the members of the Communities in light of the terms of the American Convention and international humanitarian law.[440]

3.1.2.3. Generalised Practice

179. A showing of the existence of a generalised practice that results in damage to the rights of persons and that covers the situation that is being considered by the Court may serve as a basis for the adoption of protective measures.[441] The Commission has affirmed that the existence of a generalised practice of threats and harassment directed to certain sectors of society requires the deployment of the protective mechanisms of the inter-American system. A showing of such practice served as the basis for the adoption of measures on eleven occasions

---

438 H. Faundez Ledesma, *El Sistema Interamericano de Protección de los Derechos Humanos*, San José, IIDH, 3rd ed., 2004, 567.

439 IACtHR, *Chunimá Case (Guatemala)*, Order of August 1, 1991, Explanatory Statement 7.

440 IACtHR, *Peace Community of San José de Apartadó Case (Colombia)*, Order of June 18, 2002, Preambular Paragraph 11; IACtHR, *Communities of the Jiguamiandó and of the Curbaradó Case (Colombia)*, Order of March 6, 2003, Preambular Paragraph 11and IACtHR, *Indigenous Kankuamo Community Case (Colombia)*, Order of July 5, 2004, Preambular Paragraph 11. In the 19 Tradesmen Case (Colombia), the Commission stated that the records of the case, the alleged threat and the situation of the region where the victim and her family lived showed a situation of extreme gravity and urgency. See IACtHR, *19 Tradesmen Case (Colombia)*, Order of September 3, 2004, Explanatory Statement 4(c). Although the Commission in the Mery Naranjo *et al.* Case (Colombia) referred to the armed conflict, the Court did not mention that situation in order to adopt the provisional measures.

441 H. Faundez Ledesma, *El Sistema Interamericano de Protección de los Derechos Humanos*, San José, IIDH, 3rd ed., 2004, 566.

(13,75%), eight cases concerning Venezuela, two concerning Brazil[442] and one regarding the Dominican Republic.

In the Luisiana Ríos *et al.* (Venezuela) and the Marta Colomina and Liliana Velásquez (Venezuela) Cases, the Commission contended that there were constant attacks and aggressions against those who worked in the area of social communication in Venezuela. This situation of general tension implied a continual threat to freedom of expression and to the personal integrity of journalists, cameramen and other persons who worked for the *El Observador* newscast of RCTV.[443]

The Commission also referred to the situation of human rights defenders in Venezuela.[444] In the Carlos Nieto Case (Venezuela), the Commission stated that it had received abundant information that showed a pattern of intimidation with respect to human rights defenders. The Commission stated that the intimidations directed at Mr. Nieto fell within this context, which necessitated the setting in motion of the protective mechanisms of the inter-American system to protect his life and personal integrity.[445] In referring to organisations of civil society, the Commission in the Liliana Ortega *et al.* Case (Venezuela) displayed a deep concern regarding the progressive increase in threats and attacks, which had intensified significantly during 2002, against this type of organisation. Within this context of violence, there had been acts of direct and indirect harassment and threats against members of the non-governmental organisation COFAVIC. In view of the general situation of violence against civil society organisations and, specifically, the harassment of the members of COFAVIC, the Commission requested the adoption of provisional measures.[446]

180. The Commission initially makes a general determination with respect to a situation of grave danger for a certain sector of society and then describes specifically how that situation endangers the rights of certain persons who belong

---

442 Persons imprisoned in the "Dr. Sebastião Martins Silveira" Penitentiary in Araraquara, São Paulo Case (Brazil) and Children Deprived of Liberty in the "Complexo do Tatuapé" of FEBEM Case (Brazil).

443 IACtHR, *Luisiana Ríos et al. Case (Venezuela)*, Order of November 27, 2002, Explanatory Statement 3 and IACtHR, *Marta Colomina and Liliana Velásquez Case (Venezuela)*, Order of the President of June 30, 2003, Explanatory Statement 3.

444 From 2006 the Commission has requested on four occasions provisional measures to protect people who are in prison. According to the Commission there is a general grave situation in the Venezuelan prisioner system. See Penitentiary Center of the Central Occidental Region (Uribana Prison) Case, Yare I and Yare II Capital Region Center Case, Capital El Rodeo I & El Rodeo II Judicial Confinement Center Case and Monagas Judicial Confinement Center ("La Pica") Case.

445 IACtHR, *Carlos Nieto et al. Case (Venezuela)*, Order of July 9, 2004, Explanatory Statement 3, Preambular Paragraph 8.

446 IACtHR, *Liliana Ortega et al. Case (Venezuela)*, Order of November 27, 2002, Explanatory Statement 2 (a) and (b).

to that social group. A demonstration of that situation would prove the need to adopt immediately protective measures. It is important to prove the existence of a generalised practice, because the Court relies on that to adopt the measures. Although the Commission in the Haitians and Dominicans of Haitian Origin Case (Dominican Republic) attempted to show that there was a practice of discrimination that affected a certain part of the population of the Dominican Republic, after hearing the parties, the Court held that it had not been proven that there was a State policy of massive deportations and expulsions and, therefore, it was not possible to adopt the protective measures.[447]

3.2. SUMMARY

181. Proceedings in provisional measures have special characteristics compared to procedures that are followed in the domestic order of States. This is due to the fact that there are no rules on how to prove a situation of extreme gravity and urgency[448] and that the Court usually applies flexible criteria in receiving evidence.[449] Nonetheless, the Court's action, as the Court itself has recognised, is restricted by respect for legal certainty and the procedural equality of the parties.[450]

182. Different ways have been used to demonstrate that the situation is of extreme gravity and urgency. In general terms, the evidence that has been presented to the Court may be divided into two categories: direct proof and indirect proof. In the area of direct proof one can find the judicial decisions handed down by domestic courts, judgments on the merits of the Inter-American Court and information from the mass media. In the area of indirect proof precautionary measures that did not produce the desired results, an internal armed conflict in the territory of a country and proof of a generalised practice in which it is possible to include a specific case can be found.

---

447 The Court, however, indicated that the testimony allowed it to establish a *prima facie* presumption of the frequency of the cases where the individuals were abused, and thus the provisional measures were appropriate for certain specific persons. IACtHR, *Haitians and Dominicans of Haitian Origin in the Dominican Republic Case (Dominican Republic)*, Order of August 18, 2000, Preambular Paragraphs 5 and 9.

448 E. Rey Cantor and A. Rey Cantor, *Medidas Provisionales y Medidas Cautelares en el Sistema Interamericano de Derechos Humanos*, Bogotá, Editorial Temis, 2005, 222–223.

449 IACtHR, *Velásquez Rodríguez Case (Honduras)*, Judgment on the Merits of July 29, 1988, para. 132.

450 IACtHR, *Paniagua Morales et al. and Vásquez et al. Case (Guatemala)*, Judgment on the Merits of March 8, 1998, paras. 70 and 75; IACtHR, *Loayza Tamayo Case (Peru)*, Judgment on Reparations of November 27, 1998, para. 38 and IACtHR, *Constitutional Court Case (Peru)*, Judgment on the Merits of January 31, 2001, para. 46.

Judicial decisions were presented in 40 of the 80 petitions. The sentences of national authorities were presented in the majority of the cases in which the alleged victim was a prisoner and in all the matters in which it was attempted to protect persons on death row. In some cases, the parties furnished the Court's judgments on the merits. Also serving as evidence have been complaints presented by the alleged victims to the authorities of their country and the complaints against them. The remedies exhausted before domestic judicial bodies, such as the writs of appeal, cassation, *amparo*, review and habeas corpus have also served as evidence.[451]

When a situation is covered by the mass media, the petitioners have so informed the Court. An attempt is made to show that the situation is of such gravity and notoriety that even the mass media have taken note. On 15 occasions, information was presented from the written press and on one occasion from a television program. The Court does not consider press clippings to be documentary proof in normal proceedings but does so in proceedings on provisional measures. In fact, in the Alemán Lacayo Case (Nicaragua) it was the only evidence that the Court had in adopting the provisional measures.

The Commission in twelve cases joined documents of national authorities or international bodies to the petition. They included reports of the Ombudsman, studies of the Commission itself or UN Working Groups and reports of local authorities that were directly related to the situation that was being heard by the Court. These documents have in common that they show a situation of danger regarding persons whose protection is sought. Some documents are studies on certain countries, such as for example, the report that the Inter-American Commission drafted on the human rights situation in Venezuela. The documents presented may also be those drafted by national authorities, such as the Ombudsman, which describe the grave situation of a certain sector of the population. Specifically, reports of the Ombudsman have denounced the abuses that have been committed against indigenous populations. In other cases, they are communications that call the attention to a specific situation, such as the letter sent by Amnesty International to a regional authority in Argentina, in which it expressed its concern for the situation of some prisoners.

Testimony has also served as evidence. On this topic, the Court has stated that a person who has a direct interest in the results of the proceedings or has participated as a petitioner in the procedure before the Commission may still testify.[452] As is understandable, the testimony in those situations is evaluated

---

451 Alvarez *et al.* Case (Colombia), Raxcacó Reyes *et al.* Case (Guatemala), Cesti Hurtado Case (Peru), Mendoza Prisons Case (Argentina), "La Nación" Newspaper Case (Costa Rica), Tyrone Dacosta Cadogan Case (Barbados).

452 Article 44(1) of its Rules provides that the Court may "obtain, on is own motion, any evidence it considers helpful. In particular, it may hear as a witness, expert witness, or in any other capacity, any person whose evidence, statement or opinion it deems to be relevant".

and taken into account within the totality of evidence presented. Testimony was received in eight matters.

In the area of indirect evidence, the Court has accepted precautionary measures, the existence of an internal armed conflict and proof of a generalised practice in which a specific situation could be included. A demonstration that the case pending before the Court is the subject of precautionary measures that did not give the desired results because a beneficiary had been killed, because the State refused to comply with them, or because in spite of the adoption of some measures the situation has not improved, would show the gravity of the situation and the probability that there will be irreparable damage to persons and that, therefore, protective measures must be adopted.

Another consideration is that, when there is an armed conflict in the territory of a State, it is possible to presume that a certain sector of the population may be in a grave situation that could lead to irreparable damage to their rights. An example would be the indigenous communities in zones in Colombia where different armed groups are fighting. Proving this circumstance served as grounds to adopt provisional measures in five matters. Provisional measures were also adopted in cases in which it was proved that there was a generalised practice that produced damage to the rights of persons and in which it was possible to include the situation before the Court.

Table 21. Proof

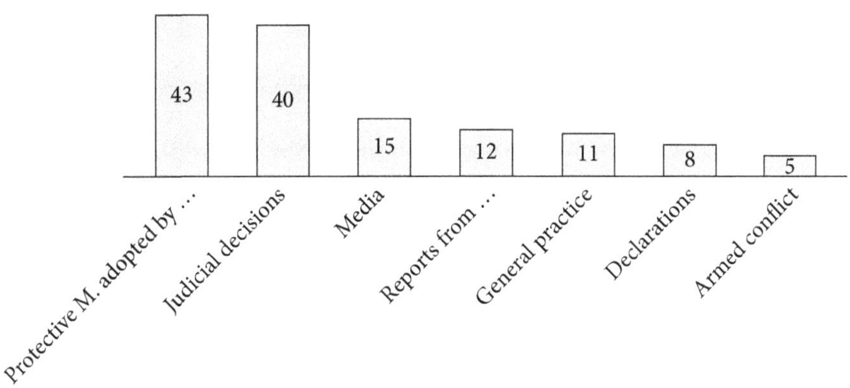

183. The evidence that has most often been presented from 1987 to 2009 (53.75% of the petitions) during the proceedings on provisional measures has been that of precautionary measures that did not fulfill the desired expectations. This was followed by judicial decisions – sentences, appeals and investigations that make it possible to prove the situation of danger that the alleged victims were encountering (50% of the petitions). Finally, indirect proof (20%), where the Court inferred that the existence of an armed conflict or the generalised practice in which a specific case could be included could be a threat to the rights of the alleged victims, has also been presented.

Information from the mass media is found in 18.75% of the cases. In a 15% of the cases the Court took into account reports of national and international bodies that describe the situation of danger that certain sectors of the population face. Finally, a smaller percentage relies on testimony and expert opinion from public hearings on the adoption of provisional measures. Although this evidence is very important because the Court has the opportunity to hear directly the circumstances and the facts of the case, it was taken into account in only 10% of the cases.

184. It is important to note that the parties normally present several means of proof at the same time. It is for this reason that the sum of the percentages cannot be 100%. In the Carlos Nieto *et al.* Case (Venezuela), the Commission presented as evidence the complaint that the presumed victim had made to the Ombudsman, the precautionary measures that were not effective and the Commission's report on the situation of human rights in Venezuela. In the Mendoza Prisons Case (Argentina), the Commission introduced writs of habeas corpus presented by the families of the inmates, local press clippings, evidence that one inmate had been killed and two had been injured while the precautionary measures were in force, written testimony of inmates, the letter of Amnesty International to the Governor of the Mendoza Province and the recommendation of the UN Working Group on Arbitrary Detentions with respect to overcrowding in the jail.

185. In general terms, it may be said that the Court accepts any evidence that shows a situation of extreme gravity and urgency, provided that the principles of legal certainty and procedural equality between the parties are respected.

4. PROCESSING OF THE REQUEST

4.1. GENERAL REMARKS

186. The procedure that is followed in adopting provisional measures is very rapid and simple because it is an exceptional mechanism that does not in any way suspend proceedings on the merits of a matter, nor does it prejudge the merits and, of course, because the type of matters submitted require a prompt decision. Article 26 of the Court's Rules provides that the request for measures may be presented to the President, any of the judges or the Secretariat by any means of communication. In any event, whoever receives the request must immediately inform the President.

187. In principle, it is the Court that resolves a request for provisional measures. When the Court is not in session, however, the President, after consulting the Permanent Commission and, if possible, the other judges, may order a government to dictate urgent measures with the aim of ensuring the efficacy of the provisional measures that the Court might subsequently order at its next session.[453]

188. In spite of the fact that Article 26 of the Rules refers to some aspects of the proceedings, none of the Rules governs the procedure that must be followed after the presentation of the petition. Indeed, the active standing, the passive standing and the means by which the petition is presented are governed by the Rules, but not the internal processing. For example, nothing is said concerning what type of cases or under what conditions the parties should be asked for their observations or in what cases a public hearing may be convoked or the time periods that must be taken into account.

189. As regards precedent, the Court has not developed specific rules, but everything seems to indicate that one or another procedure is followed depending

---

[453] Of the 80 petitions presented between 1987–2009, 28 were resolved directly by the Court. In the other 52 cases, the President of the Court first took urgent measures and subsequently submitted the petition and the measures he had adopted to the consideration of the Court. See also, A. Brewer Carias, "Introducción general al régimen del derecho de amparo a los derechos y garantías constitucionales", in *Ley Orgánica de Amparo sobre Derechos y Garantías Constitucionales,* A. Brewer Carias and C. Ayala Corao (eds.), Caracas, Editorial Jurídica Venezolana, 1988, 86, 87 and 91.

on the specific circumstances of each case. The Court has followed twelve different procedures in the 80 petitions that were presented from 1987 to 2009. Underneath one can find find an account of each of those procedures.

4.2. PROCEDURE 1: MOST COMMON PROCEDURE

Petition → President adopts urgent measures → State presents report → Commission presents observations → Court ratifies Order of President

190. This procedure was used in 22 of 80 requests (27.5%) and is the procedure that has been followed with the greatest frequency.[454] As may be seen from the diagram, the President of the Court was the first to rule on the petition. This is due to the fact that the Court was not in session when the request was made and that the gravity of the matter made it necessary that the petition be resolved as soon as possible.

191. The order that the President adopts in these cases contains a request to the State that it take whatever measures are necessary to avoid damage to persons. The President also sets a date for the State to give information on the measures that it has taken with respect to the case and requests the Commission to present its observations to the report furnished by the State. In addition, the President informs the Court of his order so that it may rule on the matter at its next session.

192. The fact that the petitioners have presented the information necessary to show that the situation described was of extreme gravity and urgency perhaps resulted in the President adopting urgent measures without previously requesting the position of the State.

193. The President took an average of 5.8 days to adopt measures under this procedure.

---

454 Bámaca Velásquez Case (Guatemala), Blake Case (Guatemala), Boyce and Joseph Case (Barbados), Chipoco Case (Peru), Cemente Teherán Case (Colombia), 19 Tradesmen Case (Colombia), Peruvian Prisons Case (Peru), Constitutional Court Case (Peru), Eloisa Barrios *et al.* Case (Venezuela), Gallardo Rodríguez Case (Mexico), Giraldo Cardona Case (Colombia), Helen Mack Chang *et al.* Case (Guatemala), James, Briggs, Noel, Garcia and Bethel Case (Trinidad and Tobago), Loayza Tamayo Case (Peru), Lysias Fleury Case (Haiti), Marta Colomina and Liliana Velásquez Case (Venezuela), Paniagua Morales *et al.* and Vásquez *et al.* Case (Guatemala) and the Velásquez Rodríguez Case (Honduras), Adrián Meléndez Quijano *et al.* Case (El Salvador), Bueno Alves Case (Argentina), Forensic Anthropology Foundation Case (Guatemala) and Tyrone Dacosta Cadogan (Barbados).

194. The Court, before resolving a petition under this procedure, may hear the views of the parties and those of the President. In every case the Court has ratified the decisions of the President, two of which rejected the measures requested because the President had found that the existence of a situation of extreme gravity and urgency had not been proved.[455]

195. The cases under this procedure had in common that they alleged a situation of extreme gravity and urgency and that the Court was not in session when the petition was presented. In addition, the majority (17) had in common allegations of death threats to the presumed victims. The rest of the cases appeared not to have a common thread; for example, eight matters were being heard by the Court and 14 being considered by the Commission when the petition was presented and twelve cases involved precautionary measures but not the other ten, and two alleged that jail conditions violated certain right(s).

4.3. PROCEDURE 2: SIMPLEST PROCEDURE

Petition → Court decides

196. This is the simplest procedure that is followed in the adoption of protective measures. As may be seen in the diagram, the Court, after receiving the request and without requesting observations of the parties, directly adopts the measures. This procedure was followed in 21 of the 80 cases (26.2%).[456]

196. In most of the cases it was affirmed that persons had received death threats and, therefore, needed their right to life be protected urgently. In 13 of the 21 cases, precautionary measures had been adopted that had not led to the desired results[457] and in eight cases it was alleged that persons associated with the cases

455 Chipoco Case (Peru) and Peruvian Prisons Case (Peru).

456 Alemán Lacayo Case (Nicaragua), Caballero Delgado and Santana Case (Colombia), Carlos Nieto *et al.* Case (Venezuela), Colotenango Case (Guatemala), Urso Branco Prison Case (Brazil), Communities of the Jiguamiandó and of the Curbaradó Case (Colombia), Indigenous Kankuamo Community Case (Colombia), Digna Ochoa y Plácido *et al.* Case (Mexico), Gómez Paquiyauri Brothers Case (Peru), Gutiérrez Soler Case (Colombia), Liliana Ortega *et al.* Case (Venezuela), Luis Uzcátegui Case (Venezuela), Luisiana Ríos *et al.* Case (Venezuela), Jorge Castañeda Gutman Case (México), Penitentiary Center of the Central Occidental Region (Uribana Prison) Case (Venezuela), Children Deprived of Liberty in the "Complexo do Tatuapé" of FEBEM Case (Brazil), Yare I and Yare II Capital Region Center Case (Venezuela), García Uribe *et al.* Case (Mexico), Gloria Giralt de García-Prieto *et al.* Case (El Salvador), Kawas Fernández Case (Honduras) and Mery Naranjo *et al.* Case (Colombia).

457 Carlos Nieto *et al.* Case (Venezuela), Colotenango Case (Guatemala), Urso Branco Prison Case (Brazil), Communities of the Jiguamiandó and of the Curbaradó Case (Colombia),

had been killed.[458] Although in principle it may be concluded that the Court did not request the State to provide its views in cases being heard by it, it is interesting to note that the great majority of these cases (16) was still under consideration by the Commission when the measures were adopted.[459]

197. As to the length of time that it takes to adopt the measures, the Court took an average of only 2.9 days.[460] It was able to decide promptly because it was in session when the petition was presented.

198. The request is sometimes presented in writing and at other times it is requested orally during a public hearing. With respect to the latter, the Court resolved the request during the hearing and notified the parties of the decision from the Bench.[461] At the hearings the judges had the opportunity to listen to

---

Indigenous Kankuamo Community Case (Colombia), Digna Ochoa y Plácido *et al.* Case (Mexico), Gutiérrez Soler Case (Colombia), Liliana Ortega *et al.* Case (Venezuela), Luis Uzcátegui Case (Venezuela), Luisiana Ríos *et al.* Case (Venezuela), Children Deprived of Liberty in the "Complexo do Tatuapé" of FEBEM Case (Brazil), Gloria Giralt de García-Prieto *et al.* Case (El Salvador) and Mery Naranjo *et al.* Case (Colombia).

458 Colotenango Case (Guatemala), Urso Branco Prison Case (Brazil), Communities of the Jiguamiandó and of the Curbaradó Case (Colombia), Indigenous Kankuamo Community Case (Colombia), Luisiana Ríos *et al.* Case (Venezuela), Penitentiary Center of the Central Occidental Region (Uribana Prison) Case (Venezuela), Children Deprived of Liberty in the "Complexo do Tatuapé" of FEBEM Case (Brazil) and Yare I and Yare II Capital Region Center Case (Venezuela).

459 Alemán Lacayo Case (Nicaragua), Carlos Nieto *et al.* Case (Venezuela), Colotenango Case (Guatemala), Urso Branco Prison Case (Brazil), Communities of the Jiguamiandó and of the Curbaradó Case (Colombia), Indigenous Kankuamo Community Case (Colombia), Digna Ochoa y Plácido *et al.* Case (Mexico), Liliana Ortega *et al.* Case (Venezuela), Luis Uzcátegui Case (Venezuela), Luisiana Ríos *et al.* Case (Venezuela) Jorge Castañeda Gutman (México), Penitentiary Center of the Central Occidental Region (Uribana Prison) Case (Venezuela), Children Deprived of Liberty in the "Complexo do Tatuapé" of FEBEM Case (Brazil), Yare I and Yare II Capital Region Center Case (Venezuela), García Uribe *et al.* Case (Mexico) and Mery Naranjo *et al.* Case (Colombia).

460 The measures were adopted on the same day they were requested in the Alemán Lacayo Case (Nicaragua), the Gutiérrez Soler Case (Colombia), the Liliana Ortega *et al.* Case (Venezuela) and the Luis Uzcátegui Case (Venezuela). The measures were adopted one day after they were requested in the Caballero Delgado Santana Case (Colombia), Penitentiary Center of the Central Occidental Region (Uribana Prison) Case (Venezuela), Gloria Giralt de García-Prieto *et al.* Case (El Salvador) and Kawas Fernández Case (Honduras) and in the Communities of the Jiguamiandó and of the Curbaradó Case (Colombia); two days after they were requested in the Carlos Nieto *et al.* Case (Venezuela), Colotenango Case (Guatemala), García Uribe *et al.* Case (Mexico), Mery Naranjo *et al.* Case (Colombia) and Yare I and Yare II Capital Region Center Case (Venezuela) and after three days in the Indigenous Kankuamo Community Case (Colombia). The Court took six, seven, nine, ten and twelve days, respectively, to adopt measures in the Digna Ochoa y Plácido *et al.* Case (Mexico), the Luisiana Ríos *et al.* Case (Venezuela), Children Deprived of Liberty in the "Complexo do Tatuapé" of FEBEM Case (Brazil), Jorge Castañeda Gutman (México) and the Urso Branco Prison Case (Brazil).

461 Gómez Paquiyauri Brothers Case (Peru) and the Gutiérrez Soler Case (Colombia).

the parties and ask the questions that they deemed timely. These were hearings on the merits and the persons who testified expressed fear of suffering harm for having appeared before the Court. The fear normally is based on the threats and intimidations that these persons have suffered during the process and are accentuated when there is about to be a decision on the merits of the matter.[462]

4.4. PROCEDURE 3: PROCEDURE WITH THE HOLDING OF A PUBLIC HEARING

Petition → President adopts urgent measures → public hearing → Court ratifies Order of the President

199. As may be seen in the diagram, this procedure is characterised by the President of the Court being the first to rule on the petition. It is also the President who, under the terms of Article 26(7) of the Rules, convokes the parties to a public hearing.[463]

200. At the hearing, which is held at the seat of the Court, the judges have the opportunity to hear the views of the parties and ask any questions that they might have.[464] Finally, depending on the information that it has at its disposal, such as the petition requesting the measures, the order of the President and the observations offered by the parties during the public hearing, the Court resolves the petition.[465] The Court has ratified the decision of the President in every case.

462 See the process employed in IACtHR, *Ivcher Bronstein Case (Peru)*, Order of October 21, 2000 and in IACtHR, *Gutiérrez Soler Case (Colombia)*, Order of March 11, 2005.

463 H. Faundez Ledesma, *El Sistema Interamericano de Protección de los Derechos Humanos*, San José, IIDH, 3rd ed., 2004, 556.

464 The Rules of Procedure of the Court of 2002 incorporated a provision by which the Court or its President, if the Court is not in session, may convoke the parties to a public hearing on provisional measures. For a complete analysis of the evolution of the Rules of the Court, see A. Cançado Trindade. "El nuevo Reglamento de la Corte Interamericana de Derechos Humanos (2000) y su proyección hacia el futuro: La emancipación del ser humano como sujeto del Derecho Internacional", in *El Futuro de la Corte Interamericana de Derechos Humanos*, A. Cançado Trindade and M.E. Ventura Robles (eds.), San José, Corte Interamericana de Derechos Humanos, UNHCR, 2003, 44–48.

465 Bustíos-Rojas Case (Peru), Cesti Hurtado Case (Peru), Carpio Nicolle Case (Guatemala), Chunimá Case (Guatemala), Peace Community of San José de Apartadó Case (Colombia), Miguel Agustín Pro Juárez Human Rights Center *et al.* Case (Mexico), Serech and Saquic Case (Guatemala), Vogt Case (Guatemala), Mapiripán Massacre Case (Colombia), María Leontina Millacura Llaipén *et al.* Case (Argentina) and Monagas Judicial Confinement Center ("La Pica") Case (Venezuela).

201. The eleven cases that followed this procedure were all under consideration by the Commission when the measures were requested, and in each of them it was argued that the presumed victims had been threatened and harassed. Precautionary measures had been adopted that had not produced the desired results in eight of them.[466]

202. Compared to Procedure 1, the President takes more time under this procedure to adopt the urgent measures – an average of 10.7 days.

203. Another difference is that here the President adopts the measures and convokes a public hearing, while in the other the President adopts the measures and requests the State and the Commission to present reports on the measures that have been adopted.

4.5. PROCEDURE 4: PROCEDURE WITH THE OBSERVATIONS OF THE PARTIES

Petition → Court requests observations → State presents observations → Commission presents observations → Court decides

204. Although the situations that are presented to the Court imply the need to adopt measures as rapidly as possible, here the Court takes a little more time since, prior to resolving the petition, it requests the State and the Commission to present their observations on the matter. There is an attempt to follow a kind of adversary proceedings before making a decision. When the Court receives the petition, it requests the State[467] and the Commission[468] to forward their views on the measures requested. The Court, taking into account the information received, then decides the request.[469]

---

466 Bustíos-Rojas Case (Peru), Cesti Hurtado Case (Peru), Carpio Nicolle Case (Guatemala), Peace Community of San José de Apartadó Case (Colombia), Serech and Saquic Case (Guatemala), Vogt Case (Guatemala), Mapiripán Massacre Case (Colombia) and María Leontina Millacura Llaipén *et al.* (Argentina).

467 On two occasions the State did not present the observations requested by the Court: "El Nacional" and "Así es la Noticia" Newspapers Case (Venezuela) and the Indigenous Sarayaku People Case (Ecuador).

468 When the representatives of the beneficiaries are the ones to request provisional measures. This occurred in the Acevedo Jaramillo *et al.* Case (Peru) and in the Mayagna (Sumo) Awas Tingni Community Case (Nicaragua).

469 Acevedo Jaramillo *et al.* Case (Peru), Raxcacó Reyes *et al.* Case (Guatemala), Mayagna (Sumo) Awas Tingni Community Case (Nicaragua), "El Nacional" and "Así es la Noticia" Newspapers Case (Venezuela), the Indigenous Sarayaku People Case (Ecuador), Guerrero Gallucci and Martínez Barrios Case (Venezuela) and Juan Humberto Sánchez Case (Honduras).

205. The Court has taken an average of 17 days to adopt measures under this procedure. This period is somewhat greater than the average, but it is understandable since the Court resolved the petitions only after seeing the observations of the parties.[470]

206. Measures were adopted in two cases in 2006,[471] four cases in 2004 and in one in 2002. Four were under consideration by the Commission and three were before the Court and three of the seven had been under precautionary measures.

4.6. OTHER PROCEDURES: RARELY USED PROCEDURES

207. In each of the following eight matters, the Court followed a different procedure, which is mostly not specifically commented upon since the procedure was used most of the times only once.

Procedure 5

Petition → President adopts urgent measures → State complies → Commission withdraws the request → Court lifts the measures of the President

208. The Court did not adopt provisional measures twice because the State, in complying with the urgent measures issued by the President of the Court, ended the situation of extreme gravity and urgency. In one case Argentina granted provisional custody of two minor children to a family and, in the other, Ecuador freed a person who had been imprisoned.[472] Since the situation of extreme gravity and urgency had disappeared, the Commission withdrew the request. The time that it took for the President to issue the measures was in one case 15 days and in the other 11 days.

---

470 In the Mayagna (Sumo) Awas Tingni Community Case (Nicaragua) the Court took 49 days; in the Acevedo Jaramillo *et al.* Case (Peru) it took nine days; in the Raxcacó Reyes *et al.* Case (Guatemala) it took 14 days; in the "El Nacional" and "Así es la Noticia" Newspapers Case (Venezuela) it took 11 days; and finally in the Indigenous Sarayaku People Case (Ecuador) the Court took 21 days.

471 The Court rejected to adopt provisional measures in the Juan Humberto Sánchez Case (Honduras).

472 Reggiardo Tolosa Case (Argentina) and the Suárez Rosero Case (Ecuador).

Procedure 6

Petition → President requests observations of State → Representatives present briefs[473] → Commission presents briefs[474] → State presents observations[475] → Court decides measures[476]

Procedure 7

Petition → President adopts measures → State presents report → Commission presents observations → Court convokes a public hearing → Court ratifies decision of the President[477]

Procedure 8

Petition → President requests observations of State[478] → President adopts measures → State presents report → Court ratifies Order of the President[479]

Procedure 9

Petition → President requests information of the Commission and State → Commission presents observations → State presents observations → Public hearing → Court requests more information → State informs → Commission presents observations → Secretariat reports that reports are contradictory → State presents brief → Commission presents observations → Court adopts measures[480]

Procedure 10

Petition → President requests information → Representatives present briefs → State presents briefs → Commission presents observations → President adopts measures → Court ratifies Order of the President[481]

---

473 On four occasions.

474 On two occasions.

475 *Ibid.*

476 Mendoza Prisons Case (Argentina), Serrano Cruz Sisters Case (El Salvador), Capital El Rodeo I & El Rodeo II Judicial Confinement Center Case (Venezuela) and the Miguel Castro-Castro Prison Case (Peru) The Court rejected to adopt provisional measures in the latest case.

477 Alvarez *et al.* Case (Colombia) and Persons imprisoned in the "Dr. Sebastião Martins Silveira" Penitentiary in Araraquara, São Paulo Case (Brazil).

478 Venezuela did not present any observations.

479 "Globovisión" Television Station Case (Venezuela).

480 "La Nación" Newspaper Case (Costa Rica).

481 Fermín Ramírez Case (Guatemala).

Procedure 11

Petition → President convokes public hearing → Commission presents brief → State presents observations → Public hearing → Court adopts measures[482]

Procedure 12

Petition → President requests observations → State presents observations → Commission presents observations → President adopts measures → Representatives inform → State informs → Representatives present observations → Commission presents observations → Court ratifies Order of the President[483]

Procedure 13

209. In one case the Court adopted provisional measures *ex officio*, after having heard the parties during the public hearing on the merits[484] and in another case, the President rejected the request and this decision was not sent to the Court.[485]

4.7. SUMMARY

210. To date the Inter-American Court has not established a specific procedure for processing requests for provisional measures. The Court has used thirteen different procedures to deal with the 80 petitions presented from 1987 to 2009. Although the Court does not have just one method to resolve the measures, an analysis of the jurisprudence shows that three of them have been employed most often: Procedures 1, 2 and 3, which have been used on 54 occasions (67.5%).

210. In many cases, it is the President of the Court who makes the initial decision. The President has ruled prior to the Court in a total of 41 matters (51.25%).[486] This is due to the fact that the Court is not in session when the petition is presented and the urgency of the situation requires the prompt adoption of measures. In any event, the Court, in accordance with Article 26(5)

482 Haitians and Dominicans of Haitian Origin in the Dominican Republic Case (Dominican Republic).
483 Plan de Sánchez Massacre Case (Guatemala).
484 Ivcher Bronstein Case (Peru).
485 Juarez Cruzzat *et al.* Case (Peru).
486 The Court ruled in 19 matters where the President had not adopted urgent measures. See Procedures 2, 4, 8, 9, 11 and 13.

of its Rules, has to ratify the decision of the President and in almost every case it has done so.[487]

211. With respect to the time from the presentation of the request until the Court or its President adopts the first order, the measures were adopted on the day that the request was presented in twelve cases, between one and five days in 32 cases, between six and ten days in 13 cases, between 11 and 15 days in nine cases and more than 16 days in nine cases. Thus, the response to a request for provisional measures is made before the sixth day in more than half of the cases.

212. The promptness in deciding reflects the urgent nature of the requests and the capacity of response of the inter-American system. The President of the Court plays a very important role here because, as has been mentioned, he must take the initial decision in a significant number of cases. If he did not have that function, the request would have to wait until the Court meets and there would be a risk of damage to the rights of presumed victims during that lapse.

213. In general, the procedures are not adversary. The Court or its President requested the State to present its observations before adopting the measures in 18 of the 80 cases, which means that in only 22.5% of the cases the position of the State was taken into account before the adoption of the initial order.[488] The usual procedure is that the President or the Court adopts the measures and then receives the observations of the State. On rare occasions, i.e. only three times (3,75%), a public hearing is convoked to receive the views of the parties before resolving the petition.[489]

214. The selection of the procedure used seems to respond more to chance than to an application of clear rules. It is impossible to ascertain the reasons why some cases follow one procedure and others another procedure in the inter-American system. We have seen that the decision does not depend on whether the case is pending before the Court or under consideration by the Commission. For example, a study of Procedure 1 shows that eight matters were pending before the Court and 14 under the consideration of the Commission; 16 were pending before the Commission and five were pending before the Court in Procedure 2; all were under consideration by the Commission in Procedure 3 and four matters

487 See Procedures 1, 3, 6, 7, 10 and 12. Bear in mind that in two cases the State, once it complied with the urgent measures, considered the situation of extreme gravity and urgency to be over. Consequently, the Court lifted the urgent measures that the President had adopted. See Procedure 5. In Juarez Cruzzat *et al.* Case (Peru) the Court did not made any pronunciation in relation with the decision taken by the President of the Court.

488 See Procedures 4 and 6–12.

489 See Procedures 9, 11 and 13.

were under consideration by the Commission and three were pending before the Court in Procedure 4.

Neither does the procedure used depend on whether the case has been under precautionary measures. Almost half of the 22 cases had precautionary procedures in Procedure 1; 13 of the 21 cases had precautionary measures in Procedure 2; eight of the eleven cases had precautionary measures in Procedure 3 and three of the eleven had precautionary measures in Procedure 4.

Neither is the choice of procedure determined by who the presumed victims are. For example, in 15 cases protection was requested for persons who were imprisoned. Almost every one of those cases followed a different procedure: four were dealt with under Procedure 1[490] and Procedure 2[491] respectively, three were dealt with under Procedure 6[492], two were dealt with under Procedure 3[493] and one was dealt with under Procedures 5[494] and 7[495] respectively. The same may be said with respect to the cases in which an attempt was made to protect persons on death row. There were a total of five cases, which followed three different procedures: the James, Briggs, Noel, Garcia and Bethel Case (Trinidad and Tobago), Boyce and Joseph Case (Barbados) and the Tyrone Dacosta Cadogan (Barbados) were dealt with under Procedure 1; the Raxcacó Reyes *et al.* Case (Guatemala) was dealt with under Procedure 4 and the Fermín Ramírez Case (Guatemala) was dealt with under Procedure 10.

Finally, it may be seen that the procedures do not follow a jurisprudential evolution. Thus, the petitions presented during the 1990s followed Procedures 1, 2, 3, 5 and 6 and those from 2000 to 2009 were resolved by using Procedures 1–4 and 6, 7 and 13.

215. Although the effective protection of rights is more important than the procedure followed, it is somewhat disquieting that the Court to date has not developed clear rules with respect to which procedure to follow. It is important that the Court indicate why it follows one or another procedure. This is relevant not only for the parties' right to procedural equality, in the sense of being treated

490 Peruvian Prisons Case (Peru), Gallardo Rodríguez Case (Mexico), Loayza Tamayo Case (Peru) and the Tyrone Dacosta Cadogan Case (Barbados).

491 Urso Branco Prison Case (Brazil), Penitentiary Center of the Central Occidental Region (Uribana Prison) Case (Venezuela), Children Deprived of Liberty in the "Complexo do Tatuapé" of FEBEM Case (Brazil) and the Yare I and Yare II Capital Region Center Case (Venezuela),.

492 Mendoza Prisons Case (Argentina), Capital El Rodeo I & El Rodeo II Judicial Confinement Center Case (Venezuela) and the Miguel Castro-Castro Prison Case (Peru).

493 Cesti Hurtado Case (Peru) and Monagas Judicial Confinement Center ("La Pica") Case (Venezuela).

494 Suárez Rosero Case (Ecuador).

495 Persons imprisoned in the "Dr. Sebastião Martins Silveira" Penitentiary in Araraquara, São Paulo Case (Brazil).

equally in the same situation, but also because the procedure followed appears to determine the time that the Court takes to adopt the measures. For example, if a comparison is made between the period to adopt measures under Procedure 2 and under Procedure 4, while the former took an average of only 2.9 days, the latter took 17 days to resolve the petition.

5. DECISION OF THE COURT

5.1. GENERAL REMARKS

216. The decision of the Court concerning a request to adopt provisional measures is manifested in an "Order of Provisional Measures." This decision, like the Court's judgments, is definitive and not subject to appeal[496] (see also *infra*, no. 224). The order contains an account of the facts and their legal consequences.

217. An order of provisional measures usually contains three parts. The first part is a description of the facts by the petitioners and, if applicable, an account of the procedural actions; for example, if there were public hearings or if observations were received from the State and the other parties. This part is followed by the "preambular part" that lays out the basis of the law and an analysis of the important points with respect to the rights guaranteed in the Convention. Finally there is an "enacting part" with the decision of the Court to adopt or not the provisional measures. In the event of adopting the measures, the Court indicates to the State that the measures must be implemented and requests that it be informed on their implementation. The Court also asks the petitioners and the Commission to present their observations to the reports of the State.

5.2. CONCURRING AND DISSENTING OPINIONS

218. When an order of provisional measures does not reflect in whole or in part the unanimous opinion of the judges, any of them may join to the order his dissenting or individual opinion. Concurring and dissenting opinions appear at the end of the order and are signed by the respective judges and the Secretary of the Court. In their concurring opinions, judges give additional reasons to support the Court's decision. To date, the judges have only added concurring opinions to the orders, which shows that the decisions on protective measures have been unanimous.

219. Concurring opinions generally appear when there is a change in the jurisprudence of the Court, when there is a situation that had not previously

496 Article 67 American Convention.

been dealt with, when the situation is extremely grave or simply when the judges wish to state their position on a particular issue.

For example, the James, Briggs, Noel, Garcia and Bethel Case (Trinidad and Tobago) presented the issue as to whether the Court maintained its jurisdiction to maintain provisional measures in a case that it knew would not be submitted to it, since the Commission had issued Articles 50 and 51 Reports. Although the Court in the order of provisional measures explained why it considered that it had jurisdiction to maintain the measures of protection, Judges García Ramírez, Cançado Trindade and de Roux Rengifo in their concurring opinions offered additional arguments on this point.

As already mentioned, concurring opinions have been written in cases on issues in which the Court has changed its jurisprudence. In the decision adopted by the Court in the Peace Community of San José de Apartadó Case (Colombia), that offered protection to a group of identifiable persons without naming them, several judges presented arguments that they felt justified the appropriateness of this type of protection.[497]

Table 22. Cases and Opinions

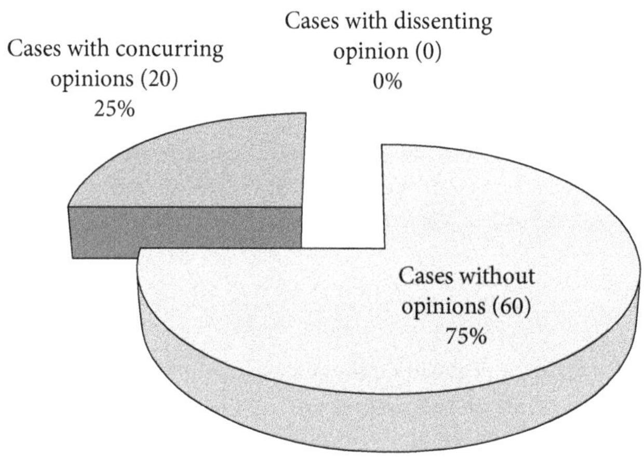

497 IACtHR, *Peace Community of San José de Apartadó Case (Colombia)*, Order of November 24, 2000, Concurring Opinions of Judges Abreu Burelli and García Ramírez. In the same case, Order of June 18, 2002, the Concurring Opinion of Judge Cançado Trindade. See also IACtHR, *Communities of the Jiguamiandó and of the Curbaradó Case (Colombia)*, Order of March 6, 2003, Concurring Opinions of Judges Abreu Burelli and García Ramírez; IACtHR, *Indigenous Kankuamo Community Case (Colombia)*, Order of July 5, 2004, Concurring Opinion of Judge García Ramírez; IACtHR, *"El Nacional" and "Así es la Noticia" Newspapers Case (Venezuela)*, Order of July 6, 2004, Concurring Opinion of Judge García Ramírez.

220. As is shown by Table 22, in 20 cases the judges have included a concurring opinion at least on one occasion. During the period studied, no dissenting opinions were issued.

Table 23. **Resolutions and Opinions**

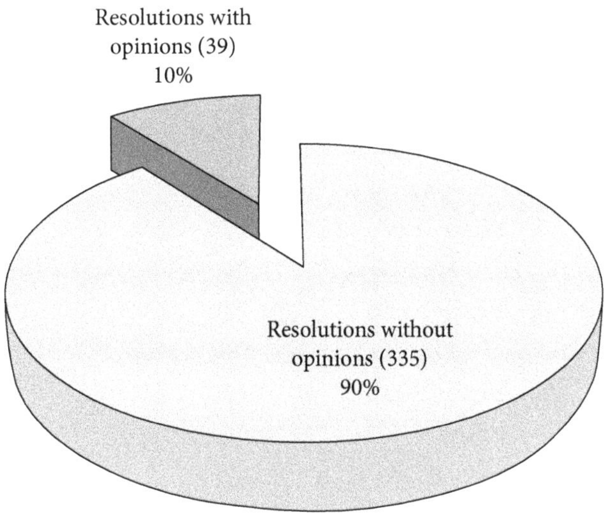

221. If one takes into account the number of resolutions instead of the number of cases, Table 23 shows that 374 resolutions were adopted, of which 39 were accompanied by concurring opinions. During the first decade of provisional measures (1987–1997), the Court adopted measures in 17 cases without any concurring opinions.[498] The majority of the opinions (11) were issued in 2005. In 2004 nine, in 2006 six and in 2008 one opinion were issued. In 2001, there were no concurring opinions were issued. The first concurring opinion appeared in the James, Briggs, Noel, Garcia and Bethel Case (Trinidad and Tobago) in 1998.[499]

498 There were 80 cases, but the number takes into account the 374 Orders. Thus, concurring opinions were presented in 20 matters and Judge Cançado Trindade presented 24 concurring opinions. This is possible because each case may have more than one order. For example, in the Peace Community of San José de Apartadó Case (Colombia), the Communities of the Jiguamiandó and of the Curbaradó Case (Colombia), the Indigenous Sarayaku People Case (Ecuador), the Eloisa Barrios *et al.* Case (Venezuela) and the Mendoza Prisons Case (Argentina), Judge Cançado Trindade presented, in each of these cases, two concurring opinions.

499 IACtHR, *James, Briggs, Noel, Garcia and Bethel Case (Trinidad and Tobago)*, Order of August 29, 1998, Concurring Opinion of Judge García Ramírez.

Table 24. Cases with concurring opinions

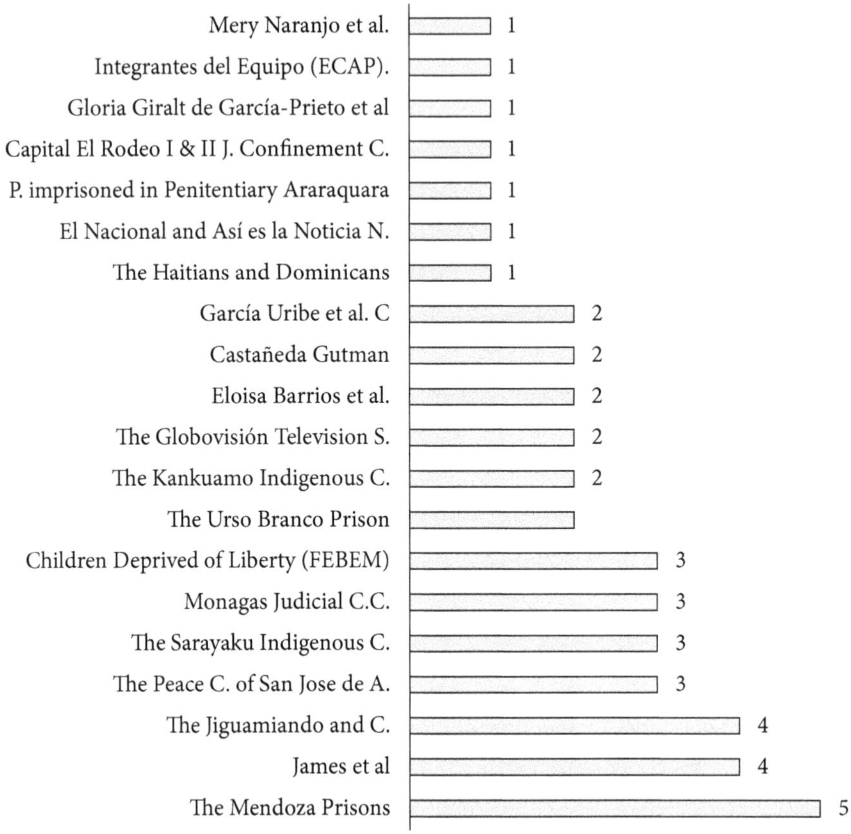

222. Table 24 shows the number of concurring opinions that were added to each case. To date, there have been 44 concurring opinions in twenty of the 80 cases.[500] The case with the most concurring opinions has been the Mendoza

[500] James, Briggs, Noel, Garcia and Bethel Case (Trinidad and Tobago), Peace Community of San José de Apartadó Case (Colombia), Haitians and Dominicans of Haitian Origin in the Dominican Republic Case (Dominican Republic), Urso Branco Prison Case (Brazil), Communities of the Jiguamiandó and of the Curbaradó Case (Colombia), Indigenous Kankuamo Community Case (Colombia), Indigenous Sarayaku People Case (Ecuador), "El Nacional" and "Así es la Noticia" Newspapers Case (Venezuela), "Globovisión" Television Station Case (Venezuela), Eloisa Barrios *et al.* Case (Venezuela), Mendoza Prisons Case (Argentina), Capital El Rodeo I & El Rodeo II Judicial Confinement Center Case (Venezuela), Monagas Judicial Confinement Center ("La Pica") Case (Venezuela), Persons imprisoned in the "Dr. Sebastião Martins Silveira" Penitentiary in Araraquara, São Paulo Case (Brazil), Children Deprived of Liberty in the "Complexo do Tatuapé" of FEBEM Case (Brazil), García Uribe *et al.* Case (Mexico), Gloria Giralt de García-Prieto *et al.* Case (El Salvador), Castañeda Gutman Case (Mexico), Integrantes del Equipo de Estudios Comunitarios y Acción Psicosocial (ECAP). Masacre Plan de Sánchez (Guatemala) and Mery Naranjo *et al.* Case (Colombia).

Prison Case (Argentina) with five, followed by the Peace Community of San José de Apartadó (Colombia) and the Communities of the Juguamiandó and of the Curbaradó (Colombia) Cases, each with four.

With regard to the case against Argentina, concurring opinions were added by the judges García Sayan, Cancado Trindade and García Ramírez. In those concurring opinions, the judges expressed their preoccupation for the situation of intra-prison violence in the Argentinean prisons and the necessity to keep the provisional measures in place until that situation would improve.

It is also interesting to see that on a number of occasions during the handling of a case, the judges express more than one concurring opinion and that from the second concurring opinion on, nothing new is being added to the first concurring opinion. In fact, one can confirm that it is almost a copy of what the judge concerned had held earlier on. Such a situation can for example be found in the case against Argentina regarding the concurring opinions of the judges Cancado Trindade and García Ramírez.

Table 25. Judges with concurring opinions

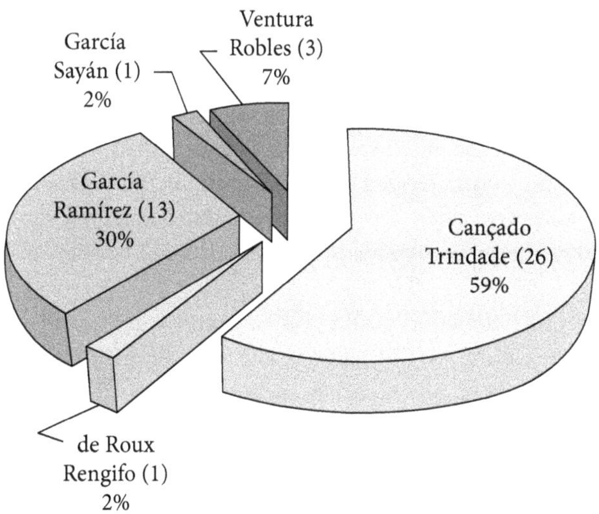

223. Sometimes judges use their opinions to state their views on the situation presented. Judge Cançado Trindade, in particular, drafts his opinions to reflect on the role of provisional measures in relation to the protection of human rights and on the need to strengthen the institution. He has also used them to write on the evolution of society in which wealth is concentrated in the hands of a few and on the increase in the number of people who are on the margins of society.[501] Judge Cançado Trindade has presented a concurring opinion on 26 occasions, thus being the judge with the most opinions. He is followed by Judge García Ramírez with 13,[502] Judge Ventura Robles with three and Judges de Roux Rengifo and García Sayán, each with one opinion.

5.3. IMPOSSIBILITY OF APPEALING THE DECISION OF THE COURT

224. Under Article 29(3) of the Rules of the Court, the judgments and orders of the Court are not subject to appeal. This implies that, with respect to provisional measures, once the decision is made to accept or reject a petition, nothing more can be done.

In any event, when the measure is rejected the petitioners may again present the request if new information is presented that allows a showing that the situation falls under Article 63(2) of the Convention.

In the Caballero Delgado and Santana Case (Colombia) when the Court decided to lift the measures of protection, the representatives of the victims requested that it review the decision because they contended that the measures should be maintained, given the dangerous situation of those who had been the beneficiaries of the measures. This petition was supported by the State, which was in agreement that the measures should be maintained while the situation of risk persisted. The Court decided that, although the petitioners had used the words review and reconsider, they were not truly challenging the decision but were asking that the protective measures be readopted because of supervening events.[503]

A request of interpretation would also be rejected since, under Article 59(1) of the Rules of the Court, it is only appropriate for judgments on the merits or on reparations. The Court on one occasion, in the *La Nación* Case, responded to an inquiry of a State regarding the enacting part of an Order of Provisional Measures. In this case a protective measure had ordered Costa Rica not to enforce the entry of the name of the beneficiary in the Judicial Registry of Delinquents until the organs of the inter-American system definitively resolved the case. It also ordered that the part of the domestic sentence that determined that a section of the judgment be published in the newspaper be suspended.

---

501 See IACtHR, Haitians and Dominicans of Haitian Origin in the Dominican Republic Case (Dominican Republic), Order of March 15, 2005, Concurring Opinion of Judge Cançado Trindade.

502 Judge García Ramírez wrote two opinions jointly with Judge Abreu Burelli.

503 IACtHR, *Caballero Delgado and Santana Case (Colombia)*, Order of April 16, 1997, Preambular Paragraph 1, Explanatory Statements 2 and 3.

Costa Rica asked whether the measures adopted involved the civil and criminal parts, or only the criminal part, of the sentence. The Court, responding to the inquiry of the State, held that the measures sought to achieve the effects indicated in the order, whether they be civil, criminal or any other type.[504]

5.4. ADOPTION OF PROVISIONAL MEASURES

225. Since the cases that are submitted to the Court require the prompt adoption of the measures, in general terms it is possible to affirm that the Court has been rather efficient in responding to the requests submitted to its consideration.

For example, 55% of the petitions were resolved within five days following their presentation, some of them were even resolved the same day that they were presented. Measures were adopted between the sixth and 15th day in 22 cases and the Court took more than 15 days in nine matters.

226. The time that the Court took in adopting protective measures depended in great part on the facts in each case. For example, in cases in which the presumed victim was condemned to death and it was alleged that he would be executed one or two days after the presentation of the petition, the Court reacted very rapidly since any delay in those circumstances might result in the loss of life of the person.[505] Although not every measure is decided on the day that it is requested, the decisions are generally made rapidly, which shows, on the one hand, the urgency of the matters and, on the other, the capacity of response of the inter-American system.

5.4.1. MEASURES ORDERED

227. Pursuant to Article 63(2) of the Convention, the Court has a broad margin of appreciation to choose the measures that it deems appropriate to remedy a situation of extreme gravity and urgency.[506] The Court determines, according to the circumstances of each case, the type of measure that is most appropriate,

---

504 IACtHR, *"La Nación" Newspaper Case (Costa Rica)*, Order of August 26, 2002, Explanatory Statement 3, Preambular Paragraph 9. Enacting Parts 1 and 2. See also H. Faundez Ledesma, *El Sistema Interamericano de Protección de los Derechos Humanos*, San José, IIDH, 3rd ed., 2004, 561–562.

505 See IACtHR, *James, Briggs, Noel, Garcia and Bethel Case (Trinidad and Tobago)*, Order of June 29, 1998. On the same matter see also, Orders of July 13, 1998 and July 24, 1998.

506 H. Faundez Ledesma, *El Sistema Interamericano de Protección de los Derechos Humanos*, San José, IIDH, 3rd ed., 2004, 571.

bearing in mind that the measures cannot prejudge the merits of the matter or convert them into a condemnation of the State before the judgment.

228. A study of the jurisprudence shows that the protective measures may be divided into two categories. A first group would be the orders that establish a general obligation of protection – those that do not determine the specific measures that the State must take to comply with its duty to protect – and a second group would be those that specify the actions that the State must take to protect the rights of the beneficiaries.

5.4.1.1. Generic Measures of Protection

229. In 32 of the 71 cases in which protective measures have been adopted, the Inter-American Court has pointed out in general terms that it is the duty of the State to protect the beneficiaries. The Court establishes the obligation to protect the rights of persons who are in a situation of extreme gravity and urgency, without specifying how the State must comply with such a requirement.

In the Reggiardo Tolosa Case (Argentina) the Court requested the State to adopt without delay all necessary measures to protect the psychological integrity of two minor children with the aim of avoiding irreparable damage. They had been born during the unlawful detention of their mother and had been registered as children of a former Federal policeman and his wife. Four years after these facts were proven, the children continued with their false parents. The Court held that this resulted in grave psychological damage and therefore requested that protective measures be adopted. The State complied with the order by means of a judicial decision that placed the children first with a substitute family and then the children were sent to live with their true relatives.

In the Miguel Agustín Pro Juárez Human Rights Center *et al.* Case (Mexico) the State complied with the order of the Court to protect the beneficiaries, by providing permanent security to the installations of the Center, furnishing the beneficiaries with 31 cellular phones, giving around-the-clock personal security to one of the beneficiaries, providing a vehicle for another and establishing a closed-circuit system in the office of another.[507]

230. Although the Court does not indicate to the State the precise actions that it must take, it has the advantage of specifying the result that it wishes: for example, to protect the right to life of the beneficiaries; that they might move freely within the national territory; that they be ensured that they might return

---

[507] IACtHR, *Miguel Agustín Pro Juárez Human Rights Center et al. Case (Mexico)*, Order of April 20, 2004, Explanatory Statement 3 (a)-(e).

to their place of residence, etc. The State, therefore, determines what measures are appropriate to comply with the general requirements of the Court.

231. In the event that the adopted measures prove to be inadequate, the Commission and the beneficiaries notify the Court and suggest the most effective options.[508] This possibility is quite positive because it places the parties in a position to oversee compliance.[509]

5.4.1.2. Specific Measures of Protection

232. The Inter-American Court has adopted specific measures of protection in 37 of the 71 cases. There is just as great a variety or forms of measures as there are requests that have been submitted because the measures should respond to the real circumstances in each State and to what is required for the effective protection of the presumed victims.[510]

233. Notwithstanding the range and diversity of the measures, for a better understanding they have been categorised according to certain themes. The first theme covers the measures related to judicial actions, the second theme covers those measures directed to provide security to the beneficiaries, the third theme covers the measures that must be complied with in prisons and the fourth and last theme covers those measures that seek to protect members of indigenous communities.

---

508 Bear in mind that the beneficiaries may only present observations as of January 1, 2004, when the new Rules came into effect. See Article 26(3).

509 J.M. Pasqualucci, "Medidas Provisionales en la Corte Interamericana de Derechos Humanos: Una Comparación con la Corte Internacional de Justicia y la Corte Europea de Derechos Humanos", *Revista del Instituto Interamericano de Derechos Humanos* 1994, no. 19, 91.

510 In the Peace Community of San José de Apartadó Case (Colombia), the Commission requested that the measures, to be effective and relevant, should be agreed to by the beneficiaries and the State. The Commission stated that there should be compatibility between the security measures offered and the nature of the Peace Community. For example, armed protection of its members could endanger the principles of collective neutrality and the humanitarian zone that were part of their experience and could generate a violent response from the armed actors in the region. IACtHR, *Peace Community of San José de Apartadó Case (Colombia)*, Order of the President of October 9, 2000, Explanatory Statement 3. In the Eloisa Barrios *et al.* Case (Venezuela), the Court specifically requested that the measures not be provided by the police force that, according to the beneficiaries, was implicated in the acts denounced. See IACtHR, *Eloisa Barrios et al. Case (Venezuela)*, Order of November 23, 2004, Enacting Part 3.

5.4.1.2.1. Measures related to Judicial Actions

234. Some measures are related to judicial actions, such as those where the Court asks the State to comply with arrest warrants for certain persons,[511] to investigate the truth of the possible link of beneficiaries to illegal groups,[512] to investigate the participation of members of the public forces in acts of violence[513] or to send a copy of the transcript of trials that are being held to shed light on the facts that gave rise to the provisional measures.[514] The Court has also requested that parts of sentences handed down by domestic judges be suspended.[515]

In the Colotenango Case (Guatemala), the Court requested that the State use all means at its disposal to comply with an arrest warrant for thirteen policemen accused as suspects for acts that occurred in Colotenango. In the Communities of the Jiguamiandó and of the Curbaradó Case (Colombia), the Court requested the State to investigate the alleged participation of members of the public forces in acts of violence and threats to the members of those Communities with the aim that the law be applied appropriately. The Court also stated that, taking into account the grave acts of violence by paramilitary groups and the increasing control of those groups in the region that moreover counted on the tolerance and indifference of the State, it was necessary that the State adopt measures to prohibit, prevent and punish the criminal activities of the paramilitary groups.[516]

The Court also pointed out that investigating, identifying and punishing those responsible for the acts that gave rise to the adoption of provisional measures is an essential element of protection. States, therefore, have the duty to investigate and inform the Court on the real and effective measures that they are implementing to punish those responsible for the acts.[517]

---

511 Colotenango Case (Guatemala) and Serech and Saquic Case (Guatemala).

512 Clemente Teherán Case (Colombia). In this case the Court requested that the State investigate the veracity of the possible link between persons protected by the measures and illegal groups, especially the three men in the armed paramilitary groups.

513 Communities of the Jiguamiandó and of the Curbaradó Case (Colombia).

514 Giraldo Cardona Case (Colombia). In this case the Court requested the State to inform it on the progress of the investigations of the persons responsible for the acts that lead to the adoption of the measures and, if possible, that it forward copies of the corresponding procedures.

515 "El Nacional" and "Así es la Noticia" Newspapers Case (Venezuela).

516 IACtHR, Communities of the Jiguamiandó and of the Curbaradó Case (Colombia), Order of March 15, 2005, Preambular Paragraph 18.

517 IACtHR, *Colotenango Case (Guatemala)*, Order of February 2, 2000, Preambular Paragraph 9; IACtHR, *Peace Community of San José de Apartadó Case (Colombia)*, Order of March 15, 2005, Preambular Paragraph 9 and IACtHR, *Gutiérrez Soler Case (Colombia)*, Order of March 11, 2005, Enacting Part 2.

This duty to investigate must be undertaken seriously and not as a mere formality intended *a priori* to fail.[518] The Court has held that the duty to investigate is related to the obligation that each State has to combat impunity by all available legal means because impunity contributes to a chronic repetition of human rights violations and a total defenselessness of the victims and their family members.[519] The investigation and punishment of those responsible, in accordance with due process of law, is the best way to combat impunity and to ensure the security, safety and life of the beneficiaries of the measures (*infra*, no. 286).[520]

The duty to investigate has been ordered in 51 of the 71 cases (71.8%).[521] When no mention is made of this duty it is due to the particular conditions of the case. An example would be cases where the Court had some doubt whether the domestic sentences were in conformity with the American Convention because it was not yet clear whether certain rights continued to be violated since the case was still under consideration. In those cases it is difficult for the Court to require a State to investigate and punish those responsible because it is not

---

518 IACtHR, *Colotenango Case (Guatemala)*, Order of September 5, 2001, Preambular Paragraphs 7–8. In this case, the Court held that it was impossible to know the true situation of the beneficiaries of the measures, since the information provided by the State was very limited. This created a situation of uncertainty for the Court, incompatible with the preventive and protective nature of the provisional measures, which required that the State send more complete information in order to determine whether it was complying with the measures. IACtHR, *Carpio Nicolle Case (Guatemala)*, Order of July 8, 2004, Preambular Paragraph 13 and IACtHR, *Miguel Agustín Pro Juárez Human Rights Center et al. Case (Mexico)*, Order of April 30, 2001, Preambular Paragraph 11.

519 IACtHR, *Bámaca Velásquez Case (Guatemala)*, Order of November 20, 2003, Preambular Paragraph 18; IACtHR, *Luis Uzcátegui Case (Venezuela)*, Order of February 20, 2003, Enacting Part 12; IACtHR, *Luisiana Ríos et al. Case (Venezuela)*, Order of February 20, 2003, Preambular Paragraph 9 and IACtHR, *Liliana Ortega et al. Case (Venezuela)*, Order of February 21, 2003, Enacting Part 9.

520 IACtHR, *Miguel Agustín Pro Juárez Human Rights Center et al. Case (Mexico)*, Order of April 30,2001, Preambular Paragraph 11 and IACtHR, *Carpio Nicolle Case (Guatemala)*, Order of September 5, 2001, Preambular Paragraph 7. In this case the Court stated that closing the investigation was an omission of the State's obligation to investigate, since it was not taking the positive and necessary measures to clarify the acts that had motivated the adoption of provisional measures.

521 See for example, Forensic Anthropology Foundation Case (Guatemala), Integrantes del Equipo de Estudios Comunitarios y Acción Psicosocial (ECAP). Masacre Plan de Sánchez Case (Guatemala), Mapiripán Massacre (Colombia), Persons imprisoned in the "Dr. Sebastião Martins Silveira" Penitentiary in Araraquara, São Paulo Case (Brazil), Persons imprisoned in the "Dr. Sebastião Martins Silveira" Penitentiary in Araraquara, São Paulo Case (Brazil), Children Deprived of Liberty in the "Complexo do Tatuapé" of FEBEM Case (Brazil), Yare I and Yare II Capital Region Center Case (Venezuela), Monagas Judicial Confinement Center ("La Pica") Case (Venezuela), Gloria Giralt de García-Prieto *et al.* Case (El Salvador), Guerrero-Gallucci y Martínez-Barrios Case (Venezuela), Mery Naranjo *et al.* Case (Colombia), Millacura Llaipén *et al.* Case (Argentina), Pilar Noriega *et al.* Case (Mexico) and Hinostroza *et al.* Case (Peru).

clear if anyone is responsible.[522] This situation occurred in every case in which measures were adopted to protect persons who were sentenced to death.[523]

On the other hand, in the *La Nación* Case (Costa Rica), the Court ordered the State to suspend the order to publish in *La Nación* newspaper a part of the sentence in which a beneficiary of the measures was found guilty.[524]

5.4.1.2.2. Measures of Personal Protection

235. In some orders the Court has asked the State to adopt measures that are directly related to the security of the beneficiaries. The Court has, for example, required that civilian authorities be placed in certain places so that they can receive the urgent communications that beneficiaries might present.[525] It has also requested a State to establish mechanisms of control and vigilance on certain illegal groups[526] and that conditions of security be ensured in specific places of the country.[527] In other cases, it has required a State to grant identity documents to the beneficiaries to prevent their expulsion or deportation or that the State refrain from expelling or deporting certain persons.[528] The Court has also asked that protection be offered around the perimeter of certain places[529] and that the

522 "La Nación" Newspaper Case or Herrera Ulloa Case (Costa Rica).

523 James, Briggs, Noel, Garcia and Bethel Case (Trinidad and Tobago), Boyce and Joseph Case (Barbados), Raxcacó Reyes *et al.* Case (Guatemala), Fermín Ramírez Case (Guatemala) and Tyrone Dacosta Cadogan Case (Barbados).

524 IACtHR, *"La Nación" Newspaper Case (Costa Rica)*, Order of August 26, 2002, Explanatory Statement 3, Preambular Paragraphs 8 and 9, Enacting Parts 1 and 2.

525 Bustíos-Rojas Case (Peru).

526 Colotenango Case (Guatemala) and Carpio Nicolle Case (Guatemala). In this case, the Court requested that the military authorities in charge of the Defense Committees be instructed to refrain from any activity that would endanger the lives or personal integrity of the beneficiaries of the measures. In the Colotenango Case (Guatemala), the Court requested that the civil patrols assigned to Colotenango be watched and controlled.

527 Peace Community of San José de Apartadó Case (Colombia). The Court requested Colombia to guarantee the necessary security measures between San José de Apartadó and Apartadó and in the place know as "Tierra Amarilla" to ensure that public transportation would not be subject to further violent attacks and that the members of the Community would be able to receive and transport their products, supplies and food efficiently and continuously.

528 Haitians and Dominicans of Haitian Origin in the Dominican Republic Case (Dominican Republic). The Court requested the State to provide six people with identification cards indicating that they were beneficiaries of provisional measures of protection ordered by the Court so that they would not be deported or expelled.

529 In the cases of Plan de Sánchez Massacre (Guatemala) and Eloisa Barrios (Venezuela), the Court required the State to adopt the necessary measures to safeguard and protect the life, integrity and personal freedom of the beneficiaries, one of the measures being the peripheral protection of their homes. IACtHR, *Eloisa Barrios et al. Case (Venezuela)*, Order of June 29, 2005, Enacting Part 5. In the "El Nacional" and "Así es la Noticia" Newspapers Case (Venezuela), the "Globovisión" Television Station Case (Venezuela) and the Luisiana Ríos *et al.* Case (Venezuela), the Court requested that peripheral protection be given to the media offices. See IACtHR, *"El Nacional" and "Así es la Noticia" Newspapers Case (Venezuela)*, Order

protection not be given by the police who, according to the beneficiaries, were involved in the acts denounced.[530]

The most requested requirement for States (eleven cases or 15.5%)[531] has been that they adopt all necessary measures of security so that the beneficiaries might continue to live in their habitual places of residence and that those who were forced to go to other zones might return to their homes with a guarantee that they would not be persecuted or threatened by government agents or by private individuals. The Court has also ordered that, by common agreement with the beneficiaries or their representatives, the State establish a permanent mechanism of supervision and security.[532]

236. Measures have also been directed at providing protection to persons who will testify before the Court or have already done so. On these occasions, the Court asks that they be provided the necessary security so that they might leave and enter their territory.[533] On other occasions, the Court has asked a State that, when the persons return to the country or go to a specific part of it, they be given the necessary protection. In the Alvarez *et al.* Case (Colombia), the Court ordered that as soon as Mr. Alvarez returned to Colombia, the State must adopt all necessary measures to protect his life and in the Clemente Teherán Case (Colombia) the Court stated that in the event that the beneficiary decided to

---

of July 6, 2004, Enacting Part 2; IACtHR, *"Globovisión" Television Station Case (Venezuela)*, Order of August 3, 2004, Enacting Part 2 and IACtHR, *Luisiana Ríos et al. Case (Venezuela)*, Order of July 27, 2004, Explanatory Statement 3.

530 Eloisa Barrios *et al.* Case (Venezuela), Guerrero-Gallucci y Martínez-Barrios Case (Venezuela), and Mery Naranjo *et al.* Case (Colombia).

531 Colotenango Case (Guatemala), Blake Case (Guatemala), Giraldo Cardona Case (Colombia), Loayza Tamayo Case (Peru), Bámaca Velásquez Case (Guatemala), Peace Community of San José de Apartadó Case (Colombia), Communities of the Jiguamiandó and of the Curbaradó Case (Colombia), Indigenous Kankuamo Community Case (Colombia) and Eloisa Barrios *et al.* Case (Venezuela). In the Loayza Tamayo Case, the Court requested that Peru adopt the necessary measures for Mrs. Loayza Tamayo to return to her country. In the Eloisa Barrios *et al.* Case (Venezuela), the Court required the State to implement effectively the necessary conditions for the members of the Barrios family, who had been forced to move, to return to their homes. See IACtHR, *Eloisa Barrios et al. Case (Venezuela)*, Order of June 29, 2005, Enacting Part 7.

532 Peace Community of San José de Apartadó Case (Colombia), Haitians and Dominicans of Haitian Origin in the Dominican Republic Case (Dominican Republic), Luisiana Ríos *et al.* Case (Venezuela), Liliana Ortega *et al.* Case (Venezuela) and Communities of the Jiguamiandó and of the Curbaradó Case (Colombia). In this last one, it was specified that among the mechanisms for protection and supervision, early alerts and other permanent communication services of immediate reaction could be used. See also Guerrero-Gallucci and Martínez-Barrios Case (Venezuela), Mery Naranjo *et al.* Case (Colombia) and Gloria Giralt de García-Prieto *et al.* Case (El Salvador).

533 Carpio Nicolle Case (Guatemala), Haitians and Dominicans of Haitian Origin in the Dominican Republic Case (Dominican Republic) and the Gallardo Rodríguez Case (Mexico).

return to her indigenous community, the State had to adopt whatever measures were necessary to protect her.[534]

237. When beneficiaries have been harassed or threatened as a result of their professional work, the Court has ordered that appropriate measures be adopted to ensure that those persons might exercise their profession without undue pressure.[535] This has or example be the case in the Colotenango Case (Guatemala) with respect to a lawyer, in the Carpio Nicolle Case (Guatemala) with respect to a Special Prosecutor who was in charge of the investigations and in the Digna Ochoa y Plácido *et al.* Case (Mexico) to protect those working for a non-governmental organisation.[536]

5.4.1.2.3. Measures in Prisons

238. Although the measures to be implemented inside prisons could be included in other sections, they are dealt with separately because they include diverse protective measures. In some cases, the States are requested not to implement domestic judicial sentences, in others they are ordered to conform prison conditions to the minimum international standards and in still others the States are requested to give adequate medical attention to inmates when their health is in danger.

The Court in three cases requested that all necessary measures be taken to preserve the life and physical integrity of certain persons on death row. The measures in those cases order the States to suspend the implementation of the sentences until the cases are resolved in the inter-American system.[537]

On the other hand, in the cases in which it is stated that the prison conditions were deplorable, the Court held that the States must adopt all necessary measures to bring the detention centers up to the standards required internationally.[538] In the Loayza Tamayo Case (Peru), the Court asked the State to change the

---

534 Alvarez *et al.* Case (Colombia) and Clemente Teherán Case (Colombia).

535 Colotenango Case (Guatemala), Carpio Nicolle Case (Guatemala) and Digna Ochoa y Plácido *et al.* Case (Mexico).

536 Colotenango Case (Guatemala); Carpio Nicolle Case (Guatemala); Digna Ochoa y Plácido *et al.* Case (Mexico).

537 This requisite is found in every case in which the beneficiaries have been sentenced to death. See, James, Briggs, Noel, Garcia and Bethel Case (Trinidad and Tobago), Boyce and Joseph Case (Barbados) and Fermín Ramírez Case (Guatemala).

538 Loayza Tamayo Case (Peru) and the Urso Branco Prison Case (Brazil). In the first case, the Court requested the State to modify the situation in which the beneficiary was held, particularly the conditions of *incommunicado* detention, in order to conform to Article 5 of the Convention. In the case against Brazil, the Court requested that the prison conditions be adjusted to the international norms of human rights protection applicable in this matter. See also Penitentiary Center of the Central Occidental Region (Uribana Prison) Case (Venezuela) and Children Deprived of Liberty in the "Complexo do Tatuapé" of FEBEM Case (Brazil).

beneficiary's situation, especially with regard to the conditions of isolation to which she was subjected, in order to conform her situation to Article 5 of the Convention. In the Urso Branco Prison Case (Brazil), the Court requested that the prison conditions be adjusted to meet the applicable international norms of human rights protection and that the inmates' weapons be confiscated.[539]

Finally, the Court has required States to provide the necessary medical treatment to inmates when it has been shown that their health is at risk. In the Loayza Tamayo Case (Peru), the Court requested that the State provide medical treatment, both physical and psychiatric, to the beneficiary as soon as possible and in the Cesti Hurtado Case (Peru) the State was ordered to permit the beneficiary to receive the medical treatment of his choosing.[540]

5.4.1.2.4. Measures in the Territory of the Indigenous Communities

239. Although in principle a threat to property does not justify the adoption of provisional measures because it does not appear to involve irreparable damage to persons, it is interesting to note that the Court has ordered States to adopt measures to protect the property of indigenous communities on three occasions.

The principal reason that the Court has protected these rights in the case of indigenous communities is because of the great importance that it has attributed to their traditions in applying the Convention. The Court has held that it is necessary to protect the property of the indigenous communities because the damage that might be produced to this right would imply placing at risk the very survival of the community.[541]

In the Mayagna (Sumo) Awas Tingni Community Case (Nicaragua), the Court asked that the State adopt without delay whatever measures that were necessary to protect the use and enjoyment of the lands and resources belonging to the indigenous community, specifically those measures that would avoid immediate and irreparable damage resulting from the activities of third persons who had invaded the territory of the Community or who had exploited the natural resources found there. In the opinion of the Court, it must be understood that the land is the fundamental basis of the culture, spiritual life, integrity and

---

539 The Urso Branco Prison Case (Brazil), Penitentiary Center of the Central Occidental Region (Uribana Prison) Case (Venezuela), Persons imprisoned in the "Dr. Sebastião Martins Silveira" Penitentiary in Araraquara, São Paulo Case (Brazil), Children Deprived of Liberty in the "Complexo do Tatuapé" of FEBEM Case (Brazil), Yare I and Yare II Capital Region Center Case (Venezuela) and Monagas Judicial Confinement Center ("La Pica") Case (Venezuela).

540 Loayza Tamayo Case (Peru) and Cesti Hurtado Case (Peru).

541 Mayagna (Sumo) Awas Tingni Community Case (Nicaragua) and the Indigenous Sarayaku People Case (Ecuador).

economic survival of indigenous communities. The relationship of the indigenous population to the land, therefore, cannot be seen as a question of possession and production but as a material and spiritual element that must be enjoyed fully to preserve their cultural legacy and transmit it to future generations. Under these conditions, damage to the land would affect the very survival of the collectivity and, thus, provisional measures may be adopted to protect the property of the indigenous peoples.[542]

In the Indigenous Sarayaku People Case (Ecuador), the State was requested to withdraw the explosive material placed in the territory where the Community was located and to ensure that the indigenous people could carry out their activities and make use of the natural resources existing in their territory.[543] In this case, like that of the Mayagna (Sumo) Awas Tingni Community Case (Nicaragua), the Court considered it important to take into account the traditions of indigenous populations. Here, however, the thinking of the Court was concentrated more on the fact that for indigenous peoples the land does not have an individual but a collective nature. The Court held that this close relationship that the indigenous peoples collectively have with the land must be taken into account in applying the Convention, because that element makes the land the basis of their subsistence, their way of life and their traditions.

In the Communities of the Juguamiandó and of the Curbaradó Case (Colombia), although the Court does not explicitly mention the necessity to protect the indigenous territory, among its considerations, it established that the State must adopt measures to cease the cultivation of African palm trees in the territory of the Communities. It was important to control the cultivation since that was the principle reason for the displacement of members of the Communities and it made the return of the families to the Communities impossible. In addition, the cultivation prevented the members from exploiting the natural resources necessary for their subsistence, which put at risk the lives and physical integrity of the beneficiaries of the provisional measures.[544]

---

542 IACtHR, *Mayagna (Sumo) Awas Tingni Community Case (Nicaragua)*, Order of September 6, 2002, Preambular Paragraphs 5, 6 and 7. The Court refers to the following jurisprudence: IACtHR, *Bámaca Velásquez Case (Guatemala)*, Reparations, Judgment of February 22, 2002, para. 81; IACtHR, *Mayagna (Sumo) Awas Tingni Community Case (Nicaragua)*, Judgment of 31 August 2001, para. 149 and IACtHR, *Aloeboetoe et al. Case (Suriname)*, Reparations, Judgment of September 10, 1993, para. 62.

543 IACtHR, *Indigenous Sarayaku People Case (Ecuador)*, Order of June 17, 2005, Preambular Paragraph 9.

544 IACtHR, *Communities of the Jiguamiandó and of the Curbaradó Case (Colombia)*, Order of March 15, 2005, Preambular Paragraphs 7 and 22.

5.5. DUTY TO INFORM

5.5.1. STATES

240. States, in addition to having to comply with all the terms of the orders, must periodically inform the Inter-American Court on the measures that they have adopted.[545] This duty to inform means more than the formal presentation of a document to the Court, but is an obligation that requires for its effective compliance the formal presentation of a document within the established period with specific, current, true and detailed information on the relevant issues.[546]

241. The jurisprudence shows that from 1987 to 1993 the Court requested only one report and in some cases it did not set a date for its presentation. In the Velásquez Rodríguez, Fairén Garbi and Solís Corrales and Godínez Cruz Cases (Honduras), the Court gave the State two weeks to inform on the measures adopted. In the Bustíos-Rojas (Peru) and the Reggiardo Tolosa (Argentina) Cases, the Court gave the States 30 days and in the Chunimá Case (Guatemala), although the first order made no reference to the duty to inform, the following order, while not setting a date for presentation, did order the State to indicate promptly the measures of protection the Court had adopted. The same occurred in the Caballero Delgado and Santana Case (Colombia).[547]

242. Beginning with the Colotenango Case (Guatemala), the Court in 1994 began to require two reports. In its initial order, the Court generally ordered that a first report be presented in a rather short term and then periodic reports to be sent less often. There is no general rule that would allow a conclusion as to what period the Court will set, since it depends somewhat on the circumstances of the case and on the discretion that the Court has. For example, when it has protected

---

545 IACtHR, *Marta Colomina and Liliana Velásquez Case (Venezuela)*, Order of December 2, 2002, Preambular Paragraph 15. See D. Padilla, "Provisional Measures Under the American Convention on Human Rights", in *Liber Amicorum Héctor Fix-Zamudio*, San José, Inter-American Court of Human Rights, 1998, 1192–1193.

546 IACtHR, *Marta Colomina and Liliana Velásquez Case (Venezuela)*, Order of December 2, 2002, Preambular Paragraph 14; IACtHR, *Liliana Ortega et al. Case (Venezuela)*, Order of December 2, 2003, Preambular Paragraph 12; IACtHR, *Luis Uzcátegui Case (Venezuela)*, Order of December 2, 2003, Preambular Paragraph 12 and Order of May 4, 2004, Preambular Paragraph 15; IACtHR, *Communities of the Jiguamiandó and of the Curbaradó Case (Colombia)*, Orders of November 17, 2004 and March 15, 2005, Preambular Paragraph 16; IACtHR, *Marta Colomina and Liliana Velásquez Case (Venezuela)*, Order of July 4, 2006, Preambular Paragraph 9; IACtHR, *Mapiripán Massacre Case (Colombia)*, Order of May 2, 2008, Preambular Paragraphs 10–13. See also H. Faundez Ledesma, *El Sistema Interamericano de Protección de los Derechos Humanos*, San José, IIDH, 3rd ed., 2004, 570.

547 The Court in its first orders did not establish a deadline to report, but began to do so in 1997. See IACtHR, *Caballero Delgado and Santana Case (Colombia)*, Order of April 16, 1997.

persons on death row whose execution is imminent, the Court has requested the first report the same day that it adopted the measures.[548] It is not possible, however, to ascertain why the Court in other cases establishes one or another period. This is the panorama: sometimes the first report must be presented in three days,[549] other times in four[550] and five days,[551] in seven days,[552] in eight days,[553] in nine days,[554] in ten days,[555] in 15 days,[556], in 16 days, in 17 days,[557] in 18 days,[558] in 19 days,[559] in 26 days,[560] in one month,[561] in 36 days[562] and on other occasions in two months.[563] Three days have been the most repeated

548 IACtHR, *James, Briggs, Noel, Garcia and Bethel Case (Trinidad and Tobago)*, Orders of June 29, 1998, July 13, 1998 and July 24, 1998. In the latter, the report was requested two days later and in the Tyrone Dacosta Cadogan Case (Barbados) the report was requested 15 days later.

549 The 19 Tradesmen Case (Colombia) and Yare I and Yare II Capital Region Center Case (Venezuela). In the last one the State had 3 days to send the first report.

550 Mapiripán Massacre Case (Colombia).

551 Paniagua Morales *et al.* and Vásquez *et al.* Case (Guatemala).

552 Eloisa Barrios *et al.* Case (Venezuela), Mendoza Prisons Case (Argentina), and Guerrero-Gallucci and Martínez-Barrios Case (Venezuela).

553 Helen Mack Chang *et al.* Case (Venezuela).

554 Fermín Ramírez Case (Guatemala) and Millacura Llaipén *et al.* Case (Argentina).

555 The Miguel Agustín Pro Juárez Human Rights Center *et al.* Case (Mexico), Plan de Sánchez Massacre Case (Guatemala), Indigenous Kankuamo Community Case (Colombia), Indigenous Sarayaku People Case (Ecuador), "El Nacional" and "Así es la Noticia" Newspapers Case (Venezuela), "Globovisión" Television Station Case (Venezuela), Carlos Nieto *et al.* Case (Venezuela), Boyce and Joseph Case (Barbados), Gutiérrez Soler Case (Colombia), Forensic Anthropology Foundation Case (Guatemala), Persons imprisoned in the "Dr. Sebastião Martins Silveira" Penitentiary in Araraquara, São Paulo Case (Brazil), Mery Naranjo *et al.* Case (Colombia), Monagas Judicial Confinement Center ("La Pica") Case (Venezuela), Masacre Plan de Sánchez Case (Guatemala) Penitentiary Center of the Central Occidental Region (Uribana Prison) Case (Venezuela), Adrian Meléndez Quijano *et al.* Case (El Salvador) and Mapiripán Massacre (Colombia).

556 Giraldo Cardona Case (Colombia), Alvarez *et al.* Case (Colombia), Clemente Teherán Case (Colombia), Digna Ochoa y Plácido *et al.* Case (Mexico), Peace Community of San José de Apartadó Case (Colombia), Ivcher Bronstein Case (Peru), Gallardo Rodríguez Case (Mexico), Urso Branco Prison Case (Brazil), Communities of the Jiguamiandó and of the Curbaradó Case (Colombia), Lysias Fleury Case (Haiti), Gómez Paquiyauri Brothers Case (Peru), Raxcacó Reyes *et al.* Case (Guatemala), Adrian Meléndez Quijano *et al.* (El Salvador), Penitentiary Center of the Central Occidental Region (Uribana Prison) Case (Venezuela), Gloria Giralt de García-Prieto *et al.* Case (El Salvador), Tyrone Dacosta Cadogan Case (Barbados) and Hinostroza *et al.* Case (Peru).

557 Bámaca Velásquez Case (Guatemala).

558 Constitutional Court Case (Peru).

559 Blake Case (Guatemala).

560 Cesti Hurtado Case (Peru).

561 Carpio Nicolle Case (Guatemala), Alemán Lacayo Case (Nicaragua), Vogt Case (Guatemala), Serech and Saquic Case (Guatemala), Suárez Rosero Case (Ecuador) and Capital El Rodeo I & El Rodeo II Judicial Confinement Center Case (Venezuela).

562 "La Nación" Newspaper Case or Herrera-Ulloa Case (Costa Rica).

563 Colotenango Case (Guatemala), Loayza Tamayo Case (Peru), Luisiana Ríos *et al.* Case (Venezuela), Liliana Ortega *et al.* Case (Venezuela), Luis Uzcátegui Case (Venezuela),

periods, ten days on 18 occasions, 15 days on 16 occasions, and two months in seven cases.

A different and lengthier term is set for periodic reports, which begins to run from the delivery of the first report. It is important to note that the Court has been more regular in setting the period for the presentation of these reports. The Court ordered in 53 cases (74.6%) that the periodic reports should be sent no later than two months. This period has been repeated since 2001.[564] In other cases, one month was given,[565] in others six months,[566] and in others 90 days.[567] Depending on how the measures are implemented and on developments in the situation of the beneficiaries, the Court has sometimes changed the dates for the presentation of the reports because the parties have asked that the period be modified since the measures were being implemented and the danger had not returned. In the Blake Case (Guatemala), the Court first indicated a period of

---

Mayagna (Sumo) Awas Tingni Community Case (Nicaragua) and the Marta Colomina and Liliana Velásquez Case (Venezuela).

564 Caballero Delgado and Santana Case (Colombia), Carpio Nicolle Case (Guatemala), Vogt Case (Guatemala), Serech and Saquic Case (Guatemala), Loayza Tamayo Case (Peru), Alvarez *et al.* Case (Colombia), Bámaca Velásquez Case (Guatemala), Paniagua Morales *et al.* and Vásquez *et al.* Case (Guatemala), Clemente Teherán Case (Colombia), Digna Ochoa y Plácido *et al.* Case (Mexico), Peace Community of San José de Apartadó Case (Colombia), Haitians and Dominicans of Haitian Origin in the Dominican Republic Case (Dominican Republic), Ivcher Bronstein Case (Peru), Gallardo Rodríguez Case (Mexico), Miguel Agustín Pro Juárez Human Rights Center *et al.* Case (Mexico), Helen Mack Chang *et al.* Case (Guatemala), Urso Branco Prison Case (Brazil), Luisiana Ríos *et al.* Case (Venezuela), Liliana Ortega *et al.* Case (Venezuela), Luis Uzcátegui Case (Venezuela), Mayagna (Sumo) Awas Tingni Community Case (Nicaragua), Lysias Fleury Case (Haiti), Marta Colomina and Liliana Velásquez Case (Venezuela), Gómez Paquiyauri Brothers Case (Peru), Plan de Sánchez Massacre Case (Guatemala), 19 Tradesmen Case (Colombia), Indigenous Kankuamo Community Case (Colombia), Indigenous Sarayaku People Case (Ecuador), "El Nacional" and "Así es la Noticia" Newspapers Case (Venezuela), "Globovisión" Television Station" Case (Venezuela), Boyce and Joseph Case (Barbados), Gutiérrez Soler Case (Colombia), Eloisa Barrios *et al.* Case (Venezuela), Mendoza Prisons Case (Argentina), Raxcacó Reyes *et al.* Case (Guatemala), Carlos Nieto *et al.* Case (Venezuela), Fermín Ramírez Case (Guatemala), Adrián Meléndez Quijano Case (ElSalvador), Integrantes del Equipo de Estudios Comunitarios y Acción Psicosocial (ECAP). Masacre Plan de Sánchez Case (Guatemala), Forensic Anthropology Foundation Case (Guatemala), Mapiripán Massacre (Colombia), Persons imprisoned in the "Dr. Sebastião Martins Silveira" Penitentiary in Araraquara, São Paulo Case (Brazil), Children Deprived of Liberty in the "Complexo do Tatuapé" of FEBEM Case (Brazil), Yare I and Yare II Capital Region Center Case (Venezuela), Monagas Judicial Confinement Center ("La Pica") Case (Venezuela), Gloria Giralt de García-Prieto *et al.* Case (El Salvador), Guerrero-Gallucci y Martínez-Barrios Case (Venezuela), Mery Naranjo *et al.* Case (Colombia), Hinostroza *et al.* Case (Peru), Pilar Noriega *et al.* Case (Mexico), Capital El Rodeo I & El Rodeo II Judicial Confinement Center Case (Venezuela) and Kawas Fernández Case (Honduras).

565 Giraldo Cardona Case (Colombia), "El Nacional" and "Así es la Noticia" Newspapers Case (Venezuela) and Communities of the Jiguamiandó and of the Curbaradó Case (Colombia).

566 Constitutional Court Case (Peru).

567 Colotenango Case (Guatemala). In this case, 45 days were given and the deadlines were then changed to every two months.

three months and then changed it to six months. This also occurred in the Giraldo Cardona Case (Colombia), when the Court initially ordered that the periodic reports be presented every 30 days and then changed it to every two months.[568]

243. On other occasions the Court, in addition to setting the periods for the presentation of the two types of reports, has asked the parties to inform it immediately of any significant developments regarding the situation.[569] Thus, when something unforeseen happens, the parties do not have to wait until the date of the report's presentation but must immediately notify the Court of any relevant fact concerning the situation of the beneficiaries. Knowing the true situation of the beneficiaries is of vital importance, because only with knowledge of the situation can the Court order, if necessary, additional measures of protection.

244. The Court has paid special attention to compliance with this obligation, either by noting that the State has presented, periodically and promptly, the reports or by indicating that the State has not complied with its duty to inform periodically on the measures that it has taken to safeguard effectively the rights of the beneficiaries. In some matters involving Venezuela,[570] Haiti,[571] Colombia[572] and Guatemala,[573] the Court declared that those States did not present the reports nor adopt the protective measures. In those circumstances, the Court normally expresses the view that since the State has not effectively implemented the measures and has not fully complied with the obligation to inform, should such situation persist the Court will apply Articles 65 of the Convention and 30 of its Statute and include the Order of Provisional Measures in its Annual Report so that the matter is brought before the OAS General Assembly.[574]

568 Blake Case (Guatemala) and Giraldo Cardona Case (Colombia).

569 IACtHR, *James, Briggs, Noel, Garcia and Bethel Case (Trinidad and Tobago)*, Order of August 29, 1998, Enacting Part 4. In the same matter see, Order of May 25, 1999, Enacting Part 2(d).

570 Marta Colomina and Liliana Velásquez Case (Venezuela), Luisiana Ríos *et al.* Case (Venezuela) and the Luis Uzcátegui Case (Venezuela).

571 Lysias Fleury Case (Haiti).

572 See IACtHR, *Mapiripán Massacre Case (Colombia)*, Order of May 2, 2008, Preambular Paragraph 10–13.

573 IACtHR, *Bámaca Velásquez Case (Guatemala)*, Order of November 20, 2003, Preambular Paragraph 20.

574 Article 26(8) Rules of Procedure of the Inter-American Court of Human Rights. See also IACtHR, *Marta Colomina and Liliana Velásquez Case (Venezuela)*, Order of December 2, 2003, Preambular Paragraphs 16 and 17 and IACtHR, *James, Briggs, Noel, Garcia and Bethel Case (Trinidad and Tobago)*, Order of December 2, 2003, Preambular Paragraphs 16 and 17.

5.5.2. BENEFICIARIES OR THEIR REPRESENTATIVES

245. Another mechanism through which the Court supervises the compliance and effectiveness of the measures are the written observations presented by the beneficiaries or their representatives. The Court requests the beneficiaries or those who represent them to present their observations to the reports of the State, as well as their views on the implementation of the protective measures.

246. These observations are very useful because they allow the Court to receive the views of the beneficiaries on how the measures are being carried out and they enable it to verify to what point the information furnished by the State is true.

In the Carpio Nicolle Case (Guatemala), the representatives of the beneficiaries informed the Court that the State had not conducted an investigation on the acts that had given rise to the measures and that the information that the State had furnished on the perimeter vigilance was not exact, since the beneficiary had never been informed of this type of protection nor did she know that it was being offered. They also reported that the State had withdrawn the police protection that a beneficiary had had at work without notification and without any justification.[575]

In the Mendoza Prisons Case (Argentina), the beneficiaries in their written observations informed the Court of what was taking place inside the prisons and suggested how the mechanisms of protection should be implemented. In their briefs, the beneficiaries reported that some prisoners had been injured and others killed. They warned that there had been no progress in the construction nor with respect to sanitation and that the pavilions lacked artificial light. The beneficiaries reiterated that the situation was grave in some pavilions where the inmates were locked up for 23 hours a day and had to share their cells with three or four persons.[576]

247. As in the case of State reports or the Commission's observations, the beneficiaries must present two types of briefs at different periods. The first time they were required was in the Helen Mack Chang *et al.* Case (Guatemala)[577] in

---

575 IACtHR, *Carpio Nicolle Case (Guatemala)*, Order of July 8, 2004, Explanatory Statement 24.

576 IACtHR, *Mendoza Prisons Case (Argentina)*, Order of June 18, 2005, Explanatory Statements 8, 9, 10, 12, 14 and 18.

577 IACtHR, *Helen Mack Chang et al. Case (Guatemala)*, Order of August 26, 2002, Enacting Part 5.

August 2002 and in the Bámaca Velásquez Case (Guatemala)[578] in December 2002. This would mean that from 1988 to 2002 the Court only received information coming directly from the Commission and the States, but not from the beneficiaries.[579]

The Court has requested that the beneficiaries present their observations in 46 of the 71 cases (64.8%). With respect to the first report, the Court has set periods that range from five days to four weeks, as may be seen from the following: in 16 cases, five days;[580] in nine cases, one week;[581] in 14 cases, four weeks,[582] in four cases, 15 days,[583] in two cases ten days[584] and in one case four days.[585]

---

578 IACtHR, *Bámaca Velásquez Case (Guatemala)*, Order of the President of December 20, 2002, Enacting Part 5.

579 This is because the beneficiaries did not have the competence to participate directly in the inter-American system. On this matter, see section regarding Competence "Measures Requested by the Victims or by their Representatives" (*supra*, nos. 32-40).

580 Carpio Nicolle Case (Guatemala), Plan de Sánchez Massacre Case (Guatemala), Indigenous Kankuamo Community Case (Colombia), Indigenous Sarayaku People Case (Ecuador), "El Nacional" and "Así es la Noticia" Newspapers Case (Venezuela), "Globovisión" Television Station Case (Venezuela), Carlos Nieto *et al.* Case (Venezuela), Boyce and Joseph Case (Barbados), Gutiérrez Soler Case (Colombia), Forensic Anthropology Foundation Case (Guatemala), Guerrero-Gallucci y Martínez-Barrios Case (Venezuela), Mapiripán Massacre Case (Colombia), Mery Naranjo *et al.* Case (Colombia), Monagas Judicial Confinement Center ("La Pica") Case (Venezuela), Hinostroza *et al.* Case (Peru) and Tyrone Dacosta Cadogan Case (Barbados).

581 Bámaca Velásquez Case (Guatemala), Helen Mack Chang *et al.* Case (Guatemala), Gómez Paquiyauri Brothers Case (Peru), Eloisa Barrios *et al.* Case (Venezuela), Mendoza Prisons Case (Argentina), Raxcacó Reyes *et al.* Case (Guatemala), Fermín Ramírez Case (Guatemala), Adrian Meléndez Quijano *et al.* Case (El Salvador) and the Penitentiary Center of *the* Central Occidental Region (Uribana Prison) Case (Venezuela).

582 Blake Case (Guatemala), Peace Community of San José de Apartadó Case (Colombia), Miguel Agustín Pro Juárez Human Rights Center *et al.* Case (Mexico), Mayagna (Sumo) Awas Tingni Community Case (Nicaragua), the Communities of the Jiguamiandó and of the Curbaradó Case (Colombia), Children Deprived of Liberty in the "Complexo do Tatuapé" of FEBEM Case (Brazil), Yare I and Yare II Capital Region Center Case (Venezuela), Capital El Rodeo I & El Rodeo II Judicial Confinement Center Case (Venezuela), Kawas Fernández Case (Honduras), Adrian Meléndez Quijano *et al.* Case (El Salvador), Penitentiary Center of the Central Occidental Region (Uribana Prison) Case (Venezuela), Forensic Anthropology Foundation Case (Guatemala), Mapiripán Massacre Case (Colombia) and Persons imprisoned in the "Dr. Sebastião Martins Silveira" Penitentiary in Araraquara, São Paulo Case (Brazil).

583 Luisiana Ríos *et al.* Case (Venezuela), Liliana Ortega *et al.* Case (Venezuela), Luis Uzcátegui Case (Venezuela) and the Marta Colomina and Liliana Velásquez Case (Venezuela).

584 Persons imprisoned in the "Dr. Sebastião Martins Silveira" Penitentiary in Araraquara, São Paulo Case (Brazil) and the Gloria Giralt de García-Prieto *et al.* Case (El Salvador).

585 Millacura Llaipén *et al.* Case (Argentina).

The Court has granted the following periods for the periodic observations: in a large number of cases (30), four weeks;[586] on seven occasions, one month;[587] once a period of ten days[588] and another time, two months.[589] The period given to the representatives of the beneficiaries to present their observations to the States' reports begins to run from the date of reception.

5.5.3. INTER-AMERICAN COMMISSION

248. The Court forwards the States' reports to the Commission so that it, within a pre-established period, might send its observations on the information furnished by the government and on the manner in which it considers that the State is implementing the provisional measures.[590] These written observations are a supervisory mechanism that allows the Court to follow up on the compliance of the measures that it has ordered. As in the case of the States' reports, the Court requires two types of reports: a first report to be furnished within a short period of time and then periodic observations that are presented in a more ample period than the first report.

In the first case where provisional measures were adopted, the Court did not request observations nor did it do so in the Reggiardo Tolosa Case (Argentina).[591]

---

586 Blake Case (Guatemala), Bámaca Velásquez Case (Guatemala), Helen Mack Chang *et al.* Case (Guatemala), Luisiana Ríos *et al.* Case (Venezuela), Liliana Ortega *et al.* Case (Venezuela), Luis Uzcátegui Case (Venezuela), Mayagna (Sumo) Awas Tingni Community Case (Nicaragua), Communities of the Jiguamiandó and of the Curbaradó Case (Colombia), Marta Colomina and Liliana Velásquez Case (Venezuela), Gómez Paquiyauri Brothers Case (Peru), 19 Tradesmen Case (Colombia), Mendoza Prisons Case (Argentina), Raxcacó Reyes *et al.* Case (Guatemala), Boyce and Joseph Case (Barbados), Fermín Ramírez Case (Guatemala), Gutiérrez Soler Case (Colombia), Miguel Agustín Pro Juárez Human Rights Center *et al.* Case (Mexico), Children Deprived of Liberty in the "Complexo do Tatuapé" of FEBEM Case (Brazil), Yare I and Yare II Capital Region Center Case (Venezuela), Capital El Rodeo I & El Rodeo II Judicial Confinement Center Case (Venezuela), Kawas Fernández Case (Honduras), Gloria Giralt de García-Prieto *et al.* Case (El Salvador), Millacura Llaipén *et al.* Case (Argentina), Pilar Noriega *et al.* Case (Mexico), Hinostroza *et al.* Case (Peru), Guerrero-Gallucci y Martínez-Barrios Case (Venezuela), Integrantes del Equipo de Estudios Comunitarios y Acción Psicosocial (ECAP). Masacre Plan de Sánchez Case (Guatemala), Mery Naranjo *et al.* Case (Colombia), Monagas Judicial Confinement Center ("La Pica") Case (Venezuela) and the Tyrone Dacosta Cadogan Case (Barbados).

587 Carpio Nicolle Case (Guatemala), Plan de Sánchez Massacre Case (Guatemala), Indigenous Kankuamo Community Case (Colombia), Indigenous Sarayaku People Case (Ecuador), "Globovisión" Television Station Case (Venezuela), Eloisa Barrios *et al.* Case (Venezuela) and the Carlos Nieto *et al.* Case (Venezuela).

588 Peace Community of San José de Apartadó Case (Colombia).

589 "El Nacional" and "Así es la Noticia" Newspapers Case (Venezuela).

590 Rules of Procedure of the Court, Article 26(6). See also D. Padilla, "Provisional Measures Under the American Convention on Human Rights", in *Liber Amicorum Héctor Fix-Zamudio*, San José, Inter-American Court of Human Rights, 1998, 1193.

591 Velásquez Rodríguez, Fairén Garbi and Solis Corrales and Godínez Cruz Cases (Honduras).

In other cases, while requesting the Commission to keep it informed, it did not indicate that the Commission should send reports nor did it set a period for them.[592] In the Caballero Delgado and Santana Case (Colombia),[593] the Blake Case (Guatemala) and the Haitians and Dominicans of Haitian Origin in the Dominican Republic Case (Dominican Republic), the Court did not ask for observations in the first order but did so at a later date.[594]

In 1994 the Court began the custom, with some exceptions, of requesting the two different reports.[595] The first period that the Court set for the observations was three months for the first report and 30 days for the following reports. In the majority of cases the Court has requested the first observations within seven days[596] and within 15 days.[597] On fewer occasions, the Court has granted a period of five days,[598] one week,[599] ten days,[600] one month,[601] six weeks[602] and two months.[603]

592 Bustíos-Rojas Case (Peru) and the Chunimá Case (Guatemala).

593 The Court did not request written submissions until after 1997.

594 Blake Case (Guatemala); Haitians and Dominicans of Haitian Origin in the Dominican Republic Case (Dominican Republic).

595 With the Colotenango Case (Guatemala).

596 Plan de Sánchez Massacre Case (Guatemala), 19 Tradesmen Case (Colombia), Indigenous Kankuamo Community Case (Colombia), Indigenous Sarayaku People Case (Ecuador), "El Nacional" and "Así es la Noticia" Newspapers Case (Venezuela), "Globovisión" Television Station Case (Venezuela), Carlos Nieto *et al.* Case (Venezuela), Boyce and Joseph Case (Barbados), Gutiérrez Soler Case (Colombia), Forensic Anthropology Foundation Case (Guatemala), Monagas Judicial Confinement Center ("La Pica") Case (Venezuela), Guerrero-Gallucci y Martínez-Barrios Case (Venezuela), Integrantes del Equipo de Estudios Comunitarios y Acción Psicosocial (ECAP). Masacre Plan de Sánchez Case (Guatemala), Mery Naranjo *et al.* Case (Colombia), Millacura Llaipén *et al.* Case. (Argentina), Hinostroza *et al.* Case (Peru) and the Tyrone Dacosta Cadogan Case (Barbados).

597 Alemán Lacayo Case (Nicaragua), Vogt Case (Guatemala), Serech and Saquic Case (Guatemala), Giraldo Cardona Case (Colombia), Paniagua Morales *et al.* and Vásquez *et al.* Case (Guatemala), James, Briggs, Noel, Garcia and Bethel Case (Trinidad and Tobago), Peace Community of San José de Apartadó Case (Colombia), Urso Branco Prison Case (Brazil), Communities of the Jiguamiandó and of the Curbaradó Case (Colombia), Lysias Fleury Case (Haiti), Gómez Paquiyauri Brothers Case (Peru), Raxcacó Reyes *et al.* Case (Guatemala), Fermín Ramírez Case (Guatemala) and the Gloria Giralt de García-Prieto *et al.* Case (El Salvador).

598 Adrian Meléndez Quijano *et al.* Case (El Salvador).

599 Helen Mack Chang *et al.* Case (Guatemala), Luisiana Ríos *et al.* Case (Venezuela) and the Marta Colomina and Liliana Velásquez Case (Venezuela).

600 Gallardo Rodríguez Case (Mexico), Miguel Agustín Pro Juárez Human Rights Center *et al.* Case (Mexico), Eloisa Barrios *et al.* Case (Venezuela), Mendoza Prisons Case (Argentina), and the Penitentiary Center of the Central Occidental Region (Uribana Prison) Case (Venezuela).

601 Loayza Tamayo Case (Peru), Alvarez *et al.* Case (Colombia), Bámaca Velásquez Case (Guatemala), Clemente Teherán Case (Colombia) and the Constitutional Court Case (Peru).

602 Digna Ochoa y Plácido *et al.* Case (Mexico), Ivcher Bronstein Case (Peru), "La Nación" Newspaper or Herrera-Ulloa Case (Costa Rica), Mayagna (Sumo) Awas Tingni Community Case (Nicaragua), Children Deprived of Liberty in the "Complexo do Tatuapé" of FEBEM Case (Brazil), Yare I and Yare II Capital Region Center Case (Venezuela), Capital El Rodeo I & El Rodeo II Judicial Confinement Center Case (Venezuela) and the Kawas Fernández Case (Honduras).

603 Cesti Hurtado Case (Peru).

A comparison of the first reports shows that the periods set for the presentation of the written observations have been more uniform. In the majority of cases (52), the Court has given a period of six weeks,[604] in seven cases one month[605] and in one case two months.[606] With respect to the years in which the measures were adopted, beginning in 2002 the Court repeatedly asked for the observations every two months.[607] In previous years, there was no rule to follow, sometimes it granted a period of one month, other times two months and in others six months. In some cases, the Court changed the dates, as in the Giraldo Cardona Case (Colombia) where it first granted 15 days, then one month and finally six weeks.[608] The period for the presentation of the observations to a

604 Carpio Nicolle Case (Guatemala), Blake Case (Guatemala), Cesti Hurtado Case (Peru), Bámaca Velásquez Case (Guatemala), Paniagua Morales *et al.* and Vásquez *et al.* Case (Guatemala), Clemente Teherán Case (Colombia), James, Briggs, Noel, Garcia and Bethel Case (Trinidad and Tobago), Digna Ochoa y Plácido *et al.* Case (Mexico), Peace Community of San José de Apartadó Case (Colombia), Haitians and Dominicans of Haitian Origin in the Dominican Republic Case (Dominican Republic), Constitutional Court Case (Peru), Gallardo Rodríguez Case (Mexico), Miguel Agustín Pro Juárez Human Rights Center *et al.* Case (Mexico), Helen Mack Chang *et al.* Case (Guatemala), Luisiana Ríos *et al.* Case (Venezuela), Liliana Ortega *et al.* Case (Venezuela), Luis Uzcátegui Case (Venezuela), Mayagna (Sumo) Awas Tingni Community Case (Nicaragua), Communities of the Jiguamiandó and of the Curbaradó Case (Colombia), Lysias Fleury Case (Haiti), Marta Colomina and Liliana Velásquez Case (Venezuela), Gómez Paquiyauri Brothers Case (Peru), Plan de Sánchez Massacre Case (Guatemala), 19 Tradesmen Case (Colombia), Indigenous Kankuamo Community Case (Colombia), Indigenous Sarayaku People Case (Ecuador), "El Nacional" and "Así es la Noticia" Newspapers Case (Venezuela), "Globovisión" Television Station Case (Venezuela), Eloisa Barrios *et al.* Case (Venezuela), Mendoza Prisons Case (Argentina), Raxcacó Reyes *et al.* Case (Guatemala), Carlos Nieto *et al.* Case (Venezuela), Boyce and Joseph Case (Barbados), Fermín Ramírez Case (Guatemala), Gutiérrez Soler Case (Colombia), Penitentiary Center of the Central Occidental Region (Uribana Prison) Case (Venezuela), Forensic Anthropology Foundation Case (Guatemala), Adrian Meléndez Quijano *et al.* Case (El Salvador), Monagas Judicial Confinement Center ("La Pica") Case (Venezuela), Mapiripán Massacre Case (Colombia), Persons imprisoned in the "Dr. Sebastião Martins Silveira" Penitentiary in Araraquara, São Paulo Case (Brazil), Children Deprived of Liberty in the "Complexo do Tatuapé" of FEBEM Case (Brazil), Yare I and Yare II Capital Region Center Case (Venezuela), Capital El Rodeo I & El Rodeo II Judicial Confinement Center Case (Venezuela), Gloria Giralt de García-Prieto *et al.* Case (El Salvador), Guerrero-Gallucci y Martínez-Barrios Case (Venezuela), Integrantes del Equipo de Estudios Comunitarios y Acción Psicosocial (ECAP) (Guatemala), Kawas Fernández Case (Honduras), Mery Naranjo *et al.* Case (Colombia), Pilar Noriega *et al.* Case (Mexico), Hinostroza *et al.* Case (Peru) and the Tyrone Dacosta Cadogan Case (Barbados).

605 Colotenango Case (Guatemala), Caballero Delgado and Santana Case (Colombia), Vogt Case (Guatemala), Serech and Saquic Case (Guatemala), Loayza Tamayo Case (Peru), "La Nación" Newspaper Case or Herrera-Ulloa Case (Costa Rica) and the Millacura Llaipén *et al.* Case. (Argentina).

606 The Urso Branco Prison Case (Brazil).

607 With the exception of the Urso Branco Prison Case (Brazil), where it requested them in two months.

608 Giraldo Cardona Case (Colombia).

State's reports and the observations of the representatives run from the date of the reception of the State's report.

249. The Court usually requests the report of the State and then forwards it to the Commission for its observations. The written observations permit the Commission to furnish the Court with its views on the compliance of the protective measures and on the reports presented by the State and the representatives of the beneficiaries. The Commission has on occasion informed that the State has not complied with the measures. In the James, Briggs, Noel, Garcia and Bethel Case (Trinidad and Tobago), the Commission informed the Court that the same day during which it had been submitting its written remarks, the State had just executed a person who was under the protective measures.[609]

250. On other occasions, the Commission has stated that the information sent by the State is not correct. The Commission in its written observations in one case informed that, contrary to what Guatemala had stated, the petitioners had informed it that the investigation on the threats and intimidations against the victims had been closed. The Commission, therefore, requested the Court to require the State to inform on the investigation and the specific progress that had been made with respect to the denounced threats.[610]

251. On still other occasions, the Commission has provided new information that shows that the situation of extreme gravity and urgency persists. In the Carpio Nicolle Case (Guatemala) the Commission stated that, while the provisional measures were in force, a beneficiary had been subjected to a series of harassments and was threatened by telephone by different persons. Some of the callers said that she was going to die. This information allowed the Court to presume that the situation of insecurity of the persons protected by the measures continued.[611]

---

609 IACtHR, James, Briggs, Noel, Garcia and Bethel Case (Trinidad and Tobago), Order of August 16, 2000, Explanatory Statement 12.

610 IACtHR, *Carpio Nicolle Case (Guatemala)*, Order of September 19, 1997, Explanatory Statement 8.

611 IACtHR, *Carpio Nicolle Case (Guatemala)*, Order of September 30, 1999, Explanatory Statement 4 and 5, Enacting Part 1.

6. DURATION OF THE MEASURES

252. As their name indicates, provisional measures are not indefinite and, therefore, should not continue any longer than the circumstances that gave rise to them.[612] Once the measures are adopted they may be maintained, broadened, lifted and also reinstated. The measures are broadened when it is necessary to extend the protection to other persons who are in a situation similar to that of the beneficiaries. The measures may be lifted when the circumstances no longer exist that gave rise to them or when they have achieved the purpose for which they were adopted. Finally, the measures may be reinstated. This implies that the provisional measures that were lifted are readopted because the situation of danger returned. Each of the aspects mentioned will now be analysed.

6.1. MAINTAINING THE MEASURES

253. Provisional measures are exceptional in nature and are ordered because of the need to protect and, once ordered, may only be maintained if the basic requirements of extreme gravity and urgency continue.[613]

254. The Court sometimes sets a period at the end of which it reviews the situation and determines whether the measures should be maintained. That period may vary from case to case. The Court has at times set a period of four

612 H. Faundez Ledesma, *El Sistema Interamericano de Protección de los Derechos Humanos*, San José, IIDH, 3rd ed., 2004, 578.

613 IACtHR, *Colotenango Case (Guatemala)*, Order of September 5, 2001, Preambular Paragraph 15; IACtHR, *Miguel Agustín Pro Juárez Human Rights Center et al. Case (Mexico)*, Order of April 20, 2004, Preambular Paragraph 9 and IACtHR, *Liliana Ortega et al. Case (Venezuela)*, Order of March 1, 2005, Preambular Paragraph 11; IACtHR, *Mapiripán Massacre Case (Colombia)*, Order of May 3, 2008, Preambular Paragraph 7; IACtHR, *Persons imprisoned in the "Dr. Sebastião Martins Silveira" Penitentiary in Araraquara, São Paulo Case (Brazil)*, Order of November 25, 2008, Preambular Paragraph 17. See also A. Cançado Trindade, "The Evolution of Provisional Measures of Protection under the Case Law of the Inter-American Court of Human Rights (1987–2002)", *Hum. Rts. L.J.* 2003, 168.

months, in others six months[614] and in others it has set a specific date.[615] On other occasions, the Court has not established a period, but simply stated that the measures would be in force as long as the dangerous situation continues. In any event, whether the Court sets a period or whether it simply conditions the length of the measures to the existence of the situation of danger, the Court asks the State for periodic reports on the measures it has taken and the Commission and the representatives of the beneficiaries for their observations on those reports. These documents allow the Court to evaluate the situation and decide whether maintaining the measures of protection is justified.

255. Although in principle the measures ordered by the Court are by definition temporary,[616] in practice some measures have lasted for years. This is due to the fact that the cases that are submitted to the Court are so grave that, in spite of the adoption of certain measures by the State, the situation of extreme gravity does not disappear.[617] It is not possible, therefore, to determine *a priori* how long the measures will remain in force. In practice, depending on how each situation develops, the measures have been maintained in some cases for periods of less than a year and in others for more than eleven years.

In the event that a State shows that it has made every effort to comply with the measures that have been ordered, but cannot prove that, in spite of its efforts, the situation of extreme gravity no longer persists, the Court has been inclined to maintain the measures because it deems that the result – avoiding irreparable damage to the rights of the beneficiaries – is what should be taken into account. In the Alvarez *et al.* (Colombia) and the Colotenango (Guatemala) Cases, the Court held that the measures should be maintained even though the States had shown a great willingness to comply with them.[618]

---

614 IACtHR, *Colotenango Case (Guatemala)*, Order of the President of December 1, 1994, Enacting Part 1; IACtHR, *Alvarez et al. Case (Colombia)*; I/A Court H.R., Order of November 11, 1997, Enacting Part 2; IACtHR, *Carlos Nieto Palma et al Case (Venezuela)*, Order of August 5, 2008, Enacting Part 1; IACtHR, *Luis Uzcátegui Case (Venezuela)*, Order of January 27, 2009, Enacting Part 1.

615 IACtHR, *Colotenango Case (Guatemala)*, Order of May 18, 1995, Preambular Paragraph 5. The Court, in this Order, extended the measures until February 1, 1996; IACtHR, *Carpio Nicolle Case (Guatemala)*, Order of February 1, 1996, Enacting Part 1. The Court, in this Order, extended the measures until September 20, 1996; IACtHR, *Alvarez et al. Case (Colombia)*, Order of June 19, 1998, Enacting Part 2. In this case, the Court extended the measures until September 6, 1998.

616 A. Cançado Trindade, *Medidas Provisionales. Prólogo del Presidente de la Corte Interamericana de Derechos Humanos al Tomo III de la Serie E.*, 2001, para. 31.

617 J.M. Pasqualucci, *The Practice and Procedure of the Inter-American Court of Human Rights*, Cambridge, Cambridge University Press, 2003, 313.

618 IACtHR, *Alvarez et al. Case (Colombia)*, Order of June 19, 1998, Preambular Paragraphs 2 and 5; IACtHR, *Alvarez et al. Case (Colombia)*, Order of February 8, 2008, Preambular Paragraphs 20 and 31.

On the other hand, provisional measures have been maintained even though the parties have reached a friendly settlement. In the Colotenango Case (Guatemala) and the Mendoza Prisons Case (Argentina), the Court held that, despite a friendly settlement that was reached to the satisfaction of the parties, it was necessary to extend the measures since it had information that showed that the beneficiaries continued to be threatened.[619]

In addition, there is no incompatibility in the coexistence of protective measures and a judgment on the merits. The jurisprudence shows that in 15 cases protective measures were maintained even though they were in force when the judgment on the merits was delivered.[620] In four cases provisional measures were even adopted for the first time after a judgment on the merits of the matter was handed down.[621]

With the same argument on the need to maintain the measures to protect persons provided that the circumstances that gave rise to them continue, the Court has ordered that they be maintained for long periods of time.[622] The Court, therefore, rejected the petition of Guatemala to lift provisional measures that had been in force for 19 months. The State argued that, due to their temporary nature, it was necessary to lift the measures so as not to distort their inherent character. The Court, however, held that the measures should be maintained until it was certain that irreparable damage would not occur to the lives and physical integrity of the protected persons.[623]

6.2. BROADENING THE MEASURES

265. Once the Court has adopted protective measures, any party may ask as many times as it wishes that they be broadened. This request may be the result of

---

619 IACtHR, *Colotenango Case (Guatemala)*, Order of April 16, 1997, Explanatory Statement 1. In this case provisional measures were lifted on July 7, 2007; IACtHR, *Mendoza Prisons Case (Argentina)*, Order of October 17, 2008, Explanatory Statement 12 and Preambular Paragraph 5.

620 Caballero Delgado and Santana Case (Colombia), Carpio Nicolle Case (Guatemala), Helen Mack Chang *et al.* Case (Guatemala), Bámaca Velásquez Case (Guatemala), Gómez Paquiyauri Brothers Case (Peru), James, Briggs, Noel, Garcia and Bethel Case (Trinidad and Tobago), Boyce and Joseph Case (Barbados), Blake Case (Guatemala), Paniagua Morales *et al.* and Vásquez *et al.* Case (Guatemala), Ivcher Bronstein Case (Peru), Cesti Hurtado Case (Peru), Loayza Tamayo Case (Peru), Constitutional Court Case (Peru), Velásquez Rodríguez Case (Honduras), Mapiripán Massacre Case (Colombia) and the Gutiérrez Soler Case (Colombia).

621 The 19 Tradesmen Case (Colombia), Mayagna (Sumo) Awas Tingni Communiy Case (Nicaragua), Mapiripán Massacre Case (Colombia) and Integrantes del Equipo de Estudios Comunitarios y Acción Psicosocial (ECAP) (Guatemala).

622 IACtHR, *Álvarez et al. Case (Colombia)*, Order of July 19, 1998, Preambular Paragraphs 2 and 5.

623 IACtHR, *Álvarez et al. Case (Colombia)*, Order of February 1, 1996, Enacting Part 4. See also H. Faundez Ledesma, *El Sistema Interamericano de Protección de los Derechos Humanos*, San José, IIDH, 3rd ed., 2004, 579.

a change of circumstances or the occurrence of new events that imply that the original situation has worsened, creating the risk of damage to the rights of other persons.[624] The measures initially adopted by the Court are, therefore, extended to other persons who are in a situation of danger.

266. As can be seen in Table 26 underneath, in 23 cases the measures were broadened,[625] This corresponds to a bit more than one third of the cases.

Table 26. Provisional Measures Broaden

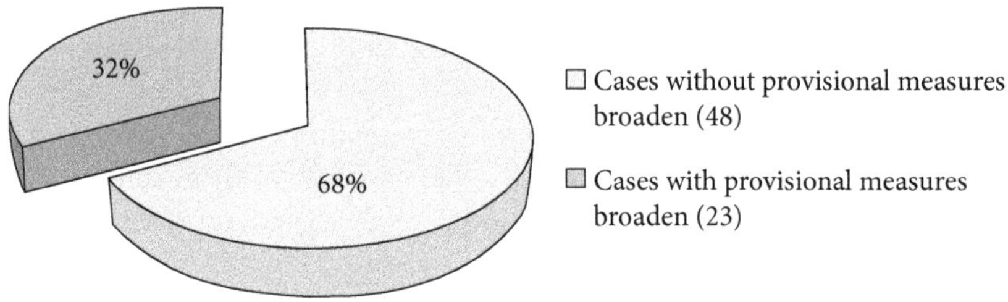

267. In the majority of the cases provisional measures were broadened to protect family members[626] and fellow workers of the presumed victims,[627] witnesses,[628] prosecutors,[629] lawyers,[630] persons on death row,[631] inmates and guards,[632] as well as members of civil society.[633]

The cases that have provoked the most requests for provisional measures are the Alvarez *et al.* Case (Colombia)[634] and the James, Briggs, Noel, Garcia and

---

624 H. Faundez Ledesma, *El Sistema Interamericano de Protección de los Derechos Humanos*, San José, IIDH, 3rd ed., 2004, 559.

625 Colotenango Case (Guatemala), Blake Case (Guatemala), Haitians and Dominicans of Haitian Origin in the Dominican Republic Case (Dominican Republic) and the Eloisa Barrios *et al.* Case (Venezuela).

626 Carpio Nicolle Case (Guatemala), Suárez Rosero Case (Ecuador), Alvarez *et al.* Case (Colombia), Cesti Hurtado Case (Peru), Bámaca Velásquez Case (Guatemala), Miguel Agustín Pro Juárez Human Rights Center *et al.* Case (Mexico), Helen Mack Chang *et al.* Case (Guatemala), 19 Tradesman Case (Colombia) and the María Leontina Millacura Llaipén *et al.* Case (Argentina).

627 Alvarez *et al.* Case (Colombia), Ivcher Bronstein Case (Peru), Luisiana Ríos *et al.* Case (Venezuela) and the Pilar Noriega García *et al.* Case (Mexico).

628 Carpio Nicolle Case (Guatemala), Bámaca Velásquez Case (Guatemala), Helen Mack Chang *et al.* Case (Guatemala) and the García Prieto *et al.* Case (El Salvador).

629 Carpio Nicolle Case (Guatemala).

630 Alvarez *et al.* Case (Colombia) and the Ramírez Hinostroza *et al.* Case (Peru).

631 James, Briggs, Noel, Garcia and Bethel Case (Trinidad and Tobago) and the Boyce and Joseph Case (Barbados).

632 The Urso Branco Prison Case (Brazil) and the Yare I and Yare II Capital Region Penitenciary Center Case (Venezuela).

633 Peace Community of San José de Apartadó Case (Colombia).

634 Alvarez *et al.* Case (Colombia).

Bethel Case (Trinidad and Tobago).[635] In the latter case, the Commission requested on seven occasions that the measures be broadened to protect other persons who had also been sentenced to death. According to the Commission, in none of the cases had the State responded to the precautionary measures that it had requested and the orders of execution were imminent. In each case, it was possible to see that the persons for whom the protection was requested were in the same situation as those who were already beneficiaries of the measures. Taking into account these considerations, the Court several times broadened the measures to protect up to an additional 38 condemned persons.

6.3. LIFTING THE MEASURES

268. Once the measures are adopted, whether *ex officio* or at the request of a party, they may be lifted only by the Court when the situation of extreme gravity and urgency and the danger of irreparable damage to the rights of the beneficiaries have ceased. Neither the Commission nor the State nor even the beneficiaries may lift them.

In the Miguel Agustín Pro Juárez Human Rights Center *et al.* (Mexico) and the Liliana Ortega *et al.* (Venezuela) Cases, the respective States informed the Court that they had lifted the measures in response to a request that had been made by the beneficiaries and the Commission. In both cases, the Court held that since it was the only body competent to decide on the permanence or the lifting of provisional measures, they were in full force and produced effects until the Court ordered them lifted.[636]

269. Unlike the position of Pasqualucci, who believes that the provisional measures must be lifted once there is a judgment on the merits or there is a friendly settlement,[637] in practice the lifting of the measures has not been conditioned on these two circumstances. In fact, in four cases the measures were adopted after a judgment on the merits[638] and in the Colotenango Case

---

635 James, Briggs, Noel, Garcia and Bethel Case (Trinidad and Tobago).

636 IACtHR, *Miguel Agustín Pro Juárez Human Rights Center et al. Case (Mexico)*, Order of April 20, 2004, Explanatory Statements 12 and 13 and IACtHR, *Liliana Ortega et al. Case (Venezuela)*, Order of March 1, 2005, Explanatory Statements 13, 16 and 17.

637 J.M. Pasqualucci, "Provisional Measures in the Inter-American Human Rights System: An Innovative Development in International Law", *Vand. J. Transnat'l L.* 1993–94, 850.

638 The 19 Tradesmen Case (Colombia), Mayagna (Sumo) Awas Tingni Community Case (Nicaragua), Plan de Sánchez Massacre Case (Guatemala) and the Integrantes del Equipo de Estudios Comunitarios y Acción Psicosocial (ECAP) Massacre Plan De Sánchez Case (Guatemala).

(Guatemala)[639] and the Mendoza Prisons Case (Argentina)[640] the measures were maintained despite the friendly settlement that the parties had reached. We share the position of the Court and Buergenthal that the essential requisite in order to lift the measures is that the situation of extreme gravity and urgency has ceased.[641] In our opinion, the measures are adopted when it has been shown that there exists a danger of irreparable damage to the rights of persons and, therefore, until that situation has terminated nothing in the Convention obliges the Court to lift the measures. In addition, as the Court has indicated on several occasions, the consideration of cases in the inter-American system does not end with a judgment on the merits since the Court maintains its jurisdiction to oversee the State's compliance of the obligations contained in the judgment.

270. Provisional measures are usually lifted when there is a fundamental change in the circumstances, either because the reasons that gave rise to them no longer exist[642] or because new facts have come to light that no longer make them indispensable.

For example, in the James, Briggs, Noel, Garcia and Bethel Case (Trinidad and Tobago), the Court lifted the measures with respect to three beneficiaries because they were no longer in a situation of extreme gravity and urgency. The Commission informed the Court in 2002 that a new trial had resulted in a reduction of the sentences of two beneficiaries from the death penalty to four years in prison and in 2005 the Commission reported that the sentence of another beneficiary had been reduced from the death penalty to seven years in prison.[643] Similarly, in the Caballero Delgado and Santana Case (Colombia), the State requested that the measures be lifted with respect to two beneficiaries because the threats had ceased. The Court, in view of these new circumstances, decided to lift the measures.[644]

---

639 Colotenango Case (Guatemala).

640 Mendoza Prisons Case (Argentina).

641 T. Buergenthal, "The Inter-American Court of Human Rights", *Am. U. L. Rev.* 1982, 241.

642 D. Padilla, "Provisional Measures Under the American Convention on Human Rights", in *Liber Amicorum Héctor Fix-Zamudio*, San José, Inter-American Court of Human Rights, 1998, 1192 and E. Rey Cantor and A. Rey Cantor, *Medidas Provisionales y Medidas Cautelares en el Sistema Interamericano de Derechos Humanos*, Bogotá, Editorial Temis, 2005, 196.

643 IACtHR, *James, Briggs, Noel, Garcia and Bethel Case (Trinidad and Tobago), Boyce and Joseph Case (Barbados)*, Order of September 3, 2002, Explanatory Statements 6 and 9. In the same case, see Order of February 28, 2005, Explanatory Statement 4, Preambular Paragraphs 6–9.

644 IACtHR, *Caballero Delgado and Santana Case (Colombia)*, Order of June 3, 1999, Explanatory Statement 2, Preambular Paragraph 2, Enacting Part 1.

271. The measures may be lifted at the request of the State,[645] the beneficiaries or their representatives,[646] the Commission[647] and *ex officio* by the Court.[648] Although any party may ask the Court to lift the measures, the Court is not obliged to do so, even if the petition comes from the petitioners themselves. The Court has lifted measures of protection even when the Commission had requested that they be maintained, as occurred in the Ivcher Bronstein (Peru)[649] and the Constitutional Court (Peru)[650] Cases. On other occasions, the measures have been maintained even though the Commission had requested that they be lifted.[651] When the Commission requests that the measures be lifted, it usually states that, in the event that measures are again necessary to safeguard rights, it will request the Court to reactivate them.[652]

272. The lifting of the measures may be total[653] or partial.[654] This means that, depending on the specific situation, the Court may decide to lift the measures for

645 Reggiardo Tolosa Case (Argentina), Blake Case (Guatemala), Loayza Tamayo Case (Peru), Cesti Hurtado Case (Peru), Colotenango Case (Guatemala), Gómez Paquiyauri Brothers Case (Peru), "El Nacional" and "Así es la Noticia" Newspapers Case (Venezuela), López Alvarez Case (Honduras) and the Persons imprisoned in the "Dr. Sebastião Martins Silveira" Penitentiary in Araraquara, São Paulo Case (Brazil).

646 Paniagua Morales *et al.* and Vásquez *et al.* Case (Guatemala) and the Plan de Sánchez Massacre Case (Guatemala).

647 Carpio Nicolle Case (Guatemala), Serech y Saquic Case (Guatemala), Suárez Rosero Case (Ecuador), Loayza Tamayo Case (Peru), Paniagua Morales *et al.* and Vásquez *et al.* Case (Guatemala), Clemente Teherán Case (Colombia), Digna Ochoa y Plácido *et al.* Case (Mexico) and the Gallardo Rodríguez Case (México).

648 Bustíos-Rojas Case (Peru), Chunimá Case (Guatemala), Ivcher Bronstein Case (Peru), Constitutional Court Case (Peru), "La Nación" Newspaper or Herrera-Ulloa Case (Costa Rica), Raxcacó Reyes *et al.* Case (Guatemala), Fermín Ramírez Case (Guatemala), Carlos Nieto Case (Venezuela), Lysias Fleury Case (Haiti), Leonel Rivero Case (Mexico), Pilar Noriega Case (Mexico) and the Mayagna (Sumo) Awas Tingni Community Case (Nicaragua).

649 Ivcher Bronstein Case (Peru).

650 Constitutional Court Case (Peru).

651 IACtHR, *Gallardo Rodríguez Case (Mexico)*, Order of the President of the Court of February 14, 2002, Explanatory Statements 5 and 6, Preambular Paragraph 6.

652 IACtHR, *Caballero Delgado and Santana Case (Colombia)*, Order of June 3, 1999, Explanatory Statement 4.

653 See for example/ Gallardo Rodríguez Case (Mexico), Carlos Nieto Case (Venezuela), Lysias Fleury Case (Haiti), Leonel Rivero Case (Mexico), Pilar Noriega Case (Mexico), Mayagna (Sumo) Awas Tingni Community Case (Nicaragua), Colotenango Case (Guatemala), Gómez Paquiyauri Brothers Case (Peru), "El Nacional" and "Así es la Noticia" Newspapers Case (Venezuela), López Alvarez Case (Honduras) and the Persons imprisoned in the "Dr. Sebastião Martins Silveira" Penitentiary in Araraquara, São Paulo Case (Brazil).

654 Caballero Delgado and Santana Case (Colombia), Carpio Nicolle Case (Guatemala), James, Briggs, Noel, Garcia and Bethel Case (Trinidad and Tobago), Miguel Agustín Pro Juárez Human Rights Center *et al.* Case (Mexico), Liliana Ortega *et al.* Case (Venezuela), Fermín Ramírez Case (Guatemala), Guerrero-Gallucci and Martínez-Barrios Case (Venezuela) and the Integrantes del Equipo de Estudios Comunitarios y Acción Psicosocial (ECAP). Masacre Plan de Sánchez Case (Guatemala).

all the beneficiaries or may decide to lift them only with respect to some of them and maintain the measures with respect to the others.

In the Carpio Nicolle Case (Guatemala), the Court stated that, in view of the State's reports and the Commission's observations, it would lift the measures with respect to four persons because they were no longer in a situation of extreme gravity and urgency, but maintain them with respect to the other two beneficiaries since they were still at grave risk of damage to their rights.[655]

273. Although the general rule is that the Court lifts the measures by means of an order, it has done so on exceptional occasions (three times)[656] in the judgment on the merits of the case.

Table 27. Provisional Measures Lifted

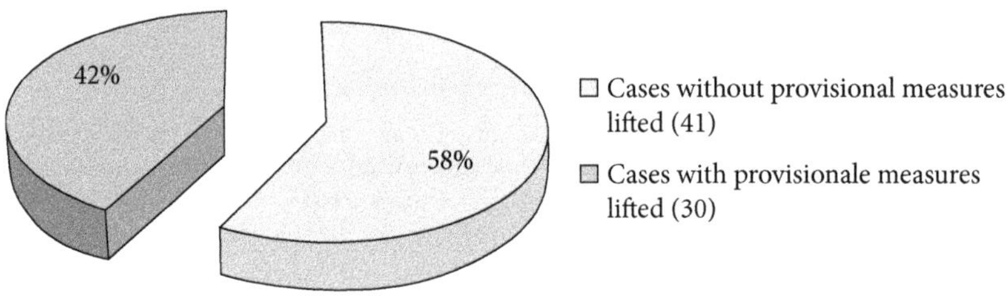

274. The Court has lifted 30 of the 71 measures that it has adopted. In general, it is not possible to determine when the Court will decide to lift the measures since everything depends on the specific circumstances of each case.

Table 28. Provisional Measures Lifted

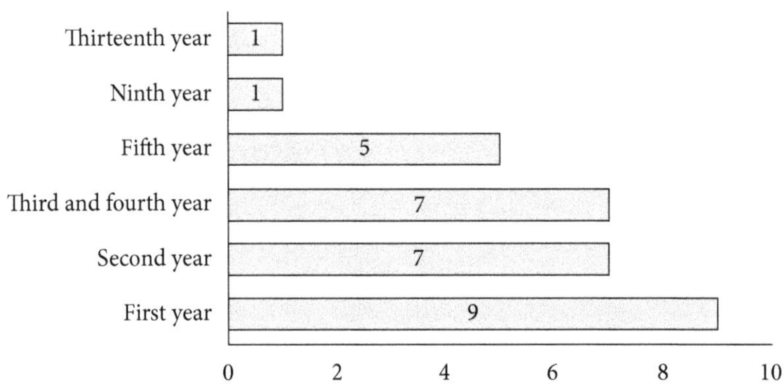

655 IACtHR, *Carpio Nicolle Case (Guatemala)*, Order of June 19, 1998, Enacting Parts 1–3.

656 IACtHR, *"La Nación" Newspaper Case or Herrera-Ulloa Case (Costa Rica)*, Judgment on the Merits of July 2, 2004; IACtHR, *Fermín Ramírez Case (Guatemala)*, Judgment on the Merits of March 12, 2005 and IACtHR, *Raxcacó Reyes et al. Case (Guatemala)*, Judgment on the Merits of September 15, 2005.

The jurisprudence shows that on nine occasions the measures were lifted during the first year,[657] in seven cases between the first and second year,[658] on seven occasions the measures were lifted during the third and fourth year,[659] in five cases during the fifth year[660], in another case in the ninth year[661] and in yet another case in the thirteenth year.[662]

6.4. REINSTATEMENT OF THE MEASURES

275. Reinstatement means that the measures that had been lifted are being restored because supervening events have placed the persons once again in a situation of extreme gravity and urgency. This circumstance is exceptional as it has only been presented in four of the 71 cases, namely cases concerning Colombia,[663] Mexico,[664] Guatemala[665] and Peru.[666]

In the Loayza Tamayo Case (Peru), the measures had been lifted in 1997 and were reinstated three years later. The provisional measures had been lifted because Mrs. Loayza had been released and she was no longer in a situation of danger. In the request for reinstatement, the petitioner argued that the health and economic situation of Mrs. Loayza was very serious and that if the State complied with the judgment on the merits and on reparations, perhaps her situation would improve. The petition stated that Mrs. Loayza was living in Chile, was not working and had gone a year without receiving the medical attention that she needed to treat the severe mental disorders that she suffered as

---

657 Bustíos-Rojas Case (Peru), Chunimá Case (Guatemala), Reggiardo Tolosa Case (Argentina), Suárez Rosero Case (Ecuador), Plan de Sánchez Massacre Case (Guatemala), Fermín Ramírez Case (Guatemala), Paniagua Morales *et al.* and Vásquez *et al.* Case (Guatemala), Ivcher Bronstein Case (Peru) and the Constitutional Court Case (Peru).

658 Alemán Lacayo Case (Nicaragua), Vogt Case (Guatemala), Serech y Saquic Case (Guatemala), Loayza Tamayo Case (Peru), Digna Ochoa y Plácido *et al.* Case (Mexico), Raxcacó Reyes *et al.* Case (Guatemala) and the Persons imprisoned in the "Dr. Sebastião Martins Silveira" Penitentiary in Araraquara, São Paulo Case (Brazil).

659 Cesti Hurtado Case (Peru) and "La Nación" Newspaper Case or Herrera-Ulloa Case (Costa Rica), Carlos Nieto *et al.* Case (Venezuela), "El Nacional" and "Asi es la Noticia" Newspapers Case, Leonel Rivero *et al.* Case (Mexico), Pilar Noriega *et al.* Case (Mexico), Children Deprived of Liberty in the "Complexo do Tatuapé" of FEBEM Case (Brazil) and the López Alvarez Case (Honduras).

660 Clemente Teherán Case (Colombia), Mayagna (Sumo) Awas Tingni Community Case (Nicaragua), Gómez Paquiyauri Brothers Case (Peru), Gallardo Rodríguez Case (México) and the Lysias Fleury Case (Haiti).

661 Blake Case (Guatemala).

662 Colotenango Case (Guatemala).

663 Caballero Delgado and Santana Case (Colombia).

664 Digna Ochoa y Plácido *et al.* Case (Mexico).

665 Carpio Nicolle Case (Guatemala).

666 Loayza Tamayo Case (Peru).

a result of the maltreatment that she had received while she was in prison. The Court ordered the State to adopt once again all necessary measures to ensure that Mrs. Loayza could return to her country and that her rights to physical, psychological and moral integrity be protected.[667]

In the Carpio Nicolle Case (Guatemala), in spite of having lifted the measures on behalf of the Special Prosecutor for the case, the Court decided to reinstate them. The Court had lifted the measures because the beneficiary and his family had preferred to leave Guatemala as a result of the threats that they had received. The beneficiary and his family later decided to return to the country and he had testified before the Inter-American Court. The Special Prosecutor stated that he was afraid that he and his family would once again receive death threats as a result of the testimony. Taking into account these facts, the Court considered it appropriate to readopt the measures of protection.

[667] IACtHR, *Loayza Tamayo Case (Peru)*, Order of the President of December 13, 2000, Explanatory Statement 1, Enacting Part 1. See also, on the same matter, Order of February 3, 2001, Enacting Part 1. See E. Rey Cantor and A. Rey Cantor, *Medidas Provisionales y Medidas Cautelares en el Sistema Interamericano de Derechos Humanos*, Bogotá, Editorial Temis, 2005, 195.

7. COMPLIANCE

276. The States have mostly complied with the measures of protection ordered by the Court. The most important advantage in employing provisional measures in the inter-American system is that they have as their purpose to protect immediately and effectively potential victims of human rights.[668] Thus, unlike the other tools available in the inter-American system, provisional measures have a true protective function because they attempt to avoid the violation of the rights of persons who are in a dangerous situation.

277. The first part of this section will deal with the means used by the States to grant protection to the beneficiaries of the measures and the second part will study the actions of the States to comply with the orders of the Court.

7.1. MEANS UTILISED TO PROTECT THE BENEFICIARIES

278. Although the means and manner of how the States grant protection to the beneficiaries are as diverse as the factual situations that are presented, the most utilised means have been assigning agents of personal security, training the beneficiaries in measures of personal self-protection and providing them with different ways of communication.

279. As can be seen in the Table, the means of protection most often used by the states, was the offer of security personnel, namely in 24 cases. In some cases, the security agents directly protected the beneficiaries and were with them 24 hours a day.[669] This type of protection was offered in the Carpio Nicolle Case (Guatemala), the Gallardo Rodríguez Case (Mexico), the Miguel Agustín Pro

---

[668] J.M. Pasqualucci, "Medidas Provisionales en la Corte Interamericana de Derechos Humanos: Una Comparación con la Corte Internacional de Justicia y la Corte Europea de Derechos Humanos", *Revista del Instituto Interamericano de Derechos Humanos* 1994, 111.

[669] IACtHR, *Carpio Nicolle Case (Guatemala)*, Order of September 19, 1995, Explanatory Statement 6; IACtHR, *Gallardo Rodríguez Case (Mexico)*, Order of February 14, 2002, Explanatory Statement 4, Preambular Paragraph 6, Enacting Part 1 and IACtHR, *Miguel Agustín Pro Juárez Human Rights Center et al. Case (Mexico)*, Order of April 30, 2001, Explanatory Statement 3. In the same matter, see Order of April 20, 2004, Explanatory Statement 3(d)-(f).

Juárez Human Rights Center *et al.* Case (Mexico), the Forensic Anthropology Foundation Case (Guatemala), the Hinostroza *et al.* Case (Peru), the Ramírez Leonel Rivero *et al.* Case (Mexico) and the Pilar Noriega *et al.* Case (Mexico). In the first of them, Guatemala, in addition to offering personal security to the beneficiaries, allowed them to choose the persons that provided the service.

Table 29. Means offered

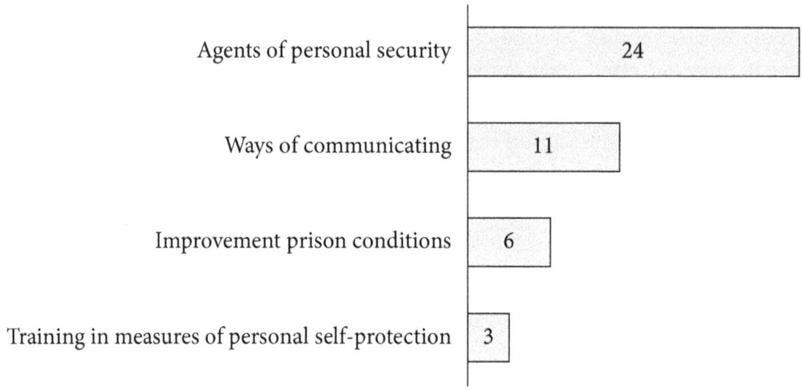

280. In a higher percentage, the protective measures offered by the States also consisted in guarding the residences and offices of the persons who were in a situation of danger.[670] This protection meant placing at least one security agent 24 hours a day in the office or home of the beneficiaries. On other occasions, the protection consisted of periodic patrols of these sites. This type of protection was given in 16 cases.

---

670 IACtHR, *Blake Case (Guatemala)*, Order of April 18, 1997, Explanatory Statement 3; Order of November 17 2004, Explanatory Statement 12; IACtHR, *Vogt Case (Guatemala)*, Order of June 27, 1996, Explanatory Statement 6; IACtHR, *Serech y Saquic Case (Guatemala)*, Order of September 19, 1997, Explanatory Statements 4 and 5, Preambular Paragraph 2, Enacting Part 1; IACtHR, *Giraldo Cardona Case (Colombia)*, Order of February 5, 1997, Explanatory Statement 4 and also Order of September 30, 1999, Explanatory Statement 6; IACtHR, *Bámaca Velásquez Case (Guatemala)*, Order of September 5, 2001, Explanatory Statement 13; IACtHR, *Paniagua Morales et al. and Vásquez et al. Case (Guatemala)*, Order of June 19, 1998, Explanatory Statement 5; IACtHR, *Clemente Teherán Case (Colombia)*, Order of August 12, 2000, Explanatory Statements 3–5 and also Order of December 1, 2003, Explanatory Statement 4; IACtHR, *Digna Ochoa y Plácido et al. Case (Mexico)*, Order of August 28, 2001, Explanatory Statements 2 and 4; IACtHR, *Miguel Agustín Pro Juárez Human Rights Center et al. Case (Mexico)*, Order of November 30, 2001, Explanatory Statement 3 and also Order of April 20, 2004, Explanatory Statement 3(d)-(f); IACtHR, *Liliana Ortega et al. Case (Venezuela)*, Order of December 2, 2003, Explanatory Statement 30(b) and IACtHR, *Plan de Sánchez Massacre Case (Guatemala)*, Order of September 8, 2002, Explanatory Statement 14. See also Millacura Llaipén *et al.* Case. (Argentina), Mery Naranjo *et al.* Case (Colombia), Integrantes del Equipo de Estudios Comunitarios y Acción Psicosocial (ECAP). Masacre Plan de Sánchez Case (Guatemala) and Adrian Meléndez Quijano *et al.* Case (El Salvador).

281. Other measures have been instructing beneficiaries in self-protection[671] and providing them with different means of communication, such as two-way radios, cellular telephones, satellite telephones and telephone lines.[672] The purpose of giving them these apparatuses was so that they could rapidly contact the security authorities in case of need.

282. Finally, the protection given in cases relating to prisons has been to improve the conditions of detention through prison reforms,[673] to contract new prison guards,[674] to organise pedagogical activities,[675] to confiscate arms[676] and to transfer beneficiaries to other detention centres.[677]

7.2. LEGAL CONSEQUENCES OF COMPLIANCE

283. On a number of occasions the compliance with the measures provided the beneficiaries to regain their liberty. On other occasions, the effects of the judicial decisions were suspended while the case was pending before the Inter-American system: in some cases, the compliance resulted in that new jurisdictional processes were instituted, this time in accordance with the American Convention; in other cases, it resulted in that beneficiaries were able to regain their work. Finally, for some beneficiaries, the threats to their life came to an end.

---

671 IACtHR, *Alvarez et al. Case (Colombia)*, Order of November 12, 2000, Explanatory Statement 13(d); IACtHR, *Giraldo Cardona Case (Colombia)*, Order of November 30, 1999, Explanatory Statement 6 and IACtHR, *Miguel Agustín Pro Juárez Human Rights Center et al. Case (Mexico)*, Order of November 30, 2001, Explanatory Statement 9(c).

672 IACtHR, *Giraldo Cardona Case (Colombia)*, Order of November 30, 1999, Explanatory Statement 6; IACtHR, *Clemente Teherán Case (Colombia)*, Order of August 12, 2000, Explanatory Statements 3–5; IACtHR, *Peace Community of San José de Apartadó Case (Colombia)*, Order of November 24, 2000, Explanatory Statement 10 and also Order of November 17, 2004, Explanatory Statements 1 and 5; IACtHR, *Miguel Agustín Pro Juárez Human Rights Center et al. Case (Mexico)*, Order of November 30, 2001, Explanatory Statement 9(c) and also Order of April 20, 2004, Explanatory Statement 3(d)-(f) and IACtHR, *Communities of the Jiguamiandó and of the Curbaradó Case (Colombia)*, Order of November 17, 2004, Explanatory Statement 2(b), Preambular Paragraph 9. See also Adrian Meléndez Quijano *et al.* Case (El Salvador), Mapiripán Massacre (Colombia), Gloria Giralt de García-Prieto *et al.* Case (El Salvador), Mery Naranjo *et al.* Case (Colombia), Ramírez Leonel Rivero *et al.* Case (Mexico) and Pilar Noriega *et al.* Case (Mexico).

673 Persons imprisoned in the "Dr. Sebastião Martins Silveira" Penitentiary in Araraquara, São Paulo Case (Brazil).

674 Children Deprived of Liberty in the "Complexo do Tatuapé" of FEBEM Case (Brazil) and Monagas Judicial Confinement Center ("La Pica") Case (Venezuela).

675 Children Deprived of Liberty in the "Complexo do Tatuapé" of FEBEM Case (Brazil).

676 Children Deprived of Liberty in the "Complexo do Tatuapé" of FEBEM Case (Brazil) and Monagas Judicial Confinement Center ("La Pica") Case (Venezuela).

677 Millacura Llaipén *et al.* Case (Argentina).

284. It is very important to emphasise that the Court has never ordered any State in whatever resolution to set any beneficiary, who is detained, free, or to return the work to the beneficiaries that had lost their work. What the Court does is ordering the States to adopt all the measures necessary to avoid that the persons who are in a situation of extreme gravity and urgency suffer irreparable harm.

In this way, it is the states that decide themselves what kind of actions they wish the take to comply with the measures ordered by the Court. A number of states decide to organise new trials, this time in accordance with the American Convention; these new trials can result in the modification of the punishment to which the beneficiaries had been condemned at the outset. Other states decide to return the work the beneficiaries had lost. Finally, a number of states offer the beneficiaries protection through personal state security personnel. Depending on the factual situation of each case and the willingness of each state, the measures ordered by the Court are complied with in many different ways.

In this sense, in the Suárez Rosero (Ecuador), the Loayza Tamayo (Peru), the Gallardo Rodríguez (Mexico) and the Cesti Hurtado (Peru) Cases, the States decided to comply with the provisional measure, hereby ordering the liberation of the beneficiaries.[678] On the other hand, in the James, Briggs, Noel, Garcia and Bethel Case (Trinidad and Tobago), the State in complying with the provisional measures, ordered a new trial that resulted in the reduction of the death sentences to four years in prison for two of the beneficiaries and for another beneficiary the modification of the death sentence to seven years in prison.[679] In this same case but with respect to other beneficiaries and in the *La Nación* (or Herrera Ulloa) Case (Costa Rica), the States suspended the execution of some sentences while the cases were being resolved in the inter-American system.[680] In the former case, the sentence of death was suspended for 39 condemned men and in the latter the entry of the beneficiary's name in the Judicial Registry of Delinquents was suspended.

---

678 IACtHR, *Suárez Rosero Case (Ecuador)*, Order of June 28, 1996, Explanatory Statement 7, Preambular Paragraph 2, Enacting Part 1; IACtHR, *Loayza Tamayo Case (Peru)*, Order of November 11, 1997, Explanatory Statements 6 and 7, Enacting Part 1 and IACtHR, *Gallardo Rodríguez Case (Mexico)*, Order of February 14, 2002, Explanatory Statement 4, Preambular Paragraph 6, Enacting Part 1 (In this case, the President of Mexico signed an agreement that reduced the jail sentence of the beneficiary and freed him); IACtHR, *Cesti Hurtado Case (Peru)*, Order of November 19, 1999, Explanatory Statement 4, Preambular Paragraph 3. Although in the latter case the order to free the beneficiary was given to comply with the judgment on the merits, this matter was also under provisional measures, and thus, in complying with the judgment, the State also complied with the provisional measures.

679 IACtHR, *James, Briggs, Noel, Garcia and Bethel Case (Trinidad and Tobago)*, Order of September 3, 2002, Explanatory Statement 6 and also Order of February 28, 2005, Explanatory Statement 4, Preambular Paragraph 10.

680 IACtHR, *"La Nación" Newspaper Case or Herrera-Ulloa Case (Costa Rica)*, Order of December 6, 2001, Explanatory Statement 16.

In other cases, compliance with the provisional measures allowed the beneficiaries to recuperate their jobs. In the Ivcher Bronstein Case (Peru), arrest warrants concerning the beneficiary were lifted and he was once again permitted to be a shareholder and President of a private television station[681] and in the Constitutional Court Case (Peru) the Congress of Peru restored the beneficiary to her post as Judge of that tribunal.[682]

The adoption of the measures also permitted persons who were endangered to return to their normal lives.[683] In some cases, once the measures were put into practice the acts of harassment and threats stopped. For example, in the Chunimá Case (Guatemala) while the measures were in force, none of the protected persons was physically harmed and two principal suspects of the violent acts were arrested.[684] Similarly, in the Alemán Lacayo Case (Nicaragua), where the

---

681 IACtHR, *Ivcher Bronstein Case (Peru)*, Order of March 14, 2001, Preambular Paragraph 4, Enacting Part 1. In the James, Briggs, Noel, Garcia and Bethel Case (Trinidad and Tobago), the suspension of the death penalty was requested for 41 persons on death row. The State complied with the order in 39 of the cases and did not do so in the other two. See IACtHR, *James, Briggs, Noel, Garcia and Bethel Case (Trinidad and Tobago)*, Order of August 16, 2000, Explanatory Statements 1–5.

682 IACtHR, *Constitutional Court Case (Peru)*, Order of March 14, 2001, Explanatory Statement 6.

683 IACtHR, *Chunimá Case (Guatemala)*, Order of August 1, 1991, Explanatory Statement 4, Preambular Paragraph 8; IACtHR, *Reggiardo Tolosa Case (Argentina)*, Order of January 19, 1994, Explanatory Statement 4 and 5, Enacting Part 1; IACtHR, *Blake Case (Guatemala)*, Order of June 14, 2005, Preambular Paragraph 10, Enacting Part 1; IACtHR, *Alemán Lacayo Case (Nicaragua)*, Order of February 6, 1997, Preambular Paragraphs 1–3, Enacting Part 1; IACtHR, *Vogt Case (Guatemala)*, Order of November 11, 1997, Explanatory Statement 4, Enacting Part 1; IACtHR, *Serech y Saquic Case (Guatemala)*, Order of September 19, 1997, Explanatory Statements 4 and 5, Preambular Paragraph 2, Enacting Part 1; IACtHR, *Suárez Rosero Case (Ecuador)*, Order of June 28, 1996, Explanatory Statement 7, Preambular Paragraph 2, Enacting Part 1; IACtHR, *Loayza Tamayo Case (Peru)*, Order of Augut 28, 2001, Explanatory Statements 3 and 4, Enacting Part 1; IACtHR, *Cesti Hurtado Case (Peru)*, Order of Augut 14, 2000, Explanatory Statement 7–9, Preambular Paragraphs 2–3, Enacting Part 1; IACtHR, *Paniagua Morales et al. and Vásquez et al. Case (Guatemala)*, Order of November 27, 1998, Explanatory Statement 4, Enacting Part 1 and IACtHR, *Clemente Teherán Case (Colombia)*, Order of December 1, 2003, Explanatory Statement 10, Preambular Paragraph 5. In this case the measures were lifted because the Commission did not have the necessary information to substantiate the existence of the assumptions that justified the adoption of the measures. IACtHR, *Digna Ochoa y Plácido et al. Case (Mexico)*, Order of August 28, 2001, Explanatory Statements 2 and 4, Enacting Part 1; IACtHR, *Ivcher Bronstein Case (Peru)*, Order of March 14, 2001, Preambular Paragraph 4, Enacting Part 1; IACtHR, *Constitutional Court Case (Peru)*, Order of March 14, 2001, Preambular Paragraph 4, Enacting Part 1; IACtHR, *"La Nación" Newspaper Case (Costa Rica)*, Order of December 6, 2001, Explanatory Statement 16 and IACtHR, *Plan de Sánchez Massacre Case (Guatemala)*, Order of June 14, 2006, Explanatory Statement 8, Preambular Paragraph 7.

684 J.M. Pasqualucci, "Medidas Provisionales en la Corte Interamericana de Derechos Humanos: Una Comparación con la Corte Internacional de Justicia y la Corte Europea de Derechos Humanos", *Revista del Instituto Interamericano de Derechos Humanos* 1994, 52. Regarding compliance of provisional measures, Cançado Trindade considers those measures to be a positive mechanism since they have allowed an effective protection of the rights of the

Court ordered the protection of a presidential candidate because his life was in danger, the provisional measures were in force for a year and during that time the danger did not reappear. Mr. Alemán had been the target of an attempt on his life while he was campaigning and the measures were lifted when he was elected President of Nicaragua.[685]

In the Blake Case (Guatemala), the Court also lifted the measures of protection because the beneficiaries had stated that they no longer received threats, that there had not been any incident that showed a situation of danger and the person responsible for the death of Mr. Blake had been tried and found guilty.[686] The same occurred in the Vogt (Guatemala), the Serech and Saquic (Guatemala), the Giraldo Cardona (Colombia), the Paniagua Morales *et al.* (Peru), the Vásquez *et al.* (Mexico) and the Caballero Delgado and Santana (Colombia) Cases,[687] among others, where the beneficiaries told the Court that because of the effective and timely intervention of the measures, the threats and harassment had lessened considerably and they were carrying out their activities normally and, thus, it was appropriate to lift the measures of protection.[688] A very important case to be mentioned is the Persons imprisoned in the "Dr. Sebastião Martins Silveira" Penitentiary in Araraquara, São Paulo Case (Brazil). In this case, the Court lifted the provisional measures because the condition of detention had improved and the situation of extreme gravity and urgency had ceased for the prisoners.[689]

285. Although the ideal is that the measures have the same effect for each beneficiary in a case, that is not always the case. The Court has sometimes declared them effective only with respect to some of the beneficiaries and, therefore, decided to lift partially the measures of protection.[690]

---

beneficiaries. See A. Cançado Trindade, "The Evolution of Provisional Measures of Protection under the Case Law of the Inter-American Court of Human Rights (1987–2002)", *Hum. Rts. L.J.* 2003, 165. See also IACtHR, *Chunimá Case (Guatemala)*, Order of August 1, 1991, Explanatory Statement 4, Preambular Paragraph 8.

685 IACtHR, *Alemán Lacayo Case (Nicaragua)*, Order of February 6, 1997, Explanatory Statement 4, Preambular Paragraphs 1–3, Enacting Part 1.

686 IACtHR, *Blake Case (Guatemala)*, Order of November 17, 2004, Explanatory Statements 10 and 11.

687 IACtHR, *Caballero Delgado and Santana Case (Colombia)*, Order of June 3, 1999, Explanatory Statements 1 and 2, Preambular Paragraph 2, Enacting Part 1.

688 IACtHR, *Vogt Case (Guatemala)*, Order of November 11, 1997, Explanatory Statement 4.

689 IACtHR, *Persons imprisoned in the "Dr. Sebastião Martins Silveira" Penitentiary in Araraquara, São Paulo Case (Brazil)*, Order of November 25, 2008, Explanatory Statements 10 and 11.

690 Caballero Delgado and Santana Case (Colombia), Carpio Nicolle Case (Guatemala), James, Briggs, Noel, Garcia and Bethel Case (Trinidad and Tobago), Miguel Agustín Pro Juárez Human Rights Center *et al.* Case (Mexico) and the Liliana Ortega *et al.* Case (Venezuela).

In the Carpio Nicolle Case (Guatemala), the Court lifted the measures for four persons because they were no longer in a situation of extreme gravity and urgency, but maintained them for the other two beneficiaries because they were still in a situation of grave risk of damage to their rights.[691] Similarly, in the James, Briggs, Noel, Garcia and Bethel Case (Trinidad and Tobago) the Court lifted the measures for three of the 41 beneficiaries.[692]

286. Until 2006 an essential element of protection was that of investigating, identifying and punishing those responsible for the acts that gave rise to the adoption of provisional measures[693] because, according to the Court, that was the best way to combat impunity and to ensure the rights of the beneficiaries of the measures.[694] Combating impunity by all available legal means was very important because impunity promotes the chronic repetition of the violations of human rights and the total defenselessness of the victims and their families.[695] Nowadays, however, the Court points out that the alleged lack of investigation on the part of a State does not constitute, *per se*, circumstances of extreme gravity and urgency that would warrant maintaining the provisional measures.[696]

287. The States have reported in some cases that they have initiated the respective judicial investigations and these investigations had culminated in some cases in the identification and punishment of those responsible for the acts

---

691 IACtHR, *Carpio Nicolle Case (Guatemala)*, Order of June 19, 1998, Enacting Part 1-3.

692 IACtHR, *James, Briggs, Noel, Garcia and Bethel Case (Trinidad and Tobago)*, Order of September 3, 2002, Explanatory Statements 6 and 9. In the same case, see Order of February 28, 2005, Explanatory Statement 4, Preambular Paragraphs 6-9. See also IACtHR, *Gómez Paquiyauri Brothers (Peru)*, Order of May 3, 2008, Explanatory Statements 6 and 9.

693 IACtHR, *Colotenango Case (Guatemala)*, Order of February 2, 2000, Preambular Paragraph 9; IACtHR, *Peace Community of San José de Apartadó Case (Colombia)*, Order of March 15, 2005, Preambular Paragraph 9 and the *Gutiérrez Soler Case (Colombia)*, Order of March 11, 2005, Enacting Part 2.

694 IACtHR, *Miguel Agustín Pro Juárez Human Rights Center et al. Case (Mexico)*, Order of April 30, 2001, Preambular Paragraph 11 and IACtHR, *Carpio Nicolle Case (Guatemala)*, Order of September 5, 2001, Preambular Paragraph 7. Regarding this case, the Court stated that closing an investigation was an omission of the State's obligation to investigate, since it was not taking the positive and necessary measures to clarify the acts that had motivated the adoption of provisional measures.

695 IACtHR, *Bámaca Velásquez Case (Guatemala)*, Order of November 20, 2003, Preambular Paragraph 18; IACtHR, *Luis Uzcátegui Case (Venezuela)*, Order of February 20, 2003, Enacting Part 12; IACtHR, *Luisiana Ríos et al. Case (Venezuela)*, Order of February 20, 2003, Preambular Paragraph 9 and IACtHR, *Liliana Ortega et al. Case (Venezuela)*, Order of February 21, 2003, Enacting Part 9.

696 IACtHR, *Colotenango Case (Guatemala)*, Order of july 12, 2007, Preambular Paragraph 11 and 14; IACtHR, *Gómez Paquiyauri Brothers (Peru)*, Order of May 3, 2008, Enacting Part 1 and 2; IACtHR, *López Alvarez et al Case (Honduras)*, Order of January 26, 2009, Preambular Paragraph 23; IACtHR, *Carlos Nieto Palma Case (Venezuela)*, Order of January 26, 2009, Preambular Paragraph 15.

that gave rise to the situation of danger and judicial investigations were on-going in others in an attempt to clarify the acts denounced.

In the Chunimá Case (Guatemala), the two principal agents of the violent acts, according to the complainants, were arrested and handed over to the judicial authorities;[697] while in the Clemente Teherán Case (Colombia) the State investigated the acts denounced and punished the persons responsible for the acts of violence against the community.[698] In the Colotenango Case (Guatemala) the State reported the capture of the killer of one of the presumed victims of the case and the arrest of another person for an attempt on another victim. It also informed the Court that 12 of the 15 former policemen had been arrested and sentenced to 25 years in prison for human rights violations against members of the Colotenango community.[699]

288. In other cases, States informed the Court that, although they had not yet punished anyone, they had initiated investigations in order to identify and punish those responsible for the dangerous situation.

In one case, a State had opened 24 criminal trials because of the denunciations presented by the beneficiaries.[700] In another case, the Prosecutor began 32 investigations for the acts that had affected the Jiguamiandó and Curbaradó Communities from 1999 to 2004. Two of the investigations were related to complaints against companies that cultivated African palm trees in the territory of the Communities for the alleged crime of invading areas of special ecological importance.[701] In another case, the State was processing the complaints regarding the deaths of the inmates of the Urso Branco Jail in Brazil and was deciding the petitions of indemnification presented by the families of the inmates who had died.[702]

While the measures were in force in the *Globovisión* Television Station Case (Venezuela), the State reported that it had opened four criminal trials with the aim of ascertaining the responsibility of policemen for the acts denounced and against members of the National Guard for the alleged non-compliance of the

697 IACtHR, *Chunimá Case (Guatemala)*, Order of August 1, 1991, Preambular Paragraph 8.

698 IACtHR, *Clemente Teherán Case (Colombia)*, Orders of August 12, 2000, Explanatory Statements 3–5 and December 1, 2003, Explanatory Statement 4.

699 The problem was that a year later these persons were freed in a violent attack by former members of the civil patrols. See IACtHR, *Colotenango Case (Guatemala)*, Orders of September 19, 1997, Explanatory Statements 10–12 and June 3, 1999, Preambular Paragraph 6, Order of September 5, 2001, Explanatory Statement 14.

700 IACtHR, *Peace Community of San José de Apartadó Case (Colombia)*, Order of November 17, 2004, Explanatory Statements 1 and 5.

701 IACtHR, *Communities of the Jiguamiandó and of the Curbaradó Case (Colombia)*, Order of March 15, 2005, Explanatory Statement 12 and Order of February 7, 2006, Explanatory Statement 13(d).

702 IACtHR, *Urso Branco Prison Case (Brazil)*, Order of September 21, 2005, Explanatory Statements 11(e) and 13.

protective measures. It also informed that it had interviewed the complainants and had taken some photographs and made on-site investigations.[703]

7.3. NON-COMPLIANCE

289. The jurisprudence shows that non-compliance with provisional measures has sometimes occurred when the beneficiaries have suffered some sort of violation to their rights or when the measures adopted rather than protecting the beneficiaries have placed them at greater risk. Still, on other occasions, non-compliance refers more to the lack of information by a State and to the failure to investigate, identify and punish those responsible for the acts that gave rise to the situation of extreme gravity and urgency.

7.3.1. VIOLATIONS OF THE RIGHTS OF THE BENEFICIARIES

290. As mentioned in the section on passive standing, States in the inter-American system have the obligation *erga omnes* to protect every person subject to their jurisdiction.[704] This general obligation, in the opinion of the Court, is imposed not only with respect to abuses of power of the State itself but also for the acts of third persons.[705] An unlawful act that violates human rights that was not initially imputable to the State because, for example, it was the work of a

[703] IACtHR, *"Globovisión" Television Station Case (Venezuela)*, Order of September 4, 2004, Explanatory Statement 7 and Order of November 23, 2004, Preambular Paragraph 10.

[704] IACtHR, *Guerrero-Gallucci and Martínez-Barrios Case (Venezuela)*, Order of November 29, 2007, Preambular Paragraph 4; IACtHR, *Ramírez Leonel Rivero et al. Case (Mexico)*, Order of November 25, 2008, Preambular Paragraph 4 and IACtHR, *Tyrone Dacosta Cadogan Case (Barbados)*, Order of December 2, 2008. With respect to the obligations *erga omnes*, of special interest are the Concurring Opinions of Judge Cançado Trindade concerning the orders of the Court on provisional measures in the Peace Community of San José de Apartadó Case (Colombia) of June 18, 2002, in the Communities of the Jiguamiandó and of the Curbaradó Case (Colombia) of March 6, 2003, and in the Indigenous Sarayaku People Case (Ecuador); IACtHR, *Children Deprived of Liberty in the "Complexo do Tatuapé" of FEBEM Case (Brazil)*, Order of November 25, 2008, Preambular Paragraph 12 and IACtHR, *Capital El Rodeo I & El Rodeo II Judicial Confinement Center Case (Venezuela)*, Order of December 2, 2008, Preambular Paragraph 11. See also A. Cançado Trindade, "The Evolution of Provisional Measures of Protection under the Case Law of the Inter-American Court of Human Rights (1987–2002)", *Hum. Rts. L.J.* 2003, 166.

[705] IACtHR, *Indigenous Sarayaku People Case (Ecuador)*, Order of July 6, 2004, Preambular Paragraph 10; IACtHR, *Plan de Sánchez Massacre Case (Guatemala)*, Order of the President of July 30, 2004, Preambular Paragraph 10; IACtHR, *Luisiana Ríos et al. Case (Venezuela)*, Order of September 8, 2004, Preambular Paragraph 12 and IACtHR, *Mendoza Prisons Case (Argentina)*. I/A Court of H.R., Order June 18, 2005, Preambular Paragraph 11.

private person or because the author of the act was not identified may be the responsibility of the State, not for the act *per se* but for the lack of due diligence in preventing the violation or for not having dealt with it in the terms of the Convention.[706] Reference will underneath be made to the cases in which there were violations of the rights of beneficiaries of the measures. In some cases, the parties argue that it was agents of the State who committed the irreparable damage, in others that it was third persons who acted with the acquiescence of the State, in still others simply third persons, as in the case of the prisons and, finally, in other cases those responsible are illegal armed groups, acting in the context of an internal armed conflict.

7.3.1.1. Violation of the Right to Life

291. Within the area of the non-compliance of the duty to protect the rights of persons there are cases in which there is a violation of the right to life.[707] These are without any doubt the most serious of all cases of non-compliance with the provisional measures of protection, since life is the primary and necessary condition for the enjoyment of all the other rights.[708]

---

706 In this context, the Court in the Caballero Delgado and Santana Case (Colombia) held that the detention and disappearance of Isidro Caballero Delgado and María del Carmen Santana had been carried out by members of the Colombian Army and by civilians operating as soldiers. See IACtHR, *Caballero Delgado and Santana Case (Colombia)*, Order of December 8, 1995, paras. 54–63. See also IACtHR, *Velásquez Rodríguez Case (Honduras)*, Judgment of July 29, 1988, paras. 164 and 169; IACtHR, *Godínez Cruz Case (Honduras)*, Judgment of January 20, 1989, paras. 173 and 178.

707 The Right to Life is contemplated in Article 4 of the American Convention in the following terms: "1. Every person has the right to have his life respected. This right shall be protected by law and, in general, from the moment of conception. No one shall be arbitrarily deprived of his life. 2. In countries that have not abolished the death penalty, it may be imposed only for the most serious crimes and pursuant to a final judgment rendered by a competent court and in accordance with a law establishing such punishment, enacted prior to the commission of the crime. The application of such punishment shall not be extended to crimes to which it does not presently apply. 3. The death penalty shall not be reestablished in states that have abolished it. 4. In no case shall capital punishment be inflicted for political offenses or related common crimes. 5. Capital punishment shall not be imposed upon persons who, at the time the crime was committed, were under 18 years of age or over 70 years of age; nor shall it be applied to pregnant women. 6. Every person condemned to death shall have the right to apply for amnesty, pardon, or commutation of sentence, which may be granted in all cases. Capital punishment shall not be imposed while such a petition is pending decision by the competent authority".

708 IACtHR, *Carpio Nicolle Case (Guatemala)*, Order of July 8, 2004, Preambular Paragraph 19; IACtHR, *Plan de Sánchez Massacre Case (Guatemala)*, Order of September 8, 2004, Preambular Paragraph 11; IACtHR, *Gutiérrez Soler Case (Colombia)*, Order of March 11, 2005, Preambular Paragraph 10 and IACtHR, *Indigenous Sarayaku People Case (Ecuador)*, Order of June 17, 2005, Explanatory Statement 31(k).

Table 30. Number of cases with violation right to life

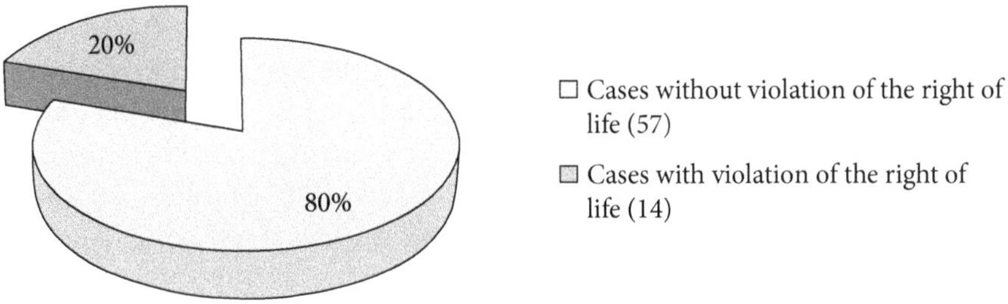

292. From 1987 to 2009 the Inter-American Court adopted measures in 71 cases and 14 of them involved the death of 102 beneficiaries, of whom six were children.[709] In terms of percentage, provisional measures were not effective because the right to life of the beneficiaries was violated from one perspective in 1% and from another in 20%.

Table 31. Number of beneficiaries killed

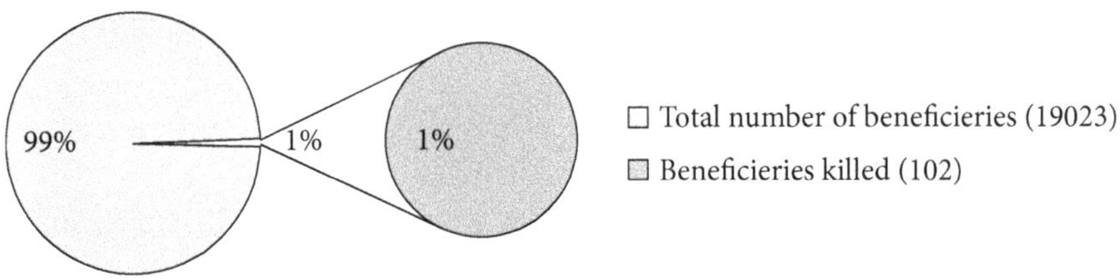

293. Considering that protection was ordered for 19,023 persons and of this total 102 persons lost their lives, then the provisional measures were not effective in 1% of the cases, but if it is taken into account that the Court ordered measures in 71 cases and that in 14 of them beneficiaries were killed, then the conclusion is that the measures were not effective in 20% of the cases. In any event, in the latter situation – the total number of cases and not the number of beneficiaries – the right to life was violated with respect to some beneficiaries and not with regard

[709] IACtHR, *Peace Community of San José de Apartadó Case (Colombia)*, Order of November 17, 2004, Explanatory Statements 10 and 13(c). In this Order, it was reported that a little girl died in the hands of the Army and a boy, 4 years old, was killed as a result of a combat between the Army and the guerrillas; IACtHR, *Communities of the Jiguamiandó and of the Curbaradó Case (Colombia)*, Order of November 17, 2004, Explanatory Statement 6(d). In this Order it was affirmed that a 3 year-old boy was killed; IACtHR, *Eloisa Barrios et al. Case (Venezuela)*, Order of June 29, 2005, Explanatory Statements 4, 6 and 8, Preambular Paragraph 13. In this Order, it was reported that a 16 year old beneficiary had been shot 8 times and as a result died a few days later; IACtHR, *Children Deprived of Liberty in the "Complexo do Tatuapé" of FEBEM Case (Brazil)*, Order of July 4, 2006, Preambular Paragraph 6. In this case, it was reported that a 16 and 17 years old beneficiaries had been killed.

to others. In those cases, the measures of protection were at the same time not effective for some and effective for others.

An example would be the James, Briggs, Noel, Garcia and Bethel Case (Trinidad and Tobago), where the State, despite the measures of protection ordered by the Inter-American Court, executed two persons who were protected.[710] The same State in the same case, but concerning other beneficiaries, subsequently decided to accept the measures and did not carry out some executions, even holding a new trial that for some persons resulted in a prison term rather than the sentence of death. This situation, in addition to showing that the provisional measures were effective only for some beneficiaries, demonstrates the importance of explaining the reasons why under certain views the measures were not effective in 1% or in 20%.

Beneficiaries were killed while under provisional measures in the Bámaca Velásquez (Guatemala), James, Briggs, Noel, Garcia and Bethel (Trinidad and Tobago), the Peace Community of San José de Apartadó (Colombia) the Urso Branco Prison (Brazil), the Communities of the Jiguamiandó and of the Curbaradó (Colombia), the Eloisa Barrios *et al.* (Venezuela), the Mendoza Prisons (Argentina), the Giraldo Cardona (Colombia), the Indigenous Kankuamo People (Colombia), the Children Deprived of Liberty in the "Complexo do Tatuapé" of FEBEM (Brazil), the Monagas Judicial Confinement Center ("La Pica") (Venezuela), the Mery Naranjo *et al.* (Colombia), the Alvarez *et al.* (Colombia) and the Millacura Llaipén *et al.* (Argentina) Cases.

The cases where the most beneficiaries were killed were the Indigenous Kankuamo People Case (Colombia) and the Urso Branco Prison Case (Brazil). During the time that the measures were in force, the Court learned of the death of 20 and 27 prisoners respectively.[711] These cases are followed by two Colombian cases, i.e. the Peace Community of San José de Apartadó Case[712] and the Communities of the Jiguamiandó and of the Curbaradó Case.[713] In the former, fifteen beneficiaries were killed and in the latter eight.

---

710 IACtHR, James, Briggs, Noel, Garcia and Bethel Case (Trinidad and Tobago), Order of August 16, 2000.

711 The first Order on this case adopted by the Court was in June 18, 2002. In August of 2009, the measures were still in force. See IACtHR, *Urso Branco Prison Case (Brazil)*, Order of March 22, 2004, Explanatory Statement 10; Order of July 17, 2004, Explanatory Statements 17, 23 and 24 and Order of September 21, 2005, Preambular Paragraph 14.

712 IACtHR, *Peace Community of San José de Apartadó Case (Colombia)*, Order of November 17, 2004, Explanatory Statements 10, 13(c) and 21; Order of March 15, 2005, Explanatory Statement 12, Preambular Paragraph 24 and Order of February 2, 2006, Explanatory Statement 12(b).

713 IACtHR, *Communities of the Jiguamiandó and of the Curbaradó Case (Colombia)*, Order of November 17, 2004, Explanatory Statements 3(a). 6(d) and 7. On the same subject see Order of March 15, 2005, Explanatory Statement 6 and Order of February 7, 2006, Explanatory Statements 17, 18(a) and 20(d).

In the Mendoza Prisons Case (Argentina) six inmates were killed while the measures were in force.[714] In the Monagas Judicial Confinement Center ("La Pica") Case (Venezuela) three beneficieries were killed.[715] In the James *et al.* Case (Trinidad and Tobago), the Giraldo Cardona Case (Colombia) and the Children Deprived of Liberty in the "Complexo do Tatuapé" of FEBEM Case (Brazil)[716] two beneficiaries were killed in each case.[717] Finally, in the Bámaca Velásquez (Guatemala), the Eloisa Barrios *et al.* (Venezuela), the Millacura Llaipén *et al.* (Argentina) and the Mery Naranjo *et al.* (Colombia) Cases one beneficiary was killed in each case.[718]

The Urso Branco Prison Case (Brazil) is of special concern not only because of the number of beneficiaries who were killed but also for the manner in which they were killed. According to the Commission, some inmates were killed publicly by other inmates, some of the bodies were cut up and pieces were thrown at the authorities and at other persons who were present in the jail.[719]

294. As can be seen in the Table, among the persons killed while under protective measures were six children, three of whom were related to two cases regarding Colombia and one regarding Venezuela and Brazil. One of the children was three years old, another four, another 17, and two more were 16 years old.[720] The latter, a witness in the Eloisa Barrios *et al.* Case (Venezuela), which was under consideration by the Commission, was gravely wounded by eight bullets, which later caused his death. In the case of the two children who died and were

---

714 IACtHR, *Mendoza Prisons Case (Argentina)*, Order June 18, 2005, Explanatory Statement 15(a)-(b) and 25(b), Preambular Paragraph 8.

715 IACtHR, Monagas Judicial Confinement Center ("La Pica") Case (Venezuela), Order February 9, 2006, Preambular Paragraph 11.

716 IACtHR, Children Deprived of Liberty in the "Complexo do Tatuapé" of FEBEM Case (Brazil), Order July 4, 2006, Preambular Paragraph 6.

717 IACtHR, *Giraldo Cardona Case (Colombia)*, Order of September 30, 1999, Explanatory Statement 4(c) and IACtHR, *James, Briggs, Noel, Garcia and Bethel Case (Trinidad and Tobago)*, Order of August 16, 2000, Explanatory Statements 4, 5 and 12.

718 IACtHR, *Bámaca Velásquez Case (Guatemala)*, Order of March 11, 2005, Explanatory Statement 17; IACtHR, *Eloisa Barrios et al. Case (Venezuela)*, Order of June 29, 2005, Explanatory Statements 4, 6 and 8, Preambular Paragraph 13; IACtHR, *Millacura Llaipén et al. Case. (Argentina)*, Order February 6, 2008, Preambular Paragraph 13 and IACtHR, *Mery Naranjo et al. Case (Colombia)*, Order January 31, 2008, Preambular Paragraph 22 and 24.

719 IACtHR, *Urso Branco Prison Case (Brazil)*, Order of April 22, 2004, Explanatory Statement 14. In the same case, see Order of July 7, 2004, Preambular Paragraph 8, where the Court expresses its great concern that, while the measures were still in effect, people had continued to die in the Urso Branco Prison, notwithstanding the fundamental purpose of the adoption of these measures to protect the life and personal integrity of all the inmates and those who were in the prison buildings.

720 The Order only mentioned that a little girl had died without stating her age. See IACtHR, *Peace Community of San José de Apartadó Case (Colombia)*, Order of November 17, 2004, Explanatory Statement 10.

included in the Peace Community Case (Colombia), the representatives of the beneficiaries reported that one was killed by the Colombian Army and another, according to the Colombian Army, had died as a consequence of a battle between the Army and the guerrillas.[721]

Table 32. Number of Children and Adults killed

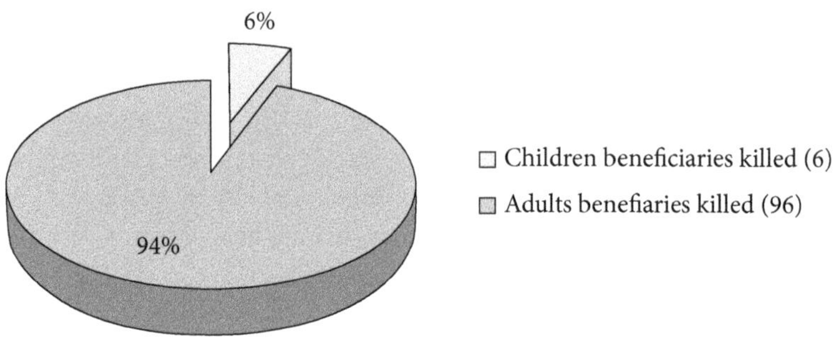

295. It is interesting to observe that in three cases the beneficiaries and the Commission itself requested that the measures be lifted since they judged that the situation of danger had ceased because the beneficiaries had changed jobs. Unfortunately, these persons were killed after the Court lifted the provisional measures. These acts occurred in the Giraldo Cardona (Colombia),[722] the Alvarez *et al.* (Colombia)[723] and the Digna Ochoa y Plácido *et al.* (Mexico) Cases.[724] In these cases, although the Commission had asked the Court to request the States that they provide information on the killings, the Court was emphatic in indicating that a State is not obligated to provide information on persons who were not beneficiaries of measures at the time they were killed. As the Court has taken this position, it is not possible to know the motive for those deaths or who was responsible, although of course there is a great probability

721 IACtHR, *Peace Community of San José de Apartadó Case (Colombia)*, Order of November 17, 2004, Explanatory Statements 10 and 13(c); IACtHR, *Communities of the Jiguamiandó and of the Curbaradó Case (Colombia)*, Order of November 17, 2004, Explanatory Statement 6(d) and IACtHR, *Eloisa Barrios et al. Case (Venezuela)*, Order of June 29, 2005, Explanatory Statements 4, 6 and 8, Preambular Paragraph 13.

722 IACtHR, *Giraldo Cardona Case (Colombia)*, Order of December 3, 2001.

723 IACtHR, *Alvarez et al. Case (Colombia)*, Order of May 30, 2001, Explanatory Statement 13, Preambular Paragraph 4. See also in the same case, Order of February 8, 2008, Preambular Paragraph 31.

724 In this case the measures were lifted at the request of the Commission. In the same year that the measures for Digna Ochoa were lifted, she was assassinated. As a result, provisional measures were ordered in the Miguel Agustín Pro Juárez Human Rights Center Case (Mexico). See IACtHR, *Digna Ochoa y Plácido et al. Case (Mexico)*, Order of August 28, 2001, Explanatory Statements 2 and 4, Enacting Part 1.

that the killings were related to the case under consideration in the inter-American system.

This position assumed by the Court, not to be concerned with the situation of former beneficiaries of the measures, is unfortunate because while it is true that the provisional measures were lifted, there is still a case under consideration in the inter-American system and it should be the responsibility of the State to ensure that every person involved in any way with cases under consideration should not have their rights infringed.

7.3.1.2. Violation of Physical Integrity

296. The right to physical integrity is of such importance that the American Convention[725] and the American Declaration[726] give it special protection by prohibiting torture, cruel, inhuman or degrading treatment and by prohibiting its suspension during states of emergency.[727]

297. Those persons or groups responsible for damage to the physical integrity of the beneficiaries, as in the case of violations of the right to life, are diverse. It is claimed that they are agents of the State or groups that act with the acquiescence of the State or third persons and other armed groups. Violations to the physical integrity of beneficiaries have been committed by different types of arms and methods, from attacks with knives to injuries from firearms.

725 Article 5 of the American Convention states the following: "Article 5. Right to Humane Treatment: 1. Every person has the right to have his physical, mental, and moral integrity respected. 2. No one shall be subjected to torture or to cruel, inhuman, or degrading punishment or treatment. All persons deprived of their liberty shall be treated with respect for the inherent dignity of the human person. 3. Punishment shall not be extended to any person other than the criminal. 4. Accused persons shall, save in exceptional circumstances, be segregated from convicted persons, and shall be subject to separate treatment appropriate to their status as unconvicted persons. 5. Minors while subject to criminal proceedings shall be separated from adults and brought before specialized tribunals, as speedily as possible, so that they may be treated in accordance with their status as minors. 6. Punishments consisting of deprivation of liberty shall have as an essential aim the reform and social readaptation of the prisoners".

726 Article 1 American Declaration.

727 IACtHR, *Gutiérrez Soler Case (Colombia)*, Order of March 11, 2005, Preambular Paragraph 11.

Table 33. Number of cases with violation of personal integrity

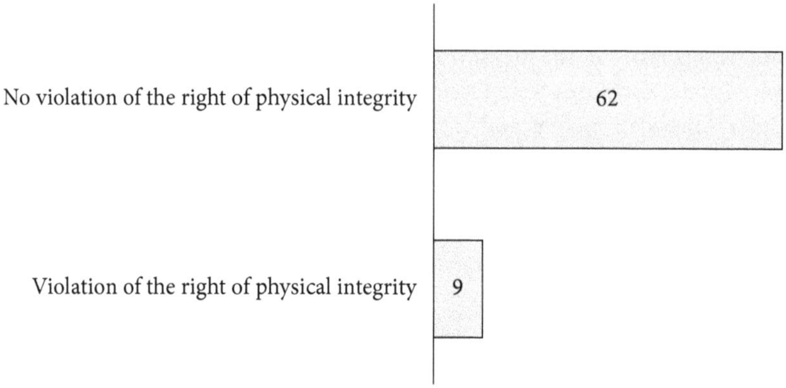

298. In nine cases, the Court was informed that beneficiaries had had their right to physical integrity infringed.[728] Except for the cases regarding prison systems, there is no pattern that would allow establishing a general rule on the circumstances in which the physical integrity of beneficiaries was affected: in the Colotenango Case (Guatemala), a beneficiary was injured with a machete after he was violently taken out of his house;[729] in the Carpio Nicolle Case (Guatemala) a beneficiary was attacked and one of the bodyguards was gravely injured;[730] in the Peace Community of San José de Apartadó Case a child[731] and two men were injured, one of them mortally, when soldiers sprayed them with gunfire and threw a hand grenade;[732] and in the Luisiana Ríos *et al.* Case (Venezuela) it was reported that a beneficiary had been wounded by gunfire in the ankle by a sniper, presumably a member of the State security forces.[733]

---

728 We do not count the Paniagua Morales *et al.* and Vásquez *et al.* Case (Guatemala), where the Court was informed that a witness had been shot twice. The protective measures were later lifted because, according to the Commission and the representatives, the attack was due to problems that the beneficiary had with a group of delinquents. See IACtHR, *Paniagua Morales et al. and Vásquez et al. Case (Guatemala)*, Order of January 29, 2001, Explanatory Statement 2. On the same subject, see Order of August 28, 2001, Explanatory Statement 5, Preambular Paragraph 1.

729 IACtHR, *Colotenango Case (Guatemala)*, Order of May 3, 1997, Explanatory Statement 3, Preambular Paragraph 3.

730 IACtHR, *Carpio Nicolle Case (Guatemala)*, Order of July 8, 2004, Explanatory Statement 29.

731 IACtHR, *Peace Community of San José de Apartadó Case (Colombia)*, Order of March 15, 2005, Explanatory Statement 9.

732 IACtHR, *Peace Community of San José de Apartadó Case (Colombia)*, Order of February 2, 2006, Explanatory Statement 16, Preambular Paragraph 21.

733 IACtHR, *Luisiana Ríos et al.Case (Venezuela)*, Order of May 4, 2004, Explanatory Statement 17(a).

299. In the Loayza Tamayo Case (Peru), as a consequence of isolation in jail and the state of incommunicado detention to which she was subjected, the victim's physical and psychological health had deteriorated. According to the Commission, she was subjected to a regime of inhumane and degrading treatment as a result of being held incommunicado and not being allowed out of her cold and humid cell of approximately two by three meters except for a half an hour a day. The beneficiary was not allowed to have a radio or newspapers or magazines and was only authorised to be outside 20 or 30 minutes each day. The cell had no direct ventilation and contained only cement shelves, a latrine and a washbasin. The cell did not have direct lighting. The light came indirectly from the fluorescent tubes in the corridor.[734] In the opinion of the Court, prolonged isolation and the forced state of incommunicado to which the victim was subjected were *per se* forms of cruel and inhumane treatment that infringed her psychological and moral integrity and the right of every detainee to the respect due the human being. Solitary confinement produces moral and psychological suffering for a detainee, places that person in a situation of special vulnerability and increases the risk of aggression and arbitrary acts in detention centers.[735]

300. On the other hand, in the Mendoza Prisons (Argentina), the Urso Branco Prison (Brazil) and the Children Deprived of Liberty in the "Complexo do Tatuapé" of FEBEM (Brazil) Cases several inmates were injured as a result of fights among them.[736] The jail conditions continued to be precarious and the security insufficient in spite of the measures adopted by the State.[737] There were also riots and it was contended that the force used by the State to resolve the situation was excessive.[738] The Court has held that States, in resolving alterations to the public order, as was reported to be the case of the prison in Brazil, must do so by following and applying its internal norms in order to restore public order,

734 IACtHR, *Loayza Tamayo Case (Peru)*, Order of September 13, 1996, Explanatory Statement 3.

735 IACtHR, *Bámaca Velásquez Case (Guatemala)*, Judgment on the Merits of November 25, 2000, para. 150; IACtHR, *Suárez Rosero Case (Ecuador)*, Judgment on the Merits of November 12, 1997, para. 90 and IACtHR, *Hilaire, Constantine and Benjamin et al. Case (Trinidad and Tobago)*, Judgment on the Merits of June 22, 2002, para. 164.

736 IACtHR, *Mendoza Prisons Case (Argentina)*, Order June 18, 2005, Explanatory Statements 15(a)-(b) and 25(b), Preambular Paragraph 8; IACtHR, *Children Deprived of Liberty in the "Complexo do Tatuapé" of FEBEM Case (Brazil)*, Order of November 30, 2005, Preambular Paragraph 10. In the Case of Monagas Judicial Confinement Center ("La Pica") (Venezuela) it was reported that one beneficiery was killed. See IACtHR, *Monagas Judicial Confinement Center ("La Pica") Case (Venezuela)*, Order of February 9, 2006, Preambular Paragraph 11.

737 IACtHR, *Urso Branco Prison Case (Brazil)*, Order of July 7, 2004, Explanatory Statements 23 and 24; Order of May 2, 2008, Preambular Paragraph 10 and IACtHR, *Mendoza Prisons Case (Argentina)*, Order of June 18, 2005, Explanatory Statements 15(a) and (b) and 25(b), Preambular Paragraph 8.

738 IACtHR, *Mendoza Prisons Case (Argentina)*, Order of March 30, 2006, Preambular Paragraph 8.

provided that these norms, and the actions taken in application of them, conform to the applicable norms of human rights protection.[739] While recognising the competence and even the obligation of the State to ensure the security of its inhabitants and to maintain public order, the power of the State is not unlimited. Its actions must respect the fundamental rights of the individual. The Court explicitly expressed its concern that the State had not adopted the measures necessary to protect the beneficiaries and dozens of them had been injured while the measures were in force. In addition, several prisoners threatened to kill themselves if the problem of overcrowding was not solved.[740]

301. Nineteen cases involved the right to psychological integrity. Most of the infringements to this right were threats made to the beneficiaries,[741] and usually

739 The Court has stated that the fact that a State faces a situation of internal unrest must not result in restrictions to the protection of the physical integrity of the person. Specifically, the Court has stressed that any "use of force that is not strictly necessary to ensure proper behavior on the part of the detainee constitutes an assault on the dignity of the person [...] in violation of Article 5 of the American Convention". See IACtHR, *Bámaca Velásquez Case (Guatemala)*, Judgment on the Merits of November 25, 2000, para. 155.

740 IACtHR, *Urso Branco Prison Case (Brazil)*, Order of April 22, 2004, Preambular Paragraph 10; Order of July 7, 2004, Explanatory Statements 23 and 24, Order of September 21, 2005, Explanatory Statement 11(d), Order of May 2, 2008, Preambular Paragraph 10.

741 IACtHR, *Colotenango Case (Guatemala)*, Order of May 18, 1995, Preambular Paragraph 4 and Order of April 16, 1997, Enacting Part 2; IACtHR, *Caballero Delgado and Santana Case (Colombia)*, Order of April 16, 1997, Enacting Part 2, Order of September 30, 1999, Explanatory Statement 4 and Order of July 8, 2004, Explanatory Statements 16 and 33; IACtHR, *Carpio Nicolle Case (Guatemala)*, Order of February 1, 1996, Explanatory Statement 3; Order of September 10, 1996, Explanatory Statement 4 and Order of July 8, 2004, Explanatory Statement 33, Preambular Paragraphs 15 and 16; IACtHR, *Blake Case (Guatemala)*, Order of June 6, 2003, Explanatory Statements 17 and 18, Preambular Paragraph 12; IACtHR, *Giraldo Cardona Case (Colombia)*, Order of February 5, 1997, Explanatory Statement 5, Order of November 27, 1998, Explanatory Statement 4(b) and (d) and Order of September 30, 1999, Explanatory Statement 4(c); IACtHR, *Alvarez et al. Case (Colombia)*, Order of September 19, 1997, Explanatory Statement 10, Order of December 22, 1997, Preambular Paragraph 3, Order of August 6, 1998, Explanatory Statement 7, Enacting Part 1, Order of August 29, 1998, Preambular Paragraph 2 and Order of October 11, 2002, Explanatory Statement 11; IACtHR, *Bámaca Velásquez Case (Guatemala)*, Order of September 5, 2001, Preambular Paragraph 10 and Order of November 20, 2003, Preambular Paragraph 15; IACtHR, *Peace Community of San José de Apartadó Case (Colombia)*, Order of June 18, 2002, Explanatory Statement 5(k) and (o), Preambular Paragraph 8, Enacting Part 2, Order of November 17 2004, Explanatory Statement 5(c), Preambular Paragraph 12, Order of March 15, 2005, Explanatory Statement 14(b) and Order of February 2, 2006, Preambular Paragraphs 21 and 23; IACtHR, *Haitians and Dominicans of Haitian Origin in the Dominican Republic Case (Dominican Republic)*, Order of May 26, 2001, Preambular Paragraph 10 and Order of February 2, 2006, Preambular Paragraph 11; IACtHR, *Gallardo Rodríguez Case (Mexico)*, Order of February 18, 2002, Explanatory Statement 8, Preambular Paragraph 6, Enacting Part 1; IACtHR, *Helen Mack Chang et al. (Guatemala)*, Order of August 26, 2002, Explanatory Statement 6, Order of February 21, 2003, Explanatory Statement 5, Preambular Paragraph 7 and Order of April 17, 2003, Explanatory Statement 4; IACtHR, *Liliana Ortega et al. Case (Venezuela)*, Order of December 2, 2003, Explanatory Statement 30(b); IACtHR, *Luis*

also affected their closest family members. That means that when the beneficiary decides as a means of protection to change his residence or even leave the country, his family members must do the same. This situation often results in the protective measures being broadened to protect the family. The family members of victims of human rights violations may also be considered under certain circumstances to be victims of violations of human rights set forth in the Convention.[742]

302. Some cases are noteworthy because of the persistence of the threats, others by the decision of several beneficiaries to abandon their homes, others for decisions to quit jobs as the only form of protection. For example, in the Carpio Nicolle Case (Guatemala) and the Blake Case (Guatemala) the beneficiaries received threats for eight straight years. In the Case of the Peace Community of San José de Apartadó (Colombia) and the Case of the Haitians and Dominicans of Haitian Origin in the Dominican Republic (Dominican Republic) the threats were made for a period of six years. In the latter case, as in the Carpio Nicolle Case and the Bámaca Velásquez Case (Guatemala), faced with the situation of insecurity the beneficiaries decided to go into exile and some of them did so with their families.[743] On the other hand, in the Luis Uzcátegui Case (Venezuela) the intimidations directed at the beneficiary obligated him to change constantly his residence.[744]

303. In the Eloisa Barrios *et al.* Case (Venezuela), as the facts showed a progressive pattern of violence and threats against the beneficiaries, one of them

---

Uzcátegui Case (Venezuela), Order of February 20, 2003, Explanatory Statements 26 and 31(b); IACtHR, *Communities of the Jiguamiandó and of the Curbaradó Case (Colombia)*, Order of November 17, 2004, Explanatory Statements 6(a)-(d) and 7(b), Preambular Paragraphs 9 and 12, Order of March 15, 2005, Explanatory Statement 10 and Order of February 7, 2006, Explanatory Statement 18(b), Preambular Paragraph 21; IACtHR, *Plan de Sánchez Massacre Case (Guatemala)*, Order of September 8, 2004, Explanatory Statement 10; IACtHR, *19 Tradesmen (Colombia)*, Order of July 4, 2006, Preambular Paragraph 13; IACtHR, *Eloisa Barrios et al. Case (Venezuela)*, Order of June 29, 2005, Preambular Paragraph 10; IACtHR, *Forensic Anthropology Foundation Case (Guatemala)*, Order of November 21, 2007, Preambular Paragraph 6 and IACtHR, *Integrantes del Equipo de Estudios Comunitarios y Acción Psicosocial (ECAP). Masacre Plan de Sánchez Case (Guatemala)*, Order of November 26, 2007, Preambular Paragraph 6.

742 IACtHR, *Gómez Paquiyauri Brothers Case (Peru)*, Judgment on the Merits of July 8, 2004, para. 118 and IACtHR, *Helen Mack Chang et al. Case (Guatemala)*, Judgment on the Merits of November 25, 2003, paras. 225 and 232.

743 IACtHR, *Carpio Nicolle Case (Guatemala)*, Order of July 28, 2004, Explanatory Statement 33, Preambular Paragraphs 15 and 16 and IACtHR, *Haitians and Dominicans of Haitian Origin in the Dominican Republic Case (Dominican Republic)*, Order of February 2, 2006, Preambular Paragraphs 11 and 19.

744 IACtHR, *Luis Uzcátegui Case (Venezuela)*, Order of December 2, 2003, Explanatory Statements 26 and 31(b).

decided to abandon his home together with his wife and son because he was afraid of being killed.[745] In the Giraldo Cardona Case (Colombia), a beneficiary and her children decided to hide in the homes of family and friends and another had to leave the city where he lived when he heard that hired killers had been asking for him at work.[746] A similar situation occurred in the Peace Community of San José de Apartadó (Colombia) and the Communities of the Jiguamiandó and of the Curbaradó (Colombia) Cases. In the former, 58 families had to move in order to protect their lives[747] and in the latter 300 families moved as a result of threats and harassments. In the latter case, the Commission reported that, when it submitted the request for provisional measures, 500 families were covered and two years later the number of families had dropped to 200.[748]

304. In the Liliana Ortega *et al.* Case (Venezuela), given the increase in threats, the beneficiaries decided to close on three occasions the office of the human rights organisation where they worked. In addition, each time that the beneficiaries made public appearances related to the defense of human rights, the acts of harassment increased to reach a level of concern.[749]

305. Of the 71 cases where measures of protection were adopted, beneficiaries were victims of some type of physical aggression in nine cases and the psychological integrity of protected persons was violated in 19 cases, which leads to the conclusion that in protecting the right to physical integrity the measures were not effective in 13% of the cases, and with respect to psychological integrity, the provisional measures were not effective in 27% of the cases.

7.3.1.3. Violation of Other Rights

306. In addition to violations of the rights to life and personal integrity, freedom of movement and residence, personal freedom, the right to education and the right to work were also affected. It is important to clarify that we are not interested in debating what type of rights may be protected by provisional

[745] IACtHR, *Eloisa Barrios et al. Case (Venezuela)*, Order of June 29, 2005, Preambular Paragraphs 10, 12 and 14.

[746] IACtHR, *Giraldo Cardona Case (Colombia)*, Order of February 5, 1997, Explanatory Statement 5.

[747] IACtHR, *Peace Community of San José de Apartadó Case (Colombia)*, Order of November 17, 2004, Explanatory Statement 5(c), Preambular Paragraph 12.

[748] IACtHR, *Communities of the Jiguamiandó and of the Curbaradó Case (Colombia)*, November 17, 2004, Explanatory Statement 7(b), Preambular Paragraphs 9 and 12, Order of March 15, 2005, Explanatory Statement 10 and Order of February 7, 2006, Explanatory Statement 18(b), Preambular Paragraph 21.

[749] IACtHR, *Liliana Ortega et al. Case (Venezuela)*, Order of June 14, 2005, Explanatory Statements 6 and 14.

measures,[750] because that was already analysed in the section on "Substantive Conditions of Admissibility" (*supra*, nos. 85-98).[751] Here we will describe the rights that were infringed while the provisional measures were in force.

307. The Indigenous Sarayaku People Case (Ecuador) was for the Court a matter of special concern because members of that community saw their rights to life, personal integrity and freedom of movement affected since they could not use their principal means of communication, nor did they have access to the place where they normally obtained their food. This situation arose as a result of conflicts that the beneficiaries had with a neighbouring community that had decided to block the free circulation of the river that was the principal means of communication in the area and because the Army and a petroleum company had placed explosives in the area where the Sarayakus traditionally hunted.[752]

308. On the other hand, in the Peace Community of San José de Apartadó Case (Colombia) the Commission argued that during four weeks not one public passenger or cargo vehicle entered or left San José de Apartadó. As a result of the lack of transportation, neither teachers nor health personnel could enter the village, the seriously ill had to be transported by mule to receive medical attention and certain products began to rot.[753] These facts implied infringements of freedom of movement because nobody could enter or leave San José; the right to education because the students could not receive classes because their professors could not enter their lands; the right to health because the ill could not receive medical attention in the infirmary of the Community and the right to work of those who were employed in public transportation.

309. In the Communities of the Jiguamiandó and of the Curbaradó Case (Colombia), several of the beneficiaries were forced to move due to the constant armed activities. This situation also meant that the family and collective plots of crops were abandoned, so that in a short time the population was without sources of food. Most of the people who were forcibly displaced ended in subhuman

---

750 One school considers that irreparable damage only concerns the rights to life, physical integrity, personal freedom and judicial guarantees inasmuch as these have direct impact on the enjoyment of others. Others consider that irreparable harm may be produced regarding any right, because nothing in the norms affirms the contrary, nor do they apply restrictions.

751 Specifically, in the Section on the "Hierarchy of the Law".

752 IACtHR, *Indigenous Sarayaku People Case (Ecuador)*, Order of June 17, 2005, Explanatory Statement 31(m), Preambular Paragraphs 8 and 12. In the Colotenango Case (Guatemala), according to the Commission, certain beneficiaries had their right to freedom of movement and circulation restricted. See IACtHR, *Colotenango Case (Guatemala)*, Order of May 18, 1995, Preambular Paragraph 4.

753 IACtHR, *Peace Community of San José de Apartadó Case (Colombia)*, Order of June 18, 2002, Explanatory Statement 5(p).

conditions in the poor zones of large and medium-size cities, which makes forced displacement a multiple, massive and continuous violation of the rights of the persons obligated to migrate.[754] Given the grave repercussions involved in any forced displacement, in this case the situation was exacerbated because it was almost impossible for the displaced to return since the sites that were abandoned were used to plant African palm trees.[755]

310. The personal freedom of some of the beneficiaries was also affected in some cases. For example, in the Peace Community of San José de Apartadó Case (Colombia) there were reports of numerous detentions of peasants and members of the Internal Council,[756] among them leaders of the Community who were detained and interrogated by the Army.[757] Similarly, in the Luis Uzcátegui Case (Venezuela) the Commission indicated that the residence of a beneficiary had been searched without a warrant by the Military Police and that he had been detained illegally for one night.[758]

7.3.2. COMPLIANCE THAT PRODUCED A SITUATION OF GREATER RISK

311. Reference will be made in this section to five cases where the measures of protection adopted by the States rather than protecting the beneficiaries, placed them in a situation of greater risk, and to other cases where the measures adopted were obviously not effective.

312. In one case, Peru in an attempt to comply with the measures, summoned the threatened persons by radio to appear at a military installation to coordinate the measures required by the Inter-American Court. According to the Commission, this measure had an intimidating and not a protective nature for the public way in which the beneficiaries were summoned – by radio – and for the place to which they were summoned – a military installation.[759]

---

754 Constitutional Court of Colombia. Plenary. Judgment of Unification SU-1150 of August 30, 2000. *Magistrado Ponente* Eduardo Cifuentes Muñoz.

755 IACtHR, *Communities of the Jiguamiandó and of the Curbaradó Case (Colombia)*, Order of March 15, 2005, Explanatory Statement 3(a) and (h).

756 IACtHR, *Peace Community of San José de Apartadó Case (Colombia)*, Order of March 15, 2005, Explanatory Statement 9 and Order of February 2, 2006, Explanatory Statement 14, Preambular Paragraph 21.

757 IACtHR, *Peace Community of San José de Apartadó Case (Colombia)*, Order of March 15, 2005, Explanatory Statement 9.

758 IACtHR, *Luis Uzcátegui Case (Venezuela)*, Order of December 20, 2003, Explanatory Statement 11.

759 IACtHR, *Bustíos-Rojas Case (Peru)*, Order of August 8, 1990, Explanatory Statement 8.

313. In the Colotenango Case, although in principle the State had complied with its obligation to investigate and punish those responsible for the acts that led to the adoption of the protective measures, the persons responsible were freed by other former policemen by violent means one year after having been sentenced to 25 years in jail for human rights violations. Two years later, the escapees were still at large and there had been no efforts to capture them.[760] This situation put the beneficiaries of the measures in more serious peril than initially, since the former policemen knew perfectly well who had been the cause of their identification and criminal trial. The situation of the beneficiaries had thus been aggravated exponentially.

314. Some of the measures adopted by the States have not been effective from the moment that they were adopted. For example, those implemented in the Carpio Nicolle Case (Guatemala), in which the State appointed a bodyguard for the beneficiaries who did not have permission to carry a gun, had no official identification, was paid very little and did not have medical insurance. In this case, the beneficiary had to supply guns to the bodyguard.[761] A similar situation occurred in the Plan of Sánchez Massacre Case (Guatemala), where the police did not have sufficient equipment to supervise the patrols of the Community.[762]

315. Another lamentable situation concerned the Liliana Ortega *et al.* Case (Venezuela), where one of the officials protecting a beneficiary had been tried for killing a leader of the opposition and, in addition, did not have a firearm to do his job.[763] This circumstance was especially grave since the petitioners argued that the danger to the beneficiaries was due to their opposition to the President of Venezuela. Similarly, in the Luis Uzcátegui Case (Venezuela) the State chose the police organisation, denounced by the beneficiaries as the cause of the dangerous situation, to be in charge of offering them protection. This was obviously unacceptable and unjustifiable.[764] Finally, in the Eloisa Barrios *et al.* Case (Venezuela) the protection consisted of visiting the residence of a beneficiary every four or ten days and asking her to sign a paper.[765]

---

760 IACtHR, *Colotenango Case (Guatemala)*, Order of June 3, 1999, Explanatory Statements 6(b) and 7, Preambular Paragraph 6 and Order of September 5, 2001, Explanatory Statement 14.

761 IACtHR, *Carpio Nicolle Case (Guatemala)*, Order of February 21, 2003, Explanatory Statement 15(g) and Order of December 2, 2003, Explanatory Statement 29.

762 IACtHR, *Plan de Sánchez Massacre Case (Guatemala)*, Order of September 8, 2002, Explanatory Statements 15 and 16.

763 IACtHR, *Liliana Ortega et al. Case (Venezuela)*, Order of June 3, 1999, Explanatory Statements 6(b) and 7.

764 IACtHR, *Luis Uzcátegui Case (Venezuela)*, Order of February 20, 2003, Explanatory Statement 17(c).

765 IACtHR, *Eloisa Barrios et al. Case (Venezuela)*, Order of June 29, 2005, Explanatory Statement 27(c). See D. Padilla, "Provisional Measures Under the American Convention on Human

7.3.3. NON-COMPLIANCE FOR NOT PRESENTING REPORTS AND INVESTIGATING

316. States did not comply at least once in 20 cases with their duty to present information on the measures of protection.[766] Non-compliance of this duty is especially grave because these reports provide the Court with knowledge of the situation of the persons who are in a dangerous situation and allow it to evaluate implementation of the measures by the State.[767] When States do not present their reports, the Court usually reminds the States of their obligation to present them and their importance. When non-compliance continues, the Court informs the OAS General Assembly of the situation in its Annual Report.

Rights", in *Liber Amicorum Héctor Fix-Zamudio*, San José, Inter-American Court of Human Rights, 1998, 1192.

766 IACtHR, *Colotenango Case (Guatemala)*, Order of September 5, 2001, Preambular Paragraphs 8 and 11; IACtHR, *Cesti Hurtado Case (Peru)*, Order of November 19, 1999, Explanatory Statement 3; IACtHR, *Bámaca Velásquez Case (Guatemala)*, Order of September 5, 2001, Enacting Part 10; IACtHR, *Clemente Teherán Case (Colombia)*, Order of December 1, 2003, Explanatory Statement 10, Preambular Paragraph 5; IACtHR, *Peace Community of San José de Apartadó Case (Colombia)*, Order of February 2, 2006, Explanatory Statement 8(a); IACtHR, *Constitutional Court Case (Peru)*, Order of August 14, 2000, Preambular Paragraph 12; IACtHR, *Carpio Nicolle Case (Guatemala)*, Order of July 26, 1995, Preambular Paragraph 1, Enacting Part 2; IACtHR, *Loayza Tamayo Case (Peru)*, Order of September 13, 1996, Preambular Paragraph 3; IACtHR, *James, Briggs, Noel, Garcia and Bethel Case (Trinidad and Tobago)*, Order of May 25, 1999, Preambular Paragraph 1(d) and (e), Enacting Part 1(b) and (e) and IACtHR, *Urso Branco Prison Case (Brazil)*, Order of April 22, 2004, Explanatory Statement 14 and Order of July 7, 2004, Preambular Paragraph 16; IACtHR, *Luisiana Ríos et al. Case (Venezuela)*, Order of November 21, 2003, Explanatory Statement 10 and Order of December 2, 2003, Preambular Paragraphs 9 and 16, Enacting Part 1; IACtHR, *Liliana Ortega et al. Case (Venezuela)*, Order of December 2, 2003, Preambular Paragraphs 9 and 16, Enacting Part 1; IACtHR, *Luis Uzcátegui Case (Venezuela)*, Order of December 2, 2003, Preambular Paragraphs 9 and 16, Enacting Part 1; IACtHR, *Communities of the Jiguamiandó and of the Curbaradó Case (Colombia)*, Order of November 17, 2004, Preambular Paragraph 16, Order of March 15, 2005, Preambular Paragraph 11 and Order of February 7, 2006, Explanatory Statement 12; IACtHR, *Lysias Fleury Case (Haiti)*, Order of December 2, 2003, Preambular Paragraph 13 and Order of November 25, 2008, Preambular Paragraphs 7 and 9; IACtHR, *Marta Colomina and Liliana Velásquez (Venezuela)*, Order of September 8, 2003, Explanatory Statement 6, Preambular Paragraphs 10 and 18, Enacting Parts 1–3, and Order of July 4, 2006, Preambular Paragraph 10; IACtHR, *19 Tradesmen Case (Colombia)*, Order of July 4, 2006, Preambular Paragraph 15; IACtHR, *Boyce and Joseph Case (Barbados)*, Order of November 25, 2004, Preambular Paragraph 12, Enacting Part 1; IACtHR, *Mapiripán Massacre Case (Colombia)*, Order of May 3, 2008, Preambular Paragraph 4,8–9; IACtHR, *Integrantes del Equipo de Estudios Comunitarios y Acción Psicosocial (ECAP). Masacre Plan de Sánchez Case (Guatemala)*, Order of November 25, 2006, Preambular Paragraph 17; Marta Colomina Case (Venezuela).

767 IACtHR, The *19 Tradesmen Case (Colombia)*, Order of July 4, 2006, Preambular Paragraph 15.

317. The duty to investigate has been imposed in 51 of the 71 cases and the Court has established non-compliance on twelve occasions.[768] In the Carpio Nicolle Case (Guatemala), the Court held that the State had not complied with its obligation because it had decided to close the investigation on the threats and intimidations that had resulted in the adoption of provisional measures.[769] In the Vogt Case (Guatemala), the Court observed that while the State had made progress in some investigations, there was non-compliance because the investigations had not been sufficient or effective.[770] In the other cases, there was non-compliance because the States simply had not begun any type of investigation.[771]

318. Until 2006 the Court held that investigating, identifying and punishing those responsible for the acts that gave rise to the adoption of provisional measures was an essential element of protection,[772] that must be done seriously and not as a mere formality intended *a priori* to fail.[773] The duty to investigate

---

768 IACtHR, *Carpio Nicolle Case (Guatemala)*, Order of September 30, 1999, Preambular Paragraph 2; IACtHR, *Vogt Case (Guatemala)*, Order of June 27, 1996, Preambular Paragraph 4; IACtHR, *Alvarez et al. Case (Colombia)*, Order of July 19, 1998, Preambular Paragraph 3; IACtHR, *Luisiana Ríos et al. Case (Venezuela)*, Order of December 2, 2003, Preambular Paragraphs 9 and 16, Enacting Parts 1 and 2; IACtHR, *Liliana Ortega et al. Case (Venezuela)*, Order of December 2, 2003, Preambular Paragraphs 9 and 16, Enacting Part 1 and IACtHR, *Luis Uzcátegui Case (Venezuela)*, Order of December 2, 2003, Preambular Paragraphs 9 and 16, Enacting Part 1. See also *Forensic Anthropology Foundation Case (Mexico)*, Mapiripán Massacre Case (Colombia), Persons imprisoned in the "Dr. Sebastião Martins Silveira" Penitentiary in Araraquara, São Paulo Case (Brazil), Children Deprived of Liberty in the "Complexo do Tatuapé" of FEBEM Case (Brazil), Yare I and Yare II Capital Region Center Case (Venezuela), Monagas Judicial Confinement Center ("La Pica") Case (Venezuela), Gloria Giralt de García-Prieto *et al.* Case (El Salvador), Guerrero-Gallucci y Martínez-Barrios Case (Venezuela), Integrantes del Equipo de Estudios Comunitarios y Acción Psicosocial (ECAP). Masacre Plan de Sánchez Case (Guatemala), Mery Naranjo *et al.* Case (Colombia), Millacura Llaipén *et al.* Case. (Argentina), Pilar Noriega *et al.* Case (Mexico) and the Hinostroza *et al.* Case (Peru).

769 IACtHR, *Carpio Nicolle Case (Guatemala)*, Order of September 30, 1999, Preambular Paragraph 2.

770 IACtHR, *Vogt Case (Guatemala)*, Order of June 27, 1996, Preambular Paragraph 4.

771 IACtHR, *Luisiana Ríos et al. Case (Venezuela)*, Order of December 2, 2003; IACtHR, *Liliana Ortega et al. Case (Venezuela)*, Order of December 2, 2003; IACtHR, *Marta Colomina and Liliana Velásquez (Venezuela)*, Order of December 2, 2003 and IACtHR, *Luis Uzcátegui Case (Venezuela)*, Order of December 2, 2003, Preambular Paragraphs 9 and 16, Enacting Parts 1 and 7. See also IACtHR, *Lysias Fleury Case (Haiti)*, Order of December 2, 2003.

772 IACtHR, *Colotenango Case (Guatemala)*, Order of February 2, 2000, Preambular Paragraph 9; IACtHR, *Peace Community of San José de Apartadó Case (Colombia)*, Order of March 15, 2005, Preambular Paragraph 9 and IACtHR, *Gutiérrez Soler Case (Colombia)*, Order of March 11, 2005, Enacting Part 2.

773 IACtHR, *Colotenango Case (Guatemala)*, Order of September 5, 2001, Preambular Paragraphs 7 and 8, where the Court held that even though it had received information on behalf of the State, it was impossible to know the true situation of the beneficiaries of the measures, since the information provided by the State was very limited. This created a situation of uncertainty

was related to the obligation that each State has to combat impunity by all available legal means.[774] The Court has expressed the view that the punishment of those responsible is important because it avoids impunity and with that the chronic repetition of human rights violations.[775] Actually, the Court pointed out that the alleged lack of investigation on the part of a State does not constitute, *per se*, circumstances of extreme gravity and urgency that would warrant maintaining the provisional measures.[776]

7.4. DIFFICULTIES TO COMPLY

319. There are many difficulties that present themselves when the object is to protect persons who are in a situation of danger. These obstacles result in the protection of the rights not being as effective as one would wish and there is often a complete failure of the efficacy of the measures. Some difficulties are related to the lack of confidence of the beneficiaries in the institutions of the State.

7.4.1. LACK OF CONFIDENCE IN THE BODIES OF PROTECTION

320. The lack of confidence in the State bodies that should provide protection is one of the principal problems that persons face when they are in a situation of

---

for the Court, incompatible with the preventive and protective nature of the provisional measures, which required that the State send more complete information in order to determine whether it was complying with the measures. IACtHR, *Carpio Nicolle Case (Guatemala)*, Order of July 8, 2004, Preambular Paragraph 13 and IACtHR, *Miguel Agustín Pro Juárez Human Rights Center et al. Case (Mexico)*, Order of April 30, 2001, Preambular Paragraph 11.

774 IACtHR, *Miguel Agustín Pro Juárez Human Rights Center et al. Case (Mexico)*, Order of April 30, 2001, Preambular Paragraph 11 and IACtHR, *Carpio Nicolle Case (Guatemala)*, Order of September 5, 2001, Preambular Paragraph 7. Regarding this case, the Court stated that closing the investigation was an omission of the State‘s obligation to investigate since it was not taking the positive and necessary measures to clarify the acts that had motivated the adoption of provisional measures.

775 IACtHR, *Bámaca Velásquez Case (Guatemala)*, Order of November 20, 2003, Preambular Paragraph 18; IACtHR, *Luis Uzcátegui Case (Venezuela)*, Order of February 20, 2003, Enacting Part 12; IACtHR, *Luisiana Ríos et al. Case (Venezuela)*, Order of February 20, 2003, Preambular Paragraph 9 and IACtHR, *Liliana Ortega et al. Case (Venezuela)*, Order of February 21, 2003, Enacting Part 9.

776 IACtHR, *Colotenango Case (Guatemala)*, Order of july 12, 2007, Preambular Paragraph 11 and 14; IACtHR, *Gómez Paquiyauri Brothers (Peru)*, Order of May 3, 2008, Enacting Part 1 and 2; IACtHR, *López Alvarez et al Case (Honduras)*, Order of January 26, 2009, Preambular Paragraph 23; IACtHR, *Carlos Nieto Palma Case (Venezuela)*, Order of January 26, 2009, Preambular Paragraph 15.

extreme gravity and urgency. This circumstance has led some beneficiaries to refuse to furnish information to the State on their activities and some to prefer to renounce the measures of protection.

321. The beneficiaries told the Court in ten cases that they were afraid to provide information on their activities and places of residence to the authorities assigned to protect them because they considered that it was precisely those authorities who were responsible for the dangerous situation. In the Giraldo Cardona Case (Colombia), the Commission pointed out that the protection of the beneficiaries had been assigned to members of the institutions that were responsible for the threats. It also pointed out that the State was pressuring the beneficiaries to accept the services of armed escorts and, if they did not want them, it was pressuring them to renounce the protection. In those circumstances, one of the beneficiaries decided to sign a document renouncing the measures for her and her daughters and then chose to hide in the homes of family and friends.[777]

In the Helen Mack Chang *et al.* Case (Guatemala), the beneficiaries indicated that they did not feel confident that the security forces would not inform on them and because groups that carried out acts of political violence belonged to the security forces.[778] Similarly, in the Indigenous Sarayaku People (Ecuador), the Eloisa Barrios *et al.* (Venezuela), the Gloria Giralt de García-Prieto *et al.* (El Salvador), the Guerrero-Gallucci and Martínez-Barrios (Venezuela) and the Integrantes del Equipo de Estudios Comunitarios y Acción Psicosocial (ECAP). Masacre Plan de Sánchez (Guatemala) Cases, the beneficiaries expressed their lack of confidence in the security agents as an institution that might provide a true protection.[779]

This situation, when persons are assigned who were involved in the acts that gave rise to the situation of danger, has resulted in some beneficiaries preferring not to cooperate with State authorities. Regarding acts that occurred in the Peace Community of San José de Apartadó Case (Colombia), the members of the Community refused to collaborate with the judicial authorities and the witnesses

777 IACtHR, *Giraldo Cardona Case (Colombia)*, Order of February 5, 1997, Explanatory Statement 5.

778 IACtHR, *Helen Mack Chang et al. (Guatemala)*, Order of August 26, 2002, Explanatory Statement 6.

779 IACtHR, *Indigenous Sarayaku People Case (Ecuador)*, Order of June 17, 2005, Explanatory Statement 31(k) and (m); IACtHR, *Eloisa Barrios et al. Case (Venezuela)*, Order of June 29, 2005, Explanatory Statement 15; IACtHR, *Gloria Giralt de García-Prieto et al. Case (El Salvador)*, Order of January 27, 2007, Explanatory Statement 10 (a); IACtHR, *Guerrero-Gallucci and Martínez-Barrios Case (Venezuela)*, Order of November 29, 2007, Preambular Paragraph 5 and IACtHR, *Integrantes del Equipo de Estudios Comunitarios y Acción Psicosocial (ECAP). Masacre Plan de Sánchez Case (Guatemala)*, Order of November 26, 2007, Preambular Paragraph 6.

were unanimous in refusing to give testimony.[780] On another occasion, when the agents of the State went to provide security to the beneficiaries, the latter stated that they did not need it and that they would not provide information on their places of residence or the telephone numbers of the persons who worked with that organization because they did not have confidence in the State authorities and because their members were always accompanied by members of the International Peace Brigades.[781]

322. While the beneficiaries' fears may be perfectly understandable since it is not unreasonable that they would not have confidence in the State body that they believed caused the situation of danger, it is true that they create a rather complicated situation that is not easy to resolve. Thus, when a beneficiary's rights are infringed, the State may argue that it could not provide adequate protection due to the lack of cooperation of those persons. This occurred in the Bámaca Velásquez Case (Guatemala), where the State, when confronted with the murder of a beneficiary, said that it had not been able to provide any type of protection because that person, like the other beneficiaries, had not wished to give the information necessary for the State to implement the measures of protection.[782]

323. Faced with the refusal of the beneficiaries to offer information on their activities, the Court has adopted three positions.

The first position the Court has taken is to invite the State to enter into a dialogue with the persons, so that together they may implement the measures of protection. In the Giraldo Cardona Case (Colombia), given the aforementioned difficult situation, the Court requested the State to communicate with the beneficiaries in order to decide on measures that would offer a serious, definitive and trustworthy protection.[783]

In other cases, the position of the Court has been that of stating that the beneficiaries have the obligation to cooperate with the State, so that the latter might adopt more effectively the pertinent provisions of security.[784]

---

780 IACtHR, *Peace Community of San José de Apartadó Case (Colombia)*, Order of February 2, 2006, Explanatory Statement 12(c), Preambular Paragraph 20 and Order of February 6, 2008, Preambular Paragraph 13 and 14.

781 IACtHR, *Alvarez et al. Case (Colombia)*, Order of November 12, 2000, Explanatory Statement 13.

782 IACtHR, *Bámaca Velásquez Case (Guatemala)*, Order of November 20, 2003, Explanatory Statement 19.

783 IACtHR, *Giraldo Cardona Case (Colombia)*, Order of November 27, 1998, Enacting Part 3; IACtHR, *Gloria Giralt de García-Prieto et al. Case (El Salvador)*, Order of January 27, 2007, Enacting Part 6.

784 IACtHR, *Alvarez et al. Case (Colombia)*, Order of August 29, 1998, Preambular Paragraph 6, Enacting Part 5.

Finally, the Court has also held that the State must ensure that the measures of protection are not provided by police who, according to the beneficiaries, were involved in the acts denounced.[785]

7.4.2. LACK OF POLITICAL WILL

324. The lack of political will is another factor that negatively affects compliance of the protective measures. This lack of will has been openly expressed in three cases involving Colombia, Venezuela[786] and Trinidad and Tobago.

With respect to Colombia, the President of that country, referring to the members of the Peace Community of San José de Apartadó, stated publicly that San José was a corridor for the Revolutionary Armed Forces of Colombia (the FARC) and that some leaders of that Community together with the international organisations who were working with them were obstructing justice.[787]

In the Liliana Ortega *et al.* Case (Venezuela), the State claimed that "the excess of democracy and the desire to subsume oneself within a participative democracy of the Venezuelan people, have made non-governmental organisations proliferate disproportionately." It also stated that no cabinet minister had the protection that the petitioners of the human rights organisation had requested.[788]

These public declarations by the Presidents of Colombia and Venezuela against the beneficiaries of provisional measures increased their risk and that of the international organisations that were aiding them. In addition, this identification and intimidation affect the credibility and transparency of persons who are in a situation of danger and create a hostile environment that ends up making relations between the State bodies and the beneficiaries of provisional measures ever more distant.

Lack of political will led Trinidad and Tobago to denounce the American Convention and to implement a domestic judgment that condemned to death two beneficiaries. Notwithstanding the fact that the Court had expressly ordered the State to suspend the sentences while the case was under consideration in the inter-American system, Trinidad and Tobago decided to execute the beneficiaries.

---

785 IACtHR, *Eloisa Barrios et al. Case (Venezuela)*, Order of November 23, 2004, Enacting Part 3 and Order of June 29, 2005, Enacting Part 9.

786 An analysis of Venezuela's position on the international law of human rights may be found in C.F. Lusverti, "El derecho internacional de los derechos humanos y los tribunales nacionales: el caso de Venezuela", *Revista CEJIL. Debates sobre Derechos Humanos y el Sistema Interamericano* 2005, 88–93.

787 IACtHR, *Peace Community of San José de Apartadó Case (Colombia)*, Order of November 17, 2004, Explanatory Statement 18.

788 IACtHR, *Liliana Ortega et al. Case (Venezuela)*, Order of February 21, 2003.

Later on, in application of Article 78 of the Convention, Trinidad and Tobago notified its denunciation of the Convention.[789]

325. There has also been a lack of political will to resolve the situation of danger involving conditions in certain prisons of Brazil and Argentina. According to the information submitted, prison conditions were precarious and security was inefficient. In the Urso Branco Prison Case (Brazil) 27 inmates were killed while the measures were in force and in the Mendoza Prisons Case (Argentina), although the State had adopted several measures tending to improve the situation, the overcrowding and the deficient conditions persisted. The acts of violence continued to the point that four persons had died in unknown circumstances. It was also claimed that while the measures were in force, there were riots and it was alleged that the force used to end them was excessive.[790]

Although in theory there is no doubt whatsoever that a State may not use situations such as those described in order not to assume its responsibility to protect every person subject to its jurisdiction and, even more so, for those persons who are in a place of detention, the described conditions are so dramatic and complex that it would not be easy for a State to comply automatically with the measures ordered by the Inter-American Court. What may occur in this type of situation, therefore, is that human rights violations continue to occur while the measures are being implemented.

In order for there to be a true change in the prison conditions it is necessary that there be a series of actions, but above all it requires a political will. The State authorities must realize that the situation in the places of detention is grave and they must also determine that this serious problem must be resolved. Only in this way will they take the profound measures necessary to change the prison conditions in those countries.

---

789 Pursuant to Article 78 of the American Convention on Human Rights, the States may denounce the Convention at the expiration of a five-year period from the date of its entry into force and by means of notice given one year in advance. Notice of the denunciation is addressed to the OAS Secretary General who informs the other States Parties. The Article also states that the denunciation does not have the effect of releasing the State Party concerned from the obligations contained in the Convention with respect to any act that may constitute a violation of those obligations and that has been taken by that State prior to the effective date of denunciation.

790 Faced with this situation, the Court stated that it was aware that the improvement of the situation in the prisons of Mendoza required short, medium and long term solutions and that, furthermore, a joint action on behalf of the federal and provincial administrative, judicial and legislative authorities was necessary to improve the conditions of the prisons and detention centers. The Court held, however, that the State could not claim reasons of internal law for not taking firm, specific and effective measures in compliance with the measures issued, so that no more deaths would occur. See IACtHR, *Mendoza Prisons Case (Argentina)*, Order of March 30, 2006, Preambular Paragraphs 8 and 11.

7.5. NON-COMPLIANCE AND THE OAS GENERAL ASSEMBLY

326. Articles 65 of the American Convention and 26(8) of the Rules of the Inter-American Court authorise the Court to inform the OAS General Assembly in its Annual Report of the cases in which it has ordered provisional measures and, when such measures have not been duly implemented, to make the recommendations that it deems pertinent.[791] In its Report, the Court describes the cases in which it has adopted provisional measures and the cases in which the State has not complied. Non-compliance is generally not reported immediately after verification, and so only persistent non-compliance is reported.[792]

327. From 1997 to 2008 the Court has informed the General Assembly of non-compliance of provisional measures in three Annual Reports. The first was its 1998 Annual Report where the Court stated that Trinidad and Tobago had not complied with the measures that it had ordered and, therefore, it requested that the Assembly urge the State to do so.[793] From 1999 to 2002 the Court did not report any type of non-compliance. In 2003 the Court informed the Assembly that in seven cases, three States had not complied with their duty to report[794] and asked the Assembly to urge Venezuela, Trinidad and Tobago and Haiti to inform it on the measures that they were implementing.[795] A year later, the Court insisted, with respect to the non-compliance of Venezuela, on the duty to

---

791 J.M. Pasqualucci, "Medidas Provisionales en la Corte Interamericana de Derechos Humanos: Una Comparación con la Corte Internacional de Justicia y la Corte Europea de Derechos Humanos", *Revista del Instituto Interamericano de Derechos Humanos* 1994, 93–94; H. Faundez Ledesma, *El Sistema Interamericano de Protección de los Derechos Humanos*, San José, IIDH, 3rd ed., 2004, 570; E. Rey Cantor and A. Rey Cantor, *Medidas Provisionales y Medidas Cautelares en el Sistema Interamericano de Derechos Humanos*, Bogotá, Editorial Temis, 2005, 203.

792 See IACtHR, *Luisiana Ríos et al. Case (Venezuela)*, Order of December 2, 2003, Preambular Paragraph 16. In this case the Court stated that since the State had not implemented the measures that it had ordered, had not investigated the acts that gave rise to the measures, had not allowed the petitioners to participate in the planning or the coordination of the means of protection and had not complied fully with the obligation of informing, if the situation were to continue it would inform the General Assembly of the OAS.

793 Organisation of American States, *Inter-American Court of Human Rights. 1998 Annual Report*, 39–40. IACtHR, *James et al. Case (Trinidad and Tobago)*, Order of May 25, 1999, Explanatory Statement 1(c).

794 Luis Uzcátegui Case (Venezuela), Liliana Ortega *et al.* Case (Venezuela), Luisiana Ríos *et al.* Case (Venezuela), Lysias Fleury Case (Haiti), James *et al.* Case (Trinidad and Tobago), Bámaca Velásquez Case (Guatemala) and the Marta Colomina and Liliana Velásquez Case (Venezuela).

795 Organisation of American States, *Inter-American Court of Human Rights. 2003 Annual Report*, 44–45.

implement the provisional measures ordered by it and to present the reports during the periods that it had indicated.[796]

328. The Court has also informed the General Assembly on those situations in which there has been partial compliance. These are cases where, although the State has adopted certain measures, they have not been sufficiently effective to avoid infringing the beneficiaries' rights or where the measures have not been sufficiently effective to protect all the beneficiaries. For example, in the 2005 Annual Report the Court expressed its concern that in seven cases there had only been partial non-compliance of the measures, because it had ordered the States to protect the rights to life and personal integrity of all the beneficiaries and some of them had been killed. The provisional measures to which reference was made involved the Peace Community of San José de Apartadó (Colombia), the Urso Branco Prison (Brazil), the Communities of the Jiguamiandó and of the Curbaradó (Colombia), the Indigenous Kankuamo People (Colombia),[797] the Eloisa Barrios *et al.* (Venezuela), the Mendoza Prisons (Argentina) and the Children Deprived of Freedom in the "Tatuapé Complex" de Febem (Brazil)[798] Cases.

329. As Faúndez Ledesma has stated, the Reports that the Court presents to the General Assembly have not had much impact since, to date, the Assembly has never ruled on the lack of compliance by States. Although the Court informed the Assembly of the lack of will of Trinidad and Tobago to adopt the requested measures and in spite of having sent two communications to the Chairman of the OAS Permanent Council and a third one to the OAS Secretary General so that the case would be considered by the Assembly and that the State be urged to comply with its international obligations, the Assembly did not issue any statement on the matter.[799] This situation can be easily criticised because the General Assembly, as the supreme organ of the OAS, could contribute to the protection of human rights through a public reproach of States that do not comply with the measures ordered by the Court.[800] Political pressure and the reproach of the international community should be a strategy that is employed

---

[796] Organisation of American States, *Inter-American Court of Human Rights. 2004 Annual Report*, 9.

[797] Although the Report of the Court states that a beneficiary had died, this information could not be reconfirmed; that is, in the Orders for provisional measures no mention is made of the death of any of the beneficiaries while the provisional measures were in effect.

[798] Organisation of American States, *Inter-American Court of Human Rights, 2005 Annual Report*, 35–36.

[799] H. Faundez Ledesma, *El Sistema Interamericano de Protección de los Derechos Humanos*, San José, IIDH, 3rd ed., 2004, 55–56.

[800] The General Assembly's powers are found in Article 54 of the Charter of the Organisation of American States.

when States refuse to comply with their international obligations and even more so when the rights of persons are in danger. It is, therefore, of great concern that reproach for non-compliance of provisional measures is not a fundamental part of the agenda of that institution.

7.6. MECHANISMS OF OVERSIGHT AND CONTROL

330. In the system designed by the American Convention, the Inter-American Court has the inherent power to oversee compliance of its own provisional measures and to issue, at the request of a party or *ex officio*, instructions for their compliance.[801]

331. The Court has followed a written procedure to oversee compliance of the measures that, in addition to allowing it to review compliance by the States, ensures respect for the principle of adversary proceedings, since the State and the Commission as well as the beneficiaries or their representatives may furnish the information that they consider relevant on compliance of the provisional measures and may also present observations to the reports presented by the other parties. Public hearings have occasionally been held to receive the views of the parties on compliance of the measures of protection.[802]

332. Oversight of compliance of its orders means that the Court may request that the State provide information on the activities it carried out to achieve compliance. The Court in its order generally sets a period for the State to present this information,[803] which is very important because it allows the Court to determine whether the State has adopted the measures of protection and also to know the true situation of the beneficiaries. Thus, the information that the States furnish must contain specific, true, detailed and current information on the implementation of the measures, on the effective investigation of the acts and on the participation

801 IACtHR, Cases of Liliana Ortega *et al.*, Luisiana Ríos *et al.*, Luis Uzcátegui, Marta Colomina and Liliana Velásquez (Venezuela), Order of May 4, 2004, Preambular Paragraph 9.

802 IACtHR, *Alvarez et al. Case (Colombia)*, Order of September 19, 1997, Explanatory Statement 10, Enacting Part 1; IACtHR, *Haitians and Dominicans of Haitian Origin in the Dominican Republic Case (Dominican Republic)*, Order of August 18, 2000, Explanatory Statement 4 and IACtHR, *"La Nación" Newspaper Case (Costa Rica)*, Order of the President of April 6, 2001, Preambular Paragraph 5, Enacting Part 2. See also Mapiripán Massacre Case (Colombia), María Leontina Millacura Llaipén *et al.* Case (Argentina) and Monagas Judicial Confinement Center ("La Pica") Case (Venezuela).

803 E. Rey Cantor and A. Rey Cantor, *Medidas Provisionales y Medidas Cautelares en el Sistema Interamericano de Derechos Humanos*, Bogotá, Editorial Temis, 2005, 199.

of the petitioners in the planning and coordination.[804] The Court has stated that a State does not comply with its duty to inform if it presents briefs that do not contain, within a certain period, the aforementioned information.

333. When the Court receives the report of the State, it is forwarded to the Commission and the beneficiaries or their representatives with two purposes: so that they might furnish the Court with their observations on the information supplied by the government and so that they might present their views on the manner in which the provisional measures are being implemented. This oversight mechanism is in practice an adversary type of proceedings that allows the Court to evaluate objectively the implementation of the measures ordered.[805]

334. When the State has sent the report and the Commission and the beneficiaries or their representatives have furnished their observations, the Court evaluates the information supplied and adopts an order on whether the State has complied with the measures of protection.[806]

---

804 IACtHR, *Colotenango Case (Guatemala)*, Order of September 5, 2001, Preambular Paragraph 5; IACtHR, *Cases of Liliana Ortega et al., Luisiana Ríos et al., Luis Uzcátegui, Marta Colomina and Liliana Velásquez (Venezuela)*, Order of May 4, 2004, Preambular Paragraphs 15–17; IACtHR, *Mapiripán Massacre Case (Colombia)*, Order of May 3, 2008, Preambular Paragraph 10.

805 H. Faundez Ledesma, *El Sistema Interamericano de Protección de los Derechos Humanos*, San José, IIDH, 3rd ed., 2004, 568–569.

806 IACtHR, *Guerrero-Gallucci and Martínez-Barrios Case (Venezuela)*, Order of November 29, 2007, Preambular Paragraph 16. In the Luisiana Ríos *et al.* Case (Venezuela), the Court held that the State had sent four reports that did not reflect the effective implementation of the measures requested. In this case, the Court declared that the State had not complied with its duty to inform. Subsequently, because of a change in attitude by the State, the Court expressed that it valued and would take into consideration the information presented by Venezuela. See IACtHR, *Luisiana Ríos et al. Case (Venezuela)*, Order of December 2, 2003, Preambular Paragraph 9, Enacting Parts 2–3 and Order of September 8, 2004, Preambular Paragraph 21. See also IACtHR, *Integrantes del Equipo de Estudios Comunitarios y Acción Psicosocial (ECAP). Masacre Plan de Sánchez Case (Guatemala)*, Order of November 25, 2006, Preambular Paragraph 17.

8. BINDING NATURE OF THE PROVISIONAL MEASURES AND INTERNATIONAL RESPONSIBILITY

8.1. GENERAL REMARKS

335. When measures are binding, States are obligated to comply with them and cannot allege domestic political or legal reasons not to implement the measures of protection that have been ordered. This binding nature of the provisional measures in the inter-American system comes first from being expressly mentioned in the Convention and, secondly, from the wording of Article 63(2) that provides for them and, finally, from the relationship of Article 63(2) with the other articles of the Convention and with the Vienna Convention on the Law of Treaties.

Faúndez Ledesma believes that there is not any doubt about the compulsory nature of provisional measures since they are expressly provided for in the Convention. Having been established in a treaty freely consented to and accepted by the States, they must be obeyed in accordance with the principle of *pacta sunt servanda*, which obligates the States to comply in good faith with the provisions of the treaties to which they are parties. The obligation to adopt provisional measures is, therefore, the result of the States' legal duty to comply with their international commitments.[807]

Given the wording of Article 63(2), the terminology employed by the Convention is also rather explicit as to the compulsory nature of the provisional measures. While the Statute of the International Court of Justice and the Rules of the European Court of Human Rights use the word "indicate," it was preferred that the American Convention indicate that the Court "shall adopt" such measures as it deems pertinent.[808] The language, plus the location of Article 63(2)

---

807 H. Faundez Ledesma, *El Sistema Interamericano de Protección de los Derechos Humanos*, San José, IIDH, 3rd ed., 2004, 586–587.

808 Article 73 of the Rules of the International Court of Justice, Article 41 of the Statute of the ICJ and Article 39 of the European Court of Human Rights. On this matter it is important to point out that the verb "indicate" used in the Statute of the ICJ generated a widespread doctrinal debate on the "binding" character of the provisional measures leading to the development of an extensive jurisprudence on the subject. In its judgment in the LaGrand Case on June 27, 2001, the ICJ concluded that its provisional measures are binding. See S. Torrecuadrada Garcia-Lozano, "La Sentencia de la Corte Internacional de Justicia del 27 de

in Chapter VIII, Section 2 on "Jurisdiction and Functions," allows the conclusion of the clear intention to grant to provisional measures a true binding force and not be simple suggestions or indications.[809]

336. Although the language employed in Article 63(2) is clear with respect to the compulsory nature of provisional measures, it is unfortunate that the Proceedings of the Specialized Inter-American Conference do not indicate whether there was any discussion on the scope and nature of provisional measures. These Proceedings contain the debate that took place on the draft Convention presented by the Inter-American Council of Jurisconsultants, which was responsible for up-dating and completing a draft, taking into account the drafts of the Inter-American Commission and those presented by Chile and Uruguay.[810]

It may be seen from the Proceedings that the Draft American Convention on the Protection of Human Rights did not provide for the figure of provisional measures in any of its provisions.[811] It was during the sixth meeting of the Second Commission, held November 19, 1969, that the delegate from Costa Rica, José Luis Redondo Gómez, proposed that the Court act in grave and emergency situations. The delegate took into account that this function was common in

junio de 2001", *Boletín Mexicano de Derecho Comparado* 2004, n° 109, 207–260; A. Cançado Trindade, *Medidas Provisionales. Prólogo del Presidente de la Corte Interamericana de Derechos Humanos al Tomo III de la Serie E.*, 2001, para. 6.

809 R. Nieto Navia, "Las medidas provisionales en la Corte Interamericana de Derechos Humanos", in *La Corte y el Sistema Interamericano de Derechos Humanos*, R. Nieto Navia (ed.), San José, Inter-American Court of Human Rights, 1994, 392; A. Cançado Trindade, , *Medidas Provisionales. Prólogo del Presidente de la Corte Interamericana de Derechos Humanos al Tomo III de la Serie E.*, 2001, paras. 13 and 21; J.M. Pasqualucci, *The Practice and Procedure of the Inter-American Court of Human Rights,* Cambridge, Cambridge University Press, 2003, 318; J.M. Pasqualucci, "Medidas Provisionales en la Corte Interamericana de Derechos Humanos: Una Comparación con la Corte Internacional de Justicia y la Corte Europea de Derechos Humanos", *Revista del Instituto Interamericano de Derechos Humanos* 1994, 96–97; J.M. Pasqualucci, "Provisional Measures in the Inter-American Human Rights System: An Innovative Development in International Law", *Vand. J. Transnat'l L.* 1993–94, 823, 824, 849.

810 R. Nieto Navia, "Las medidas provisionales en la Corte Interamericana de Derechos Humanos", in *La Corte y el Sistema Interamericano de Derechos Humanos*, R. Nieto Navia (ed.), San José, Inter-American Court of Human Rights, 1994, 380.

811 See Conferencia Especializada Interamericana sobre Derechos Humanos, San José, Costa Rica, Nov. 7–22, 1969, Actas y Documentos, OEA/Ser.K/XVI/1.2, 13–35. A study on the *travaux préparatoires* of the American Convention compared to that of the European Convention may be found in T. Buergenthal, "The European and Inter-American Human Rights Courts: Beneficial Interaction", in *Protecting Human Rights: The European Perspective, Studies in memory of Rolv Ryssdal,* P. Mahoney, F. Matscher, H. Petzold and L. Wildhaber (eds.), Köln, Carl Heymanns Verlag, 2000, 123–133.

every tribunal in the world. He proposed that there be included before Article 57 a text that would state the following:

> "The Court shall take the provisional measures that it deems pertinent in emergency situations and when there is sufficient cause that justifies it to protect the right that is claimed to be infringed."[812]

When the amendment was voted upon, it was rejected by one vote in favor, none against and 16 abstentions. Two days later, on November 21, during the third plenary session, once again the delegate of Costa Rica, this time José Francisco Chaverri, when Article 63 was being considered, proposed that a paragraph be added, nearly the same as that presented previously, with the following text:

> "In cases of extreme gravity and urgency, and when necessary to avoid irreparable damage to persons, the Court shall adopt such provisional measures as it deems pertinent in matters it has under consideration. With respect to a case not yet submitted to the Court, it may act at the request of the Commission."[813]

According to the minutes of the Third Plenary Session (summary version) the proposal was considered and it was decided to incorporate a Paragraph 1 into the text presented. The minutes say nothing of the arguments of the Costa Rican delegate nor as to whether there were comments by the delegates of the other States nor the results of the voting. This was the text that was incorporated into the Convention.[814]

---

812 See Conferencia Especializada Interamericana sobre Derechos Humanos, San José, Costa Rica, Nov. 7–22, 1969, Actas y Documentos, OEA/Ser.K/XVI/1.2, Doc. 85, 361.

813 See Conferencia Especializada Interamericana sobre Derechos Humanos, San José, Costa Rica, Nov. 7–22, 1969, Actas y Documentos, OEA/Ser.K/XVI/1.2, Doc. 83, 457.

814 Conferencia Especializada Interamericana sobre Derechos Humanos, San José, Costa Rica, Nov. 7–22, 1969, Actas y Documentos, OEA/Ser.K/XVI/1.2, Doc. 83, 457. See also Article 63(2) of the American Convention on Human Rights.

8.2. POSITION OF THE INTER-AMERICAN COURT

337. The jurisprudence shows that the Court has relied on Articles 1(1),[815] 2,[816] 33,[817] 62(1)[818] and 68(1)[819] of the American Convention and Articles 26 and 27 of

---

815 Article 1(1) of the American Convention specifies the obligation of the State parties to respect the rights and freedoms recognized therein and to ensure to all persons subject to their jurisdiction the free and full exercise of those rights and freedoms. See IACtHR, *Caballero Delgado and Santana Case (Colombia)*, Order of December 7, 1994, Preambular Paragraph 2; IACtHR, *Carpio Nicolle Case (Guatemala)*, Order of June 4, 1995, Preambular Paragraph 3; IACtHR, *Serech and Saquic Case (Guatemala)*, Order of June 28, 1996, Preambular Paragraph 1; IACtHR, *Giraldo Cardona Case (Colombia)*, Order of the President of February 5, 1997, Preambular Paragraph 1; IACtHR, *James et al. Case (Trinidad and Tobago)*, Order of November 24, 2000, Preambular Paragraph 5; IACtHR, *Urso Branco Prison Case (Brazil)*, Order of August 29, 2002, Preambular Paragraph 5; IACtHR, *Bámaca Velásquez Case (Guatemala)*, Order of February 21, 2003, Preambular Paragraph 5; IACtHR, *Gómez Paquiyauri Brothers Case (Peru)*, Order of May 7, 2004, Preambular Paragraph 5; IACtHR, *19 Tradesmen Case (Colombia)*, Order of September 3, 2004, Preambular Paragraph 4 and IACtHR, *Mendoza Prisons Case (Argentina)*, Order November 22, 2004, Preambular Paragraph 6.

816 According to Article 2 of the Convention, the State Parties undertake to adopt the legislative or other measures as may be necessary to give effect to the rights or freedoms contemplated in the Convention. IACtHR, *Blake Case (Guatemala)*, Order of August 16, 1995, Preambular Paragraphs 1 and 3; IACtHR, *James et al. Case (Trinidad and Tobago)*, Order of May 25, 1999, Preambular Paragraph 2(g); IACtHR, *Constitutional Court Case (Peru)*, Order of August 14, 2000, Preambular Paragraph 4; IACtHR, *Ivcher Bronstein Case (Peru)*, Order of November 21, 2000, Preambular Paragraphs 1 and 5; IACtHR, *Helen Mack Chang et al. (Guatemala)*. Order of August 14, 2002, Preambular Paragraph 4 and IACtHR, *Plan de Sánchez Massacre Case (Guatemala)*, Order of the President of July 30, 2004, Preambular Paragraphs 1 and 4.

817 Pursuant to Article 33 of the Convention, the States parties recognise the Court and the Commission as the competent organs to ensure the object and purpose of the Convention; *i.e.* the protection of human rights and in the case of the Court, its contentious jurisdiction when it has been accepted. See IACtHR, *Liliana Ortega et al. Case (Venezuela)*, Order of May 4, 2004, Preambular Paragraph 2.

818 Pursuant to Article 62(1), the States declare that they recognise as binding, *ipso facto*, and not requiring special agreement, the jurisdiction of the Court on all matters relating to the interpretation or application of the American Convention. See IACtHR, *Carpio Nicolle Case (Guatemala)*, Order of June 4, 1995, Preambular Paragraph 1; IACtHR, *Giraldo Cardona Case (Colombia)*, Order of February 5, 1997, Preambular Paragraph 1; IACtHR, *Urso Branco Prison Case (Brazil)*, Order of August 29, 2002, Preambular Paragraph 1; IACtHR, *Helen Mack Chang et al. Case (Guatemala)*, Order of June 6, 2003, Preambular Paragraph 1; IACtHR, *Mendoza Prisons Case (Argentina)*, Order of November 22, 2004, Preambular Paragraph 1 and IACtHR, *Liliana Ortega et al. Case (Venezuela)*, Order of May 4, 2004, Preambular Paragraph 1.

819 According to Article 68(1) of the American Convention, the State parties undertake to comply with the judgment of the Court in any case to which they are parties. See IACtHR, *James et al. Case (Trinidad and Tobago)*, Order of August 16, 2000, Preambular Paragraph 10; IACtHR, *Lysias Fleury Case (Haiti)*, Order of December 2, 2003, Preambular Paragraph 7; IACtHR, *Liliana Ortega et al. Case (Venezuela)*, Order of December 2, 2003, Preambular Paragraph 2 and IACtHR, *Luisiana Ríos et al. Case (Venezuela)*, Order of December 2, 2003, Preambular Paragraph 10.

the Vienna Convention on the Law of Treaties as to the binding effect of provisional measures.[820]

Taking into account the aforementioned articles, the Court has held that compliance of provisional measures does not depend on the discretion or good will of States. Provisional measures are binding because they are explicitly set forth in the Convention, and the States as Parties to the Convention have the duty to comply with all the provisions in that treaty.[821] This is also true for those who believe that the Court may only adopt provisional measures with respect to the States that have accepted its contentious jurisdiction,[822] because they believe that the measures are binding since the States have made an express declaration in which they recognise as binding the Court's jurisdiction in all cases concerning the interpretation and application of the Convention.[823] The States are, thus, committed to comply with all the decisions of the Court,[824] including, naturally, orders of provisional measures.[825]

The Court has also held that the obligation to comply with its decisions corresponds to a basic principle of the law of international responsibility, according to which States must fulfill their obligations under international treaties in good faith (*pacta sunt servanda*) and, in conformity with Article 27 of the Vienna Convention on the Law of Treaties of 1969, they cannot for domestic reasons fail to assume their already established international responsibility.[826] The measures are, therefore, compulsory even in situations of internal armed conflict. In the Communities of the Jiguamiandó and of the Curbaradó (Colombia) and the Peace Community of San José de Apartadó (Colombia) Cases, the Court held that the State must guarantee the protection of the

---

820 Article 26 of the Vienna Convention on the Law of Treaties of 1969 provides that the States must comply with their treaty-based obligations in good faith (*pacta sunt servanda*). Under Article 27 of the same Convention, States may not invoke the provisions of their internal law as justification for their failure to perform their international responsibilities. See IACtHR, *Lysias Fleury Case (Haiti)*, Order of December 2, 2003, Preambular Paragraph 7; IACtHR, *Liliana Ortega et al. Case (Venezuela)*, Order of December 2, 2003, Preambular Paragraph 7; IACtHR, *James et al. Case (Trinidad and Tobago)*, Order of December 2, 2003, Preambular Paragraph 6 and IACtHR, *Luis Uzcátegui Case (Venezuela)*, Order of December 2, 2003, Preambular Paragraph 14.

821 See Article 1(1) and 2 of the American Convention. See also A. Cançado Trindade, "The Evolution of Provisional Measures of Protection under the Case Law of the Inter-American Court of Human Rights (1987–2002)", *Hum. Rts. L. J.* 2003, 163–164.

822 T. Buergenthal, R. Nieto Navia, J.M. Pasqualucci and H. Gros Espiell. See the section on "Passive Standing: The States", *supra* nos. 57–60.

823 See Article 62(1) of the American Convention.

824 See Article 68(1) of the American Convention.

825 IACtHR, *James, Briggs, Noel, Garcia and Bethel Case (Trinidad and Tobago)*, Order of September 25, 1999, Preambular Paragraph 10 and Order of November 26, 2000, Preambular Paragraph 10.

826 IACtHR, *Luisiana Ríos et al. Case (Venezuela)*, Order of December 2, 2003, Preambular Paragraph 11. See also Articles 26 and 27 of the Vienna Convention on the Law of Treaties.

beneficiaries of the measures in the light of the provisions of the American Convention as well as the norms of international humanitarian law. The Court called upon Colombia to ensure that said norms were respected by all the actors of the armed conflict and urged it to guarantee the principle of distinction in international humanitarian law with respect to the members of the Peace Community, who were civilians not involved in the internal armed conflict.[827]

338. In summary, the binding nature of provisional measures signifies that the States may not for any reason fail to assume the international responsibility that they acquired by freely ratifying the American Convention and they must, therefore, adopt the measures of protection that have been ordered.[828] This binding nature applies also in situations of internal armed conflict, given that the purpose of the measures is to protect civilians who find themselves in the middle of the conflict. A State may be internationally responsible for failure to comply with the provisional measures of protection. The Court has held that Article 63(2) of the Convention, interpreted in light of the principle of the law of international responsibility, according to which States must fulfill their treaty obligations in good faith (*pacta sunt servanda*), obliges the States to comply with the measures of protection ordered by the Court. Thus, non-compliance of an order to adopt provisional measures may result in the international responsibility of the State.[829]

Taking into account these circumstances, the Court declared in its judgment on the merits in the Hilaire, Constantine and Benjamin *et al.* Case (Trinidad and Tobago) the international responsibility of that State. The Court held that the State had violated Article 4 of the Convention and that this violation was aggravated by the non-compliance of the provisional measures with respect to

---

827 IACtHR, *Peace Community of San José de Apartadó Case (Colombia)*, Order of November 17, 2004, Preambular Paragraph 13 and IACtHR, *Communities of the Jiguamiandó and of the Curbaradó Case (Colombia)*, Order of March 15, 2005, Preambular Paragraphs 15 and 28.

828 A. Aguiar, "Apuntes sobre las Medidas Cautelares en la Convención Americana sobre Derechos Humanos", in *La Corte y el Sistema Interamericano de Derechos Humanos*, San José, Inter-American Court of Human Rights, 1994, 112. See also IACtHR, *Colotenango Case (Guatemala)*, Order of September 5, 2001, Preambular Paragraph 5; IACtHR, *Luisiana Ríos et al. Case (Venezuela)*, Order of February 20, 2003, Preambular Paragraph 10; IACtHR, *Bámaca Velásquez Case (Guatemala)*, Order of November 20, 2003, Preambular Paragraph 17; IACtHR, *James, Briggs, Noel, Garcia and Bethel Case (Trinidad and Tobago)*, Order of December 2, 2003, Enacting Parts 1 and 2; IACtHR, *Liliana Ortega et al. Case (Venezuela)*, Order of May 24, Preambular Paragraph 11; IACtHR, *Luis Uzcátegui Case (Venezuela)*, Order of May 4, 2004, Preambular Paragraph 7; IACtHR, *"Globovisión" Television Station Case (Venezuela)*, Order of September 4, 2004, Preambular Paragraph 21 and IACtHR, *Bámaca Velásquez Case (Guatemala)*, Order of March 11, 2005, Preambular Paragraph 8.

829 IACtHR, *Communities of the Jiguamiandó and of the Curbaradó Case (Colombia)*, Order of February 7, 2006, Preambular Paragraph 7 and IACtHR, *Mendoza Prisons Case (Argentina)*, Order March 30, 2006, Preambular Paragraph 10.

Joey Ramiah,[830] who had been found guilty of murder and sentenced to death under the obligatory death penalty penal law. By order of May 25, 1999, the Court required Trinidad and Tobago to adopt whatever means were necessary to preserve his life so as not to frustrate consideration of the case in the inter-American system. Notwithstanding the measure of protection expressly ordered by the Court, the State executed the beneficiary on June 4, 1999, thus applying the death penalty despite the protective measure.

The Court considered that the execution of a person protected by a provisional measure that expressly indicated that the execution should be postponed until the case was resolved in the inter-American system constituted an arbitrary deprivation of the right to life. The Court held that the State had caused irreparable harm in the case of Joey Ramiah by having ignored the direct order of the Court and its deliberate decision to execute him. The Court found that the State was responsible for the aggravated violation of Article 4 of the American Convention. Additionally, the Court found that the execution of the beneficiary had also prejudiced three other persons: the woman who bore his child, his child and his mother. Therefore, the Court established, on the grounds of equity, that Trinidad and Tobago had to award an indemnity to repair the non-pecuniary damage presumably suffered by those persons due to the execution of Joey Ramiah.[831]

8.3. INTENTIONAL NON-COMPLIANCE BY SOME STATES

339. So far, Trinidad and Tobago (in 1999) has been the only State that has intentionally violated an order of interim measures, more specifically in the Case of James and others, where the State had effectively implemented the death penalty against two beneficiaries, notwithstanding a provisional measure issued by the Inter-American Court to suspend the implementation.

The respondent State argued in the case of the death of Anthony Briggs that, since the Commission had decided to publish the reports mentioned in Articles 50 and 51 of the Convention, there was no case anymore relating to that person before the Commission, or capable of being submitted to the Court. In this sense, this body had, according to the State, lost all power to adopt interim measures.

830 IACtHR, *Hilaire, Constantine and Benjamin et al. Case (Trinidad and Tobago)*, Judgment of June 21, 2002, paras. 190–191, 196–200, 216, Enacting Part 7. See also IACtHR, *Eloisa Barrios et al. Case (Venezuela)*, Order of June 29, 2005, Separate Opinion of Judge Cançado Trindade, para. 8.

831 IACtHR, *Hilaire, Constantine and Benjamin et al. (Trinidad and Tobago)*, Judgment of June 21, 2002, para. 216.

Thus, the order made after the publication of that report was invalid because the Court had no jurisdiction.

In the opinion of the Court however, the State was bound by the interim measures, whether the case was sent to it or not, because the situation of extreme gravity and urgency provided the foundations necessary to maintain the measures to protect the rights of the petitioner. It also found that, although, following the publication of the reports on the matter the proceedings before the Commission had ended, the same could not be said with regard to the case of the Court, because from the moment that the Court had received the request for interim measures, the case was under its jurisdiction. In this regard, the study of the case had not been completed under the inter-American System. Once the Commission requests interim measures, the only restriction in Article 63(2) to the jurisdiction of the Court is that the situation of extreme gravity and urgency should continue and that the measures are indeed necessary to avoid damage to the rights of persons.[832]

Regarding the other beneficiary (Joey Ramiah) who had been executed, the State pointed out that it had not received any order to adopt protective measures in favour of Joel Ramiah. In its judgment the Inter-American Court considered his execution by Trinidad and Tobago to be an arbitrary deprivation of the right to life that was aggravated because the victim was protected by provisional measures that it had ordered, indicating that his execution should be stayed pending the resolution of the case by the inter-American human rights system.[833]

340. In this regard, it is also worth to mention the behaviour of Venezuela in the Liliana Ortega *et al.*, the Luisiana Ríos *et al.*, the Luis Uzcátegui and the Marta Colomina and Liliana Velásquez Cases. Venezuela stated that the provisional measures ordered with respect to these four cases have to be consistent with the Constitutional norms that grant sovereign competences exclusively to the public powers. According to Venezuela, these attributes could not be delegated to non-Venezuelan institutions, such as the Inter-American Commission and the Inter-American Court, which by definition were not supranational.[834] It also argued that it was enough for the State, should it so decide, to adopt the provisional measures requested by the Court in the manner in which the State considered sufficient in objective terms, and, therefore, it should cease automatically its international cooperation with the Court.

---

832 *Ibid.*

833 IACtHR, *Hilaire, Constantine and Benjamin Case (Trinidad and Tobago)*, Judgment of June 21, 2002, paras. 33, 84, 197–200.

834 IACtHR, *Liliana Ortega et al. Case (Venezuela)*, Order of May 4, 2004, Explanatory Statement 11.

The Inter-American Court stated that the obligation to comply with its decisions corresponded to a basic principle of the law of international State responsibility, supported by international jurisprudence, according to which States must comply with their obligations under international treaties in good faith (*pacta sunt servanda*). In addition, under Article 27 of the Vienna Convention on the Law of Treaties of 1969, States may not invoke domestic reasons in order to avoid their international responsibilities. Finally, the Court stated that the position of Venezuela, in affirming that States could decide at their own discretion and autonomously whether to comply with the decisions of the Court, ignored the principles that govern both international law and the inter-American system.[835]

[835] IACtHR, *Cases of Liliana Ortega et al., Luisiana Ríos et al., Luis Uzcátegui, Marta Colomina and Liliana Velásquez (Venezuela)*, Order of May 4, 2004, Preambular Paragraph 7.

BIBLIOGRAPHY

BOOKS

BERNHARDT, R., *Interim Measures Indicated by International Courts*, BERNHARDT, R. (ed.), Berlin, Springer Verlag, 1994, 154 p.

BUERGENTHAL, T., NORRIS, R. and SHELTON, D., *Protecting Human Rights in the Americas, Selected Problems,* Strasbourg, International Institute of Human Rights, 1990, 473 p.

COLLINS, L., *Provisional and protective measures in international litigation*, Dordrecht, Martinus Nijhoff, 1993, 234 p.

FAÚNDEZ LEDESMA, H., *El Sistema Interamericano de Protección de los Derechos* Humanos, San José, IIDH, 2004, 1053 p.

GARCÍA RAMIREZ, S., *La jurisdicción interamericana de derechos humanos*, Mexico D.F., Comisión de Derechos Humanos del Distrito Federal & Corte Interamericana de Derechos Humanos, 2006, 300 p.

GONZÁLEZ NAPOLITANO, S., *Las medidas provisionales en Derecho Internacional ante las Cortes y Tribunales Internacionales*, Buenos Aires, La Ley, 2004, 245 p.

GROS ESPIELL, H., *Estudios sobre Derechos Humanos II,* Madrid, Instituto Interamericano de Derechos Humanos, Editorial Civitas, 1988, 383 p.

HARRIS, D.J. and LIVINGSTONE, S. (eds.), *The Inter-American System of Human Rights*, Oxford, Oxford University Press, 1998, 616 p.

HERNÁNDEZ GÓMEZ, I., *Sistemas Internacionales de Derechos Humanos,* Madrid, Dykinson, 2002, 320 p.

MEDINA QUIROGA, C., *The Battle of Human Rights. Gross, Systematic Violations and the Inter-American System*, Dordrecht, Martinus Nijhoff, 1988, 246 p.

NIKKEN, P., *La Protección Internacional de los Derechos Humanos, Su desarrollo progresivo*, San José / Madrid, Instituto Interamericano de Derechos Humanos & Editorial Civitas, 1987, 321 p.

NOWAK M., *U.N. Covenant on Civil and Political Rights, CCPR Commentary*, 2005, 1277 p.

ORLIN, TH.S. and SCHEININ, M. (ed.), *The Jurisprudence of Human Rights Law: A Comparative Interpretative Approach*, Institute for Human Rights/Abo Akademi University, Turku/Abo, 2000, 323 p.

PASQUALUCCI, J. M., *The Practice and Procedure of the Inter-American Court of Human Rights,* Cambridge, Cambridge University Press, 2003, 488 p.

REY CANTOR, E. and REY CANTOR, A., *Medidas Provisionales y Medidas Cautelares en el Sistema Interamericano de Derechos Humanos,* Bogotá, Temis, 2005, 353 p.

ARTICLES

AGUILAR, A., "Procedimiento que debe aplicar la Comisión Interamericana de Derechos Humanos en el exámen de las peticiones o comunicaciones individuales sobre presuntas violaciones de Derechos Humanos", in *Derechos Humanos en las Américas. Homenaje a la Memoria de Carlos A. Dunshee de Abranches,* Washington D.C., CIDH, 1984, 199–216.

AGUIAR, A., "Apuntes sobre las Medidas Cautelares en la Convención Americana sobre Derechos Humanos," in *La Corte y el Sistema Interamericano de Derechos Humanos,* R. NIETO NAVIA (ed.), San José, Costa Rica, 1994, 19–31.

BECERRA RAMIREZ, M., "Las Decisiones Judiciales como Fuente del Derecho Internacional de los Derechos Humanos", in *Liber Amicorum Héctor Fix-Zamudio,* San José, Inter-American Court of Human Rights, 1998, p. 431–446.

BUERGENTHAL, T., "The American and the European Conventions on Human Rights: Similarities and Differences, *Am. U.L. Rev.* 1980–1981, 155–166.

BUERGENTHAL, T., "The Inter-American System for the Protection of Human Rights", in *Human Rights in International Law, Legal and Policy Issues.* TH. MERON (ed.), Oxford, Clarendon Press, 1984, 439–493.

BUERGENTHAL, T., "El Sistema Interamericano para la Protección de los Derechos Humanos", *Anuario Jurídico Interamericano 1981,* Washington D.C., Secretariat General of the OAS, 1982, 110–130.

BUERGENTHAL, T., "The Inter-American Court of Human Rights", *Am. U. L. Rev.* 1982, 231–245.

BUERGENTHAL, T., "The European and Inter-American Human Rights Courts: Beneficial Interaction", in *Protecting Human Rights: The European Perspective, Studies in memory of Rolv Ryssdal,* P. MAHONEY, F. MARSCHER, H. PETZOLD, and L. WILDHABER (eds.), Koln, Carl Heymanns Verlag, 2000, 123–133.

BUERGENTHAL, T., "The Evolving International Human Rights System", *Am. U. L. Rev. 2006,* 783–807.

BURBANO HERRERA, C. and HAECK, Y., "Leaving States Unpunished? The Paradox of the Legal Consequences following State Non-compliance with Provisional Measures in the Inter-American and European Human Rights Systems", *N.Q.H.R.* 2010, No. 2.

CANÇADO TRINDADE, A., "El nuevo Reglamento de la Corte Interamericana de Derechos Humanos (2000) y su proyección hacia el futuro: La emancipación del ser humano como sujeto del Derecho Internacional", in *XVIII Curso de derecho internacional,* Washington, D.C., OEA; Comité Jurídico Interamericano, 2002, 33–92.

CANÇADO TRINDADE, A., "The Evolution of Provisional Measures of Protection under the Case Law of the Inter-American Court of Human Rights (1987–2002)", *Hum. Rts. L.J.* 2003, 162–168.

CORTE INTERAMERICANA DE DERECHOS HUMANOS, "Prólogo del Presidente de la Corte Interamericana de Derechos Humanos (Juez FIX-ZAMUDIO H.)", in *Medidas Provisionales,* Serie E, 1996.

CORTE INTERAMERICANA DE DERECHOS HUMANOS, "Prólogo del Presidente de la Corte Interamericana de Derechos Humanos (Juez CANÇADO TRINDADE A.)", in *Medidas Provisionales,* Serie E, 2001.

Garcia Ramírez, S.,"Una reflexión pragmática sobre el Sistema Interamericano", *Revista CEJIL, Debates sobre Derechos Humanos y el Sistema Interamericano* 2005, 5–11.

Harris, D., "Regional Protection of Human Rights: The Inter-American Achievement", in *The Inter-American System of Human Rights*, D. Harris, and S. Livingstone (eds.), Oxford, Oxford University Press, 1998, 1–29.

Kolb, R., "Note on New International Case-Law concerning the Binding Character of Provisional Measures", *Nordic journal of international law: acta scandinavica juris gentium* 2005, 117–129.

Kunz, J.L., "The Bogotá Charter of the Organisation of American States", *A.J.I.L.* 1948, 568–589.

Lusverti, C., "El derecho internacional de los derechos humanos y los tribunales nacionales: el caso de Venezuela," *Revista CEJIL, Debates sobre Derechos Humanos y el Sistema Interamericano* 2005, 88–93.

Mendez, J., and Dulitzky, A. "Medidas Cautelares y Provisionales", in *Protección Internacional de Derechos Humanos: Nuevos Desafíos,* Mexico, Porrua, 2005, 67–93.

Nieto Navia, R., Las medidas provisionales en la Corte Interamericana de Derechos Humanos, in R. Nieto. (ed.) *La Corte y el Sistema Interamericano de Derechos Humanos*, San José, Costa Rica, 1994, 369–398.

Padilla, D.J, "Provisional Measures Under the American Convention on Human Rights", in *Liber Amicorum Héctor Fix-Zamudio,* San José, Corte Interamericana de Derechos Humanos, 1998, 1189–1196.

Pasqualucci, J.M., "Provisional Measures in the Inter-American Human Rights System: An Innovative Development in International Law", *Vand. J. Transnat'l L.* 1993-1994, 803–863.

Pasqualucci, J.M., "Medidas Provisionales en la Corte Interamericana de Derechos Humanos: Una Comparación con la Corte Internacional de Justicia y la Corte Europea de Derechos Humanos", *Revista IIDH* 1994, 47–112.

Rodríguez Pinzon, D., "Jurisdicción y Competencia en las Peticiones Individuales del Sistema Interamericano de Derechos Humanos", in: <www.wcl.american.edu/pub/humright/red/articulos/JurisdccionCompetencia.htm>, 1–22.

Rodríguez Rescia, V., "El Sistema Interamericano de Protección de Derechos Humanos", in: <www.iidh.ed.cr/BibliotecaWeb>, 1–23.

Salvioli, F.O., "Derechos, acceso, y rol de las víctimas", in *El futuro del sistema interamericano de protección de los derechos humanos*, Costa Rica, IIDH. 1998, 293–342.

Segares, R.E., "Jurisprudencia de la Corte Interamericana de Derechos Humanos sobre las Medidas Provisionales", in *Justicia Libertad y Derechos Humanos: ensayos en Homenaje a Rodolfo E. Piza*, San José, IIDH, 2003, 287–357.

Shelton, D., "Discussion", in *Mesures conservatoires et droits fondamentaux*, G. Cohen-Jonathan and J.F. Flaus. (eds.), Brussels, Bruylant, 2005, 165–176.

Ventura Robles, M., "La Corte Interamericana de Derechos Humanos: la necesidad inmediata de convertirse en un tribunal permanente", *Revista CEJIL, Debates sobre Derechos Humanos y el Sistema Interamericano* 2005, 12–26.

CASES INTER-AMERICAN SYSTEM

Velásquez Rodríguez, Fairén Garbi and Solis Corrales, and Godínez Cruz and others (Honduras). 1988.
Bustíos-Rojas (Peru). 1990.
Chunimá (Guatemala). 1991.
Los Penales Peruanos (Peru). 1992.
Chipoco (Peru). 1992.
Reggiardo Tolosa (Argentina). 1993.
Colotenango (Guatemala). 1994.
Caballero Delgado and Santana (Colombia). 1994.
Carpio Nicolle (Guatemala). 1995.
Blake (Guatemala). 1995.
Suárez Rosero (Ecuador). 1996.
Loayza Tamayo (Peru). 1996.
Vogt (Guatemala). 1996.
Serech and Saquic (Guatemala). 1996.
Giraldo Cardona (Colombia). 1996.
Alemán Lacayo (Nicaragua). 1996.
Álvarez and others (Colombia). 1997.
Cesti Hurtado (Peru). 1997.
Paniagua Morales y Otros y Vásquez and others (Guatemala). 1998.
Clemente Teherán (Colombia). 1998.
James, Briggs, Noel, García and Bethel (Trinidad and Tobago). 1998.
Bámaca Velásquez (Guatemala). 1998.
Digna Ochoa and Plácido and others (Mexico). 1999.
The Peace Community of San José de Apartadó (Colombia). 2000.
Tribunal Constitucional (Peru). 2000.
Ivcher Bronstein (Peru). 2000.
Haitians and Dominicans of Haitian Origin in the Dominican Republic (Dominican Republic). 2000.
Gallardo-Rodríguez (Mexico). 2001.
Periódico "la Nación" (Herrera Ulloa) (Costa Rica). 2001.
Miguel Agustín Pro Juárez Human Rights Center (Mexico). 2001.
Urso Branco Prison (Brasil). 2002.
Comunidad Mayagna (Sumo) Awas Tingni (Nicaragua). 2002.
Helen Mack Chang and others (Guatemala). 2002.
Luisiana Ríos and others (Venezuela). 2002.
Liliana Ortega and others (Venezuela). 2002.
Luis Uzcátegui (Venezuela). 2002.
The Communities of the Jiguamiambó and of the Curbaradó (Colombia). 2003.
Lysias Fleury (Haití). 2003.
Marta Colomina and Liliana Velásquez (Venezuela). 2003.
Kankuamo Indigenous Community (Colombia). 2004.
Raxcacó and others (Guatemala). 2004.

Sarayaku Indigenous Community (Ecuador). 2004.
"El Nacional" and "Así es la Noticia" Newspapers (Venezuela). 2004.
Carlos Nieto (Venezuela). 2004.
"Globovisión" Television Station (Venezuela). 2004.
Boyce and Joseph (Barbados). 2004.
Eloisa Barrios and others (Venezuela). 2004.
Las Penitenciarias de Mendoza (Argentina). 2004.
19 Tradesmen (Colombia). 2004.
Gómez Paquiyauri (Peru). 2004.
Fermín Ramírez (Guatemala). 2004.
Masacre Plan de Sánchez (Salvador Jerónimo and others) (Guatemala). 2004.
Acevedo Jaramillo and others (Peru). 2004.
Gutiérrez Soler (Colombia). 2005.
Pilar Noriega et al. (Mexico). 2005
Mapiripán Massacre (Colombia). 2005
Children Deprived of Liberty in the "Complexo do Tatuapé" of FEDEM (Brazil). 2005
Ramírez Hinostroza et al. (Peru). 2005
Gloria Giralt de García-Prieto et al. (El Salvador). 2006
Juan Humberto Sánchez (Honduras). 2006
Juarez Cruzzat et al. (Peru). 2006
Forensic Anthropology Foundation (Guatemala). 2006
Integrantes del Equipo de Estudios Comunitarios y Acción Psicosocial (ECAP). Masacre Plan de Sánchez (Guatemala). 2006
Yare I and Yare II Capital Region Center (Venezuela). 2006
Monagas Judicial Confinement Center ("La Pica") (Venezuela). 2006
Guerrero-Galucci y Martínez-Barrios (Venezuela). 2006
Mery Naranjo et al. (Colombia). 2006
Persons imprisoned in the "Dr. Sebastião Martins Silveira" Penitentiary in Araraquara, São Paulo (Brazil). 2006
Millacura Llaipén et al. (Argentina). 2006
Serrano-Cruz Sisters (El Salvador). 2006
Penitentiary Center of the Central Occidental Region (Uribana Prison) (Venezuela). 2007
Adrián Meléndez Quijano et al. (El Salvador). 2007
Miguel Castro-Castro Prison (Peru). 2007
Capital El Rodeo I & El Rodeo II Judicial Confinement Center (Venezuela). 2008
Leonel Rivero et al. (Mexico). 2008
Tyrone Dacosta Cadogan (Barbados). 2008
Kawas Fernández (Honduras). 2008

www.ingramcontent.com/pod-product-compliance
Ingram Content Group UK Ltd.
Pitfield, Milton Keynes, MK11 3LW, UK
UKHW051922100926
8556IPUK00021B/1324

9 789400 000377